The Hebraic Tongue Restored

[Volume Two]

The Hebraic Tongue Restored

And the True Meaning of the Hebrew
Words Re-established and Proved
by their Radical Analysis

[Volume Two]

By

Fabre d'Olivet

Done into English by

Nayán Louise Redfield

יתות

"He who can rightly pronounce it, causeth
heaven and earth to tremble, for it is the
NAME
which rusheth through the universe."

Hermetica

San Rafael, Ca

Second, facsimile edition
Hermetica, 2007
First edition, G.P. Putnam's Sons, 1921

For information, address:
Hermetica, P.O. Box 151011
San Rafael, California 94915, USA

Library of Congress Cataloging-in-Publication Data

Fabre d'Olivet, Antoine, 1767–1825.
The Hebraic tongue restored and the true meaning of the
Hebrew words re-established and proved by their radical analysis /
Fabre d'Olivet; translated by Nayán Redfield. — Reprint ed.

v. cm.
Originally published: New York: G.P. Putnam's Sons, 1921.
ISBN 978-1-59731-204-2 (vol 1, pbk.: alk. paper)
ISBN 978-1-59731-205-9 (vol 1, hardback: alk. paper)
ISBN 978-1-59731-206-6 (vol 2, pbk.: alk. paper)
ISBN 978-1-59731-207-3 (vol 2, hardback: alk. paper)
1. Hebrew language—Grammar. I. Redfield, Nayán Louise. II. Title.
PJ4563.F25 2007
492.4'82421—dc22   2007027592

The Hebraic Tongue Restored

Part Second.

CONTENTS

OF PART SECOND

———

3

PRELIMINARY DISCOURSE

If, instead of Hebrew, I had chosen Chinese or Sanskrit as the basis of my labour, having reached this point of my work I might have mastered the greatest difficulties; for, after having developed the principles of these tongues by explaining their constitutive elements and their radical forms, there would only remain for me to show the attentive and unprejudiced reader, the excellence of these same principles in applying them to the translation of certain chapters from the Kings or the Vedas. But the choice that I have made of Hebrew places me in quite a contrary position. The difficulties increase even where they should be lessened; what might have been a sort of complement, an easy result, becomes the principal object, awakens, fixes the attention, arouses and excites the reader; whereas he would have remained calm, and might have followed me with an interest which, being keen, would have been impartial. This is the effect of the translation which I have felt impelled to make of the Sepher of Moses. I have realized it and have foreseen all the consequences. I was even inclined to make this translation the principal title of my work, naming it simply *The Cosmogony of Moses;* but then I would have placed the Hebraic tongue in the background and my first plan was that it should occupy the foreground; since it was while seeking the origin of speech that I encountered this tongue and considered it particularly as one of those whose grammatical principles could more safely lead to this unknown origin and unveil its mysteries.

I shall not repeat what I have said in my Dissertation concerning this tongue itself, its culture, its perfection among the ancient Egyptians, and its transplantation,—effect of the providential emigration of the Hebrews; neither shall I speak of the rapid degeneration of its expressions, which from metaphorical, intelligible, and

5

universal had become literal, sentient and particular; neither of its utter loss, nor of the insurmountable obstacles which the temporal state of things brought about in its reëstablishment: I have taken care to prove these diverse assertions as much as the obscurity of the centuries and the lack of monuments have permitted: I have established my Grammar upon principles whose simplicity exemplifies its veracity and strength. Now it is only a question of applying these principles. The Sepher is presented. But what a host of phantoms move by its side!

Child of the past and teeming with the future, this book, inheritor of all the sciences of the Egyptians bears still the germs of future sciences. Fruit of divine inspiration it contains in few pages the elements of that which was, and the elements of that which shall be. All the secrets of Nature are entrusted to it. All. It assembles in the Beræshith alone, more things than all the accumulated books in European libraries. Whatever is most profound, most mysterious in Nature, whatever wonders can be conceived in the mind; whatever is most sublime in the understanding, this book possesses it.

The Sepher is the basis of the Christian and Mussulman religions, as well as that of the Judaic, which claims justly the name of their common mother; but this basis is equally unknown to all three, as far as the vulgar teaching is concerned; for I know that among the Israelites there exist certain successors of the Essenes who possess the oral traditions, and among the Christians and Mussulmans certain men more advanced than others in the interpretation of the Sacred Books. The versions which these three religions possess are all made in the spirit of that of the Hellenists which has been their model: that is to say, that they deal with the exterior forms of the work of Moses, with the grossest and most material sense only, the one which this theocrat had destined as a veil for the spiritual sense, the knowledge of which he reserved for the initiates. Now to what point ought one to reveal this basis upon which repose the three dominating cults of the earth? To what point ought one to lighten the mysterious darkness by which it has with purpose been surrounded?

These are the stumbling blocks that I have long since foreseen and whose principle I have already attacked in my Dissertation; for if it is true, as everything convinces me, that Providence, opening the portals of a New Day, is pushing minds on toward the perfecting of knowledge, is recalling Truth designedly eclipsed, and is hastening the downfall of prejudices which had served it in less happy times; what are these stumbling blocks whose aspect terrifies? Vain phantoms that the breath of Truth ought to dissipate and will dissipate.

Europe, after long darkness and keen agitations, enlightened by the successive efforts of the sages of all nations, and taught by her misfortunes and her own experiences, seems at last to have arrived at the moment of enjoying in peace the fruit of her labours. Escaped from the moral winter whose thick mists had long obscured her horizon she has for several centuries experienced the productive warmth of spring. Already the flowers of thought from all parts have embellished the reigns of Alphonso, of the Medicis and of Louis XIV*. Her spiritual summer draws nigh and the fruit is about to succeed the flowers. Minds more advanced demand more solid food.

The ancient religions and particularly that of the Egyptians, were full of mysteries, and composed of numberless pictures and symbols, sacred work of an uninterrupted chain of divine men, who, reading in the book of Nature and in that of the Divinity, translated into human

---

* I call the age of Alphonso, that in which the Oscan troubadours appeared. Alphonso X, king of Leon and Castile, through his love for the sciences merits the honour of giving his name to the age which saw them renascent in Europe. In my younger days I consecrated to the memory of the Oscan troubadours, a work in which I tried to do for them what Macpherson had already done for the bards of the North. I was at that time quite far from the ideas which occupy me now.

language, the ineffable language. Those whose dull glance, falling upon these pictures, these symbols, these holy allegories, saw nothing beyond, were sunk, it is true, in ignorance; but their ignorance was voluntary. From the moment that they wished to leave it, they had only to speak. All the sanctuaries were opened to them, and if they had the necessary constancy and virtue, nothing hindered them from passing from knowledge to knowledge, from revelation to revelation to the sublimest discoveries. They might, living and human, according to the force of their will, descend among the dead, rise to the gods and penetrate everything in elementary nature. For religion embraced all these things, and nothing of that which composed religion remained unknown to the sovereign pontiff. The one, for example, at the famous Egyptian Thebes, reached this culminating point of the sacred doctrine only after having passed through all the inferior grades, having exhausted in succession the portion of science allotted to each grade, and having proved himself worthy of attaining to the highest.

The king of Egypt alone was initiated by right, and by the inevitable course of his education, admitted to the most secret mysteries. The priests had the instruction of their order, their knowledge increased as they rose in rank and all knew that their superiors were not only much higher but much more enlightened. So that the sacerdotal hierarchy like a pyramid seated upon its base, offered always in its theocratic organization, knowledge allied with power. As to the people, they were, according to their inclination whatever they wished to be. Knowledge offered to all Egyptians was forced upon none. The dogmas of morality, the laws of politics, the restraint of opinion, the yoke of civil institutions were the same for all; but the religious instruction differed according to the capacity, virtue and will of each individual. They were not prodigal with the mysteries, and did not profane the knowledge of the Divinity; in order to preserve the Truth, it was not given indiscriminately.

This was the condition of things in Egypt, when Moses, obedient to a special impulse from Providence followed the path of sacerdotal initiation, and with such constancy as perhaps only Pythagoras later displayed, passed through all tests, surmounted all obstacles and braving the death threatening each step, attained at Thebes the highest degree of divine knowledge. This knowledge which he modified by a particular inspiration, he enclosed entire in the Beræshith, that is to say, in the first book of his Sepher, reserving as its safe-guard the four books which follow, and which give to the people who should be its trustee, ideas, institutions and laws which would distinguish them essentially from all other peoples, marking them with an indelible character.

I have already related the various revolutions undergone by the Sepher, in order to show that the condition of things in Europe and in all parts of the earth, wherever the Judaic cult and its two derivatives—the Christian and Islamic, have extended, is precisely the inverse of what it was in Egypt at the epoch when the germ of this cult was detached from it and entrusted to the Hebrew people. The *Beræshith* which contains all the secrets of elementary and divine Nature, offered to peoples, to the heads of peoples, to the priests themselves, under its most material covering, commands their faith in this state, and presents as basis of their religion a sequence of pictures and symbols that human reason, at the point which it has attained can only grasp with great difficulty.

It cannot be said, as in Egypt, that the understanding of these pictures or the revelation of the symbols may be given to whomsoever desires it. Not at all. The Judaic priesthood, destined to guard the Sepher of Moses, has not been generally destined to comprehend it and still less to explain it. Possessor of the profoundest mysteries, this priesthood is to these mysteries as the Egyptian people were to theirs: with this difference, that the position of this priesthood does not allow it to penetrate these mysteries; for in order to do this it would have to recognize superiors and address itself to the Essenes whose doctrine it condemns and whose traditions it does not admit as authentic. Moreover these Essenes, isolated, unknown and often persecuted, no longer offer today a sufficient guarantee. Thus this priesthood, whose devotion to the exterior forms of the Sepher, is in keeping with its fidelity to the purpose of its institution, is further from divine knowledge in the highest of its priests than in its humblest; for its purpose, as I have said, being to preserve and not to comprehend, it had to be limited to transmitting intact the sacred storehouse which had been confided to its keeping, and this obligation it has fulfilled with a force, constancy and rectitude beyond all eulogy.

Has the Christian priesthood in receiving this storehouse from the hands of the Judaic priesthood, contracted the same obligations? That is to say, is it bound to transmit it faithfully from generation to generation without ever being permitted to open it? It is not my purpose to determine this question. But in the state of civilization and enlightenment which Europe has attained since the invention of printing, the Sepher of Moses has not remained a book entirely theological. Spread broadcast in all classes of society, thanks to this admirable invention, it has been examined by all sorts of persons and subjected to the rigorous analysis of savants. All sects have taken possession of it and vying with one another, have sought reasons for defending their belief. The numberless disputes brought forth by the various interpretations of which the text has been believed susceptible, has made this text more and more popular; so that one may say with reason that this book has also become a classic. It is under this last relation that the lay writers consider it in Europe today, and that I myself consider it*.

---

* The study of the Sepher of Moses, very widespread in Germany and in England, and the examination of the divers parts of which it is composed, has brought forth in these countries a new science known by the modern savants under the name of *Exegesis*.

I have therefore translated the *Cosmogony of Moses* as *littérateur,* after having restored, as grammarian, the tongue in which this Cosmogony was written in its original text.

Therefore it is not for the theologian that I have written, but for the *littérateur,* for the people of the world, for the savants, for all persons desirous of knowing the ancient mysteries and of seeing to what point, the peoples who have preceded us in the course of life, had penetrated into the sanctuary of nature and into that of knowledge; for I believe I have expressed quite strongly, my opinion concerning the origin of the Sepher: this book is, according to the proofs which I have given in my Introductory Dissertation, one of the genetical books of the Egyptians, issued, as far as its first part called *Beræshith* is concerned, from the depths of the temples of Memphis or of Thebes; Moses, who received extracts therefrom in the course of his initiations had only arranged them, and added according to the providential will which guided him, the enlightenment of his own inspiration, so as to confide this storehouse to the people by whom he was recognized as prophet and theocratic lawgiver.

My translation of the *Cosmogony of Moses* should be considered only as a *literary work* and by no means as a *theological work.* I have not intended it to command the faith of anyone and still less to distress anyone. I have carefully put aside from my notes all that which might have any reference to theological disputes; limiting myself to prove grammatically the meaning that I have given to the words and to show the strong connection of this meaning with what followed or with what had preceded. I have purposely omitted any commentary; leaving the reader to make his own comparisons.

However it is not through timidity nor through ignorance of reasons which I might use, that I have evaded theological controversy; it is through respect for the Christian church which must know perfectly to what point she ought or ought not to adopt the new ideas that I present. These ideas, purely literary, as long as they remain in my book, might become theological, and would become irresistibly so, by passing into the books of theologians and being subjected to their interpretations.

Whatever may be the fate of my book, I think that it will not be from the Reformed Christians, Lutherans or Calvinists that I shall find slanderers. For, is there in Germany, in England or elsewhere, a Protestant even slightly instructed in the motives of the Reformation who has not learned early to weigh the authorities and appreciate them at their just value? What disciple of Luther or Calvin does not know that any version whatsoever of the Sepher can never be made a rule in the matter of faith, and in no case should usurp the place of the original text and be followed in preference? If he pretended otherwise, would he not deny the fundamental principle of his sect and would he not repudiate its authors? What have Luther, Zwingli and Calvin said, and before them John Huss, Wycliff and Berenger; that the Scripture alone was and ought to be the rule of faith; that every man of sane understanding and just mind, became its legitimate interpreter after his studies had given him such power, or when God had deigned to grant him the inspiration? Now of which Scriptures did these promoters of the Reform speak, these proud antagonists of sacerdotal authority? Was it of the Scriptures of the Hellenists or that of Saint Jerome? Assuredly not; but of the original Scriptures: and this is so true that, suspecting these imperfect copies, with just reason, of not being sufficiently confirmed, nearly all of them undertook a new translation of the text. If they did not succeed in the interpretations which they gave of the Sepher, it was because the means and not the will was lacking. The temporal state of things at that time was opposed to their desires. They have attempted it, and that is enough to legitimatize my efforts in the eyes of the Reformers as this is all that I have claimed to do.

If among the Catholic priesthood there are men judicious enough to consider, in this purely literary work, what it has useful to morality and to religion in general, and who, ready to receive the truth if it were shown them, await only a legal authority to sanction an examination; I could give them satisfaction: for it is not for want of proofs that I avoid controversies but for want of inclination. Here are two authorities that cannot be challenged. The first, that of Saint Paul, the wisest of the apostles, proves that already in his time, it was an acknowledged opinion that the Jews no longer understood the text of the Sepher, and had not the power to raise the veil which Moses had spread over his doctrine.

The second, that of Saint Augustine, the most learned of the Fathers of the Church, proves my entire translation in giving to the first two verses of the Beræshith, exactly the same meaning as I have given; a meaning wholly contrary to the Vulgate.

"But our sufficiency is of God; who also hath made us able ministers of the New Testament; not of the letter, but of the spirit . . . Seeing then that we have such hope, we use great plainness of speech: and not as Moses which put a veil over his face, that the children of Israel could not steadfastly look to the end of that which is abolished: but their minds were blinded: for until this day remaineth the same veil untaken away in the reading of the Old Testament; which veil is done away in Christ. But even unto this day, when Moses is read, the veil is upon their heart". . . *.

---

* *Epist. Corinth.* II. ch. 3. Here is this remarkable passage of Saint Paul in its Hellenistic text, with an interlinear interpretation in Latin.

'Αλλ' ἡ ἱκανότης ἡμῶν ἐκ τοῦ Θεοῦ, ὃς καὶ ἱκάνωσεν ἡμᾶς διακόνους καινῆς
Sed sufficientia nostra ex Deo, qui et idoneos fecit nos ministros novi

διαθήκης; οὐ γραμμάτος, ἀλλὰ πνεύματος...... ἔχοντες οὖν τοιαύτην ἐλπίδα,
testamenti; non litteræ, sed spiritus...... habentes igitur talem spem,

πολλὺ παῤῥεσία χρώμεθα: καὶ οὐ καθάπερ Μωυσῆς, ἐτίθει κάλυμμα ἐπὶ τὸ προ-
multa libertate utimur: et non sicut Moyses, ponebot velamen super fa-
    fiducia

Saint Augustine, examining the question of the creation in his book of Genesis, against the Manichæans, expresses himself thus: "It is said: *in principle, God made heaven and earth;* not that this was in effect, but because this was in power of being; for it is written that heaven was made afterward. It is thus, that considering the *seed* of a tree, we say that it has there the roots, trunk, branches, fruit and leaves; not that all these things are formally there, but virtually, and destined to be brought forth. Just as it is said, *in principle God made heaven and earth;* that is to say, the seed of heaven and earth; since the matter of heaven and earth was then in a state of confusion. Now, as it is certain that from this matter the heaven and the earth must be brought forth, that is why this matter was already called potentially the heaven and the earth" . . . .**

It seems to me difficult to add anything more to texts so concise. I refrain from all commentary upon that of Saint Paul; my design moreover not being, as I have said,

σωπον ἑαυτοῦ πρὸς τὸ μὴ ἀτενίσαι τοὺς υἱοὺς Ἰσραὴλ εἰς τὸ τέλος τοῦ καταρ-
ciem suam ad non intueri filios Israel in finem hujus abro-
mysterium

γουμένου. Ἀλλ' επωρώθη τὰ νοήματα αὐτῶν; ἄχρι γὰρ τῆς σήμερον τὸ αὐτὸ
gati. Sed obduruerunt cogitationes eorum; usque enim hodie id ipsum

κάλυμμα ἐπὶ τῇ ἀναγνώσειτῆς παλαῖας διαθήκης μένει μὴ ἀνακαλυπτόμενον, ὅ τι
velamen super lectionem veteris testamenti manet non revelatum, quod

ἐν Χριστῷ καταργεῖται. Ἀλλ' ἕως σήμερον ἡνίκα ἀναγινώσκεται Μωυσῆς, κάλυμμα
in Christo abrogatur. Sed donec hodie, cum legitur Moyses, velamen

ἐπὶ τὴν καρδίαν αὐτῶν κεῖται....
super cor eorum positum est....

** I give the text itself of Saint Augustine so that it may be compared with my translation.

"Dictum est: *In principio fecit Deus cœlum et terram;* non quia jam hoc erat, sed quia hoc esse poterat: nam et cœlum scribitur postea factum. Quemadmodum si *semen* arboris considerantes, dicamus ibi esse radices, et robur, et ramos, et fructus, et folia, non quia jam sunt, sed quia inde futura sunt. Sic dictum est: *in principio fecit Deus cœlum et terram*, quasi semen cœli et terræ, cum in confuso adhuc esset cœli et terræ materia: sed quia certum erat inde futurum esse cœlum et terram, jam et ipsa materia, cœlum et terra appellata est. (L. I. c. 3 *num.* 11.)

to enter into discussion with the theologians. But I believe it necessary to say that Saint Augustine, still quite young when he composed his books of Genesis against the Manichæans, and when he might have been accused of being carried away by flights of his imagination, was so far from repudiating afterward the opinion that I have just quoted, that, recalling it in the confessions of his old age, he still regarded it as a divine inspiration; "Is it not Thou, O Lord, who hast taught me, that before fashioning this unformed matter and distinguishing its parts, it was nothing in particular, no colour, no form, neither body nor spirit? . . . "

And further on: "If I confess, O Lord, both by tongue and pen, what Thou hast taught me concerning this matter . . . what Thou hast revealed to me upon this difficult question . . . my heart ceases not to render homage to Thee for this, and to offer up its hymns of praise for the things that it knows not how to express."

But this is sufficient for the judicious men of whom I speak; the others will not be wanting in reasons for perverting the truth of the text of Saint Paul and for invalidating what Saint Augustine said. Let them guard carefully without ever opening the mysterious coffer which has been confided to them; but, since this coffer, through the irresistible progress of things, has become the patrimony of a multitude of persons of every nation and every cult, let them at least permit those among them who, far from the service of altars, devote themselves to the study of the sciences and strive to draw from it new principles and learning which may be used for the advancement of knowledge and the welfare of humanity. The times now are no longer those in which the simplest truths could not be shown without veils. Natural philosophy and mathematics have made such great strides, and have in such a manner, uncovered the secret resources of the Universe, that it is no longer allowable for moral and metaphysical sciences to drag after them the cradle blankets of infancy. It is necessary that the harmony which has been interrupted between these two principal branches of human understanding be reëstablished. This is what the savants, ordained to know nature in its double sanctuary, must endeavour to do with necessary prudence and precaution; for every divulgation has limits that one must know how to respect.

So much for the two difficulties of which I have spoken at the beginning of this Discourse. Both are dispelled before what I have just said: first, because minds long since open to the light of reason, furnish no more food for religious conflagrations; afterward, because the rays of truth purified today by the prism of science, enlighten the souls and burn them no more. Moreover, the form that I have given my work and the scientific staging with which I have been forced to surround it, will hinder its popularity.

This staging is immense. The reader has already seen it in the first part: that is to say, the radical Vocabulary where all the Hebraic roots explain themselves readily; the Grammar whose principles are attached to those of speech, and an Introductory Dissertation wherein I have explained my thought upon the origin of Hebrew, upon that of the Sepher, upon the divers revolutions experienced by this book, and upon the versions which have been made of it, particularly that of the Hellenists, vulgarly called Septuagint*.

In the second part is the *Cosmogony of Moses*. Now what I call the *Cosmogony of Moses* is included in the first ten chapters of the *Berœshith*, the first of the five books of the Sepher. These ten chapters form a kind of sacred decade in which each of the ten chapters bears the character of its number as I shall show. It has been assumed that the divisions of the Sepher, in books, as well as in chapters and verses, were the work of Esdras. I do not think so. These ten chapters which contain the whole, and whose

---

* There will be found here several phrases already inserted in the prospectus of this work; but these repetitions were unavoidable.

number indicates the summary, prove to me that the *Science of Numbers* was cultivated long before Pythagoras, and that Moses having learned it from the Egyptians, used it in the division of his work.

The entire Cosmogony, that is to say, the origin of the Universe, that of the beings, from the elementary principle to man, their principal vicissitudes, the general history of the earth and its inhabitants, is contained in these ten chapters. I have not deemed it necessary to translate further; inasmuch as this suffices to prove all that I have advanced and nothing prevents anyone from applying my grammatical principles and continuing the exploration of the Sepher.

The Hebraic text which I quote is that contained in the Polyglot of Paris. I have scrupulously preserved all the characters without altering any under pretext of re-forming it. I have likewise preserved of the Chaldaic punctuation, all that has appeared to me necessary for the reading of the text or required by grammatical rules; I have suppressed only the Masoretic minutiæ and the musical notes, called improperly accents, of which I have said often in my Grammar, that I regarded its usage as absolutely foreign to the sense, and useful only for the Jews of the synagogue who wish to continue singing psalms in a tongue lost for twenty-five centuries.

I have considered this text as correct, and I have avoided the paradoxical spirit of those who have claimed that the Jews had designedly falsified their Scriptures. I know that among the Fathers who have sustained this paradox, are cited Saint Justin Martyr, Saint Irenus, Tertullian and others: but besides the fact that these Fathers always mean by the Hebrew text which they disparage, the Greek version of Aquila, or that of Symmachus, versions made in opposition to that of the Septuagint, it is unfortunate that they did not know a word of Hebrew. For, how can persons who do not know a tongue say that a book written in this tongue, an original, is not worth the translation which has been made of it? In order to sustain such an assertion, they must quote the falsified passages and prove that its words, that its style, are obviously altered. This is what they were incapable of doing.

When one knows with what religious care, with what scruples, with what excess of attention the Jews copy the sacred text of the Sepher, and preserve it, such ideas cannot be admitted. One can see in Maimonides, what the prescribed rules are in this respect. They are such that it is impossible that the least error, that the least oversight, can ever creep into the manuscripts destined for the use of the synagogues. Those who have not seen these manuscripts can have no idea what patience assisted by religious zeal can accomplish. Father Morin and Vossius, who have adopted the paradox of the Fathers of the Church, prove by that, to what point prejudice can obscure knowledge and render it vain. If the original text offers certain errors, they are slight, and are always anterior to Esdras, or at least to the Septuagint version. It is true that the manuscripts of the synagogues are without any kind of vowel points or accents; but, as I have repeated often enough, the meaning never depends upon these points. The meaning depends upon the root, upon the sign which rules it and upon the place that the word occupies.

It is always necessary, before determining the signification of any Hebrew word whatsoever, to interrogate the primitive meaning of the root, which is easy if it is a simple root; if the word is compound, it is necessary to refrain from any interpretation before having made the grammatical analysis according to the rules that I have given and upon which the use of my notes will shed much light. The primitive meaning of the root being always generic, it must first be modified by the sign, or signs, by which this same root may be accompanied and never particularized, according to the advice of the wise Maimonides, without long meditation upon the subject of which it treats, upon the occasion which brings about the expression, upon the thought of the writer, upon the movement of the style, literal or figurative and upon all the circumstances which, among a great number of significations, incline the word to one rather than to another. The usefulness of the vowel points is limited to giving the vulgar pronunciation of the word and determining its grammatical forms whether as noun, verb or relation.

I have transcribed the original text in English characters to facilitate the reading for persons little familiar with the Hebraic characters; I have tried, as far as possible in this transcription to reconcile the primitive orthography with the Chaldaic punctuation. I have, for that reason, given carefully and in conformity with the comparative Alphabet inserted in my grammar, the value of the consonants; I have indicated the presence of the first four mother vowels א, ו, ו, ו, by a circumflex accent on the corresponding vowels *â, oû, ô, î;* and those of the other three ה, ה, ע, by the aspiration *h, h* and *h.* When the mother vowels ו, ו, ע, have appeared to be consonants I have expressed them by *w, j* and *gh,* or *wh.* I have indicated the vague vowel of the Chaldaic punctuation by the corresponding English vowels without accent. When I have found a vague vowel opposing a mother vowel, I have amalgamated them, forming thereby a sort of diphthong *æ, æ aï, ao,* etc.

It has seemed to me advisable before giving the correct translation of the Hebraic text, to approach as near as possible by a literal *word-for-word,* which would make my readers understand the exact value of each term of the original with its grammatical forms, according to the tongue of Moses. This was very difficult because of the signification of the words, which, nearly always metaphorical, and not being found contained in modern tongues in simple and analogous terms, requires a periphrasis. The Asiatic tongues, in general and particularly Hebrew, cannot be paralleled word-for-word with European tongues, and this is easy to conceive; for, in a word-for-word translation it would be necessary that the same literal ideas should be developed, the same ideas represented, or that the same universal ideas should have sprung from the same particular ideas; which is impossible in tongues so opposed, so diverse, spoken by peoples so different, so distant from one another in times and customs.

In order to obviate this difficulty as much as possible, I resolved to compose two literal versions, the one French and the other English; so that the word-for-word of the one, throwing light upon the word-for-word of the other, they are mutually sustained and together lead the reader to the desired end. I have chosen from among all the European tongues, the English tongue, as one of the most simple and the one whose grammar less rigid, allows me more facility in the construction. I believe I have no need of saying that one must not seek for elegance or grammatical purism in these two versions where I have purposely taken the greatest license.

I have supported these two versions with numerous notes, in which, applying the principles developed in my Grammar, I have proved the signification given to each word of the original text, in the strongest manner, taking one by one, each of these words, I have analyzed it by its root, reduced it to its elementary principles, modified it by the sign, decomposed, recomposed and, every time it has been necessary, confronted it with the corresponding word in Samaritan, Chaldaic, Syriac, Arabic, Ethiopic even, and Greek.

Thus I have prepared the correct translation of the *Cosmogony of Moses* with which I terminate this work. I venture to believe that it would be difficult to prepare this result by means more fitting to demonstrate its truth, to establish it upon bases more solid, or to attain this end after efforts more sustained and less subject to illusion.

Therefore, in going back to the principles of Speech, and finding on this path the thought of Moses, I have interpreted and set forth in suitable language, the work of this great man whose energetic influence exerting itself for thirty-four centuries has, under sundry names, directed the destiny of the earth. My intention having been steadfastly sincere I trust that its results will be felicitous.

Through this translation which I give of the Sepher, Moses will no longer be the stumbling-block of reason and the dismay of the natural sciences. Those shocking contradictions, those incoherencies, those ridiculous pictures which furnish weapons so terrible for its enemies shall be no more seen in his Cosmogony. Nor shall one see in him, a limited man attributing to the Being of beings the narrowest views and passions, refusing his immortality to man and speaking only of the soul which passes away with the blood; but a sage, initiated in all the mysteries of Nature, uniting to the positive knowledge which he has imbibed in the sanctuaries of Thebes, the knowledge of his own inspiration. If the naturalist interrogates it, he will find in his work the accumulated observations of a sequence of incalculable centuries, and all the natural philosophy of the Egyptians summed up in a few words: he will be able to compare this imposing natural philosophy with that of the moderns and judge in what the one resembles, surpasses or is inferior to the other. The metaphysician will have nothing to compare with it since real metaphysics does not exist among us. But it is the philosopher especially who will discover in this book analogies worthy of his curiosity. If he desires it, this book will become in his hands a veritable *criterion*, a touchstone, by means of which he will be able to recognize, in any system of philosophy whatsoever, the truth or error it contains. He will find there finally, what the philosophers have thought most just or most sublime from Thales and Pythagoras, to Newton and Kant. My notes will furnish him with much data in this respect.

Besides I have had constantly before me, during the long composition of these notes, *the four original versions*: that of the Samaritans, the Chaldaic targums, the Hellenistic version called the Septuagint, and the Latin Vulgate of Saint Jerome. I have quoted them when it has been necessary. I have paid little attention to other versions; for it is proved, for example, that the Syriac version, made from that of the Hellenists and which agrees with the Greek whilst the latter differs materially from the Hebrew, has been the text for the Arabic version; so that neither has authority. But it is useless to return incessantly to things that have been sufficiently explained.

Cosmogony of Moses

SEPHER BERÆSHITH
A.

סֵפֶר בְּרֵאשִׁית א׃

1. BERÆSHITH barà Ælo-
hîm æth-ha-shamaîm w'æth-
ha-âretz.

בְּרֵאשִׁית בָּרָא אֱלֹהִים אֵת־
הַשָּׁמַיִם וְאֵת־הָאָרֶץ ׃

---

v. 1. בְּרֵאשִׁית *At-first-in-principle....* In these notes, it is not my
intention either to examine or discuss the opinions which the savants
of past centuries, Jews or Christians, have put forth upon the hidden
meaning of this word or of those which follow. It would be a task quite
as long as tedious. I shall explain, but I shall not comment; for this
is not a system that I am establishing upon conjectures or probabilities
more or less happy, but the tongue itself of Moses, that I am interpreting according to its constitutive principles.

Therefore, setting aside the sundry interpretations good or bad,
which have been given to the word בְּרֵאשִׁית, I shall say that this
word, in the position which it occupies, offers three distinct meanings: the literal, the figurative, and the hieroglyphic. Moses has used
all three, as is proved in the course of his work. He has followed in
this, the method of the Egyptian priests: for these priests had three
ways of expressing their thought. The first was clear and simple,
the second, symbolic and figurative, the third sacred or hieroglyphic.
They made use of three kinds of characters, but not of three dialects,
as might be imagined. The same word took at their pleasure, the
literal, figurative or hieroglyphic sense. Such was the genius of
their tongue. Heraclitus has expressed perfectly the difference of these
three styles, in designating them by the epithets, *spoken, significant*
and *hidden.* The first two ways, that is to say, those which consisted
of taking words in the literal or the figurative sense, were spoken;
but the third, which could only receive its hieroglyphic form by means
of the characters of which the words were composed, existed only for
the eyes, and was used only in writing. Our modern tongues are
entirely incapable of making this distinction. Moses, initiated in all
the mysteries of the Egyptian priesthood, made use of these three

GENESIS 1.

1. AT-FIRST-IN-PRINCIPLE, he - created, Ælohim (he caused to be, he brought forth in principle, HE-the-Gods, the-Being-of-beings), the-selfsameness-of-heavens, and - the - selfsameness - of - earth.

COSMOGONIE 1.

1. PREMIÈREMENT - EN - PRINCIPE, il créa, Ælohîm (il détermina en existence potentielle, LUI-les-Dieux, l'Être-des-êtres), l'ipséité-des-cieux et-l'ipséité-de-la-terre.

---

ways with unbounded skill; his phrase is almost invariably constituted in such a manner as to present three meanings: this is why no kind of word-for-word can render his thought. I have adhered as much as possible to expressing the literal and figurative sense together. As to the hieroglyphic, it would often be too dangerous to give it; but I have made every effort to furnish the means of attaining it, by stating its principles and by giving examples.

The word בראשית, which is here in question, is a modificative noun formed from the substantive ראש, *the head, the chief, the acting principle*, inflected by the mediative article ב, and modified by the designative ending ית. It signifies literally, *in the beginning, before all;* but figuratively *in principle, in power of being.*

Thus one can deduce the hieroglyphic sense. What I am about to say will serve as example for what follows. The word ראש, from which is formed the modificative בראשית, signifies indeed *head;* but only in a restricted and particular sense. In a broader and more generic sense, it signifies *principle.* Now, what is a principle? I shall state in what manner the earliest authors of the word ראש, conceived it. They conceived a sort of absolute power, by means of which every relative being is constituted such; they expressed their idea by the potential sign א, and the relative sign ש, united. In hieroglyphic writing it was a point at the centre of a circle. The central point unfolding the circumference, was the image of every principle. The literal writing rendered the point by א, and the circle by ס or ש. The letter ס represented the sentient circle, the letter ש the intelligible circle which was depicted winged or surrounded with flames.

2. W'ha-âretz haîthah thohoû wa-bohoû, w'hoshèch hal-phenî th'hôm, w'roûah Ælohîm merahepheth hal-phenî ha-maîm.

וְהָאָרֶץ הָיְתָה תֹהוּ וָבֹהוּ וְחֹשֶׁךְ
עַל־פְּנֵי תְהוֹם וְרוּחַ אֱלֹהִים
מְרַחֶפֶת עַל־פְּנֵי הַמָּיִם :

A principle thus conceived was, in an universal sense, applicable to all things, both physical and metaphysical; but in a more restricted sense it was applied to elementary fire; and according as the radical word אש was taken literally or figuratively, it signified *fire*, sentient or intelligible, that of matter, or that of spirit.

Next, taking this same word אש, whose origin I am about to explain, it was made to govern by the sign of proper and determining movement ר, and the compound word ראש was obtained; that is to say, in hieroglyphic language, every principle enjoying a proper and determining movement, and of a force innately good or bad. This letter ר is rendered in sacred writing by the image of a serpent, upright or crossing the circle through the centre. In the common language one saw in the word ראש, a chief, a guide, the head of such a being, of such a thing, whatever it might be: in the figurative language, is understood the *primum mobile*, an acting principle, a good or evil genius, a right or perverse will, a demon, etc; in the hieroglyphic language, it signalized the universal, *principiant principle*, the knowledge of which it was not permitted to divulge.

These are the three significations of the word ראש, which serves as basis for the modificative בראשית. It is obvious that it would be impossible for me to enter into similar details concerning all the words which are to follow. I could not do it without going beyond the limits of prudence. But I shall endeavour, in amalgamating the three significations, to give the intelligent reader all the facilities that he could desire.

Here are the four original versions of this important word. The Samaritan version reads ꚠꙭ꙼ꚒꙮꟼꝐ that is to say, *in substantiality, in corporeity, in the beginning.* The Chaldaic targum reads בקדמין, which can be translated, *in the culminating point of the universal assimilations; in the anteriority of times.* The Hellenists translate 'Εν ἀρχῇ, and the Latins, "in principio." The former is more akin to the

2. And-the-earth was contingent-potentiality in-a-potentiality - of - being: and - darkness (hard-making-power)-was on-the-face of-the deep (fathomless-contingent-potentiality of being); and-the-breath of-HIM-the-Gods (a light-making-power) was-pregnantly-moving upon-the-face of-the-waters (universal passiveness).

2. Et-la-terre e x i s t a i t puissance-contingente-d'être dans-une-puissance-d'être : et -l'obscurité (force compressive et durcissante)-était sur-la-face de l'abîme (puissance universelle et contingente d'être); et-le-souffle de-LUI-les-Dieux (force expansive et dilatante) était-génératiment-mouvant sur-la-face des-eaux (passivité universelle).

Samaritan, and the latter to the Chaldaic. Which is natural, for, as I have said, the Hellenists consulted frequently the Samaritan version, while Saint Jerome and the rabbis of Tiberias adhered to the targums.

ברא, *he created*.... It would be not only long but useless to dwell upon the numerous disputes concerning this word; they are all reduced to this, namely, whether the verb ברוא signifies *to make something from nothing*, or simply, *to make something from something*. The rabbis of the synagogue and the doctors of the church, have indeed proved by these wordy struggles, that not any of them understood the tongue over which they disputed: for otherwise they would have seen that they were very far from the point of the question. I have already had occasion to bring out the true etymology of this famous verb, and I have proved that it signified, *to draw from an unknown element; to make pass from the principle to the essence; to render same that which was other*, etc., as can be seen in chapter VII of my Grammar. I have derived it from the sign of movement proper ר, united to that of interior action ב. The Arabs have translated it by خلق, whose root خل signifies a thing rare and tenuous, a thing without form and without consistency, a void, a nothingness. The Greeks have rendered it by ἐποίησεν, *he made*, and the Latins by "creavit," *he created*. This last expression, clearly understood, is not far from the Hebrew, for it comes from the same elementary root אר, raised from the sign of movement proper ר. It is the word "re," indicating *the thing*, by means of which one acts, which is governed by the assimilative sign כ used very extensively by the Etruscans. This word, having become

3.   Wa-îâomer Ælohîm   וַיֹּאמֶר אֱלֹהִים יְהִי־אוֹר וַיְהִי־
îehî-âôr,   wa-îehî-âôr.   אוֹר :

---

the verb c-re-are, takes in this new state, a sense which can only be
rended exactly by coining the verb to thing. The Samaritans have
expressed the Hebrew by 𝕎𝕒𝕑2𝕍 which signifies literally to render
dense and compact; as is proved by the Chaldaic טלם. The targum
has preserved the primitive word ברא.

אלהים, Ælohim.... This is the plural of the word אלה, the name
given to the Supreme Being by the Hebrews and the Chaldeans, and
being itself derived from the root אל, which depicts elevation, strength
and expansive power; signifiying in an universal sense, GOD. It is a
very singular observation that this last word applied to the Most
High, is however, in its abstract sense only the relative pronoun he
employed in an absolute manner. Nearly all of the Asiatic peoples
have used this bold metaphor. הוא (hoa), that is to say, HE, is in
Hebrew, Chaldaic, Syriac, Ethiopic and Arabic, one of the sacred names
of the Divinity; it is evident that the Persian word خدا (Goda), GOD,
which is found in all the tongues of the North, is derived also from
the absolute pronoun خود, HIM-self. It is known that the Greek
philosophers and Plato particularly, designated the Intelligent Cause
of the Universe in no other way than by the absolute pronoun τὸ Αὐτό.

However that may be, the Hebraic name Ælohim has been obviously composed of the pronoun אל and the absolute verb הוה,
to be-being, of which I have spoken at length in my Grammar. It
is from the inmost root of this verb that the Divine Name יה (Yah)
is formed, the literal meaning of which is Absolute-Life. The verb
itself, united to the pronoun אל, produces אלוה (Æloah), that-HE
who-IS, the plural of which Ælohim, signifies exactly HE-they-who-
ARE: the Being of beings.

The Samaritan says 𝟑𝟒2𝕒 (Alah), whose root אל is found still
in the Arabic الله (Allah), and in the Syriac ܐܠܗܐ (Æloha). The
Chaldaic alone departs from this root and translates ייי (Iaii), the
Eternity-of-eternities, which it also applies to the Ineffable Name
of GOD, יהוה (Ihoah), of which I shall speak further on; also of the
words שמים, the heavens, and ארץ, the earth.

3. And-he-said (declaring his will), HE-the-Being-of-beings: there-shall-be light; and-there-(shall be)-became light (intellectual elementizing).

3. Et-il-dit (déclarant sa volenté), L U I-l'Être-des êtres: sera_faite-lumière; et-(sera)-fut-faite lumière (élémentisation intelligible).

---

v. 2. וּבֹהוּ תֹהוּ, *contingent-potentiality in-a-potentiality-of-being*.... If one examines the sense of the four original versions, a great difference is found between what they say and what I say. The Samaritan version reads ⵏⵎⵎⵏⵯⵎⵏ⸱ⵯⵏⵯⵎ, *distended to incomprehensibility and most rare*. The Chaldaic targum says צָדְיָא וְרֵקָנְיָא, *divided to annihilation and vain*. The Hellenists translate ἀόρατος καὶ ἀκατασκεύαστος, *invisible and decomposed*. Saint Jerome understood "inanis et vacua" *unanimated and vague*, or *unformed and void*. The error into which all these translators have fallen depends here upon a prior one very slight in appearance, but whose consequences becoming more and more complicated pushes them into an abyss from which nothing can draw them. This first error depends upon the manner in which they have understood the first word of the Sepher, the famous בְּרֵאשִׁית. This word, having impressed them neither in its figurative nor in its hieroglyphic sense, has involved all that follows, in the literal and material sense that they have given to it. I pray the reader to give strict attention to this, for upon this depends all the incoherences, all the absurdities with which Moses has been reproached. In fact, if the word בְּרֵאשִׁית signified simply, in the beginning, in the beginning of time, as it was said, why did not the heavens and the earth, created at that epoch, still exist at that time; why should there be need of a successive development; why should they have rested an eternity in darkness; why should the light have been made after the heavens and before the sun; can one conceive the heavens without light, light without the sun, an earth invisible, inanimate, vain, formless, if it is material; etc., etc. But what can remedy all this? Absolutely nothing but an understanding of the tongue which is translated and seeing that בְּרֵאשִׁית means not only *in the beginning*, ἐν ἀρχῇ, "in principio," but clearly *in principle*; that is to say, not yet in action but in power; as Saint

4.   Wa-îara Ælohîm æth-
ha-aôr čhi tôb, wa-îabeddel
Ælohîm beîn ha-âôr w'beîn
ha-hoshečh.

וַיַּרְא אֱלֹהִים אֶת הָאוֹר כִּי טוֹב
וַיַּבְדֵּל אֱלֹהִים בֵּין הָאוֹר וּבֵין
הַחֹשֶׁךְ :

Augustine interpreted it. This is the thought of Moses, profound thought
which he expresses admirably by the words תהו ובהו, in which he depicts
with masterhand that state of a thing, not only in contingent power
of being, but still contained in another power of being; in short,
without form, in germ in a germ. It is the famous χαός of the Greeks,
that *chaos* which the vulgar have also gradually materialized and
whose figurative and hieroglyphic signification I could very easily demonstrate were it necessary.

The Hebraic words תהו ובהו belong to those words which the sages
create in learned tongues and which the vulgar do not comprehend.
Let us now examine their figurative and hieroglyphic sense.

. We know that the sign ה is that of life. We have seen that this
sign being doubled, formed the essentially living root הה, which, by
the insertion of the luminous sign, became the verb הוה, *to be-being*.
But let us imagine now that, wishing to express, not an existence in
action, but only in power, we restrict the verbal root in the sole sign
of life and extinguish the luminous sign ו to bring it back to the
convertible ו; we shall have only a compressed root wherein the
being will be latent and as it were, in germ. This root הו, composed of the sign of life, and of that which, as we know, is the link
between nothingness and being, expresses marvelously well that in-
comprehensible state of a thing when it exists no more, and when it
is, nevertheless, in power of existing. It is found in the Arabic هو
in which it depicts a desire, a tendency, a vague, indeterminate existence. It is sometimes an unfathomable depth, هوه; sometimes a
sort of physical death هوي ; sometimes an ethereal space هوا, etc.

Moses, after the example of the Egyptian priests, taking this root
and making it rule by the sign of mutual reciprocity ת, formed the
word תהו by means of which he expressed a contigent and potential
existence contained in another potential existence בהו; for here he
inflects the same root by the mediative article ב.

4. And-he-did-ken, ʜᴇ-the-Gods that-light as good; and-he-made-a-division (he caused a dividing motion to exist) ʜᴇ-the-Gods, betwixt the-light (intellectual ele-mentizing) and-betwixt the-darkness (hard-making pow-er).

4. Et-il-considéra, ʟᴜɪ-les-Dieux, c e t t e lumière comme bonne; et-il-fit-une-solution (il détermina un moyen de séparation) ʟᴜɪ-les-Dieux, entre la-lumière (élémentisation intelligible) et entre l'obscurité (force compressive et durcissante).

Thus, there is no need of conceiving the earth invisible, de-composed, vague, void, formless, which is absurd or contradictory; but only as existing still in power, in another seed-producing power, which must be developed in order that it may be developed.

חֹשֶׁךְ, *darkness*.... This word is composed of the two contracted roots חֹשׁ-אָךְ It is remarkable in its figurative and hieroglyphic sense. In its figurative sense, it is a compressing, hardening movement; in its hieroglyphic, it is a combat, a violent opposition between the con-trary principles of heat and cold. The root חשׁ expresses a violent and disordered movement caused by an inner ardour which seeks to distend. The root אָךְ depicts on the contrary, a sentiment of con-traction and tightening which tends to centralize. In the composition of the word it is the compressive force which prevails and which en-chains the inner ardour forced to devour itself. Such was the idea that the Egyptian priests formed of *darkness*.

תהום, *the deep*.... This is the root הו which I have already analyzed, modified now by the reciprocal sign ח, and endowed with the collective sign ם, which develops its power in infinite space.

רוח, *the breath*.... It is figuratively, a movement toward ex-pansion, toward dilation. Hieroglyphically, it is strength opposed to that of *tenebræ*. And if the word חֹשֶׁךְ characterizes a compressive power, a compression, the word רוח will characterize an expansive power, an expansion. In both will be found this eternal system of two opposed forces, which the sages and savants of all the centuries, from Parmenides and Pythagoras to Descartes and Newton, have seen in Nature, and signalized by different names.

5. Wa-îkerâ Ælohîm la-
âôr Iôm, w'la-hoshèċh karâ
laîlah, wa-îehî hereb, wa-
îehî-boker, Iôm æhad.

וַיִּקְרָא אֱלֹהִים לָאוֹר יוֹם וְלַחֹשֶׁךְ
קָרָא לָיְלָה וַיְהִי־עֶרֶב וַיְהִי־בֹקֶר
יוֹם אֶחָד :

The Hebraic word רוח is composed of the sign of movement proper ר, united to that of elementary existence ה, by the universal, convertible sign ו. The root which results contains all ideas of expansion and exaltation, of ethereal breath, inspiration, animation, etc. It is found in the Chaldaic רוח, in the Syriac ܪܘܚ and in the Arabic روح.

מרחפת, *pregnantly-moving*.... Moses, by a turn of phrase frequently adopted by him, uses here, to express the action of the breath, of which he was about to speak, a verb which is derived from the same root; that is to say, which is always attached to the word רוח, and which depicts, as I have already said, an expansive and quickening movement. The sign פ which terminates it now, adds the idea of active generation of which it is the hieroglyphic symbol. The Samaritan makes use of the word 𐤓𐤇𐤐 whose root being the same as that of the Hebrew נשם, gives the sense of agitating with a vital movement, of *animating*. Finally, the Hebraic verb רחם is the same as רחב, with the sole difference of the character פ being substituted for the character ב: it signifies, *to dilate, to expand, to agitate prolifically*. The Arabic رحب has the same sense.

See Radical Vocabulary for the word מים, root ים and מה.

v. 3. ויאמר, *And-he-said*.... It can be seen by the etymology which I have given of this important verb in chapter VII of my Grammar, that it signifies not only *to say*, but according to the occasion, it can attain a signification much more exalted. Now, is this occasion more important than that in which the Being of beings manifests his creative will? To understand it in the literal sense only, is to degrade it, and is detrimental to the thought of the writer. As the judicious Maimonides said, it is necessary to spiritualize the sense of this word and to guard against imagining any sort of speech. It is an act of the will and as is indicated by the hieroglyphic composition of the verb אמור, a power which declares, manifests and reflects itself without, upon the being which it enlightens.

אור, *light*.... I cannot repeat too often that all words of the Hebraic tongue are formed in such a way as to contain within them-

5. A n d-he-assigned-for-name, HE-the-Gods, to-the-light, *Day* (universal manifestation) ; and-to-the-darkness, he-assigned-for-name, *Night* (naught manifested, all-knitting) : and-there-was west-eve ; and-there-was east-dawn (o v e r and b a c k a g a i n); Day the-first (light's first manifestation).

5. Et-il-assigna-nom, Lui-les-Dieux, à-la-lumière, *Jour* (manifestation univer-selle) ; et-à-l'obscurité il-as-signa-nom *Nuit* (négation manifestée, nutation des choses) ; et-fut-occident, et-fut-orient (libération et itération) ; Jour premier (première manifestation phé-noménique).

---

selves the reason of their formation. Let us consider the word אוֹר *light;* it is derived directly from the word אוּר *fire.* The only dif-ference between them is, that in the word which designates fire, it is the universal convertible sign וֹ which forms the link between the sign of power א, and that of movement proper ר: whereas in the second, it is the intelligible sign וֹ. Let us proceed further. If, from the words אוּר and אוֹר, one takes away the median sign וֹ or וֹ there will remain the elementary root אר, composed of power and movement, which in all known tongues signifies by turns, *earth, water, air, fire, ether, light,* according to the sign joined thereunto. See also, Radical Vocab. root אר.

ויהי, *and-there* (*shall be*)-*became....* I must not neglect to say, that Moses, profiting by the hieroglyphic genius of the Egyptian tongue, changing at will the future tense into past tense, depicts, on this occasion, the birth of light, symbol of intelligible *corporeity,* with an animation that no modern tongue can render except the Chinese. He writes first יהי־אוּר *there-shall-be light;* then repeating the same words with the single addition of the convertible sign וֹ, he turns suddenly the future into the past, as if the effect had sustained before-hand the outburst of the thought ויהי־אוֹר *and there-*(*shall be*)-*became light.*

This manner of speaking figuratively and hieroglyphically, always comes from the primitive meaning given to the word בראשית: for the heavens and the earth created in principle, and passing from power into action, could unfold successively their virtual forces only as far as the divine will announced in the future, is manifest in the past.

6. Wa-îâomer   Ælohîm îehî rakîwha bethôch ha-maîm w'i̱hî mabeddil beîn maîm la-maîm.

וַיֹּאמֶר אֱלֹהִים יְהִי רָקִיעַ בְּתוֹךְ הַמָּיִם וִיהִי מַבְדִּל בֵּין מַיִם לָמָיִם :

The Being of beings knows no time. The Egyptian tongue is the only one in which this wonderful trope can take place even in the spoken tongue. It was a spoken effect which, from the hieroglyphic style passed into the figurative, and from the figurative into the literal.

v. 4. וירא, *And-he-did-ken*.... Moses continues to make the Being of beings, the universal Creator, speak in the future, by turning the expression of his will into the past by means of the convertible sign. The verb ראות which is used by Moses on this occasion, signifies not only *to see*, but *to ken*, by directing voluntarily the visual ray upon an object. The root רו or רי composed of the sign of movement proper united to the convertible, or to that of manifestation, develops every idea of a stroke, ray, or trace, of anything whatever, being directed in a straight line. It is joined to the root או or א, expressing the goal, the place, the object toward which the will inclines, there where it is fixed, and forms with it the compound ראה, ראי or ראות, that is to say, *the vision*, the action of seeing and the very object of this action.

ויבדל, *and-he-made-a-division*.... The verb בדל springs from the two contracted roots בד־דל. By the first בד, should be understood every idea of individuality, of peculiarity, of isolation, of solitary existence: by the second דל, every kind of division, of opening, of disjunction. So that the verb here alluded to, signifies literally the action of particularizing, of isolating one from another, of making solution of things, distinguishing them, separating them, etc. Moses employs it here according to the intensive form to give it more force.

v. 5. ויקרא, *And-he-assigned-for-name*.... This verb is produced from the root קר which signifies literally a character, a characteristic sign, an engraving.

The Samaritan word 𐤒𐤓𐤀 has lost the early expression and signifies only *to cry out, to emit the sound of the voice.*

יום, *Day*.... The root ים contains every idea of heap, of gather-

6. And-he-said, HE-the-Gods, there-shall-be a-rare-fying (a slackening, loosening action) in-the-centre of-the-waters: and-there-shall-be a-separating-cause (a lone-making action) betwixt the-waters toward-the-waters.

6. Et-il-dit, LUI-les-Dieux il-sera-fait une-raréfaction (un desserrement, une force raréfiante) au-centre des-eaux: et-il-sera-fait un-fai-sant-séparer (un movement de séparation) entre-les-eaux envers-les-eaux.

---

ing, of pile; it is in this relation that it constitutes the masculine plural of Hebraic nouns. In its natural state it provides, by restriction, the name of the sea, and denotes then, the mass of waters, the piling of the waves. But if the luminous sign וֹ is inserted in this root, it is no longer the mass of waters that it expresses; it is, so to speak, the mass of light, the gathering of the intelligible element; it is יוֹם, the universal manifestation, *day*. See Rad. Vocab. root יֹ and יֵם.

It is unnecessary, I think, for me to say how very essential is this grammatical training. But I must warn the reader that the Chaldaic punctuation having suppressed almost invariably the sign וֹ of the word יוֹם, especially in the plural יָמִים, it has caused the same characters יֵם or יָמִים to signify, according to the circumstance, *day or sea; days or seas*.

לֵילָה, *Night*.... The formation of this word demands particular attention. Refer to Rad. Vocab. root לֹא, לוֹ and לֹל. It is the amalgamation of these three roots that forms the word in question. The words *naught* and *knot*, holding to the same root as the word *night*, portray very felicitously the figurative and hieroglyphic sense attached to the Hebrew word לֵילָה.

עֶרֶב, *west-eve*.... This name famous in all the ancient mythologies, is the *Erebus* which we have drawn from the Greek ἐρεβός, and whose origin has so greatly troubled the savants. Its signification is not doubtful. It always recalls to the mind something obscure, distant, out of sight. The Hellenists who have rendered it in this passage by ἐστέρα and the Latins by "vespere," *evening*, have visibly weakened the meaning. It signifies the occident, and all ideas which are related to it, not only in Hebrew, but in Chaldaic, Syriac, Ethiopic and in Arabic.

7. Wa-îahash Ælohîm æth-ha-rakîwha wa-îabeddel beîn ha-maîm âsher mith-ahath la-rakiwha, w'beîn ha-maîm âsher mehal la-raki-wha, wa-îehî čhen.

וַיַּעַשׂ אֱלֹהִים אֶת־הָרָקִיעַ וַיַּבְדֵּל בֵּין הַמַּיִם אֲשֶׁר מִתַּחַת לָרָקִיעַ וּבֵין הַמַּיִם אֲשֶׁר מֵעַל לָרָקִיעַ וַיְהִי־כֵן :

The name of the last mentioned people is derived therefrom, as I have already stated in my Introductory Dissertation.

בקר, *east-dawn*.... This word, produced from the root קר, governed by the sign ב, indicates a thing whose course is regulated, and which presents itself ever the same; a thing which is renewed unceasingly. The Arabic reads بقر . This word is found sometimes used to express, light. The Syriac ܒܩܪ contains often the idea of inspection, of exploration. The Hellenists in restricting its signification to the word πρωΐ, *morning*, have followed purposely the literal and vulgar sense. The Samaritan version was less restricted; it translates ערב and בקר, by ᛘᛉᚦᚢ and ᚦᛄᚻ; that is to say, that which lowers, falls, ends, and that which rises, begins, signals. The Chaldaic targum says the same thing: רמש and צפר. The English words *over and back*, hold to the same roots as the Hebraic words, and vividly express the figurative sense.

v. 6. רקיע, *a-rarefying*.... The Hellenists have translated this word by the Greek ζερέωμα, which signifies a firm, solid thing; Saint Jerome has imitated them in saying "firmamentum," *firmament*. This version grossly misinterprets Moses, who never thought that ethereal space was either firm or solid, as he has been made to say; on the contrary, the root רק, from which he draws this expression contains the idea of tenuity and expansion. The verb רוק or ריק, which comes from it, signifies *to be rarefied* or *rendered void*. Finally the compound word רקע, whence the word referred to is derived, presents only the sense of expanding and attenuating. It is difficult to understand how the Hellenists have been able to see in all this, their solid ζερέωμα; at least assuming the idea of Richard Simon who thinks that they have followed, on this occasion, the rude jargon that was spoken at that time in Jerusalem. (*Hist. crit.* L. II. ch. 5). The Samaritan version translates the word רקיע by ᚦᛰᛉᚼᛣ , that is to say, *order, harmony, arrangement of parts;* an idea very far from solidity. Per-

7. **And-he-made**, HE-the-Gods, that-self-sameness-of--t h e-rarefying (loosening power, ethereal expanse): and-he-did-effect-a-separating-cause betwixt the-waters which-were below by-the-rarefying (sinking down) and-betwixt the-waters which-were above by-the-rarefying (raising up) and-it-was-so.

7. **Et-il-fit**, L U I - l e s - D i e u x , cette-ipséité-de-la-raréfaction (cette force raréfiante, l'espace éthéré) ; et-il-fit-exister-une-séparation entre les-eaux que-étaient par-en-bas (affaissées) de-l'espace-éthéré et-entre les-eaux qui-étaient par-en-haut (exaltées) de l'espace-éthéré: et-ce-fut-ainsi.

---

haps the Hellenists have deemed it proper to materialize this expression. However that may be, the Arabic رق, even the Syriac ܪܩ, and the Ethiopic analogue ⵤⵗⵗ (*rakk*), confirm all the ideas of subtlety, tenuity and spirituality which is in the Hebrew.

כתוֹך המים, *in-the-centre of-the-waters....* This is to say, in examining the roots and the figurative and hieroglyphic sense, *in the sympathetic and central point of universal passivity;* which agrees perfectly with a rarefying and dilating force such as Moses understood. But the Hellinists having considered it proper to change this intelligible force into a sentient solidity, have been led to change all the rest. The word מבדל, which is obviously a continued facultative, according to the excitative form, expressing the action of making a separation exist among divers natures, they have changed into a substantive, and have seen only a separation produced by a kind of wall that they have created. The Arabic verb بدل which is attached to the same root as the Hebrew בדל, expresses a mutation of nature or of place.

v. 7. את הרקיע, *that-selfsameness-of-the-rarefying....* It was doubtless seen in the first verse of this chapter, that I gave according to the occasion, a particular meaning to the designative preposition את having rendered את השמים word-for-word by *the selfsameness-(objectivity)-of-the-heavens:* it is true, as I have taken pains to state in my Grammar (ch. IV, § 3), that this preposition expresses often more than a simple designative inflexion, and that it characterizes, especially when it is followed by the determinative article ה, as in this instance,

8. Wa-îkerâ Ælohîm la-rakîwha shamaîm, wa-îehî hereb, wa-îehî boker Iôm shenî.

וַיִּקְרָא אֱלֹהִים לָרָקִיעַ שָׁמָיִם וַיְהִי־עֶרֶב וַיְהִי־בֹקֶר יוֹם שֵׁנִי :

9. Wa-îâomer Ælohîm îkkawoû ha-maîm mitha-hath ha-shamaîm æl-makôm æhad, w'thera æth ha-îaba-shah, wa-îehî-chen.

וַיֹּאמֶר אֱלֹהִים יִקָּווּ הַמַּיִם מִתַּחַת הַשָּׁמַיִם אֶל־מָקוֹם אֶחָד וְתֵרָאֶה הַיַּבָּשָׁה וַיְהִי־כֵן :

---

the substance itself, the ipseity, the objectivity, the selfsameness of the thing which it designates.

מתחת, *below*.... מעל, *above*.... These two adverbial relations have, in this instance, a figurative and hieroglyphic sense, very essential to understand. The first מתחת, has the root תה, containing every idea of shock, terror, restraint. This root, governed by the sympathetic sign ת, becomes in an abstract sense, the expression of that which is worn out and inferior. The root of the second of these relations is, on the contrary על, which draws with it every idea of distention, and of sentient exaltation. It is the reinforcement of the root הל, which develops a sentiment of joy and merriment.

v. 8. שמים, *heavens*.... Later on I shall give the etymology of this word. But I beg the reader to observe here, that the heavens are developed only successively, and after the formation of ethereal space: which proves that they were at first created only in principle, as I have said.

v. 9. יקוו, *they-shall-drive*.... The root קו, whence comes the verb קוה, expresses every leaning, every inclination, every movement of blind but irresistible force toward a goal. The figurative sense of this expression, which Moses uses according to its intensive verbal

8. And-he-assigned-for-name, HE-the-Being-of-beings, to-the-e t h e r e a l-expanse, *Heavens* (exalted and shining waters) : and-there-was west-eve, and-there-was east-dawn (over and back again), Day the-s e c o n d (light's second manifestation).

8. Et-il-assigna-nom, LUI l'Être-des-êtres à-l'espace-éthéré, *Cieux* (les eaux éclatantes, élevées) : et-fut-occident, et-fut-orient (libération et itération), Jour second (seconde manifestation phénoménique).

9. And-he-said, HE-the-Gods, they-shall-drive (tend to) the-waters from-below (from the sinking down) the-heavens toward a-driving-place, one (single) ; and-there-shall-be-seen the-dryness : and-it-was-so.

9. Et-il-dit, LUI-les-Dieux, elles tendront-fortement (inclineront, se détermineront par un movement irrésitible) les-eaux par-en-bas (de l'affaissement) d e s-c i e u x, vers un-lieu-déterminé, unique; et se-verra-l'aridité : et-ce-fut-ainsi.

---

form, has been corrupted by the Samaritans who restrict it to the literal sense, and make use of the verb ‮נב‬ , according to the reflexive form ‮התאבנע‬ ; that is to say, *they shall be confluent, the waters....*

‮אל-מקום‬, *toward a driving-place....* This word, which Moses uses after the verb ‮קוה‬, holds to the same root. It is a figure of speech which this hierographic writer never lacks, and which proves the inner knowledge that he had of his tongue: one always finds the verb derived from the substantive or the substantive derived from the verb, proceeding together as if to confirm and sustain each other. In this instance, the root ‮קו‬ which expresses the tendency toward a goal, the force which drives with power in action, produces at first the verb ‮קוה‬, which depicts the movement toward that goal: this one taking on the character ‮ם‬ as collective sign, becomes the verb ‮קום‬ whose meaning is, to substantialize, to establish in substance, to drive with power in action. This same verb, being inflected in its turn by the sign of exterior action ‮מ‬, becomes the very place, the goal of the movement, the action resulting from the power.

10.   Wa-îkerâ Ælohîm la-
îabashah aretz, w'l'mikweh
ha-maîm karâ îammîm, wa-
iaræ Ælohîm chi-tôb.

וַיִּקְרָא אֱלֹהִים לַיַּבָּשָׁה אֶרֶץ
וּלְמִקְוֵה הַמַּיִם קָרָא יַמִּים וַיַּרְא
אֱלֹהִים כִּי־טוֹב :

Thus the waters, moved in the centre by an expansive and rarefying force which tends to make a separation of the subtle parts and
of the dense parts; the waters, image of universal passivity, rise from
the one side to form ethereal space, and fall on the other to be united
in the gulf of seas. I know not what the modern savants will think
of this physics; but this I do know, that it is neither ridiculous nor
contemptible. If I did not fear to display in these notes an erudition out of place, I would repeat what I have already said pertaining
to the system of the two opposed forces, admitted not only by the ancients but also by the moderns: forces which Parmenides called *ethereal
fire* and *night;* Heraclitus, *the way upward* and *the way downward;*
Timæus of Locri, *intelligence* and *necessity;* Empedocles, *love* and
hate; Plato, *himself* and *that which is not him;* Descartes, *movement*
and *resistance;* Newton, *centrifugal force* and *centripetal force,* etc.

v. 10. יבשה, *the dryness....* Here, the root אש, whose meaning
I have already explained, is found preceded by the sign of interior
action ב, and by the sign of manifestation and of duration י, giving
evidence of the inner and continuous action of this igneous principle.
Thus, it is a thing not only dried by *fire,* but a thing that *fire* continues to burn interiorly, which is revealed through the irresistible
force which makes the waters tend toward a determined place.

ארץ, *earth....* I make the same remark with respect to the
earth, that I have made with respect to the heavens, and pass on to
its etymology. The primitive root אר, contains the united signs,
almost always violent, of stable power and of continued movement
proper. These two signs which appear opposed to each other, produce
an elementary root which is found again in all tongues, and which,
expressing that which pertains to the elementary principle or to nature
in general, signifies, following the new modifications that it receives,
light, ether, fire, air, water, earth and even *metal.* The Hebraic
tongue which is no other than the primitive Egyptian, possesses this

10. And-he-assigned-for-name, HE-the-Gods, to-the-dryness, *earth* (terminating element) ; .and-to-the-driving-place of-the waters, he-assigned-for-name, *seas* (waterish streaming) : and-he-did-ken, HE-the-Being-of-beings, that-as-good.

10. Et-il-assigna-nom, LUI-les-Dieux, à-l'aridité, *terre* (élément terminant et bornant) ; et-à-la-tendance des-e a u x, il-assigna-nom, *mers* (immensité acqueuse, manifestation de l'universelle passivité) : et-il-considéra, LUI-les-Dieux, cela-ainsi-bon.

---

root in all its modifications, as can be seen in the Rad. Vocab. root בר, אר, etc.

Without there being need for examining here the diverse modifications of this important root, let it suffice for me to say, that whether one adds the signs of compression and material sense, as the Chaldeans and Samaritans in their words ארק, ארע, or אֶרֶע or whether one places there, as the Hebrews, the sign צ, which expresses the term and end of all substance, one finds equally *earth*, that is to say, the element which is limited, figured, tactile, compressive, plastic, etc.

It must be remarked that in augmenting the force of the root אר in its potential character א, one makes it חר or חרי, that which burns, that which inflames, either literally, or figuratively; in doubling its movement as in ארר, that which is execrable and cursed; and חרר that which is steep, rough, hilly, etc.

ימים, seas.... That is to say, *aqueous immensity:* for the word which designates *seas*, is only the word מים, *waters* preceded by the sign of manifestation י. As to the word מים itself, the following is the history of its formation.

The root מה, מו or מי, contains the idea of passive relation, of plastic and movement. It is perceived in the Arabic words ماء . ماد.ماج all of which have reference to this idea. The Hebrews have made much use of it in the vulgar idiom, without entirely penetrating its meaning; however, they, as well as the Chaldeans and Syrians, employed the verb מוט to express the mutation of things, and their relative movement. The name which they gave to water, in general, although expressed by the root of which I speak, was rarely in the singular, and as if their sages had wished to show in

11.   Wa-îâomer Ælohîm, thadeshæ ha-âretz deshæ hesheb mazeriha zerah, hetz pherî hosheh pherî le-mînoû, âsher zareh' ô-b'ô, hal-haâretz, wa-îehî-čhen.

וַיֹּאמֶר אֱלֹהִים תַּדְשֵׁא הָאָרֶץ דֶּשֶׁא עֵשֶׂב מַזְרִיעַ זֶרַע עֵץ פְּרִי עֹשֶׂה פְּרִי לְמִינוֹ אֲשֶׁר זַרְעוֹ־בוֹ עַל־הָאָרֶץ וַיְהִי־כֵן :

12.   Wa-thôtzæ ha-âretz deshæ hesheb mazeriha zerah le-mînehoû w'hetz hosheh pherî, âsher zareh'ô-b'ô le mînehoû: wa-îaræ Ælohîm čhi-tôb.

וַתּוֹצֵא הָאָרֶץ דֶּשֶׁא עֵשֶׂב מַזְרִיעַ זֶרַע לְמִינֵהוּ וְעֵץ עֹשֶׂה פְּרִי אֲשֶׁר זַרְעוֹ־בוֹ לְמִינֵהוּ וַיַּרְא אֱלֹהִים כִּי־טוֹב :

---

that way the double movement which it contains, or that they knew its inner composition, they gave it almost always the dual number: מַיִּם , *double waters*.

Yet, a very singular thing which ought not to escape the archæologists is, that from the Chinese to the Celts, all peoples may draw from the word which, in their tongue designates water, the one which serves as indeterminate pronominal relation. The Chinese say *choui* water, and *choui*, who, what? The Hebrews מַה or מִי water and מַה or מִי who, what? The Latins, *aqua*, water, and *quis, quæ, quod*, who, what? The Teutons and Saxons, *wasser*, water, and *was* or *wat*, who, what? etc.

I am taking up here, the etymology of the word שָׁמַיִם *heavens*, because it is attached to the one I have been explaining in this article, and because it signifies literally, the waters, raised, brilliant and glorified; being formed from the word מַיִם, *waters*, and from the root שָׁם which is united to it. This root contains the idea of that which rises and shines in space, that which is distinguished and noticeable by its elevation or its splendour. The Hebrew and Chaldaic שָׁמָה means, happy, transported with joy; the Arabic سام , has almost the same sense.

11. And-he-said (declaring his will) HE-the-Gods; shall-cause-to-grow, t h e-earth, a-growing grass, seed-yielding-seed, (sprout-yielding-sprout) vegetable-substance and-fructuous, yielding-fruit, after-the-kind-its-own which-has the-seed-its-own unto-itself, upon-the-earth : and-it-was-so.

12. And-it-did-shoot-out, (yield forth), the earth, a-growing-grass seed-yielding-seed after-the-kind-its-own, and-a-vegetable-substance and-fructuous, which the-seed its-own unto-itself (has), after-the-kind-itself; and he-viewed, HE-the-Being-of-beings, that-as-good.

11. Et-il-dit (déclarant sa volonté), LUI-les-Dieux; fera-végéter la-terre, une-végétante herbe, germifiant-germe, substance fructueuse faisant-fruit, selon-l'espèce-sienne qui-ait semence-sienne dans-soi, sur-la-terre: et-ce-fut-ainsi.

12. Et - elle - fit - sortir (provenir, naître), la terre, une végétante herbe, germinant-germe, d'après-l'espèce -sienne, et une-substance fructuese qui semence-sienne dans-soi, (avait et aura) selon l'espèce-sienne; et-il-vit, LUI-l'Être-des-êtres, c e l a-ainsi-bon.

/

---

v. 11. תדשא, *shall-cause-to-grow*.... This is the verb רשא *to grow*, used according to the excitative form, active movement, future tense. The Hebraic phrase has a delicacy and precision that is almost impossible to make understood even in the word-for-word, where I allow myself the greatest license, not only in the form but also in the concatenation of the words. There exists only the difficulty which rises from the idiomatic genius and from the turn of phrase affected by Moses. This turn of phrase consists, as I have already said, in drawing always the noun and the verb from the same root, and in repeating them under diverse modifications. One can perceive in this verse and in those following, the singular grace and picturesque beauty. I venture to hope even through the perplexity of the French and English word-for-word rendering, that by adhering to the literal sense, one will see here many things that the Hellenists or Latin translators had not allowed even to be suspected.

v. 12. והוצא, *and-it-did-shoot-out*.... It is the verb יצא, *to come*

13.   Wa-îehî-hereb,   wa-îehî-boker, iôm shelîshî.

וַיְהִי־עֶרֶב וַיְהִי־בֹקֶר יוֹם שְׁלִישִׁי:

14.   Wa-îâomer Ælohîm îehî maôroth bi-rekîwha ha-shamaîm le-habeddil beîn ha-îôm w'beîn ha-laîlah w' haîoû le-âothoth w'l'môha-dîm w'l'îamîm w'shanîm.

וַיֹּאמֶר אֱלֹהִים יְהִי מְאֹרֹת בִּרְקִיעַ הַשָּׁמַיִם לְהַבְדִּיל בֵּין הַיּוֹם וּבֵין הַלַּיְלָה וְהָיוּ לְאֹתֹת וּלְמוֹעֲדִים וּלְיָמִים וְשָׁנִים:

---

forth, to proceed, to be born, used according to the excitative form, in the future tense made past by the convertible sign. I beg the reader to observe here again this hieroglyphic expression. GOD speaks in the future and his expression repeated, is turned suddenly to the past. Let us examine this important verb and proceed to the analysis of its elements. The first which offers itself is the sign צ, expressing every terminative movement, every conclusion, every end. Its proper and natural place is at the end of words: thence the roots אץ or הץ, in Arabic اصر containing every idea of corporeal bourns and limits, of re-pressing and concluding force, of term. But if, instead of terminating the words, this sign begins them; then, far from arresting the forms, it pushes them, on the contrary, toward the goal of which it is itself the symbol: thence, the opposed roots צא, in Syriac ܐܠ, and in Arabic ﻇ , whose idea is, leaving the bourns, breaking the shackles of the body, coming outside, being born. It is from this last root, verbalized by the initial adjunction י, that the verb which is the subject of this note, is derived. It signifies *to appear, to come outside by a movement of propagation,* as is demonstrated unquestionably, by the substantive nouns which are derived therefrom, צִא *a son,* and צאצא *a numerous progeny.*

v. 13.   There are no further remarks to be made here.

v. 14.   מְאֹרֹת, *sensible lights....* This is the root אוֹר *light,* de-termined into form by the plastic sign מ. I have restored to this word the mother vowels which the Chaldaic punctuation had sup-pressed; I have done the same in the following: but I must state that

13. And-there-was-west-eve, and - there - ,was - east-dawn (over and back again) day the-third (light's third manifestation).

14. And-he-said, HE-the-Gods: sensible-lights-and-local there-shall-be in-the-ethereal-expanse of-heavens, for - causing-a-separation-to-be-made betwixt the-day, and-betwixt the-night; and they-shall-be-in-futurity, for-the-divisions-of-time, and-for-the-revolutions-of-light's-universal - manifestations, and - for - the - ontological-changes-of-beings.

13. Et-fut-occident, et-fut-orient (libération et it-ération) jour troisième (tro-isième manifestation phé-noménique).

14. Et-il-dit, LUI-les Di-eux: il-existera des-clartés-extérieures (lumières sensi-bles) dans-l'expansion-éthé-rée des-cieux, pour-faire-le-partage (le mouvement de séparation) entre le jour et-entre la-nuit: et-elles-se-ront-en-signes-à-v e n i r et-pour-l e s-divisions-temporel-les et-pour-les manifesta-tions-phénoméniques-univer-selles, et-pour-les-mutations-ontologiques-des-êtres.

---

the suppression of these vowels is here necessitated by the hiero-glyphic style. For the Divine Verb always expressing itself in the future, and the accomplishment of the will of the Being of beings, following likewise in the convertible future, the creation remains always in power, according to the meaning of the initial word בראשית. This is why the word מארת is deprived of the luminous sign not only in the singular, but also in the plural.

לאֹתֹת. *in-signs-to-come (in-futurity)* .... The Hellinists have trans-lated simply ἐνιαυτοῖς, and Saint Jerome has said "in signa," *in signs.* But this word comes from the continued facultative אֹותֹה, *to be com-ing,* inflected by the directive article ל.

ולמוֹעדים, *and-for-the-divisions-of-times....* This word springs from the root עד, governed by the sign of exterior action מ, and inflected by the directive article ל. It is necessary to consult the Radical Vocab. concerning this important root, as well as the roots of the two following words יֹם and שנה.

As the Greek and Latin translators have seen in these three words

15. W'haîoû li-maôroth bi-rekiwha ha-shamaîm l'-haîr hal-ha-âretz wa-îhî ḋhen.

וְהָיוּ לִמְאוֹרֹת בִּרְקִיעַ הַשָּׁמַיִם לְהָאִיר עַל־הָאָרֶץ וַיְהִי־כֵן ׃

16. Wa-îahash Ælohîm æth-sheni ha-mâoroth ha-gheddolîm, æth-ha-mâôr ha-gaddol le-memesheleth ha-îôm w'æth-ha-mâôr ha-katon le-memesheleth ha-laîlah, w'æth-ha-ḋhôḋhabîm.

וַיַּעַשׂ אֱלֹהִים אֶת־שְׁנֵי הַמְּאֹרֹת הַגְּדֹלִים אֶת־הַמָּאוֹר הַגָּדֹל לְמֶמְשֶׁלֶת הַיּוֹם וְאֶת־הַמָּאוֹר הַקָּטֹן לְמֶמְשֶׁלֶת הַלַּיְלָה וְאֶת־הַכּוֹכָבִים ׃

---

only days, months and years, it will be well for me to dwell upon this; but I shall find the occasion to do so further on.

v. 15. להאיר, *for-causing-brightness-to-shine*.... This is the root אוֹר, *light*, or hieroglyphically, *intellectual coporeity*, which, having become verb, is employed here according to the excitative form: so that it appears evident by the text of Moses, that this hierographic writer regarded the celestial luminous centres, as sensible lights destined to propagate intellectual light and to excite it upon the earth. Physics of this kind offers much food for reflection.

v. 16. את־שני, *those twain*.... It must be observed that Moses does not employ here שנים *two*, as the Greek and Latin translators have rendered it, which would separate the two luminaries of which he speaks; but that he employs the word שני, inflected by the designative preposition את, *that same twain, that couple, that gemination*: thus uniting them under one single idea.

לממשלת, *for-a-symbolical-representation*.... The Hellenists have translated this, εἰς ἀρχάς, which is the most restricted interpretation; for in short, it is evident that the sun and the moon rule over the day and night. Indeed Moses would be but little understood if one were to stop at an idea so trivial. The verb מָשַׁל means, it is true, *to be ruler, judge* or *prince*; but it signifies much oftener *to be the model, the representative, the symbol of something; to speak in alle-*

15. And-they-shall-be as-sensible-lights (sparkling foci) in-the-e t h e r e al -expanse of-heavens, for-causing-brightness-to-shine (intellectual light) upon-the-earth : and-it-was-so.

16. And-he-made, HE-the-Gods, those-twain (that couple, that pair) of-central-lights the-great : ' the-self-sameness-of-the-central-light the-greater, for-a-symboli-cal-representation of-day, and-the-self-sameness-of-the -central-light the-lesser, for-a-symbolical - representation of-night; and-the-selfsame-ness-of-the-stars (world's virtual faculties).

15. Et-elles-seront-com-me-des-lumières sensibles (des foyers lumineux) dans-l'expansion-éthérée des-cieux pour-faire-briller (exciter la lumière intellectuelle) sur-la-terre : et-cela-fut-ainsi.

16. Et-il-fit, LUI-les-Di-eux, cette-duité (cette gé-mination, ce couple) de-clartés-extérieures les-gran-des : l'ipséité-de-la-lumière-centrale, la-grande, pour-représenter-symboliquement le-jour (la-manifestation universelle), et-l'ipséité-de-la-lumière-centrale la-peti-te, pour-représenter symboli-quement-la-nuit (la néga-tion-manifestée) ; et-l'ipséi-té-des-étoiles (facultés vir-tuelles de l'univers).

---

gories, *in parables; to present a similitude, an emblem, a figure.* This verb is produced from the root שׁר which, containing in itself every idea of parity, similitude and representation, is joined to the signs מ and ל, to express its exterior action and its relative movement In the phrase with which we are occupied, this verb is used according-ing to the intensive form, and consequently invested with the con-tinued facultative of the sign מ, which doubles the force of its action.

The word ꔢ2ꔢ ꔢ, made use of by the Samaritan version in this instance, signifies likewise *to speak allegorically, to use parables.*

ואת־הכוכבים, *and-the-selfsameness-of-the-stars....* The word כּכב, vulgarly translated *star,* is composed of the root כּוֹה, which is related to every idea of strength and of virtue, physically as well as morally, and of the mysterious root אוֹב which develops the idea of the fe-

17. Wa-ítthen   âotham
Ælohîm bi-rekîwha ha-sha-
maîm l'haîr hal-ha-âretz.

וַיִּתֵּן אֹתָם אֱלֹהִים בִּרְקִיעַ
הַשָּׁמַיִם לְהָאִיר עַל־הָאָרֶץ :

18. W'li-meshol   ba-îôm
w'-ba-l a î l a h   w'l'habeddîl
beîn ha-âôr w'beîn ha-hosh-
ech, wa-îeræ Ælohîm chî-
tôb.

וְלִמְשֹׁל בַּיּוֹם וּבַלַּיְלָה וּלְהַבְדִּיל
בֵּין הָאוֹר וּבֵין הַחֹשֶׁךְ וַיַּרְא
אֱלֹהִים כִּי־טוֹב :

19. Wa-îehî hereb, wa-
îehî boker, îôm rebîhî.

וַיְהִי־עֶרֶב וַיְהִי־בֹקֶר יוֹם רְבִיעִי :

20. Wa-îâomer Ælohîm
îshertzoû ha-maîm sheretz
nephesh haîah, w'hoph îwho-
pheph hal-ha-âretz, hal-pheneî rekîwha ha-shamaîm.

וַיֹּאמֶר אֱלֹהִים יִשְׁרְצוּ הַמַּיִם שֶׁרֶץ
נֶפֶשׁ חַיָּה וְעוֹף יְעוֹפֵף עַל־
הָאָרֶץ עַל־פְּנֵי רְקִיעַ הַשָּׁמָיִם :

---

cundation of the universe. Thus according to the figurative and hieroglyphic sense, the word כוכב signifies not only *star*, but *the virtual and
fecundating force* of the universe. Therein can be found the germ of
many ancient ideas, whether relative to astrological science, concerning which it is known that the Egyptians thought highly, or whether
relative to the Hermetic science. As my intention is not, at this time,
to comment upon the thought of Moses, I shall not draw from the explanation of this hieroglyphist, all the inferences that I might; I am
satisfied to do in this instance as I have already done, and as I shall
be forced to do more and more, that is, giving only the literal and
figurative meaning, and as much as is possible for me, the hieroglyphic,
leaving to the sagacity of the reader the task of making the applica-
tions. The Samaritan and Chaldaic versions do not differ here from
the Hebrew.

17. And-he-laid-out them, HE-the-Gods, in-the-dilating-power (ethereal expanse) of-heavens, for-c a u s i n g-b r i g h t n e s s (intellectual light)-to-shine (perceptibly) upon-the-earth.

18. And-for-acting (as symbolical types) in-the-day and in-the-night; and-for-causing-a-separation-to-be-made betwixt the-light and-betwixt the-darkness: and-he-did-ken, HE-the-Being-of-beings, that-as-good.

19. And-there-was-west-eve, a n d-t h e r e-was-east-dawn, d a y-t h e-f o u r t h (light's fourth mainfestation.)

20. And-he-said, HE-the-Gods, (declaring his will) shall-spring-forth-plentiful-ly, the-waters, the-plentiful-wormlike soul-of-life and-the-fowl flying-about above-the-earth on-the-face of-the-ethereal-expanse-of-heavens.

17. Et-il-préposa elles, LUI-les-Dieux, dans-la-force-raréfiante (l'expansion éthérée) des-cieux, pour-ex-citer-la-lumière (élémenti-sation intellectuelle)-à-bril-ler-d'une-manière sensible, sur-la-terre.

18. Et-pour-représenter-symboliquement dans-le-jour et-dans-la-n u i t; et-p o u r-faire-le-partage entre-la-lu-mière et-entre-l'obscurité: et-il-vit, LUI-l'Être-des-êtres, cela-ainsi-bon.

19. Et-fut-occident, et-fut-orient, jour-quatrième (quatrième manifestation phénoménique).

20. Et-il-d i t, L U I-l e s Dieux, (déclarant sa volon-té) : origineront-à-foisons, les-eaux, l'originante-vermi-forme âme-de-vie et-le-vola-tile veloci-volant au-dessus-de-la-terre sur-la-face de-l'ex p a n s i o n-é t h é r é e-d e s-cieux.

---

v. 17. וַיִּתֵּן, *And-he-laid-out*.... This is the verb נָתַן *to set forth, to put, to leave;* which, employed according to the intensive form, as on this occasion, signifies *to assign, to lay out, to ordain.*

v. 18 and 19. There is nothing more to observe here than what has already been said.

v. 20. וַיֹּאמֶר, *And-he-said*... I refer the reader to v. 3. of this chapter, and beg also to call attention to the effect of the convertible sign וֹ, which turns the future to the past. It is very important in

21. Wa-îberâ Ælohîm
æth-ha-thanînîm ha-gheddolîm, w'æth-ĉhol-nephesh ha-
haîah ha-romesheth âsher
shartzoû ha-maîm le-mîne-
hem w'æth-ĉhol-hoph ĉha-
naph le-mîne-hou, wa-îaræ
Ælohîm ĉhitôb.

וַיִּבְרָא אֱלֹהִים אֶת־הַתַּנִּינִם
הַגְּדֹלִים וְאֵת כָּל־נֶפֶשׁ הַחַיָּה
הָרֹמֶשֶׂת אֲשֶׁר שָׁרְצוּ הַמַּיִם
לְמִינֵהֶם וְאֵת כָּל־עוֹף כָּנָף
לְמִינֵהוּ וַיַּרְא אֱלֹהִים כִּי־טוֹב :

---

this instance where, (the modern tongues not permitting in any fashion
an imitation of this hieroglyphic trope) I am constantly obliged to
put in the simple past that which, in Hebrew, is in the convertible
future.

יִשְׁרְצוּ, *shall-spring-forth-plentifully....* The Samaritan version says
𐤉𐤔𐤓𐤑𐤅 𐤁𐤌𐤀 𐤉𐤔𐤓𐤑𐤅𐤌. *the waters shall emit prolifically
in prolific emission...* The Chaldaic targum gives ירחשון מיא רחשא *the
waters shall ferment a ferment....* Thus can be seen that even in the
literal sense, the Hellenists have been weak, for in saying ἐξαγαγέτω τα
ὕδατα ἑρπετά, *the waters shall bring forth reptiles,* they have distorted
not only the thought, but the expression of Moses, which has here a
picturesque forcefulness. The verb שָׁרוֹץ which he employs, springs
from two contracted roots שר־רץ; the first, שר, composed of the signs
of relative and proper movement, or circular and rectilinear, indicates
an emission, a liberation, a detachment, a separation. The second,
רץ, characterizes a sort of movement, of vibration, recommencing and
finishing, reptilian, being propagated by being divided: thus the compound שרץ contains every idea of propagative emission, of motive
origin, of generative separation. This is the figurative and hieroglyphic meaning. In the literal sense, it is a reptilian movement, and
in a wholly restricted and materialized sense, *a reptile.*

עוֹף, *fowl....* This expression, which depends still upon the verb
ישרצו, *shall-spring-forth,* and which is connected with the substantive
המים, *the waters,* proves, as the authors of the Samaritan version and
the Chaldaic targum have very well perceived, that Moses regarded
the waters as specially charged with furnishing the first elements of
vital movement to reptilian and flying animals. The root רץ, of which
I spoke above and the one now in question, are both linked to this
same motive principle designated by the root שר; but whereas, by

21. And-he-did-frame-out, HE-the-Being-of-beings, the-selfsameness-of those-huge-bulked-bodies, the-largest (flocking throngs of enormous whales) and-that-of-all-soul of-life, trailing-along and-swimming, which produced-plentifully the-waters after-the-kinds-their-own; and-that-of-all-quick and strong-winged-fowl, after-the-kind-its-own: and-he-did-ken, H E-t h e-G o d s, that-as-good.

21. Et-il-produisit-et-forma (il créa), LUI-l'Être-des-êtres l-existence-individuelle d e-ces-amplitudes-c o r p o-relles les-grandes (légions de monstres marins), et-celle-de-toute-âme d e-v i e mouvante d'un mouvement-contractile, laquelle origi-naient-à-foisons les-eaux; selon-l'espèce-à-eux; et-cel-le-de-tout-volatile à l'aile-forte-et-rapide, selon-l'espè-ce-sienne; et-il-vit, LUI-les-Dieux, cela-ainsi-bon.

רִיץ, should be understood, a laborious movement attached to the earth, by עִוֹף, should be seen, an easy, soaring movement in the air. The one is heavy and rapid, the other light and swift. Both receive existence from the vital principle brought forth by the waters.

This verse and the one following, present in Hebrew, a series of expressions whose harmony and force are inimitable. The Samaritan version gives the same impression, as the copy of a picture by Raphael would produce compared with the original.

v. 21. הַתַנִינִם, *those-huge-bulked-bodies....* This word is derived from the root נוּן, which contains every idea of extension, of amplifi-cation in bodies, whether in number or in volume. This root, governed by the sign of reciprocity ת, is applied to cetacea, and in general, to marine animals, either on account of their mass, or on account of their prodigious fecundity.

נֶפֶשׁ הַחִיה, *soul-of-life....* The word נֶפֶשׁ, which is used by Moses to designate, in general, the soul and the animating life of being, merits much more serious attention, as this great man has been accused by very superficial writers who have never read him, or by very prejudiced sectarians who have read him only to misunderstand him, of having denied the existence of this spiritual essence.

The root from which the word נֶפֶשׁ comes, is without doubt

22.   Wa-îbarech aôtham Ælohîm l'æmor, phroû w're-boû w'milaoû æth-ha-maîm ba-îamîm w'ha-hoph îreb ba-âretz.

וַיְבָרֶךְ אֹתָם אֱלֹהִים לֵאמֹר פְּרוּ וּרְבוּ וּמִלְאוּ אֶת־הַמַּיִם בַּיַּמִים וְהָעוֹף יִרֶב בָּאָרֶץ :

23.   Wa-îhî-herb,   wa-îhî-boker, îôm hamîshî.

וַיְהִי־עֶרֶב וַיְהִי־בֹקֶר יוֹם חֲמִישִׁי :

---

material, for there is no word possible, in any tongue possible, whose elements are not material. As I have said in my Grammar it is the noun which is the basis of speech. Everytime that man wishes to express an intellectual and moral thought, he is obliged to make use of a physical instrument, and to take from elementary nature, material objects which he spiritualizes, as it were, in making them pass, by means of metaphor or hieroglyphic, from one region into another.

Three distinct roots compose this important word and are worthy of the closest attention. The first נ presents the idea of an in-spiration, an infusion, a movement operated from without, within: it is literally *an inspiring breath*. The second פה, which is only the reaction of the first, is attached to the idea of expansion, of effusion, of movement operated from within, without: it is literally *the mouth, the expiring breath, the voice, the speech*, etc. The third finally אש, characterizes the *principiant principle* of which I have already spoken in v.l. of this chapter. It is *fire*, and that which is igneous, ardent, impassioned, etc.

Such is the hieroglyphic composition of the word נפש, *the soul*, which, formed of the three roots נ־פה־אש, presents the symbolic image of a thing that the Egyptian priests regarded as belonging to a triple nature. This is known to be the idea of Pythagoras and Plato, who had drawn it from the Egyptian sanctuaries. Those priests, in-structors of Moses, saw in נ, the *partie naturante* of the soul, in פה the *partie naturée*, and in אש, the *partie naturelle*. From this ele-mentary triad resulted a unity whose immortality they taught, accord-ing to all the ancient sages.

22. And-he-blessed-them, HE-the-Being-of-beings, pursuing-to-say: beget and-multiply, and-fill the-waters in-the-seas; and-the-fowl shall-multiply in-the-earth.

23. And-there-was-west-eve, and-there-was-east-dawn (over and back again), day the-fifth, (light's fifth manifestation).

22. Et-il-bénit-eux, LUI-l'Être-des-êtres, en-disant: propagez et-multipliez-vous, et-remplissez les-eaux, dans les-mers, et-l'espèce-volatile se-multipliera en-la-terre.

23. Et-fut-occident, et-fut-orient (libération et itération), jour cinquième (cinquième manifestation phénoménique).

The Hebrew text, the Samaritan version, the Chaldaic targum, and even the Syriac and Arabic, employ the same word; only, they give, following their genius, different significations to the verb which is formed of it. Among the Hebrews, נֶפֶשׁ signifies *to live* and *breathe;* among the Chaldeans, *to grow, to multiply, to fill space;* the Samaritan verb נגג, expresses *to dilate, to develop, to manifest;* the Syriac دهـا *to give life, to heal;* the Arabic نفش , *to expand, to evaporate*, etc.

הרמשת, *trailing-along and-swimming....* By the word רמש Moses intends, in general, all animal kind, the individuals of which either aquatic, or terrestrial, lack the exterior members which support bipeds and quadrupeds, or which serve them only in *trailing*, after the manner of reptiles, or *swimming*, after the manner of fishes. This word proceeds from the root מש, which expresses that which touches itself, gathers to itself, or withdraws into itself; a root to which the sign ר is used only to give a new motive force.

v.22. פרו ורבו ומלאו *beget, and-multiply, and-fill....* Here are the roots of these three verbs: פר, generative movement, in general; in particular a bull, symbol of generation; in the Arabic فرا , a wild ass: רב that which is great, abundant, extended, either in number or in volume: מל, that which is full, that which has attained its highest elevation. See, Rad. Vocab.

v.23. All these terms are understood.

24. Wa-îâomer Ælohîm, thôtzæ ha-âretz nephesh haîah le-mine-ha, behemah wa-remesh w'haîthô-æretz le-mine-ha, wa-îhî-ċhen.

וַיֹּאמֶר אֱלֹהִים תּוֹצֵא הָאָרֶץ נֶפֶשׁ חַיָּה לְמִינָהּ בְּהֵמָה וָרֶמֶשׂ וְחַיְתוֹ־אֶרֶץ לְמִינָהּ וַיְהִי־כֵן :

25. Wa-îahash Ælohîm æth-haîath ha-âretz le-mine-ha, w'æth-ha-behemah le-mine-ha, w'æth-ċhol-remesh ha-âdamah le-mine-hou, wa-îara Ælohîm ċhi-tôb.

וַיַּעַשׂ אֱלֹהִים אֶת חַיַּת הָאָרֶץ לְמִינָהּ וְאֶת־הַבְּהֵמָה לְמִינָהּ וְאֵת־כָּל־רֶמֶשׂ הָאֲדָמָה לְמִינֵהוּ וַיַּרְא אֱלֹהִים כִּי־טוֹב :

---

v.24. הוֹצֵא, *shall-yield-forth*.... See v. 12.

בהמה, *quadrupeds*.... That is to say, according to the idea of Moses, that part of the animal kingdom whose individuals are neither winged as birds, nor crawling nor swimming as the terrestrial reptiles or the fishes. For it is obvious that this hierographic writer divides the animal kingdom into three great series according to the locomotive movement which he points out in the divers kinds which compose this kingdom.

The first of this great series, comprises the animals of the first origin, vermiform, crawling upon the earth, swimming in the waters or flying in the air, which he calls, in general שרץ חיה, *primitive life, vermiform*. He divides this first series into two kinds: the aquatic and the aerial kind. The first of these kinds, retains the original name שרץ, that is to say *vermiform;* the second is called עוֹף עוֹפֵף *fowl-flying*.

The second of this great series consists of the animals of the second origin, which Moses designates in general, by the name of נפש חחיה *soul of life*. These are the genera which are distinguished from the first original series, by their bulk, their strength and the different relations which they already have with terrestrial animals. The marine animals of this series are called תנינים, *the-huge-bulked-bodies*: the aerials bear the name of עוֹף כנף, that is to say, *quick-and-strong-winged-fowl*.

Finally, the third series is composed of animals called, in general.

24. And-he-said, HE-the-'
Gods, shall-yield-forth, the-
earth, a-soul-of-life (an animality) according-to-the-
kind-its-own, quadrupedly-
walking and-creeping, and-
earthly-living, after-the-kind
-its-own: and-it-was-so.

24. Et-il-dit, L U I-les-
Dieux fera-provenir-la-terre,
une-âme-de-vie (une animalité), selon-l'espèce-sienne,
quadrupède (à la marche él-
evée et bruyante) se-mou-
vant et-vivant-d'une-vie-ter-
restre, selon-l'espèce-sienne:
et-cela-fut-ainsi.

25. And-he-made, HE-the-
Gods, that-life earth-born,
according-to-the - kind - its -
own, and-the-quadruped-ex-
istence after - the - kind - its-
own, and-all-trailing-along-
m o t i o n from-the-adamic
(homogeneal)-ground, aft-
er-the-kind-its-own; and-he-
did-ken, HE-the Being-of-beings, that-as-good.

25. E t-i l-f i t, L U I-l e s-
Dieux, cette-animalité terrestre, selon-l'espèce-sienne,
et-ce-genre-quadrupède selon
l'espèce sienne, et-l'univer-
salité de-tout-mouvement-vi-
tal de-l'élément-adamique
(homogène), selon l'espèce-
sienne; et-il-vit, LUI-l'Être-
des-êtres, cela-ainsi-bon.

חיתו־ארץ, *terrestrial animality.* In this series are contained all
the terrestrial animals whose locomotive movement is neither trailing,
nor swimming, nor flying; but which is executed progressively by
the aid of appropriate members. This series contains also two particular genera; namely, the animals which creep along like lizards,
רמש , and those which support themselves like quadrupeds, called
בהמה. I have already explained the first of these names, which is
applied to whatever moves itself by a trailing and contractile movement. As to the second, it is formed from the root בא, expressing all
progressive and sustained movement, and from the onomatopoeia
הם, which depicts that which is raised and loud.

Before finishing this note I wish to say that these three classes
of animals, considered abstractly, and under figure of three moral
beings, have been named by the Hebrew poets: לויתן, *Leviathan;*
that is to say, the universality of marine monsters; עון, *Hozan,* the
universality of birds; and בהמות, *Behemoth,* the universality of terrestrial animals. The savants who sought for the signification of

26.   Wa-îâomer Ælohîm nahasheh Adam be-tzalle-me-noû chi-de-mouthe-noû, w'îreddou bi-deggath ha-îam-w'be-hoph ha-shamaîm, w'-ba-behemah,   w'bechol-ha-âretz   w'be-chol-ha-remesh ha-romesh hal-ha-âretz.

וַיֹּאמֶר אֱלֹהִים נַעֲשֶׂה אָדָם בְּצַלְמֵנוּ כִּדְמוּתֵנוּ וְיִרְדּוּ בִדְגַת הַיָּם וּבְעוֹף הַשָּׁמַיִם וּבַבְּהֵמָה וּבְכָל־הָאָרֶץ וּבְכָל־הָרֶמֶשׂ הָרֹמֵשׂ עַל־הָאָרֶץ :

---

these words, brought into their researches too much scholastic prejudice to draw from it any fruit.

I shall refrain from saying anything in regard to the three grand divisions which Moses established in the animal kingdom; I shall only observe that there is as much precision and more true philosophy in drawing methodical distinctions from the kind of movement in animals, as there is in drawing these same distinctions from their legs or from the temperature of their blood.

v. 25.   האדמה, *from the-adamic-ground....* See following note.

v. 26.   אדם, *Adam....* I beg those who are reading this without partiality, to observe that Moses does not fall here into the modern error which has made of man a particular species in the animal kingdom; but only after having finished all that he wished to say concerning the elementary, the vegetable and the animal kingdom, he passes on to a kingdom distinct and higher that he names אדם, Adam.

Among the savants who have searched for the etymology of the word *Adam*, the majority went no further than its grossest exterior; nearly all of them have seen only red clay, or simple clay, because the word אדום, signifies *red* or *reddish;* because by ארמה, *the earth* in general, has been understood; but they have failed to see that these words themselves are compounds, and that they can only be the roots of words still more compound; whereas the word אדם being more simple cannot come from it.

The Egyptian priests, authors of this mysterious name, and of a

26. And-he-said, HE-the-Gods, (declaring his will) we-will-make *Adam* in-the-shadow-of-us, by-the-like-making-like-ourselves; and-they-shall-hold- the - sceptre, (they shall rule, they, *Adam*, universal man) in-the-spawn breeding-kind- of - the - seas, and-in-the-flying-kind of-the-heavens, and-in-the quadrupedly-walking-kind, and-in-the-whole- earth - born - life, and - in - all - moving - thing crawling - along upon - the - earth.

26. Et-il-dit, LUI-les-Dieux (déclarant sa volonté), nous-ferons *Adam* en-ombre-nôtre, comformément -à - l'action - assimilante - à - nous : et - ils - tiendront - le - sceptre, (ils régneront, eux, *Adam*, l'-homme universel), dans-les-poissons des-mers, et - dans - les - oiseaux des - cieux, et-dans-le-genre-quadrupéde, et dans-toute-l' animalité-terrestre, et-dans-toute-mouvante-vie se-mouvant-sur-la-terre.

---

great part of those employed by Moses, have composed it with an infinite art. It presents three meanings, as do the greater part of those which enter into the composition of the Beræshith. The first, which is the literal meaning, has been restricted more and more, in proportion as the ideas of the Hebrews have been narrowed and materialized; so that it is doubtful whether it was understood in its purity even at the epoch of the Babylonian captivity, at least by the vulgar. The Samaritan version, the most ancient of all, is also the one which conserves best its signification. It is seen in the efforts made by the translator to find a corresponding expression. After having copied the name itself **ᘓᎢᗺ** , he sought a synonym for it in **ᗌᙏ ᒍᙏ** , *man;* but feeling that this synonym did not render the Hebrew, he chose the word **ᘓᒕᎢᐁ**, *universal, infinite*: an opportune word which proves the anteriority and the superiority of the Samaritan version over the Chaldaic targum; for the author of this targum, in interpreting אדם, does not go beyond the material meaning and confines himself constantly to the word אינשא, *man*. The Hellenists who follow quite voluntarily the Samaritan have abandoned it on this occasion. They would have exposed too much the spiritual meaning which they wished to hide. They were content to copy the Chaldaic and translate אדם, by ἀνθρώπος, *man;* in which they have been imitated by Saint Jerome and his successors.

27. W a-î b e r â Ælohîm
æth-ha-Adam, be-tzallem-ô,
be-tzellem Ælohîm barâ âoth
-ô, zaċhar w'nekebah barâ
âoth'am.

וַיִּבְרָא אֱלֹהִים אֶת־הָאָדָם בְּצַלְמוֹ
בְּצֶלֶם אֱלֹהִים בָּרָא אֹתוֹ זָכָר
וּנְקֵבָה בָּרָא אֹתָם :

The name given to Adam   אדם, signifies not only "homo," *man*,
but it characterizes, as the Samaritan had clearly seen in rendering
it by   **32QV**, *universal*, that which we understand by mankind,
and which we would express much better by saying *kingdom of
man*: it is collective man, man abstractly formed of the assemblage of
all men. This is the literal meaning of אדם.

The figurative meaning is indicated by the constant practice which
Moses follows, of making the noun always accompanied by a verb
from the same root. Now what is the verb here which follows the
word אדם ?   It is רמות, used constructively in the enunciative
nominal, inflected by the assimilative article כ and bearing the affix
of the first person plural כרמותנו : that is to say, word-for-word and
grammatically, *conformable-to-our-action-of-assimilàting*.   This comparison of the verb and the noun, gives us the root from which both
spring. This root is דם which carries with itself every idea of assimilation, of similitude, of homogeneity.   Governed by the sign of
power and stability א, it becomes the image of an immortal assimilation, of an aggregation of homogeneous and indestructible parts.
Such is the etymology of the name *Adam*,   אדם, in its figurative sense.

I shall enlarge less upon the hieroglyphic meaning, which Moses
allows nevertheless, to be understood in the same verse, and to which
he makes allusion, by causing this same noun, which is singular, to
govern the future plural verb ירדו : quite contrary to the rule which
he had followed, of making the noun of the Being of Beings אלהים
which is plural, govern always the singular verb.   The hieroglyphic
root of the name *Adam*, אדם is אר, which, composed of the sign of
unitary, principiant power, and that of divisibility, offers the image
of a relative unity, such as might be expressed, for example, by
means of the simple although compound number 10.   This root being
endowed with the collective sign כ, assumes an unlimited develop-

27. And-he-did-frame-out, HE-the-Gods, the-self-same-ness-of-*Adam,* (original similitude, collective unity, universal man), in-the-shadow-his-own, in-the-shadow-of HIM-the-Being-of beings, he-created-him (Adam); male and-female he-created the-universal-self-of-them.

27. Et-il-créa, LUI-les-Dieux, l'ipséité-d' *Adam* (similitude première, unité collective, homme universel) en-ombre-sienne, en-ombre-de LUI-l'Être-des-êtres, il-créa-lui (Adam); mâle et-femelle il-créa l'existence-universelle-à-eux.

---

ment: that is to say, the symbolic number 10, being taken to represent the root אר, the sign ם will develop its progressive power to infinity, as 10; 100; 1000; 10,000, etc.

בצלמנו *in-the-shadow-universal-ours....* This figurative expression, very difficult to render was already materialized at the epoch when the Samaritan version was written. Here is the sentence word-for-word.

·ꝋꝘꞪ ·Ꝙ𝈙Ꝇ ·Ꝙ2Ɦ ·Ꝙ𝈝Ɦ𝈙 "And-he-said," HE GOD, "let-us-
·ꝆꞪ𝈝ꝏ𝈙ꞪꝌ ·𝈝Ɦ9Ꝇ𝈡ꝏ "work-upon Adam, in-the-form-
"exterior-ours, and after-the-ac-
"tion-ours-of-us-composing."

The Chaldaic targum copies the Hebrew; but everything proves that it is misinterpreted. The Hellenists say, κατ'εἰκόνα, *in the image;* the Hebraic root צל is obvious; it expresses always an idea of a shadow thrown upon something, a veil, an appearance, a protection. The collective sign ם, which terminates the word צלם, universalizes its meaning.

כדמותנו, *by-the-like-making-like-ourselves....* I have already explained the root of this verb and its composition.

v. 27 זכר ונקבה, *male and female....* The root of the first of these words is כר, which expresses that which is apparent, eminent; that which serves as monument or as character, to preserve the memory of things. It is the elementary root אר united to the assimilative sign כ, and ruled by the demonstrative sign ז.

The second of these words has for root קב, whose meaning, entirely opposed to that of כר, is applied to that which is hidden and not apparent; to that which is graven, hollowed out, enveloped. The sign נ which rules it is the image of passive action.

28. Wa-îbarèch âoth'am Ælohîm, wa-iâomer la-hem Æ l o h î m, p h r o û w'reboû w'milâoû æth-ha-âretz w'chi-beshu-ha, w'redoû bi-deg-gath ha-îam w'bi-hôph ha-shamaîm, w'bi-chol-haîah ha-romesheth hal-ha-âretz.

וַיְבָרֶךְ אֹתָם אֱלֹהִים וַיֹּאמֶר לָהֶם אֱלֹהִים פְּרוּ וּרְבוּ וּמִלְאוּ אֶת־הָאָרֶץ וְכִבְשֻׁהָ וּרְדוּ בִּדְגַת הַיָּם וּבְעוֹף הַשָּׁמַיִם וּבְכָל־חַיָּה הָרֹמֶשֶׂת עַל הָאָרֶץ :

29. Wa-iâomer Ælohîm, hinneh nathathî la-chem æth-chol-heshcb zoreha ze-rah âsher hal-pheneî chol-ha-âretz, w'æth-chol ha-hetz âsher-b'ô pherî, hetz zoreha zerah la-chem îhîeh la-âche-lah.

וַיֹּאמֶר אֱלֹהִים הִנֵּה נָתַתִּי לָכֶם אֶת־כָּל־עֵשֶׂב זֹרֵעַ זֶרַע אֲשֶׁר עַל־פְּנֵי כָל־הָאָרֶץ וְאֶת־כָּל־הָעֵץ אֲשֶׁר־בּוֹ פְרִי עֵץ זֹרֵעַ זָרַע לָכֶם יִהְיֶה לְאָכְלָה :

30. W'l-chol-haîah ha-âretz, w'l'-chol-hôph ha-sha-maîm, w'l'chol-romesh hal-ha-âretz, âsher b'ô nephesh haîah, æth-chol îerek hesheb l'âchelah, wa-îhî-chen.

וּלְכָל־חַיַּת הָאָרֶץ וּלְכָל־עוֹף הַשָּׁמַיִם וּלְכָל־רוֹמֵשׂ עַל־הָאָרֶץ אֲשֶׁר־בּוֹ נֶפֶשׁ חַיָּה אֶת־כָּל־יֶרֶק עֵשֶׂב לְאָכְלָה וַיְהִי־כֵן :

It must be observed that the verb ברא, *to create*, which in the Hebrew text, expresses the action of the Supreme Being creating man male and female, is rendered in the Samaritan version by צֶבֶ, which, as can be judged by the Hebrew and Chaldaic analogue כון, preserved in Syriac and Ethiopic, signifies *to identify, to naturalize*.

v. 28. ויברך, *and-he-blessed*.... The root רך contains the idea of bending, of extenuation, of feeling compassion, physically as well as morally. This root, become verb, signifies in the Samaritan ᏕᎦᎯ

28. And-he-blessed the-self-sameness-of-them (universal) HE-the-Gods, and-he-said unto-them : beget and-multiply and-fill the-earth; and-subdue-it, and-hold-the sceptre (rule) in-the-fish of-the-seas, and-in-the-fowl of-h e a v e n s, and-in-all-life crawling-along u p o n-the-earth.

29. And-he-said, HE-the-Being-of-beings : behold ! I-h a v e-given-unto-you t h e-whole grass seed-yielding-seed which-is upon-the-face of-all-the-earth, and-the-vegetable-substance which-has in-itself fruit; substance seed-y i e l d i n g-seed to-you shall-be-for food.

30. And-unto-all-animal-ity earth-born, and-unto all-fowl of-heavens, and-unto-all-moving-life c r e e p i n g-along upon-the-earth, which has-in-i t s e l f an-animated-breath-and-living, (I have given) the-whole verdant grass for-food: and-it-was-so.

28. Et-il-bénit l'existence-universelle-à-eux, LUI-les-Dieux, et-il-dit-à-eux : en-gendrez et-multipliez et-remplissez la-terre et-capti-vez-la, et-tenez-le-gouvernail (régnez) dans-le-poisson des-mers, et-dans-l'oiseau des-cieux, et-dans-toute-chose mouvante-d'un-mou-vement-vital sur-la-terre.

29. Et-il-dit, LUI-l'Être-des-êtres; voici ! J'ai-donné-à-vous en-totalité l'herbe germinant-g e r m e qui-est sur-la-face de-toute-la-terre, et-en-totalité la-substance-végétale qui-a-dans-soi fruit; substance germinant-germe, à-vous sera pour-aliment.

30. Et-à-toute-vie de-la-terre, et-à-tout-volatile des-cieux, et-à-tout-être repti-forme-se-t r a î n a n t sur-la-terre, qui-a dans-soi souffle-animé de-vie, (j'ai-donné) en-t o t a l i t é la-verdoyante herbe pour aliment : et-cela-fut-ainsi.

---

or in the Arabic ﻙﺭ, the action of bending, of extending the hands over someone. It is, by employing this word with the paternal sign ב, image of active and interior action, that the verb בּרךְ to bless, has been formed; properly speaking, it is to lay on the hands with a paternal sentiment of tenderness and kindness.

31. Wa-îaræ Ælohîm æth-
ĉhol-âsher w'hinneh-tôb mâ-
ôd, wa-îhî-hereb, wa-îhî-boker, îôm-ha-shîshî.

וַיַּרְא אֱלֹהִים אֶת־כָּל־אֲשֶׁר עָשָׂה
וְהִנֵּה־טוֹב מְאֹד וַיְהִי־עֶרֶב וַיְהִי־
בֹּקֶר יוֹם הַשִּׁשִּׁי :

---

v. 29.   עֵץ, *vegetable-substance....*   This important word which
the Hellenists have rendered by ξύλον, *wood*, will be explained further
on, when it will be more essential to penetrate its real meaning.

אָכְלָה, *food....*   This word will also be explained in its place.

v. 30.   It should be observed in this verse, that the Supreme Being,
speaking of the food accorded to animals, makes no mention of the
substance   עֵץ, of which he had spoken in the preceding verse with
respect to man. The very profound reason for this reticence will later
on be shown.

v. 31.   מְאֹד, *as-much-as-possible....*   That is to say, filling its
fixed and determined unity, its whole measure. This word springs from
the root אֵר, רֹהַר or חַר , *unity*, the power of divisibility. It is governed by the determining, local and plastic sign, מ.

31. And-he-did-ken, HE-the-Gods, the-whole-that-he-had-made, and-lo! good as-much-as-possible (in its own nature) : and - there - was - west-eve, and-there-was-east-dawn (over and back again), day the-sixth (light's sixth manifestation).

31. Et-il-vit, LUI-les-Dieux, ce-tout lequel il-avait-fait, et-voici! bon autant-que-possible (selon sa mesure), et-fut-occident, et-fut-orient (libération et itération) jour sixième (sixième manifestation phénoménique).

I have not dwelt upon the Hebrew words which enter into the composition of the last verses of this chapter, because they offer no grammatical difficulty. I might have expatiated at length, if I had wished to comment upon them; but, for the moment, it is enough to re-establish the meaning of the words and to explain what may have been obscure, without examining in particular all the inferences that might be drawn.

SEPHER BERÆSHITH
B.

ספר בראשית ב ·

---

1. Wa-îchuloû ha-sha-maîm w'ha-âretz, w'chol-tzebâ'am.

וַיְכֻלּוּ הַשָּׁמַיִם וְהָאָרֶץ וְכָל־
צְבָאָם :

2. Wa-îchal Ælohîm ba-îom ha-shebîhî melacheth-ô âsher hasah, wa-îsheboth ba-îôm ha-shebîhî mi-chol milâcheth-ô âsher hashah.

וַיְכַל אֱלֹהִים בַּיּוֹם הַשְּׁבִיעִי
מְלַאכְתּוֹ אֲשֶׁר עָשָׂה וַיִּשְׁבֹּת
בַּיּוֹם הַשְּׁבִיעִי מִכָּל־מְלַאכְתּוֹ
אֲשֶׁר עָשָׂה :

---

v. 1. וַיְכֻלּוּ, and-(shall become)-thus-were-wholly-finished.... This is the verb כלה, employed according to the passive movement of the enunciative form, convertible future. The word כל, the whole, from which it is derived, is composed of the assimilative sign כ, united to the root כל, containing the idea of that which is raised, stretched to infinity, without limits. It is important to observe here, the future tense turned to the past. This trope is hieroglyphic.

The Samaritan makes use of the verb 2Ꞛ▽, to complete, to achieve, employed according to the reflexive form Ꞛ2Ꞛ▽ᴧᴧ, they were achieved; they were made perfect. That which is always attached to the idea contained in the initial word בראשית, and marks a successive development, a passing from power into action.

צבאם, and-the-ruling-law-of-them........ This remarkable word has not been understood by any of the translators. The Hellenists have said ὁ κόσμος, and the Latins "ornatus." The Samaritans have translated Ꞛᴧᴧ℘2Ꞛᴧ, the parts, the divisions, the distributions. The Chaldaic targum reads חיליהון, the force, the universal faculty, the army. This is only the material meaning.

The roots of the Hebrew word employed in this place by Moses, are צו, which contains within itself every idea of order, of commandment, of direction impressed toward an end, and אב, which

GENESIS II

1. And-(shall become) thus- were - wholly - finished (completed) the - heavens and-the-earth, and-the-whole ruling - law - of - them (elementizing nature).

2. And-he-fulfilled, HE-the-Gods, in-the light's manifestation-the-seventh, the-sovereign-work (act of his almighty power) which-he-had-performed; and-he-restored-himself, (he returned in his former divine self) in-t h e-l i g h t' s-manifestation the-seventh, from-the-whole-sovereign-work - which - he - had-performed.

COSMOGONIE II

I. Et-(seront) ainsi-furent - accomplis (totalisés, parfaits) les-cieux et-la-terre, et-toute l'ordonnance-conductrice-à-eux (la nature régulatrice).

2. Et-il-accomplit, LUI-les-Dieux, dans la-manifestation-phénoménique la-septième, l'acte-souverain qu'il-avait-exercé; et-il-se-restitua (il se rétablit dans son ineffable séité) la-manifestation - lumineuse - universelle la-septième, après-tout-l'acte-de-sa-souveraine-puissance, qu'il-avait-exercé.

---

expresses every organizing and efficient will. The entire word צבא is related to law, to innate, principiant force, to universal nature finally, which being developed with the universe, must lead it from power into action, and raise it from development to development to its absolute perfection.

v. 2. מלאכתו, *the-sovereign-work*.... The Samaritan is the sole translator who has understood that this word, 'ࠌࠋࠀࠊࠕࠅ', signifies *a sovereign work accompanied with all royal majesty.* The Hebrew word is obviously derived from the verb מלוך *to rule,* whose etymology I have explained sufficiently in my Grammar (ch. VII. §2).

וישבת, *and-he-restored himself*.... This is the root שוב, containing in itself the idea of every kind of re-establishment, of return to a primitive state, united to the sign ת, which is that of sympathy and of reciprocity, sign *par excellence*, and image of per-

3.　　Wa-îbareċh Ælohîm æth-îôm ha-shebihî, wa-îkaddesh âoth'-ô ċhi b'ô shabath mi-ċhol-melâċheth-ô　âsher barâ Ælohîm, la-hashôth.

וַיְבָרֶךְ אֱלֹהִים אֶת־יוֹם הַשְּׁבִיעִי וַיְקַדֵּשׁ אֹתוֹ כִּי בוֹ שָׁבַת מִכָּל־מְלַאכְתּוֹ אֲשֶׁר־בָּרָא אֱלֹהִים לַעֲשׂוֹת :

4.　　Ælleh thô-ledôth ha-shamaîm w'ha-âretz b'hibbarâ'm ba-îôm hashôth Ihôah Ælohîm æretz w'shamaîm.

אֵלֶּה תוֹלְדוֹת הַשָּׁמַיִם וְהָאָרֶץ בְּהִבָּרְאָם בְּיוֹם עֲשׂוֹת יְהֹוָה אֱלֹהִים אֶרֶץ וְשָׁמָיִם :

---

fection. The translators who have seen in this verb the idea of resting, have not understood the Hebrew. The error concerning this word has been general, and the Samaritan has been unfortunate enough to render it by **בטל**, which signifies *to rest idle*, as can be seen by the Chaldaic בטל, and the Arabic بطل , which have the same meaning.

השביעי, *the-seventh*.... This is the number of complete restitution, of cyclic fullness. It is true that שבע signifies *seven*, and that שביעי can be taken for *seventh* or *septenary;* but the name of this number draws with it in the Hebraic tongue, the idea of the consummation of things, and of the fullness of times. One of the roots of which it is composed שוב, and of which I am about to speak, expresses the idea of return to the place from which one had departed, and the one which is joined to it by contraction עו, indicates every kind of curve, of inversion, of cycle.

The Hebrews make use of the verb שבע, to express the oath by virtue of which they affirm that a thing promised will be fulfilled.

All names of number have, in Hebrew, particular and often very deep significations: the abundance of new things upon which I was obliged to dwell in beginning, has forced me to neglect them; but as soon as I shall have more leisure, I shall make amends for my silence in this respect, as well as in some others.

v. 3. All these terms have been explained.

v. 4. תוֹלְדוֹת *the sign*....*of the progenies*.... The root תו contains every idea of sign, of symbol, of hieroglyphic character: it is taken, in a restricted sense, for the same thing symbolized, and for

3. And-he-blessed, HE-the-Gods, that-day the-seventh (seventh light's manifestation); and-he-did-sanctify its-selfsameness, because-that in-it, he-reëstablished-himself (he returned into his unspeakable self), from - the - sovereign - work whereby he-created, HE-the-Being-of-beings, according to-his-performing.

4. Such-is-the-sign (symbolical monument) - of - the progenies of-the-heavens and -of-the-earth, in-their-being-created - them at - the - day, (light's manifestation) of-the-producing of-IHOAH, HE-the-Being-of-beings, earth-and heavens.

3. Et-il-bénit, LUI-les-Dieux, ce-jour le-septième (s e p t i è m e manifestation phénoménique); et-il-sanctifia l'existence-sienne-à-jamais, à-cause-que dans-elle, il-se-restitua (il retourna dans son ineffable séité). après-tout -l'acte - souverain durant lequel-il-avait-créé, LUI-l'Être-des-êtres, s e l o n-l'action-de-faire-à-lui.

4. Tel-est-le-signe (l'emblème, le monument sacré, hiéroglyphique) des-générations - des - cieux et - de - la-terre, dans-l'acte d'être-créés-eux, au-jour (la manifestation lumineuse) de-l'action-de-faire de-IHOAH, LUI-l'Être-des-êtres, la-terre et-les-cieux.

---

that which serves to symbolize: it is then, a narration, a fable, a speech, a table, a book, etc. The Samaritan, Hellenist and Arabic translators have expressed in some degree this important word which the Latins have neglected absolutely.

יהוה, IHOAH.... This is the proper name that Moses gives to GOD. It appears here for the first time, and only when the Being of beings, having accomplished the sovereign act whose thought he had conceived, re-establishes himself in his Immutable Seity. This name is never pronounced by modern Jews in their synagogues, the majority attaching thereunto great mysteries, and especially the rabbis whom we name Kabbalists, on account of the Hebraic word קבל, *the transmission.* By this word, they understand the oral law left by Moses and claim to be the guardians of it: which is true only of a very small part of them. I shall relate presently why both of these, who always read the Hebraic books without points, refuse to pronounce

5. W'chol shîah ha-she-dah terem îhîeh ba-âretz w'chol hesheb ha-shadeh te-rem îtzemath chi-loâ hime-tîr IHÔAH Ælohîm hal-ha-âretz, w'Adam aîn la-habod æth-ha-âdamah.

וְכֹל שִׂיחַ הַשָּׂדֶה טֶרֶם יִהְיֶה בָאָרֶץ וְכָל עֵשֶׂב הַשָּׂדֶה טֶרֶם יִצְמָח כִּי־לֹא הִמְטִיר יְהוָה אֱלֹהִים עַל־הָאָרֶץ וְאָדָם אַיִן לַעֲבֹד אֶת־הָאֲדָמָה :

---

this name. Let us now analyze it and see with what infinitely mar-vellous art it has been composed by Moses, or by the ancient sages who have communicated it to him.

This noun offers first, the sign indicative of life, doubled, and forming the essentially living root הה. This root is never used as noun, and it is the only one which enjoys this prerogative. It is, in its formation, not only a verb, but an unique verb, of which all the other are only derivatives: it is in short, the verb הוה to-be-being. Here, as can be seen, and as I have taken pains to explain in my Gram-mar, the sign of intelligible light ו, is in the middle of the root of life. Moses, taking this verb *par excellence*, to form the proper name of the Being of beings, adds the sign of potential manifestation and of eternity to it, and he obtains יהוה, IHOAH, in which the facultative *being*, is found placed between a past without origin and a future with-out limit. This wonderful noun therefore, signifies exactly, *the-Being-who-is-who-was-and-who-will-be.*

Sometimes this noun is written אהוה ÆHOAH, and in this case, the sign of potentiality is substituted for that of duration. It becomes much more mysterious as first person of the future, replacing the third, and seems to belong only to the being which bears it and by which it is uttered; then it signifies, *I-the-Being-who-is-who-was-and-who-will-be.*

The Samaritan version does not alter in the least this Divine Name which it renders by ꓵꓵꓵ. The Chaldaic targum renders it by ꙗꙗꙗ, the three Eternities, or the Eternity of eternities. The Syriac has ܠܡܪܝܐ, and the Greek, κύριος, both of which mean *Lord*, or rather according to its etymology, *the Glorious* and *the Lumi-nous.*

Now, let us approach the delicate question of knowing why the Jews of the synagogues and the kabbalistic rabbis either refrain from pronouncing it, or make a mystery of its pronunciation.

5. And-all-the-produce of-nature before it-will-be in-the-earth; and-all-the-growing-grass of-nature, before-it-will-grow: because-of-not causing-to-rain IHOAH, HE-the-Gods, upon-the-earth; and-*Adam* (collective man) not-being-existing to-labour t h e-a d a m i c-selfsameness (homogeneal ground).

5. Et-toute-la-conception-de-la-nature, avant-qu'elle-existera en-la-terre; et-toute-la-végétation-de-la-nature, avant-qu'elle-germera: car-non-faire pleuvoir IHOAH, LUI-les-Dieux, sur-la-terre; et-*Adam* (l'homme universel) non-être (non-exister en acte) pour-travailler la-substance-adamique (l'élément homogène, similaire à *Adam*).

If one recalls what I have said in my Grammar pertaining to the hardening of the vowels, and their transformation into consonants (ch. II. §. 2), he will not be far from the idea which I have disclosed concerning the ravage that this revolution had brought about in the primitive signification of words. Now, the most important of all the vocal sounds, those whose meaning is the most spiritual, ו and י, are also those which are most easily influenced by this revolution, and upon which it operates the greatest changes. The changes are such, that these spiritual signs, becoming materialized in the name given to GOD by Moses, this name (pronounced *Jehovah*, according to the Chaldaic punctuation יְהֹוָה), is far from expressing the divine perfections which I have stated, and signifies no more than a calamity, an unfortunate existence, whose origin or whose limit is unknown: for such is the meaning of the word הֹוָה, materialized, as one can be convinced by opening the first Hebrew lexicon.

This is the reason, known or unknown, why the Jewish people are not permitted to utter this Name, and why only the writings without points are admitted in the synagogues; inasmuch as the pronunciation which results from these points, alters sometimes the original signification of the words, rendering them unrecognizable.

As my intention is not to profane the secrets of any sect, I desire that those which I have disclosed thus far, or which I shall reveal as we go on, will disturb no one. If contrary to my expectation, some sectarians are found who might take offense at the publicity which I give to certain mysteries, I repeat to them what I have already inti-

6. W'æd îahaleh min-â-
retz w'hishekah æth-chol-
pheneî ha-âdamah.

וְאֵד יַעֲלֶה מִן־הָאָרֶץ וְהִשְׁקָה
אֶת־כָּל־פְּנֵי הָאֲדָמָה :

---

mated, that since I did not receive them from any person nor from any society, and have acquired them by my own studies alone, I can publish them without betraying any kind of oath.

v. 5.   שִׂיחַ, *the-produce*.... By this word should be understood all creative travail. It springs from the root שׂח, which expresses the effort of the soul toward any goal whatsoever. The facultative שׂוֹחַ, which comes from it, signifies *to be-producing* or *uttering one's thoughts*, whether by travail, or by speech. The Hellenists, and Saint Jerome who has followed them, have seen in this word only a tender herb, a shrub; χλωρόν or "virgultum," *a young shoot*.

הַשָּׂדֶה, *of-nature*.... Following this same idea, these translators have seen in the word שָׂדֶה, applied to generative and fostering Nature, only *a field*, thus taking the Hebraic word in its most material and most restricted meaning. But how, in this energetic expression composed of the contracted roots שׂו־דִי, of which the first שׂו contains the idea of equality and distributive equity, and the second דִי that of abundance; how, I say, can they not recognize Nature, always ready to load men with her gifts? How fail to see in the word שַׂד, *mammal*, her sacred symbol among the Egyptians? How, with only the slightest attention are they unable to perceive that the name of שַׁדִּי, given to GOD Himself to express his munificence and the abundance of his gifts, could not be directly formed from that of a field, but from that of Nature? Besides if one examines the corresponding idioms, he will see that the Chaldaic שְׂרָא signifies *fusion; profusion, ejaculation;* that the Syriac ܣܐܕܘ, characterizes *fortune, the demon of the earth; the state* or *nature of things;* that the Arabic شد or شديد indicates that which is constant, firm in its progress; that which is abundant, nourishing; that the Ethiopic ሸዪ (*shadi*) expresses *benignity, good nature*, etc. When one ponders upon these things he can only believe, that the Jews of Alexandria, the Essenes, if they had not had very strong reasons for suppressing the truth,

6. But-a-virtual-effluence went-up from-out the-earth, and-bedewed that-the-whole-face of-the-adamic (homogeneal ground).

6. Mais-une - émanation-virtuelle s'élevait-avec-énergie du-sein de-la-terre et-abreuvait cette-toute-la-face de l'élément-adamique.

---

would never have rendered the word שׂדה, terminated here with the emphatic article ה sign of life, by the Greek word ἀγρός, a *field*.

ואדם אין, *and-Adam-not-being....* It is assuredly difficult to read attentively this verse without finding the convincing proof, that the figurative meaning given to the initial word בראשית is of rigorous exactitude, and that it is indeed, only *in principle*, that the Being of beings had at first determined the creation of the heavens and the earth, containing them תהו ובהו, *in contingent power of being, in another power of being.* It would seem that Moses, wishing to make this profound truth clearly understood, has written designedly the beginning of this chapter. In the first verse, he speaks of the natural law צבאם which must lead this creation of power in action to its highest development. He repeats carefully several times, that this creation has been made לעשׂות *according to the efficient action of* יהוה אלהים Ihoah, *the Being of beings.* Finally he gives the word, and says openly, that every conception of productive Nature had been created before Nature existed, and all vegetation, before anything had germinated; furthermore, after having announced the formation of Adam, he declared expressly that Adam did not exist, ואדם אין.

It is true that the Hellenist translators have wished to see in the natural law, where the Samaritan version and the Chaldaic targum at least, see *an acting force*, and *a host*, only an embellishment, κόσμος, and in the conception of productive nature, only an herb of the field, χλωρὸν ἀγροῦ : but no doubt they had their reasons for that; as well as for making the Being of beings say ποιήσωμεν ἄνθρωπον *let us make man*, instead of *we will make Adam*, נעשׂה אדם as is given in the original text, which is very different. The determined resolution of veiling the spiritual meaning of the Sepher, and above all of the Beræshith, placed them at every turn in difficult positions and forced them to distort the clearest phrases. A single word badly disguised would have been sufficient to make their preparations crumble away. They preferred to risk the grossest mistransla-

7. Wa-îîtzer IHÒAH Ælo-
hîm æth-ha-Adam haphar
min ha-âdamah w'îphah bi-
âphi-ô nishemath haîîm wa-
îehî ha-Adam le-nephesh
haîah.

וַיִּיצֶר יְהוָֹה אֱלֹהִים אֶת־הָאָדָם
עָפָר מִן־הָאֲדָמָה וַיִּפַּח בְּאַפָּיו
נִשְׁמַת חַיִּים וַיְהִי הָאָדָם לְנֶפֶשׁ
חַיָּה :

---

tions and make Moses fall into palpable contradictions, rather than expose its mysteries.

What, for example, could be more incoherent than what they
made him say? According to their version, man, already created in
v. 26 of the preceding chapter, does not exist in v. 6 of this one; and
presently in v. 7, this same man comes to be created anew. How
can this be?

The first creation takes place only in principle. The days, or the
luminous manifestations, are only the efficient epochs, the phenomenal
phases; Moses states it in a manner so precise that one must voluntarily close the eyes in order not to see its light. The conception of
Nature had been created before Nature itself; the vegetation before the
vegetable; Adam was not. The Being of beings had said only, *we will
make Adam;* and Adam, universal man had been made in power.
Soon he appears in action, and it is by him that effective creation begins. Profound Mystery! upon which I shall endeavour to throw as
much light as is possible.

את־האדמה *the-adamic-selfsameness....* This word which is
formed from that of *Adam*, and partakes of all its significations, figuratively as well as hieroglyphically, has undergone continuous restrictions,
until it signifies only *the earth*, properly speaking; in the same manner
that one has been brought to see in אדם, universal man, *the kingdom
of man*, only a material man of flesh and blood. The name of *Adam*,
being well understood, leads the mind easily to that of *Adamah*, its
elementary principle, homogeneous earth, and like unto *Adam;* primitive earth, very far from that which is obvious to our senses, and as
different from *the earth*, properly so-called, as intelligible, universal
man, אדם , is different from particular and corporeal man, אֱנוֹשׁ .

v. 6.   ואר , *But-a-virtual-effluence....* The Hellenists have seen in

7. And-he-formed (framed, elementized for an everlasting end) IHOAH, HE-the-Being - of - beings, the - self-sameness of-*Adam* (collective man), by-rarefying (sublimating the principle) of-the-adamic (homogeneal ground); and-he-inspired into-the-inspiring-faculty-of him, a-being-exalted (an essence) of-the-lives, for-being-made Adam (collective man) according-to-the-soul of-life.

7. Et-il-forma (substantialisa, en déterminant les éléments vers un but) IHOAH, LUI - l'Être - des - êtres, l'ipséité d'*Adam* (l'homme universel) en-r a r é fi a n t (sublimant le principe) de-l'élément-adamique; et-il-inspira dans la-faculté-inspirante-à-lui un-étant-é l e v é (une essentialité) des-vies; a fin-qu'il-fût cet-homme-universel (Adam) selon-l' âme-vivante.

πηγή , *a fountain*, as has also Saint Jerome. It would be difficult to disparage more the expression of Moses. This expression, in the figurative sense in which it must be taken, indicates every kind of force, of faculty, by means of which any being whatsoever manifests its power exteriorly; a good power if it is good, and bad if it is bad.

One finds in the Arabic اد or ايد signifying force, power, vigour; the victory which follows them: a thing unprecedented, happy or sad, an emanation sympathetic or evil. ادا is the thing produced; ادي the productive thing, the instrument. In Samaritan, ᛋᚾ , in Ethiopic ᚼᛈ (ad) both signify *the hand*, instrument of man, symbol of his power. The Syriac says ܐܝܕ , and the Chaldaic יד . The Hebrew also says יד *the hand*: this word, ruled by the sign of power and stability א , becomes איד, that is to say, every corroboration, every virtual emanation, every faculty, good or evil, according to the being by which it is produced.

If one takes this last word איד, and in order to give it an hieroglyphic sense, eliminates the sign of manifestation י , the word אד , preserving all the acceptations of the radical איד will become purely intelligible; it will be, as I have translated it, *a virtual emanation*. Moses has employed it in this sense. But this sense, too sublime to be easily understood, is materialized in the imagination of a gross and ignorant people. The word אד in its degeneration, signifies no more

8. Wa-îttah Iнôaн Ælo-
hîm gan-bi-heden mi-kedem,
wa-îâshem   sham   æth-ha-
Adam âsher-îatzar.

וַיִּטַּע יְהוָֹה אֱלֹהִים גַּן־בְּעֵדֶן
מִקֶּדֶם וַיָּשֶׂם שָׁם אֶת־הָאָדָם
אֲשֶׁר יָצָר:

---

than *a smoke, a vapour, a mist, a cloud.* The Samaritan and Chaldaic
translators understood it thus. This interpretation is defective no
doubt, but it is better than that of *fountain,* given by the Hellenist
Jews.

v. 7   וַיִּיצֶר, *and-he-formed....* This is one of the most difficult
words in the Hebraic tongue. Its primitive root is אר, the elementary principle whose analysis I have given in v 3, ch. I. This root,
ruled by the determinative sign צ, and animated by the convertible
sign ו, offers in the verb צוּר, the idea of figuring, forming, coördinat-
ing, fixing and binding the constitutive elements of a thing. If this
radical verb, employed according to the intensive form, doubles its
final character ר, image of proper and frequentative movement, as in
צוּרר ; then it signifies to tighten and to press forcibly, to oppress:
but if the convertible sign passes to the condition of hard consonant,
as in   צָעֹר; then the material compression has attained its height,
and this verb contains only the idea of agony, of ignominy, and of very
sharp pain.

In the present case, Moses has used the simple root   צר, which
expresses coördination, elementary configuration, by giving it for
initial adjunction, the sign of manifestation and duration י, thus
forming the compound radical verb יצר, *he substantiated, formed,
fastened; and fashioned for eternity.*

עָפָר, *by-rarefying....*This continued facultative, which has been
taken for a simple substantive by the Latin translator, has not been by
all the Hellenists, who at least say   χοῆν λαβών, *taking the dust:*
imagining, *dust* where there was none: but still, it is better to imagine dust, than *mud* and *mire.*

The Samaritan renders עָפָר by ᛞᛜᛕᛊ which is to say, *a volatile,
essential spirit;* as is shown by the Ethiopic analogue ጸፈ
(tzawphe), signifying literally *new wine;* and the Arabic word   ضوا,
which presents the idea of that which is inflamed rapidly, of that

8. And - he - appointed, IHOAH, HE-the-Gods, an-enclosure (an organical boundary) in-the-temporal-and-sensible-sphere extracted-from - the - boundless - and - foregoing (time); and-he-laid-up there that-same-*Adam* whom-he-had-framed-forever.

8. Et-il arrêta (traça), IHÔAH, LUI-les-Dieux, une-enceinte (une circonférence organique) dans-la-sphère-sensible-et-temporelle extra-ite - de - l'antériorité - uni-verselle (des temps); et-il-plaça là ce-même-*Adam* qu'il-avait-formé-pour l'éterni-té.

---

which exhales an odour, of that which moves with vivacity; as is proved by its derivatives اضواع · تضوع · ضوع, etc.

The word עֻף here in question, offers the two roots united עוּף־אר, the first of which עוּף contains the idea of all rapid, volatile, aerial movement; the second, as we have already seen, is applied to the elementary principle.

וַיִּפַּח בְּאַפָּיו, *and-he-inspired into-the-inspiring-faculty-of-him* . . . . Following the custom of Moses, the verb and the substantive, drawn from the same root, succeed and enlighten each other. This root is פא, or פִי, which signifies literally *the mouth* and the breath which it exhales; figuratively, *speech* and intelligence which is its source.

נשמת, *a-being-exalted*.... This is the verb שׂמֹח, whose root שׂם expresses that which is exalted, employed according to the enunciative form, passive movement, as continued facultative, feminine construction.

v. 8. גן, *an enclosure*.... The Hellenist translators have copied here the Samaritan word ꟼ, *paradise·* Let us take up this Samaritan word, whose root רך, so little understood, expresses the idea of circular movement, steady and easy as that of a wheel; it can be perceived in the verb רוך, which expresses the action of that which unfolds around something and envelops it in its enclosure. Also, the Syriac ܪܕܝܐ, the Chaldaic and Hebrew רדיד, have signified alike a woman's garment, a light mantle enveloping a person with its undulating folds. The Samaritan word ꟼ, has had most

9.   Wa-îatzemah IHÔAH
Æ l o h î m, min-ha-âdamah
chol-hetz nehmad l'mæh,
w'tôb l'maâchal, w'hetz ha-
haîim b'thôch ha-gan, w'hetz
ha-dahath tôb wa-rawh.

וַיַּצְמַח יְהֹוָה אֱלֹהִים מִן־הָאֲדָמָה
כָּל־עֵץ נֶחְמָד לְמַרְאֶה וְטוֹב
לְמַאֲכָל וְעֵץ הַחַיִּים בְּתוֹךְ הַגָּן
וְעֵץ הַדַּעַת טוֹב וָרָע :

---

assuredly the same signification; what proves it beyond rejoinder, is
that the word גִּ, whose emphatic version, by means of the sign כ
or ם added at the head, has never had any other meaning than that
of an envelope, a protecting enclosure.   This word which partakes of
the nature of the same name given to woman by a great number
of peoples, signifies still a covering, in the Italian *gonna*, in the
English *gown*, in the French *gaine* and even in the ancient Celtic *gun*
or *goun*.   It can signify *a garden* only in the sense wherein one considers a garden as enclosed and surrounded with hedges.   But this restricted signification is belied here by the Samaritan *paradise*, whose
analogues all respond to the meaning of *enclosure*, *sphere*, *veil*, and
ORGAN which I give to it.

Here is the hieroglyphic etymology of the word גָּן.   This mysterious word comes evidently from the root גּוּ, expressing every idea
of an object, enveloping and containing without effort, opening and extending itself to contain and to receive, and which terminates with
the final, extensive sign ן.   See Rad. Vocab. roots גּוּ and גָּן .

בְעֶרֶן, *in-the-sensible-sphere*....   Since this word has been rendered by those of *pleasure* and *sensual desire*, it has been so only by
a sequence of gross ideas which are attached to that which is sentient and temporal.   The root from which it springs is evident: it is
עוּר, which expresses every kind of limited period.   Thence, עַר   and
עֶרֶן *the actual time*, the temporal; things sentient and transitory,
etc.

מִי־קְרָם, *extracted-from-the-foregoing*....   If the Hellenist translators had wished to understand the word עֶרֶן, they would have understood this one likewise; but having eluded the sense of the one
they have necessarily missed the sense of the other.   It is always the
root עַר which precedes and which is used according to the usage of
Moses, but considered under another relation and modified by the
initial sign of the greatest agglomerating and compressing force ק ,
and by the final collective sign ם.   It must be stated here that the
Egyptian priests conceived two eternities: קְרָם, that of this side of

9. And-he-caused-to-shoot-out, IHOAH, HE-the-Gods, from-the-adamic (homogeneal-ground) a l l-g r o w t h (every vegetative-faculty) fair-at-its-highest-rate, to-the-sense-of-sight, and-good to-the-sense-of-taste; and-a-growth of-lives, in-the-bosom of - the - organic - enclosure; and-a-growth (a vegetative faculty) of-the-knowledge of-good and-evil.

9. Et - il - fit - développer, IHOAH, LUI-les-Dieux, de-cet -élément-adamique (homogène) toute-substance-végétative belle-autant-que-possible selon-la-vue, et-bonne selon-le-goût; et-u n e-s u b-stance des-vies dans-le-centre de l'enceinte-organique; et-une-substance-végétative d e-l a-connaissance du-bien et-du-mal.

---

time, and עולם, that of the other side of time: that is to say, anterior eternity and posterior eternity.

v. 9. עץ, a *growth....* The root עו or עי develops every idea of growth, excrescence, tumour; anything which accumulates. The sign ץ which terminates it, marks the aim, the end to which all things tend. Seeing only *a tree*, in the word עץ, as the Hellenists or as Saint Jerome who has copied them, testifies to a great desire to suppress the truth or to show great ignorance. The Samaritan has been more happily chosen, or less cautiously. The word ᎷᏜᏠᎲ which it uses expresses a *vegetation of elementary nature;* it comes from the root עול or עיל, and terminates with the extensive sign ן. The Chaldaic reads אילן, which amounts to nearly the same. It is *an extensive force, an invading power;* in short, *matter in travail*: it is what the Greeks name ὕλη, and the Latins "sylva." Now, observe that ὕλη and "sylva" have likewise signified *tree*, or *wood*, in a very restricted sense.

The mistake that the translators committed here appears to me voluntary and calculated; for otherwise it would be ridiculous: that of Saint Jerome was forced. Having once followed these untrustworthy guides in one point, he was obliged to follow them in all. After having seen a *garden*, in an intelligible enclosure that we would today name *an organic sphere of activity*, it was quite natural that he should see *sensual desire* in what was *sentient* and *temporal; morning*, in what was *anteriority of time; a tree*, in what was *matter in travail*, etc., etc.

10. W'nahar îotzæ me-he-
den l'ha-shekôth æth-ha-gan,
w'mi-sham îophared, w'haîah l'arbahah rashîm.

וְנָהָר יֹצֵא מֵאֶרֶן לְהַשְׁקוֹת אֶת־
הַגָּן וּמִשָּׁם יִפָּרֵד וְהָיָה לְאַרְבָּעָה
רָאשִׁים :

11. Shem ha-æhad phî-
shôn, houâ hassobeb æth-
chol-ha-æretz   ha-hawilah,
âsher-sham ha-zahab.

שֵׁם הָאֶחָד פִּישׁוֹן הוּא הַסֹּבֵב
אֵת כָּל־אֶרֶן הַחֲוִילָה אֲשֶׁר־שָׁם
הַזָּהָב :

12. W'zahab ha-âretz ha-
hiwâ tôb sham ha-beddolah
w'æben ha-shoham.

וּזֲהַב הָאָרֶן הַהוּא טוֹב שָׁם
הַבְּרֹלַח וְאֶבֶן הַשֹּׁהַם :

---

v. 10. לְאַרְבָּעָה, *according-to-the-four-fold-power*.... The root of
this mysterious number is רִב, which, formed of the sign of movement proper ר, and that of generative action, contains all ideas of
grandeur and of multiplication. If the last character is doubled as
in רכב, this word acquires an endless numerical extent; if it is followed by the sign of material sense, as in רבע, it becomes the expression of solidity, of physical force, and of all ideas attached to the
cube. It is in this state that it represents the number *four*. But in
the above example, it begins one part with the sign of power א, and
terminates with the emphatic article ה, which attaches to it the
hieroglyphic meaning of the *four-fold power* or *quaternary*.

v. 11. פִּישׁוֹן, *Phishon*.... This is the root יש, which, formed by
the signs of manifestation and of relative movement, expresses every
idea of reality and of physical substantiality. It is governed by the

10. And -a-flowing-efflu-ence (an emanation) was-running from-this temporal-and-sensible-place, for-be-dewing that-same-organic-enclosure; and-thence, it-was-dividing in-order-to-be-henceforth suitable-to-the-four-fold-generative-power.

10. Et-un-fleuve (une émanation) était-coulant de-ce-lieu-temporel-et - sensible, pour-l'action-d'abreuver cet-te-même-sphère - organique; et-de-là, il-était-se-divisant afin-d'être-à-l'avenir selon-la - puissance - quaternaire - multiplicatrice-des - princi - pes.

11. The-name of-one (of-those generative effluences) -was-*Phishon* (real exist-ence) that-which-is sur-rounding the-whole-earth-of *Hawilah* (virtual energy) which-is the-native-spot of-gold (light's reflection).

11. Le-nom- du - premier (de ces principes émanés)-était-*Phishon* (la réalité physique, l'Être apparent) lui - qui - est circonscrivant toute - la - terre- de *Hawilah* (l'énergie virtuelle) laquelle -est-le lieu-propre de-l'or (la réflexion lumineuse).

12. And-the-gold of-the-earth that-self-same, good; proper-spot of - *Bedellium* (mysterious dividing) and-of-the-*Stone Shoam* (univer-sal sublimation).

12. Et-l'or de - la - terre icelle, bon; lieu-propre du-*Bedellium* (sèparation mys-térieuse), et-de-la-*pierre shohâm.* (sublimation uni-verselle).

---

emphatic sign of speech כ, and is terminated by the augumentative syllable ון, which carries to its highest degree, the extent of every produced being. One can recognize in this proper name and in all the following ones, the genius of the Egyptian tongue.

הֲחֵוִילַה, *Hawilah....* Here the root חל, הול or חיל, is related to the idea of effort, of tension, or virtual travail, of trial, etc. This root is used as continued facultative, with the emphatic article ה. Refer to the Rad. Vocab. concerning this root, and the preceding one.

v. 12. I suspect this verse was at first a marginal note which has crept into the text, either by the carelessness of Esdras, or by that of

13.   W'shem ha-nahar ha-shenî Gîhôn, houâ hassobeb æth-ĉhol-æretz Choush.

וְשֵׁם הַנָּהָר הַשֵּׁנִי גִּיחוֹן הוּא הַסֹּבֵב אֵת כָּל־אֶרֶץ כּוּשׁ :

14.   W'shem ha-nahar ha-shelîshî Hiddekel, houâ ha-holeĉh kidemath âshoûr, w' ha-nahar ha-rabîhî houâ phrath.

וְשֵׁם־הַנָּהָר הַשְּׁלִישִׁי הִדֶּקֶל הוּא הַהֹלֵךְ קִדְמַת אַשּׁוּר וְהַנָּהָר הָרְבִיעִי הוּא פְרָת :

15.   Wa-îkkah Ihôah Ælohîm æth-ha-Adam, wa-înnihe - hou be - gan - heden l'habed-ha w'l'shamer-ha.

וַיִּקַּח יְהֹוָה אֱלֹהִים אֶת־הָאָדָם וַיַּנִּחֵהוּ בְגַן־עֵדֶן לְעָבְדָהּ וּלְשָׁמְרָהּ :

---

some earlier copyist.   What leads me to suspect this is, that it inter-rupts visibly the narration, by an hermetic allegory, very crude, which is neither the style nor the manner of Moses.

v. 13.   גִּיחוֹן , *Gihon*.... Consult again the Rad. Vocab. for the root גה. This root is employed here in the intensive verbal form with the augmentative syllable וֹן.

כּוּשׁ, *Chush*.... The elementary root אשׁ, which signifies in general, the *igneous principle*, being verbalized by the signs ו or י has produced the word אוֹשׁ or אִישׁ ; that is to say, *fire*, physical or moral: and this word contracted by the assimilative sign כ, has given rise to the one of which we are speaking.   This name which is found in the sacred books of the Brahmans, and whose origin is consequently

13. And-the-name of-the-effluence the-second, was-*Gihon* (determining motion) that-very-one-which-is encompassing the - whole - earth *Chush* (fire-like, ethereal principle).

14. And-the-name of-the-effluence the-third was-Hiddekel (nimble and swift-propagator, universal fluid) the -same-that-is the-producing-cause of-the-eternal-principle of-happiness (harmony, lawful rule) and-the-effluence the-fourth, the-same-that - is the - fecundating - cause.

15. And-he-took, IHOAH, HE - the - Gods, that - same - *Adam* (collective-man) and-he-placed-him in - the - temporal-and - sensible - sphere, for dressing-it and-over-looking-it-with-care.

13. Et-le - nom-du-fleuve (du principe émané) deuxième, était-*Gihon,* (le mouvement déterminant) lui-qui-est entourant toute-la-terre *Choush* (le principe igné).

14. Et-le-nom du-fleuve (de l'émanation) troisième, était Hiddekel (le rapide et léger propagateur), le fluide électrique, magnétique, galvanique, etc.) lui-qui-est le-faisant-aller (le moyen de propagation) du-principe-primitif de-la-félicité (de l'ordre, de l-harmonie) et-le-fleuve (l'émanation) quatrième-était lui-qui-est le-fécondateur.

15. Et-il-prit, IHOAH, LUI - les - Dieux, ce - même - *Adam* (l'homme universel), et-il-laissa-lui dans-la-sphère -temporelle-et-sensible, pour ellaborer-elle, et-pour-la-surveiller-avec-soin.

---

very ancient, has been rendered by that of *Æthi-ops,* which is to say, the sympathetic fire of the globe. All the allegorical names of which Moses makes use, come evidently from the Egyptian sanctuaries.

v. 14. הִדֶּקֶל *Heddekel.* . . . This name is formed of two words הדה, *emitting, propagating,* and קל *light, rapid.* It is used in the intensive form.

הוא פרת, *that-is the-fecundating-cause.* . . . The Hellenists having

16. Wa-îtzaw IHÔAH Ælohîm hal-ha-Adam, l'æ-mor, mi-ċhol hetz-ha-gan âċhol thâoċhel.

וַיְצַו יְהֹוָה אֱלֹהִים עַל־הָאָדָם לֵאמֹר מִכֹּל עֵץ־הַגָּן אָכֹל תֹּאכֵל:

17. W'me-hetz ha-dahath tôb wa-rawh loâ thâoċhal mi-men-oû ċhi b'îôm âċal-ċha mi-men-oû, môt ha-môth.

וּמֵעֵץ הַדַּעַת טוֹב וָרָע לֹא־ תֹּאכַל מִמֶּנּוּ כִּי בְּיוֹם אֲכָלְךָ מִמֶּנּוּ מוֹת תָּמוּת:

---

seen the Tigris in the allegorical river הדקל *the swift propagator* spoken of by Moses, have not failed to profit here, by a slight resem-blance in the sound of the words, to see the Euphrates, in הוא פרת, *that which fecundates;* without concerning themselves with what they had said of the two preceding rivers: but only a little attention is needed to see that הוא is a masculine pronoun which governs the nominal verb פרת, *the action of fecundating.*

v. 15. All these terms are simple or known.

v. 16. ויצו, *and-he-prescribed....* The root צו expresses every kind of line traced toward an end, of which the sign צ is the symbol. This root, having become the verb צוה, according to the intensive form, signifies *to conduct with rectitude, to guide well,* etc.

מכל־עץ, *the whole growth....* Turn to v. 9. of this chapter.

אכל האכל, *feeding thou-mayst-feed-upon....* Here is a word, which, as the result of contraction, has become very difficult to understand, on account of the resemblance that it has acquired with certain different words which come from another root, and with which it can easily be confused. Its proper root must be sought for carefully, for Moses has attached great importance to this point. One can see by the pains that he has taken to repeat twice the same verb, first, as continued facultative, and afterward, as temporal future.

This root is עול, *elementary matter,* unknown substance, symbol-

16. And - he - prescribed, IHOAH, HE-the-Gods (enacting, settling) toward-*Adam*, by - declaring: from - the - whole growth-of-the-organic -enclosure, feeding thou-mayst-feed-upon.

16. Et-il-prescrivit, IHO-AH, LUI-les-Dieux, (statua, régla), envers-*Adam*, selon-l'action-de déclarer (sa parole): de-toute substance-végétative-de-l'enceinte - or - ganique, alimentant tu-peux -t'alimenter.

17. But-from-the-growth (growing might) of-the-knowledge of-good and-evil, not-shalt - thou - feed - upon any-of-it; for-in-the-day of-the-feeding-thine upon-some -of-it, dying thou-shalt-die (thou shalt transmute to another state).

17. Mais-de-la-substance -physique de-la-connaissance du-bien et-du-mal, non-pas tu-consommeras de-quoi-d' elle; car dans-le-jour de-la-consommation-à-toi de-quoi-d'elle, mourant tu-mourras (tu passeras à un autre état).

---

ized here by the universal convertible sign placed between those of physical sense and expansive movement. This root which is conserved wholly in the Syriac ܠܘܳܐ and in the Greek ὕλη, was famous among the Egyptians who made it play an important rôle in their mythology. One finds in Ethiopic the word አኅል (*achal*) signifying *substance, essence, matter, nourishment*. Element and **aliment,** hold to this through their common root.

Furthermore, this root is used in Hebrew only in a restricted sense, and as it were, *to nurse an infant*, to give it its first nourishment. One finds עֹלֵל, to designate, an infant at the breast. When the Chaldaic punctuation materializes completely this root in making consonantal the mother vowel ו, then it develops ideas of injustice, crime and perversity.

But if, instead of materializing this vowel, the character of the physical sense ע, is softened by substituting the sign of assimilated life כ; then this root written thus, כּוּל, expresses ideas of apprehension, of violent shock; of measure, of substantiation; if it is reduced to the single characters כל, one obtains by this contraction, the analogous ideas of assimiliation, of substance, and of consummation, whether one considers the action of consummating or of consuming.

18. Wa-îâomer I ʜ ô ᴀ ʜ, Ælohîm, loâ-tôb heiôth ha-Adam l'badd'-ô æhesheh-l'ô hezer b'neghed-ô.

וַיֹּאמֶר יְהֹוָה אֱלֹהִים לֹא־טוֹב הֱיוֹת הָאָדָם לְבַדּוֹ אֶעֱשֶׂה־לּוֹ עֵזֶר כְּנֶגְדּוֹ׃

19. Wa-îtzer IʜôАʜ, Æ-lohîm min-ha-Adamah čhol-h a î a t h ha-shadeth w'æth čhol hôph ha-shamaîm, wa-îabæ ael-ha-Adam l'r â ô t h mahîkerâ-l'ô w'čhol âsher îkerâ-l'ô ha-Adam, nephesh haîah houâ shem-ô.

וַיִּצֶר יְהֹוָה אֱלֹהִים מִן־הָאֲדָמָה כָּל־חַיַּת הַשָּׂדֶה וְאֵת־כָּל־עוֹף הַשָּׁמַיִם וַיָּבֵא אֶל־הָאָדָם לִרְאוֹת מַה־יִּקְרָא־לוֹ וְכֹל אֲשֶׁר יִקְרָא־לוֹ הָאָדָם נֶפֶשׁ חַיָּה הוּא שְׁמוֹ׃

It is at this point that Moses has taken it, and giving it the exalted meaning which he conceived, he has made it rule by the sign of power א . In this state, the verb אָכֹל , which is formed, has signified *to feed upon*, that is to say, *to assimilate to one's self elementary matter as food.*

It must be remembered that the root עוּל of which we are speaking, is precisely the same as that which the Samaritan translator used to render the substance called עֵץ , by Moses, and the object of alimentation expressed by the verb אָכֹל . Refer again to v. 9. of this chapter and to Rad. Voc. root כֹּל and עֹל.

v. 17. הרעת , *of the knowledge*.... דע is a root which con-tains every idea of exposition, explanation, demonstration; being formed by contraction of the roots יד *the hand*, that which shows, and עה. *the superficies*, the curve, the exterior form of things.

The Samaritan word 𐤑𐤁𐤏𐤕 holds to the Hebraic root חק , which is related to that which grasps forms interiorly and which fixes them, as for example *taste*. Thus *knowledge*, indicated by the He-brew text, is that which depends upon *judgment* and upon exterior forms, and that indicated by the Samaritan translator, is that which

18. And-he-said, IHOAH, HE-the-Being-of-beings, not-good the-being-*Adam* (collective m a n) in-lonesomeness-his; I-will-make-to-him, an-auxiliary-might (a prop, a mate) unto-the-reflecting-light-his-own.

19. And-he-had-elementized (by compacting the elements toward an end), IHOAH, HE-the-Being-of-beings, from-the-adamic (homogeneal ground) every-life of-nature - earth - born, and - every fowl of-the-heavens; and-he-brought unto-*Adam*, to see what he-would-assign-for-name in-relation-to-himself-unto-it: and-all-that he as-signed - for - name - unto - it (after him), *Adam* (collective man), soul-of-life was-the-n a m e-its-own-suitable-to-him.

18. Et-il-dit, IHOAH, LUI-l'Être - des - êtres, pas - bon être-*Adam* (l'homme-universel) dans-la-solitude-sienne: Je-ferai-à-lui, une-force-auxiliaire (un s o u t i e n, un aide, une corroboration, une doublure) en-r e fl e t-lumineux-de-lui.

19. Et-il-avait-formé (en coordonnant les é l é m e n s vers un but), IHOAH, LUI-l'Être-des-êtres du-s e i n-de-l'adamique, (élemént homogène) toute-vie de-la-nature-terrestre et-toute-espèce-de-volatile d e s-cieux; et-il-fit-venir vers-*Adam*, pour-voir q u e l il-assignerait-nom-à-cela (selon lui) : et-tout-ce-qu' il-a s s i g n a-nom-à-cela (selon lui), *Adam* (l'homme universel), âme-de-vie ce-fut-le-nom-sien-de-lui.

---

results from *taste* and from interior forms. The Latin word *sapientia* has the same expression as the Samaritan. The French *connaissance* holds a medium between the two. The word *knowledge* and the Greek γνῶσις are derived from the Celtic word *ken* or *kan*, which signifies to conceive, to comprehend, to embrace in a glance, etc.

מות תמות. *dying, thou-shalt-die*.... I shall explain later on the root of this word. See Rad. Vocab. root מת.

v. 18. עור, *an-auxiliary-might*.... This energetic word has been formed of the root עז, which expresses every force, every means added, every strengthening, and of the elementary sign of movement

20. Wa-îkerâ ha-Adam shemôth-l'čhol ha-behemah w'l'hôph ha-shamaîm w'l' čhol haîath ha-shadeh, w'l' Adam lôa-matzâ hezer čh' neghed'-ô.

וַיִּקְרָא הָאָדָם שֵׁמוֹת לְכָל־ הַבְּהֵמָה וּלְעוֹף הַשָּׁמַיִם וּלְכֹל חַיַּת הַשָּׂדֶה וּלְאָדָם לֹא־מָצָא עֵזֶר כְּנֶגְדּוֹ :

21. Wa-îaphel IHÔAH, Ælohîm thareddemah hal-ha-Adam, wa-îîshan, wa-îk-kah âhath mi-tzal-hothaî-ô, wa-îsseggor bashar thahathe-nah.

וַיַּפֵּל יְהֹוָה אֱלֹהִים תַּרְדֵּמָה עַל־ הָאָדָם וַיִּישָׁן וַיִּקַּח אַחַת מִצַּלְעוֹתָיו וַיִּסְגֹּר בָּשָׂר תַּחְתֶּנָה :

---

proper ר. The Samaritan word ᴪᴧⱯ, which translates it, means *a support, a counsel, a kindness;* as is proved by the corresponding Arabic word سِعد. The Chaldaic targum says סָמִיךְ, *a conjunction.*

כְּנֶגְדּוֹ, *unto-the-reflecting-light-his-own....* The root נג is applied to every kind of light reflected like a mirror. Thence the ideas of manifestation and opposition, of object presented and put in juxtaposition, which is found in the word נֶגֶר, wherein the root נג is rendered still more expressive by the addition of the sign ר. The mediative article כ, which inflects this word shows the application. I shall only state here that, following the narrative of Moses, the Being of beings, creating Adam, forms him in his likeness; that creating *Eve,* he forms her in the light of *Adam,* or of that which is the same thing, in the luminous reflection of *Adam.*

v. 19. לוֹ, *unto it (after him)....* Here is a grammatical trope that I wish to point out, as this verse merits particular attention, on account of the actual formation of the animals in which Adam takes part. This trope contains two meanings. Moses who uses it quite readily, appears to have imitated the hieroglyphic style in which no doubt, it was often used. In this verse, for example, the word לוֹ composed of the nominal affix ו, belonging to the third person mascu-

20. And - he - assigned *Adam*, names to-the-whole quadruped-kind, and-to-the-fowl of-heavens, and-to-the-whole living-nature earth-born and-for-*Adam* (collective man) not-to-meet with--an-auxiliary-mate as-a-reflected-light-of-him.

20. Et-il-assigna *Adam*, des-noms à-toute-l'espèce-quadrupède, et-à-l'espèce-volatile des-cieux, et-à-toute l'animalité de-la-nature-terrestre : et-pour-*Adam* (l'homme universel) non-pas trouver un-aide (une force auxiliaire) comme-un-reflet-lumineux-de-lui.

21. And - he-caused - to - fall, IHOAH, HE-the-Gods, a-sympathetic-slumber (mysterious and deep) upon *Adam* (collective man) who -slept : and-he-broke-off one of-the-involutions (that sheltered him) and-he-covered-with-care (he coloured) with-shape and-corporeal-beauty the-weakness (inferiority) of-her.

21. Et - il-laissa - tomber IHOAH, LUI-les-Dieux, un-sommeil-sympathique (mystérieux et profond) sur-*Adam* (l'homme universel) qui-dormit : et-il-rompit-de-l'unité une des-enveloppes-siennes (extérieures) et-il-couvrit-avec-soin (il colora) forme-et - beauté - corporelle la-faiblesse (l'infériorité)-à-elle.

---

line, and of the directive article ל, is placed with reference to the thing to which Adam is to give a name, and to Adam himself, who will give this name according to him; that is to say, according to the relations that he shall discover between him and that thing.

This trope is remarkable because it is from the examination of the relations which it indicates, that the names result, which Adam, universal man, gives to the divers animals, according to their relations with the living soul whence their existence issues.

שמו, *the-name-its-own-suitable-to-him* . . . . The same trope continued, makes the affix ו, belong both to the thing which received the name, and to Adam who gives it.

v. 20. All these terms are understood.

v. 21. תרדמה, *a-sympathetic-slumber* . . . . This is a kind of lethargy or *somnambulism*, which takes possession of the sentient

22. Wa-îben IHÔAH, Ælohîm æth-ha-tzellah âsh-er lakah min-ha-Adam l'âis-hah, wa-îbiæha æl-ha-Adam.

וַיִּבֶן יְהֹוָה אֱלֹהִים אֶת־הַצֵּלָע אֲשֶׁר־לָקַח מִן הָאָדָם לְאִשָּׁה וַיְבִאֶהָ אֶל־הָאָדָם׃

---

faculties and suspends them; as is testified by the Chaldaic נרהם and even the Arabic ندم . The hieroglyphic composition of the Hebrew word is remarkable. It can cause strange reflections anent certain modern discoveries. The two contracted roots רד־דם, ex-press, the first, that which extends and takes possession by a proper movement; the other, that which is similar, homogeneous and con-formable to universal nature. The sign of mutual reciprocity ר and the emphatic article ה are here at the beginning and the end, to increase the energy of this mysterious word.

After the analysis of this word, one cannot fail to recognize that extraordinary condition, to which the moderns have given the name of *magnetic sleep*, or *somnambulism*, and which one might perhaps desig-nate, as in Hebrew, *sympathetic sleep*, or simply *sympatheticism*. I must moreover state that the Hellenists who say ἔκστασις, *a trance*, are not so far from the truth as Saint Jerome who merely says "soporem" *a deep sleep*.

אחת, *one*.... This word does not signify here only *one*, but it characterizes also *unity*. Moses employs it in two senses, by means of the grammatical trope of which I spoke in v. 19, of this chapter.

מצלעתיו, *of-the-involutions-of-him*.... One cannot, in a word wherein are formed so many different images, choose an idea more petty and more material, than that which the Hellenists have rendered by the word πλευρά, *a rib*. Saint Jerome who has said in bad Latin "unam de cotis," could not do otherwise, because the course of error was irresistibly marked out. The word צלע can only be composed of one root and of one sign, or of two contracted roots. If it is the first, it is צל־ע, for לע, is not an Hebraic root; if it is the second, it is צל־עו, in either case, the meaning is the same, for the root עה or עוה is only an extension of the sign ע.

According to this data, let us examine the ideas contained in the root צל. They are those of shadow, of an object extending above,

22. And-he-restored (in its former state) IHOAH, HE -the-Being-of-beings, the-selfsameness-of-the - shelter-ing-windings which he-had-broken, from *Adam* (collective man) for-(shaping) *Aishah* (intellectual woman, man's faculty of volition) and-he-brought-her to-him-*Adam*.

22. Et - il - reconstruisit (consolida, rétablit dans son premier état) IHOAH, LUI-l'Être-des-êtres, la sub-stance-de-l'enveloppe-extéri-eure, laquelle il-avait-rom-pue d'*Adam* (l'homme uni-versel) pour-(baser) *Aishah* (la femme intellectuelle, la faculté volitive d'*Adam*) et-il-amena-elle à-lui-*Adam*.

---

and making shadow as a canopy, a curtain, a screen, hangings, roof, etc.

Now what is the meaning of the root עה? Is it not that which is attached to all curving, all circumferential form, to all exterior superficies of things, as I stated in v. 17 of this chapter?

Therefore the word צלע signifies exactly an envelope, an ex-terior covering, a protecting shelter. This is what the facultative צלע proves, *to be enclosing, covering, enveloping*: this is what is proved also by the word ⳹⳾, by which the Samaritans have ren-dered it. This word which is derived from the root על, characterizes a thing raised to serve as covering, canopy, etc. The Chaldaic makes use of the word עלע, analogous to the Samaritan and having the same signification.

בשר, *shape-and-corporeal-beauty*.... I omit analyzing סגּור em-ployed here according to the intensive form, because, in reality, there is nothing very difficult in it. The word בשר demands also all of our attention, notwithstanding the length of this note; seeing that the Hellenist translators, always restricted to the material mean-ing, have rendered it by σαρξ, an ignoble word which Saint Jerome has copied in "caro," *the flesh.* Now סר or שׁור, is an Hebraic root which contains in itself all ideas of movement toward consistency, cor-poreity, elementary form and physical force, as is sufficiently de-noted by the signs of which it is composed. The sign of interior ac-tivity ב, governs this same root, and constitutes the verb בשׁור which always signifies *to inform; to announce a thing, to bring glad tidings;* as is proved by the Arabic بشر which adds to this signification,

23.   Wa-îâomer ha-Adam zoâth ha-phahain hetzem me-hetzama-î, w'bashar me-be-shar-î, l'zaôth îkkarâ âîshah chi me-aîsh lukahah-zaôth.

וַיֹּאמֶר הָאָדָם זֹאת הַפַּעַם עֶצֶם מֵעֲצָמַי וּבָשָׂר מִבְּשָׂרִי לְזֹאת יִקָּרֵא אִשָּׁה כִּי מֵאִישׁ לֻקֳחָה־זֹאת :

---

that of showing a pleasant physiognomy, and of pleasing by its beauty: moreover the word بَارَة, in the latter tongue, is always applied to physical beauty. Now, if the Hebraic word בשׁר designates the *flesh*, among the vulgar, it has been only by a shocking abuse, and by a continuation of that unfortunate inclination which the Jews had of restricting and materializing everything. It signified first, *form*, *configuration, exterior appearance, corporeal beauty, animal substance*. The Samaritan version and the Chaldaic targum use the analogous word ᛈᚷᛒ or בסר. It is difficult to say today what meaning the Samaritans attached to this word on account of the few documents which remain to us in their tongue; but we cannot doubt that the Chaldeans deduced from it all ideas relative to exterior forms, ideas more or less agreeable according to the point of view under which they considered these forms. Thus, for example, they understood by the nominal בסר the action of informing, announcing, evangelizing, preaching, scrutinizing, disdaining, scorning, etc.

v. 22. לאשׁה, *for-(shaping) Aishah....* Here again is the trope of repetition, of which I have spoken. This trope is here of the highest importance in the hieroglyphic sense, and even in the literal sense, which remains incomplete if it is not admitted. In order to understand, it must be recalled that the root אשׁ develops all ideas attached to the first principle; so that the verb אשׁה which is derived from it signifies *to begin, to establish in principle, to shape*, etc. Now, the grammatical trope in question consists of this; the word אשׁה taken at the same time as verb and as substantive, expresses on the one hand, the action of shaping, of beginning, and on the other, characterizes the very object of this action, *Aishah*, the principiant volitive faculty of Adam, his intellectual spouse. I shall relate presently what should be understood by this faculty, in analyzing the name

23. And-he-said *Adam* (declaring his thought): this-is actually universal-substance of-the-substance-mine and-corporeal-shape of -the-shape-mine: to-this he-assigned-for-n a m e *Aishah* (principle of volition, intellectual woman) because out-of-the-volitive-principle *Aish* (intellectual man) she-had-been-taken-selfsameness.

23. Et-il-dit *Adam* (déclarant sa pensée) celle-ci-est actuellement substance-universelle de-la-substance-à-moi, et-forme-corporelle-de-la - forme - corporelle - à - moi : à-celle-là-même il-as-signa-nom *Aishah* (volonté principiante, femme intellectuelle) à-cause-que-du-principe-volitif *Aish* (l'homme intellectuel) elle-avait-été-détachée-ipséité-même.

---

given to intellectual man, אֵישׁ, (*aish*) in opposition to universal man, אָדָם (*Adam*).

v. 23. עֶצֶם, *universal-substance*.... This is the well-known root עֶץ, used here with the collective sign ם. An attentive reader should see two things in this word: the first, that the root עֶץ does not signify *tree*, as the Hellenists have said; the second, that the sign ם has really the universal expression that I have given to it. This last observation will be very useful to him as we proceed.

אֵישׁ, *intellectual man*.... Here is a new denomination given to man. It appears for the first time, when the Being of beings, having declared that it was not good for universal man, *Adam*, to live alone in the solitude of his universality, has effected his individuality, in giving him an auxiliary force, a companion, created in his light and destined for him to reflect his image.

I beg the reader to remark first of all, that Moses, giving a name to this companion, does not derive it from that of Adam; for *Adam* considered as universal man, could not know a companion. The Hebraic word אָדָם has no feminine. The word אֲדָמָה which appears to be it, does not signify *universal woman*, as one might think; but, as I have said, the elementary principle of Adam. אָדָם, *universal man*, possesses the two sexes. Moses has taken care to repeat it several times so that one shall not be deceived. What therefore is this companion, this auxiliary force, as the word עֵזֶר expresses it? It

24.   Hal-čhen îawhazab aîsh æth-âbi-ô w'æth âim-ô w'dabak b'âisheth-ô w'haîoû l'bashar æhad.

עַל־כֵּן יַעֲזָב־אִישׁ אֶת־אָבִיו וְאֶת־אִמּוֹ וְדָבַק בְּאִשְׁתּוֹ וְהָיוּ לְבָשָׂר אֶחָד :

25. W'îhîoû sheneî-hem haroûm-mîm, ha-Adam w' âisheth-ô, w'loâ-îthboshas-hoû.

וַיִּהְיוּ שְׁנֵיהֶם עֲרוּמִים הָאָדָם וְאִשְׁתּוֹ וְלֹא־יִתְבֹּשָׁשׁוּ :

---

is the volitive faculty developed by the Being of beings: it is the intellectual woman of universal man; it is the will proper which in-dividualizes him, and in which he is reflected and which, rendering him independent, becomes the creative force by means of which he realizes his conceptions, and makes them pass from power into action. For, this truth must come out from the darkness of the sanctuaries: the will was creator with universal man. Whatever this man willed was when and how he willed it. The power and the act were indivisible in his will.

Such is the difference between the Hebraic words אדם and איש. The one characterizes man universalized by his homogeneous essence, the other designates man individualized by his efficient will. The hieroglyphic etymology of the first of these names is already known, let us examine the second, which is also important.

This name springs from two contracted roots אי־אש. I have explained them both. אי develops every idea of desire, of inclination, of appetite, of election: אש is the power of movement, the elementary principle, fire, considered in the absence of all substance. The word איש which results from the contraction of these two roots only dif-fers from the word אוש, which indicates natural, substantialized fire, by the median sign. In the former it is that of manifestation and duration; in the latter it is the bond between nothingness and being, which I name convertible. The one is a movement, intelligent, volitive, durable; the other, a movement, appetent, blind, fugacious.

Here is the hieroglyphic meaning of the word איש *intellectual man*. It is a new development of *universal man*, a development, which,

24. So-that shall-leave the-intellectual-man, the-father-his-own, a n d - t h e - mother-his-o w n, a n d-h e-shall-cleave unto-the-intellectual-wife-of-him; and-they-shall-be, as-to-the-exterior-form, one.

24. Sur-ce-donc il-quittera, l'homme-intellectuel, la-père-même-s i e n, e t-l a-mère-sienne, et-il-se réunira (ne fera qu'un être) avec-la-femme - intellectuelle - à - lui : et-ils-seront-s e l o n-l a-forme-extérieure, un.

25. And-they-were both-themselves entirely-uncovered (bare-bodied), *A d a m* (collective man) and-the-intellectual-wife-of-him and-not-they-shamed-one-anoth - er.

25. Et - ils - étaient - les-deux-eux-mêmes, *Adam* (l' homme universel) et-la-femme -intellectuelle - à - lui entièrement-découverts; et-non-pas-se-faisaient - honte - entr'eux.

---

without destroying his universality and his homogeneity, gives him, nevertheless, an independent individuality, and leaves him free to manifest himself in other and particular conceptions, by means of a companion, an auxiliary force, intended to reflect his image.

It is therefore with profound reason that Moses having especially in mind, in this companion, the volitive faculty which constitutes universal man, *intelligent-being*, that is to say, the faculty which renders him capable of willing and of choosing, draws its name from the same name of intellectual man, אִישׁ. In this derivation, he has caused the sign of manifestation י, to disappear, and has replaced it with the final sign of life, in order to make it understood that it is not the volitive principle which resides in אִשָּׁה, but the principiant will, existing, no longer in power, but in action.

v. 24 and 25. These two verses appear to me to be the reflection of some commentator, written at first on the margin of the text, and in the course of time, inserted in the text itself. They bear neither the style nor the form of Moses. The two words alone עַל-כֵּן *so-that*, suffice to prove their intercalation. However little one may be impressed with what has preceded, one is well aware that these two verses are not connected with the cosmogonical narrative, and above all that they have not come from the Egyptian sanctuary.

SEPHER BERÆSHITH
G.

ספר בראשית ג׃

1. W'ha - Nahash haîah
haroum miċhol haîah ha-
shadeh âsher ha-shah Iᴀ0ᴀн
Ælohîm, wa-îâomer æl-ha-
Aishah âph ċhî-âmar Ælo-
hîm loâ-thâo-ċheloû mi-ċhol
hetz ha-gan.

וְהַנָּחָשׁ הָיָה עָרוּם מִכֹּל חַיַּת
הַשָּׂדֶה אֲשֶׁר עָשָׂה יְהוָֹה אֱלֹהִים
וַיֹּאמֶר אֶל־הָאִשָּׁה אַף כִּי־אָמַר
אֱלֹהִים לֹא־תֹאכְלוּ מִכֹּל עֵץ
הַגָּן ׃

---

v. 1. וְהַנָּחָשׁ. *Now-eager-Covetousness....* It is well known that
the Hellenists and Saint Jerome, have seen here only a snake,
a serpent, properly speaking: indeed according to the former a very
wise serpent, ὄφις φρονιμώτατος, and according to the latter, a serpent
very skillful and very cunning, "serpens callidior". This wretched
interpretation appears to go back to the epoch of the captivity of
Babylon and to coincide with the total loss of the Hebraic tongue:
at least, it is true that the Chaldaic paraphrase has followed it. He
says הוּיא חכים *a most insidious serpent.* I do not know if any one
can entirely exonerate the author of the Samaritan version: for,
although he employs the word 𝕹𝕬𝕾, which corresponds to the
Hebrew נחש, it is very doubtful whether he understood it exactly,
not having known how to render the word עָרוּם, which follows, as I
shall explain hereafter.

But all those authorities who support this error, cannot prevent
the truth from being seen. The word נחש, as it is employed in this
case, cannot mean *a serpent.* It is an eager covetousness, self-con-
ceited, envious, egoistic, which indeed winds about in the heart of
man and envelops it in its coils, but which has nothing to do with
a serpent, other than a name sometimes given metaphorically. It
is only by restricting this figurative expression more and more, that
ignorant people have been able to bring it to the point of signifying
only a serpent. The Hellenists have followed this crude idea; but
could they have done otherwise? If, through delicacy of sentiment
or respect for Moses, they had wished to raise the veil in this passage,
what would have become of the garden, the tree, the rib, etc. etc.?
I have already said, in the part they had taken, they had to sacrifice
all to the fear of exposing the mysteries.

GENESIS III.

1. Now-eager-Covetous-ness (self-conceit, envy, concupiscence) was a-gen-eral-ruling-passion (blind principle) in-the-whole life of-Nature which had-made IHOAH, HE-the-Gods: and-it-said (that grovelling pas-sion) unto-*Aishah* (*Adam's* volitive faculty) because of-what declared, HE-the-Gods, not-shall-you-feed from-the whole-growth of-the-organ-ic-enclosure?

COSMOGONIE III.

1. Or-l'Ardeur-c u p i d e (l'intérêt, l'envie, l'égo-isme) était une-passion-générale (un principe aveu-gle) parmi-toute l'anima-lité de-la-Nature-élémen-taire laquelle avait-faite IHOAH, LUI-les-Dieux: et-elle dit (cette passion) à-*Aîshah* (la faculté volitive d'*A d a m*) à-cause de-quoi déclara LUI-les-Dieux, non-pas - vous - vous-alimenterez de-toute substance de-l'en-ceinte-organique?

Let us examine the word שׁחנ with the attention it merits, in order to prove the meaning contained in its root, not only by means of all the analogous idioms which possess it, but also by its own hieroglyphic composition.

This root is חש, which, as I have said in explaining the word חשׁך, *darkness*, indicates always an inner covetousness, a centralized fire, which acts with a violent movement and which seeks to distend itself. The Chaldaic, derives a great many expressions from it, all of which are related to anxiety, agony, sorrow and painful passions. It is literally, *a torrefaction;* figuratively, *an eager covetousness*, in the Arabic بشر. It is *a suffering, a grievous passion*, in the Syriac ܚܫ or ܚܫ. It is finally, *a turbulent agitation*, in the Ethiopic ሐውሰ (*housh*). This root verbalized in the Hebraic חוש, depicts the action of being precipitated, of being carried with violence toward a thing. The analogous verbs have the same meaning in Arabic, Ethiopic and Syriac. There is nothing in these which restricts us to the idea of a serpent.

The hieroglyphic analysis can perhaps give us the key to this mystery. The reader will doubtless remember that I have several

2. W a t h â o m e r   h a-   וַתֹּאמֶר הָאִשָּׁה אֶל־הַנָּחָשׁ מִפְּרִי
A î s h a h æl-ha-Nahash mi-
pheri hetz ha-gan nâochel.   עֵץ הַגָּן נֹאכֵל :

---

times set down two different roots, אר and אש, to designate equally,
the first principle, the elementary principle and the unknown prin-
iple of things.   I shall now state the important difference that the
Egyptian priests conceived between these two roots, and in what
manner they expressed this difference.

They attached to both, the idea of movement; but they considered אר as the symbol of movement proper, rectilinear; and אש
as that of relative movement, circular. The hieroglyphic character
which corresponded to these two movements was likewise *a serpent*:
but a serpent sometimes straight and passing through the centre of
a sphere, to represent the principle אר; sometimes coiled upon itself
and enveloping the circumference of this sphere, to represent the
principle אש. When these same priests wished to indicate the union
of the two movements or the two principles, they depicted a serpent
upright, uncoiling itself in a spiral line, or two serpents interlacing
their mobile rings. It is from this last symbol that the famous
caduceus of the Greeks has come.

The priests were silent as to the inner nature of both these
principles; they used indifferently the radicals אר or אש to characterize the ethereal, igneous, aerial, aqueous, terreous, or mineral
principle; as if they had wished to make it understood that they
did not believe these simple and homogeneous things, but the composite
ones.   Nevertheless, among all these several significations, that which
appeared the most frequently was that of fire. In this case, they
considered the igneous principle under its different relations, sentient
or intelligible, good or evil, and modified the radical word which
represented it, by means of the signs. Thus, for example, the primitive אר became אור to designate *elementary fire*, אור *light*, איר
intelligible brightness, etc.   If the initial vowel is hardened, it takes
a character more and more vehement. הר represented *an exaltation*,
literally as well as figuratively: חר, *a burning centre*, ער *a passionate, disordered, blind ardour*. The primitive אש was nearly the same.

2. And-she-said, *Aishah* (*A d a m*'s volitive faculty) to-that-covetous (passion): the-fruit, growing-substance of-the-organic-enclosure, we-may-feed-upon.

2. Et-elle-dit *A i s h a h* (la faculté volitive) à-cette-ardeur-cupide: du fruit, substance de-l'enceinte-organique, nous-nous-pouvons-alimenter.

The movement alone still distinguished the two principles, whether they were exalted or whether they were debased. The rectilinear movement inherent in the primitive אר, prevented the confusing of its derivatives with those of the primitive אש, in which the gyratory movement dominated. The two radicals דר and חש represented alike *a central fire;* but in the first הר, it was a central fire from which the igneous principle radiated with violence; whereas in the second הש, it was, on the contrary, a central fire from which this same principle being moved in a circular movement, was concentrated more and more and destroyed itself.

Such was the hieroglyphic meaning of this root which I have already examined under its idiomatic relations. This coincidence ought not to leave any doubt in the mind of the reader. Now the sign which governs it in the word נחש, is that of passive action, individual and corporeal; so that the devouring ardour expressed by the root חש, becomes by means of this sign, a passive ardour, cold in its vehemence, contained, astringent and compressive. Literally, it is every hard and refractory body; everything acrid, cutting and corroding; as *copper,* for example, which this word signifies in a very restricted sense; figuratively, it is every sentiment, painful, intense or savage, as *envy, egoism, cupidity,* it is, in a word, *vice.*

This is the real signification of the word נחש. I have been obliged to extend my proofs more than usual; but its importance demands it. It can be clearly seen that it does not signify simply a serpent. Moses, who has spoken so much of the reptilian life, in the beginning of the Beræshith, was careful not to employ it. The word שרץ which he uses, is that which, in his idiom, indicates veritably *a serpent.* One can easily recognize here the source of the French and Latin word, and that of the Celtic *sertz,* which is preserved without alteration in the modern Oscan.

ערום, *the-blind-and-general-passion....* What proves that the Sa-

3. W'mi-pheri ha-hetz âsher bethôch ha-gan âmar Ælohîm loâ-thoâcheloû mi-men-noû, w'loâ-thigghehoû b'ô, phen themutthoûn.

וּמִפְּרִי הָעֵץ אֲשֶׁר בְּתוֹךְ־הַגָּן אָמַר אֱלֹהִים לֹא־תֹאכְלוּ מִמֶּנּוּ וְלֹא תִגְּעוּ בּוֹ פֶּן תְּמֻתוּן:

4. Wa-îâomer ha-Nahash æl-ha-Aishah loâ-môth the-mutthoûn.

וַיֹּאמֶר הַנָּחָשׁ אֶל־הָאִשָּׁה לֹא־ מוֹת תְּמֻתוּן:

---

maritan translator has not understood the word ערום, is that he has completely missed the meaning of it. He renders it by 2ꭑᱡ, keen, cunning, subtle, and makes it agree thus, with the strange idea that he appears to have really had, that נחש signified a serpent. The word ערום was nevertheless easy, very easy to explain; but how it could be said that a serpent is a passion, a vehemence, a blindness, and so to speak, an universal impulse in productive nature? This is, however, what is found in the root ער or עור. This root is none other than the primitive אר, of which I have just spoken at consider-able length, and which Moses causes to govern here by the sign of material sense ע; a sign almost always taken in the bad sense. The final sign ם, which he adds to it, indicates that the idea is generalized and should be taken in the broadest sense.

All the derivatives of the root עור, present a certain calamitous idea; first, it is ער a violent adversary; עור a privation of sight; then, it is ערום or עירם a desert, a barrenness, a complete naked-ness, literally as well as figuratively; it is מערה a devastated place, an abyss, a cavern; it is finally מערון, an absolute blindness, a total abandonment. In the sequence of these words can be placed the name that the Persians gave to the infernal adversary غريمن (hariman) which is nothing else than the word ערום referred to in this note, with the augmentative syllable ון.

v. 2. All these terms have been explained.

3. But-from-the-fruit of-the growth-itself, which-is-in-the-bottom-of the-organic-enclosure, he-declared, HE-the-Gods: not-may-you-feed upon-any-of-it and-not-may-you-dive (aspire, breathe out your soul) into-it; lest you-might-cause your un-avoidable-dying.

3. Mais-du-fruit de-la-substance-même laquelle-est au-centre de l'enceinte-organique, il déclara, LUI-les-Dieux: non-pas vous-pourrez-vous-alimenter de-quoi-de-lui, et-n o n-p a s-v o u s-pourrez-plonger (aspirer votre âme) dans-lui; de-peur-que vous-vous-fassiez inévitablement-mourir.

4. And-it-said, eager-covetousness, unto-*A i s h a h* (*A d a m*'s volitive faculty) not-in-dying will-you cause-your-unavoidable-dying.

4. Et-elle-dit, la passion - ardente - de - la - convoitise, à *Aishah* (la faculté volitive d'*Adam*) non-pas-mourant vous-vous-ferez-inévitablement-mourir.

---

v. 3. ולא־תגעו, *and-not-may-you-dive*.... That is to say, it is not permitted you to stretch out, to aspire, to have your desires. It is the verb נגע, employed here according to the enunciative form, active movement, future tense. The root גוע, from which this verb springs, is remarkable: it signifies literally, in its verbal state, to expire, to bear its soul wholly into another life.

תמתון, *you-might-cause-your-unavoidable-dying*.... This is the verb מות, *to die*, used according to the intensive form, passive movement, second person plural, future tense, with the extensive sign ן. This final sign whose effect is always to extend the physical and moral sense, is used in this instance by Moses, to augment the force of the intensity and to depict imminent future. We shall see in time, the character ם, giving to active movement, the same extension that the one of which I have been speaking, gives to passive movement.

Finally the verb מות, is raised from the root מת, whose literal meaning is a fusion, a sympathetic extension, a passing, a return to the universal seity, according to the expression that its signs involve. Thus the idea that is contained in the Hebraic verb מות *to die*, has no connection with anything which pertains to destruction or anni-

5.   Chi iôdeha Ælohîm
èhi b'iôm aèhale-èhem mi-
m e m - n o û, w'niphekehoû
heînéi-èhem w'îhithem èhe-
Ælohîm iôdeheî tôb wa-
rawh.

כִּי יֹדֵעַ אֱלֹהִים כִּי בְּיוֹם אֲכָלְכֶם
מִמֶּנּוּ וְנִפְקְחוּ עֵינֵיכֶם וִהְיִיתֶם
כֵּאלֹהִים יֹדְעֵי טוֹב וָרָע ׃

6.   Wa-theræ ha-Aishah
èhi-tôb ha-hetz l'maâèhal
w'èhî thaâwa houâ la-heîn-
aîm wa-nihe-mad ha-hetz
l'hashèhîl,   w a - t h i k k a h
mi-pherî-ô, wa-thâoèhal wa-
thitthen gam-l'Aîsh-ha him-
ha, wa-îao-èhal.

וַתֵּרֶא הָאִשָּׁה כִּי טוֹב הָעֵץ
לְמַאֲכָל וְכִי תַאֲוָה הוּא לָעֵינַיִם
וְנֶחְמָד הָעֵץ לְהַשְׂכִּיל וַתִּקַּח
מִפִּרְיוֹ וַתֹּאכַל וַתִּתֵּן גַּם־לְאִישָׁהּ
עִמָּהּ וַיֹּאכַל ׃

---

hilation, as Moses has been accused of having thought; but, on the
contrary, to a certain transmutation of the temporal substance. See
Rad. Vocab. root אֵת and מֻת .

    v. 4. לֹא־מוֹת, *not-in-dying*....   It is essential to notice the
repetition that Moses makes of the verb מוּת which I have just
explained.

    v. 5. יֹדֵת, *knowing*.... I have spoken of the formation of this
facultative in v. 17, of the preceding chapter.   I shall only state here
that when it appears in the verse for the second time in the constructive plural יֹדְעֵי, the luminous sign וֹ has disappeared, as hieroglyphic index of the catastrophe which is about to follow.

    וְנִפְקְחוּ, *shall-be-opened-to-light*....   This is the verb פֹקֹה
used according to the enunciative form, passive movement, third
person plural, past tense, rendered future by the convertible sign וֹ.
The root קֹה presents the idea of an effort that one makes toward
a thing; a comprehension. This root verbalized in קוֹח signifies *to be
extended, to be dilated,* in every way: governed by the sign פ , as it
is in the example in question, it expresses every solution, every opening, especially that of the eyes and the ears, or the mouth.

5. For knowing, HE-the-Gods, that-in-the-day, food-for-yourselves, upon-some-of-it, (you will use) that-shall-be-opened-to-light the-eyes-yours; and-you-shall-be like-HE-the Gods, comprehending-good and-evil.

6. A n d-she-did-observe *Aishah,* that-good-was the-natural-g r o w t h for the-sense-of-taste, a n d-t h a t both-desired-it-was for-the-eyes, and-pleasing t o-t h e-highest-rate, that-growth, for-causing to-generalise-intelligence (to become universal); a n d-s h e-took-off some fruit-from-it and-she-did-feed-thereupon, a n d-she-gave-designedly also-to the - intellectual - principle-h e r-o w n, in-coalescence-with her; and-he-did-feed-thereupon.

5. Car sachant, LUI-les-Dieux, que dans-le-jour, aliment à vous de-quoi-de-lui, (vous ferez) seront-ouverts - à - la - lumière, les-yeux-à-vous, et-vous-serez tels-que LUI-les-Dieux, connaissant-le-bien et-le-mal.

6. Et-elle-considéra *Aishah,* que bonne-était la-sub-stance-élémentaire selon-l e-goût, et-que mutuellement-désirée-elle-était selon-les-yeux, et-agréable autant-que-p o s s i b l e cette-sub-stance, selon-l'action-d'uni-versaliser-l'intelligence; et-elle-prit du-fruit-sien, et-elle-s'alimenta, e t-e l l e-donna-avec-intention aussi-à-l'être-intellectuel-sien, ré-uni-à-elle; et-il-s'alimenta.

---

v. 6. האוה, *both-desired....* I make note of this only to call attention to the action of the sign ה; its root is או or אי, which expresses every desire, as can be seen in the Rad. Vocab.

להשכיל, *for-causing to-generalize-intelligence....* The verb שכל signifies, *to come to perfection, to achievement, to the fullness of things.* It is used on this occasion according to the excitative force, as nominal verb, inflected by the directive article ל. Its root כל expresses the totality, the universality of things, as I have explained in v. 1. of chapter II. This root, being verbalized, is found governed by the sign of relative movement ש, which augments its force, and gives it an usurping expression, physically as well as morally.

v. 7. כי עירמים, *that-void-of-light....* Refer to first verse of this

7.   Wa-thipkahena heî-
nî shenei-hem, wa-îedĉhoû
ĉhi hirummîm hem, wa-
îthepheroû haleh thænah,
waîa-hashoû la-hem ha-go-
roth.

וַתִּפָּקַחְנָה עֵינֵי שְׁנֵיהֶם וַיֵּדְעוּ כִּי
עֵירֻמִּם הֵם וַיִּתְפְּרוּ עֲלֵה תְאֵנָה
וַיַּעֲשׂוּ לָהֶם חֲגֹרֹת :

---

chapter. It is always the same root עוּר, containing the idea of ardour,
of a vehement fire, literally as well as figuratively. Formed from the
root אוּר, which presents the idea of luminous corporeity, it becomes
its absolute opposite. The one is a tranquil action; the other, a
turbulent passion: here, it is an harmonious movement; there it is
a blind, disordered movement. In the above example, the sign of
manifestation י, has replaced the sign of the mystery of nature, and
in this way Moses has wished to show that this terrible mystery was
unveiled to the eyes of universal man, Adam. I can go no further
in my explanation: the earnest reader must investigate for himself,
the force and the concatenation of the Hebraic expressions; I have
furnished him with all the means. The word ⸘⸘⸘⸘⸘⸘ , by which
the Samaritan translator has rendered עירמים, belongs to the root עֵה,
image of *darkness*, united to the root שׂם, which develops all ideas of
inflation, of vacuity, of vanity. The word עֵם, which is formed from
it, signifies *an enormous excavation*, and also *a savage, voracious
animal*.

ויתפרו, *and-they-yielded-forth* .... In this instance, the Hellenists
have obviously and with deliberate purpose, exaggerated the vulgar
sense, so as to thicken more and more the veil which they had resolved
to throw over the Sepher, for it is evident that the verb פרות, used
here according to the reflexive form, signifies, *to produce, to bring
forth, to fecundate*, and not *to sew*. I do not see how they dared to
take this ridiculous expression and still less why Saint Jerome agreed
with them. The Samaritan version and the Chaldaic targum offered
him quite an easy way. Here are their verbal translations.

⸘⸘⸘⸘ ⸘⸘⸘⸘⸘⸘⸘
⸘⸘⸘⸘

"And-they-condensed a-condensation (a
    thick veil), elevation of sorrow-
    mutual-and-of-mourning."

וחטיטו להון טרפי תאנין :

"And-they-excited-profoundly   in-them
    a-trouble (a confusion obscure) of
    sorrow-mutual-and-of-mourning."

7. And-were-opened the-eyes of-them-b o t h ; and-they-knew that-void-of-light (barren, unveiled in their dark origin) they-were, and-they-yielded-forth a-dark-covering (thick veil) with-s a d n e s s-a n d - mourning-formed; and-they-made-for-themselves-pilgrim-coats.

7. Et-furent-ouverts les-yeux à eux-deux; et-ils-con-nurent que d é n u é s-de-lum.ière (stériles, révélés dans leur obscur principe) ils-étaient; et-ils-se-firent-n a î t r e une-élévation-om-breuse (un voile) de-tris-t e s s e-mutuelle-et-de-deuil; et-ils-firent-à-eux-des-péleri-nes (des vêtemens de voya-ge).

One can see nothing in them which can excuse the extravagant Greek and Latin phrase: καὶ ἔρραψαν φύλλα συκῆς, "et consuerunt folia ficus," *and they sewed fig-leaves!*

For the Hebraic word עלה signifies neither *a leaf*, nor *leaves*, but a shadowy elevation, a veil; a canopy, a thing elevated above another to cover and protect it. It is also *an elevation; an extension; a height*. The root על develops all these ideas. As to the word תאנה, I admit that, in the ignorance which prevailed concerning the Hebraic tongue, it was a little difficult to explain. Yet what was the question? Only to distinguish the sign ה, a sign that the most ordinary grammarians have distinguished as an *héémanthe* or *paragogic*, and to which they have attributed, under these two relations, the faculty of expressing the continuity of things and their reciprocity. This distinction made, the word אנה has no longer the least difficulty. It is an expression of grief not only in Hebrew, but in Samaritan, Chaldaic, Syriac, Arabic and Ethiopic. It is formed of an onomatopoetic root which depicts the groans, sobs, pain and the *anhelation* of a person who suffers. This expressive root belongs to all tongues. One finds it united to the sign ה on several occasions, and especially to express a deep, mutual sorrow. It is presumable that the fig-tree has received the metaphorical name of תאנה on account of the mournfulness of its foliage, from which lactescent tears appear to flow from its fruits. However that may be, the onomatopoetic figure which is here presented for the first time, although it may be somewhat rare in Hebrew, is

8. Wa-îshamehoû æth-
kôl IHÔAH Ælohîm mithe-
halleĉh b'gan l'roûah ha-
îôm, wa-îthehabbæ ha-Adam
w'âisheth-ô mi-phenei
IHÔAH Ælohîm be-thôĉh
hetz ha-gan.

וַיִּשְׁמְעוּ אֶת־קוֹל יְהוָֹה אֱלֹהִים
מִתְהַלֵּךְ בַּגָּן לְרוּחַ הַיּוֹם וַיִּתְחַבֵּא
הָאָדָם וְאִשְׁתּוֹ מִפְּנֵי יְהוָֹה
אֱלֹהִים בְּתוֹךְ עֵץ הַגָּן:

9. Wa-îkerâ IHÔAH Ælo-
hîm æl-ha-Adam, wa-îâomer
l'ô aîe-ĉhah.

וַיִּקְרָא יְהוָֹה אֱלֹהִים אֶל־הָאָדָם
וַיֹּאמֶר לוֹ אַיֶּכָּה:

10. Wa-îâomer æth-kôle-
ĉha shamahethî ba-gan, wa-
âîrâ ĉhî-heirom ânoĉhî, wa-
æhabæ.

וַיֹּאמֶר אֶת־קוֹלְךָ שָׁמַעְתִּי בַּגָּן
וָאִירָא כִּי־עֵירֹם אָנֹכִי וָאֵחָבֵא:

---

far from being wholly foreign as the Rad. Vocab. has shown. It is
at first, in Hebrew, as in the Arabic ان or وا ا , only a kind of excla-
mation as *alas!* but, transformed into a verb by means of the convertible sign וֹ, it becomes אוֹן or אֲנוֹה whose meaning is, to be plunged
in grief, to cry out with lamentations. Thence אֲנוֹה , sorrow, affliction; and finally תַּאֲנָה or תַּאֲנוֹה deep and concentrated grief
that one shares or communicates.

v. 8. מִתְהַלֵּךְ, *causing-itself-to-be-carried-to-and-fro*.... This is the
verb הָלֹךְ employed here according to the reflexive form, as continued facultative. The two roots which compose it הָל־אָךְ depicting
the two opposed movements, excentric and concentric, of going away
from and drawing near to. The Hellenists have so disfigured the
meaning of this facultative, that instead of attributing it to the voice
of God, they have applied it to God Himself, and have not hesitated
to say that the Being-of-beings walked in the garden in the cool of
the day: περιπατοῦντος ἐν τῷ παραδείσῳ πρὸς τοδειλινόν.

8. And-they-did-hear the-voice-of I H O A H, HE-t h e-Being-of-beings, causing-it-self-to-be-carried-to-and-fro, in-the-o r g a n i c - enclosure with-the-s h i n i n g of-day-l i g h t: and-he-hid-himself, *A d a m* (collective m a n) and-the-intellectual-wife-of-him (his volitive faculty) from-the-face-of IHOAH, HE-the-Gods, in-the-b o s o m of-the generative-substance of-the-organic-sphere.

8. Et-ils-entendirent-la-voix-même-de IHOAH, LUI-l'-Être-des-êtres, se-portant-en tous-sens, dans-l'enceinte-or-ganique, selon-le-s o u f f l e-spiritueux du-jour: et-il-se-cacha, *Adam* (l'homme uni-versel) et-la-femme-intellec-tuelle-à-lui (sa faculté voli-tive) de-la-face-de IHOAH, LUI-les-Dieux, au-centre de-la-substance de-la-sphère-organique.

9. And-he-uttered-t h e-name, IHOAH, HE-the-Gods, to-him-*Adam;* and-he-said to-him, where-of-thee (where has brought thee thy will)?

9. Et-il-prononça-le-nom, IHOAH, LUI-les Dieux, à-lui-*Adam;* et-il-dit-à-lui: où-de-toi (où t'a porté ta volon-té)?

10. And-he-said (answer-ing *Adam*), that-voice-thine, I-did-hear by-the-organic-enclosure, and-I-d i d-k e n-that void-of-light (unveiled in my blindness) I-was: and-I-hid-myself.

10. Et-il-dit (répondant *Adam*) cette-voix-t i e n n e j'ai-entendue en-l'enceinte-organique et-j'ai-vu-que dé-nué-de-lumière (révélé dans mon obscurité) j'étais: et-je-me-suis-caché.

---

v. 9. אֵיכֹה, *where-of-thee?*.... The root אֵי contains not only all ideas of desire, will, inclination; but it designates also the place, the object toward which all these ideas tend, so that Moses in uniting to this root the nominal affix of the second person כֹה with its em-phatic termination, has made one of the strongest and most forceful ellipses that has ever been made in any human tongue.

v. 10. All of these terms are understood.

v. 11. הֲמִי, *but-from-that*.... Moses, by another very bold

11. Wa-îaomer mî higgîd l'cha chî-heirom âthah, ha-min-ha-hetz âsher tziwîthi-cha lebilethî âchal mimen-noû âchaletha.

וַיֹּאמֶר מִי הִגִּיד לְךָ כִּי־עֵירֹם אַתָּה הֲמִן־הָעֵץ אֲשֶׁר צִוִּיתִיךָ לְבִלְתִּי אֲכָל־מִמֶּנּוּ אָכָלְתָּ :

12. Wa-îaomer ha-Adam, ha-Aîshah âsher nathathah himmad-î hiwâ natthanah l'î min-ha-hetz, wa-âochel.

וַיֹּאמֶר הָאָדָם הָאִשָּׁה אֲשֶׁר נָתַתָּה עִמָּדִי הִוא נָתְנָה־לִּי מִן־הָעֵץ וָאֹכֵל :

---

ellipsis, takes as substantive the extractive preposition מִן, and applies to it the determinative article ה, thus making it the cause of the collusion of Adam.

v. 12. הָאִשָּׁה, *Aishah*. . . . I have spoken sufficiently of the word אִישׁ whence comes the word אִשָּׁה, but I beg the reader to observe closely here, with what force and what justice the cosmogonical ideas of Moses are connected and developed.

Universal man אָדָם, being unable to remain in his universality, without remaining also in the volitive homogeneity of the Being-of-beings אֱלֹהִים, and consequently in a sort of relative necessity, leaves this close dependence, when receiving a new development which individualizes and makes him an intelligent being אִישׁ; that is to say, a being susceptible of willing and of choosing freely for himself. The faculty which gives him power, emanates from himself; it is his intellectual companion אִשָּׁה, his creative force: for it is by it that he creates; it is by means of this volitive faculty that he realizes his conceptions. He wills; and that which he wills exists. But this faculty is not homogeneous with the universal creative faculty of the Being-of-beings; for if it were, it would not exist, or *Adam* would be GOD. It has only the degree of force and extent that is given it, by the degree that *Adam* occupies in the order of the divine emanations. It can do all, except to create itself in going back to its principle and taking possession of it. It is essential that universal man should know

11. And-he-said (Ælo-him) : who has-taught-thee that-thus bare-thou-w a s t? but-f r o m-t h a t-n a t u r a l growth which-I-prescribed-unto-thee not-to-feed-upon-any-of-it.

12. And-he-said *Adam* (collective man) : *A i s h a h* (the volitive faculty) whom t h o u-didst-give, propping-mate-of-mine, it-is-that gave -to-me from-that-elementary -growth, and-I-have-fed-up-on.

11. Et-il-dit (Ælohim), qui a-enseigné-à-toi qu'ainsi-dénué tu étais? sinon-de-cette-substance-physique de-laquelle j'avais-prescrit-à-toi de nullement-t'-alimen-ter de-quoi-d'elle.

12. Et-il-dit-*Adam* (l'-homme universel) : *Aishah* (la faculté volitive) que-tu-donnas-compagne-à-moi, el-le-est-celle-qui a-donné à-moi de-cette-substance-phy-s i q u e; et-je-m'en-suis-ali-menté.

---

this important point at which his power is arrested, so that he does not lose himself through abuse of his liberty, and the retrograde movement of his volitive faculty. Moses takes the precaution of caus-ing him to be instructed by the mouth of GOD Himself, not under the form of an absurd and despotic command, as the ignorant translators have made it understood, but in the form of a counsel, a paternal warning. *Adam* can make use of everything in the immense radius of the organic sphere which is allotted to him; but he cannot without risking his intellectual existence, touch the centre: that is to say, by wishing to seize the double principle of good and evil, upon which stands the essence of his intellectual being.

In all this, there is no question of planted garden, tree, fruit, rib, woman, or serpent, because, I cannot repeat too often, *Adam* is not, in the thought of Moses, a man of blood, of flesh and bones; but a man, spiritually and universally conceived, an intellectual being, of which *Aishah* is the creative faculty, that which realizes his concep-tions in causing them to pass from power into action by his will.

Although this doctrine is assuredly to my liking, I do not pretend to be answerable for it; because I am, at this time, only translator. I give the Hebraic expressions as nearly as is possible for me to do;

13. Wa-îâomer I H O A H
Ælohîm la-Aishah mah-
zâoth hashîth, wa-thâomer
ha-Aishah ha-Nahash his-
hiâ-nî, wa-âoċhel.

וַיֹּאמֶר יְהוָֹה אֱלֹהִים לָאִשָּׁה מַה־
זֹּאת עָשִׂית וַתֹּאמֶר הָאִשָּׁה
הַנָּחָשׁ הִשִּׁיאַנִי וָאֹכֵל :

14. Wa-îâomer I H O A H
Ælohim æl-ha-Nahash, ċhî-
hashîtha zâoth, ârour athah !
mi-ċhol ha-behemah, w'mi-
ċhol haîath ha-shadeh, hal-
ghehon-ċha theleċh, w'haphar thâoċhal ċhol-îemeî haîî-
ċha.

וַיֹּאמֶר יְהוָֹה אֱלֹהִים אֶל־הַנָּחָשׁ
כִּי־עָשִׂיתָ זֹּאת אָרוּר אַתָּה מִכָּל
הַבְּהֵמָה וּמִכֹּל חַיַּת הַשָּׂדֶה עַל־
גְּחֹנְךָ תֵלֵךְ וְעָפָר תֹּאכַל כָּל־יְמֵי
חַיֶּיךָ :

---

but I give them as grammarian. I affirm that it is this very thing
that Moses has said, without affirming that it is this very thing which
is. To establish a system is one thing; to explain a doctrine, another.

I regard Moses as a very great man, as a man chosen and inspired
by Providence to fulfill a vast plan; but I am far from believing him
infallible, exempt from every kind of error. It is for his Book, restored in its veritable expressions, to speak for him, and to defend
him. All that I have endeavoured to do is to put the reader within
reach of understanding it, freed from the thick veil which disguised
it.

As to my translation, I leave it to itself. Let my readers judge
whether it is not more conformable, not only to the genius of such
a man as Moses, learned in all the sciences of the Egyptians, but also
to simple human reason, to conceive a covetous passion, fermenting
in elementary nature, which insinuates itself in the volitive faculty
of the intelligent being, excites his pride, and persuades him to obtain
possession of the very principle of his existence, in order to exist in
an absolute manner, and to rival the Being of beings, than to see
a serpent, the most subtle of the beasts of the field, crawling before

13. And-he-said, IHOAH, HE-the-Gods, unto *A i s h a h* (*Adam's* volitive faculty) why-this hast-thou done? a n d-*Aishah*-said (answering) eager-self-c o n c e i t (groveling passion) caused-me-to-become-delirious and-I-did-feed.

14. And-he-said, IHOAH, the-Being-of-beings, u n t o-t h a t-covetous-passion, because thou-hast-done that, cursed be-thou! amidst-all-terrestrial-animality, a n d-amidst-all-life of-nature: according-to-the-o b l i q u i t y-thine thou-shalt-grovelling-ly-proceed and-earth-exhalements thou-shalt-feed-upon all the-days of-the life-thine.

13. Et-il-dit, IHOAH, LUI-les Dieux, à *Aishah* (la faculté volitive d'*Adam*) pourquoi-cela fis-tu? et-elle-dit (répondant) *Aishah*, l'orgueil-cupide (cette insidieuse passion) fit-délirer-moi, et-je-m'alimentai.

14. Et-il-dit, IHOAH, l'-Être-des-êtres), à-ce-vice-insidieux (passion cupide) puisque tu-as-fait cela, maudit sois-tu parmi-tout-le-règne-animal et-parmi-toute-vie-de-la-nature-élémentaire. D ' a p r è s-l'inclination-tor-tueuse - tienne tu - agiras-bassement et-d'exhalaisons-physiques tu - alimenteras tous-les-jours-de l'existence-à-toi.

---

a woman, seducing her and causing her to eat of the fruit of a certain tree, planted in a certain garden, so as to become equal to the gods.

v. 13. הִשִּׁיאַנִי, *caused-me-to-become-delirious*.... The real root of this word has never been perceived. Nearly all the translators have seen a certain verb נָשָׁא, which has never existed. It is simply the substantive שׁוֹא, which expresses the idea of disorder, and of void in the thoughts, employed as verb according to the excitative form, active movement, with the verbal affix נִ. The root proper of the substantive is שָׁא, symbol of all whirling, frenzied, frantic movement. It appears to be formed by the reversing of the primitive אַשׁ .

v. 14. גְחֹנְךָ, *thine-obliquity*.... It was quite natural that those who had seen only a serpent in an insidious passion, should see only a belly where they ought to see the turnings, the inclination, of this same passion. The word גָחֹן holds to the root גַ, of which I have already spoken in v. 8. ch. II, and which, being found at that time relating to universal man, has been taken for *a garden*. The sign of

15. W'æîbah âshith beîn-
ĉha w'bein ha-Aishah, w'-
bein zareh-ĉha w'bein zareh-
ha hoûa îshouph-ĉha roâsh
w'âthah thesouphe-noû ha-
keb.

וְאֵיבָה אָשִׁית בֵּינְךָ וּבֵין הָאִשָּׁה
וּבֵין זַרְעֲךָ וּבֵין זַרְעָה הוּא יְשׁוּפְךָ
רֹאשׁ וְאַתָּה תְּשׁוּפֶנּוּ עָקֵב :

---

elementary existence which is here added to the root in question,
depicts admirably the idea of Moses. But, in order that I may not
be accused of having seen inappropriately in the word גָּחֹן, a moral
bending, *an inclination*, I must state that the Hebrew verb גָּחֹן, which
is derived from it, signifies *to bend, to incline*, and that it is the same
in the Chaldaic, and in the Arabic جحن. As to the verb following תלך
thou-shalt-grovellingly-proceed, which all the translators have believed
to be from the verb הלך *to go and come, to walk up and down*, it is
derived from the compound-radical לכֹך or from the radical לוּך both
of which signify literally *to get dirty, to wallow*, and figuratively, *to
behave iniquitously, basely*.

וְעָפָר *and-earth-exhalements....* That is to say, *igneous spirits,
elementary vapours*, and perhaps also *corporeal illusions*. I have
explained the roots of which this word is composed, in v. 7. ch. II.
I shall only observe that this word was then used as facultative,
instead of substantive as it is here.

v. 15. יְשׁוּף, *shall repress....* The verb שׁוּף signifies *to centralize*, to act from the the circumference to the centre, as is proved
by the signs שׁ and פ, of which the one expresses relative movement,
and the other, interior action, particularly in its relations with the
paternal sign ב, which it often replaces. This verb is used here
according to the positive form, active movement, future tense. It is
governed by the third person masculine, because the word ורע, which
signifies literally *seed*, and which I have rendered in this instance by
the word, *progeny*, is masculine in Hebrew.

רֹאשׁ, *the-principle....* This word signifies not only *the head* or
the principle, as I have already said: but it also signifies *the source
of evil, the venom*. In this case the elementary root אשׁ is taken in
the bad sense, and the sign ר, which governs it, is regarded as symbol
of disordered movement.

עקב, *the-bad-consequences (of evil)....* Those who have seen
in this same verse the bruised head of a serpent, have seen here the

15. A n d-a n-antipathy (natural averseness I-will-put between-thee and-between *Aishah* (*Adam's* volitive faculty) and-between the seed-thine, and-between the-seed of-it: it-shall (that-s e e d) repress-to-thee t h e-venomous-principle; and-thou shalt-repress the-bad consequences (of evil).

15. E t-u n e-antipathie-profonde, je metterai entre-toi et-entre *Aishah* (la faculté volitive d'*Adam*) et-entre la-propagation-à-toi, et-e n t r e-la-propagation-à-elle: elle (cette même propagation) comprimera (restreindra)-à-toi le-principe venimeux et-toi, tu-comprimeras-à-elle les-suites (du mal).

---

bitten heel of a woman: but how can the verb שׁוּף, signify at the same time *to bruise*, that is to say, to trample upon, and *to bite?* For Moses was careful to repeat this verb twice. If the modern Hebraists had wished to detach themselves a moment from the Hellenists, they might have seen that the word עָקֵב used here as the antithesis of ראשׁ, could not mean simply *the heel*, except in the most restricted sense; but that, in its most ordinary signification, it expresses *the consequences, the traces of a thing*, and particularly of evil, whose material sign ע it, moreover, bears. Indeed, this can be proved by a great number of Hebrew and Chaldaic passages, in which this word signifies *fraud, perversity, malice* and all the evil qualities generally, which belong to vice.

v. 16. עצבון, *the-woeful-natural-hindrances....* The word עצב employed twice in this verse merits a particular attention. It springs from the two contracted roots עץ־צב. The first עץ should be known to us. It is the same one which forms the name of that mysterious substance whose usage was forbidden to *intellectual man*. It is not difficult to recognize in it, sentient, corporeal substance, and in general, the emblem of that which is physical, in opposition to that which is spiritual. The second צב contains the idea of that which is raised as hindrance, swells with wrath, arrests, prevents a thing, opposes with effort, etc.

Moses employs first, the word עצבון, after having added the ex-

16. Al-ha-Aishah âmar, ha-rebbah ha-rebbeh hittze-bône-che w'herone-che, b'-hetzeb theledî banîm w'æl-Aîshe-che theshoukathe-che, v'houâ îmoshal ba-che.

אֶל־הָאִשָּׁה אָמַר הַרְבָּה אַרְבֶּה עִצְּבוֹנֵךְ וְהֵרֹנֵךְ בְּעֶצֶב תֵּלְדִי בָנִים וְאֶל־אִישֵׁךְ תְּשׁוּקָתֵךְ וְהוּא יִמְשָׁל־בָּךְ :

---

tensive syllable וֹן, wishing to indicate the general obstacles which shall be opposed henceforth to the unfoldment of the will of intellectual man, and which shall multiply its conceptions, forcing them to become divided and subdivided *ad infinitum*. He then makes use of the simple word עֶצֶב, to depict the pain, the torment, the agony which shall accompany its least creations. This hierographic writer would have it understood, that the volitive faculty shall no more cause intellectual conceptions to pass from power into action, without intermediary; but that it shall experience, on the contrary, deviations without number and obstacles of all sorts, whose resistance it shall be able to overcome, only by dint of labour and of time.

It is not necessary to say how the Hellenists have interpreted this verse. It is well known in what manner the ideas of Moses were materialized, and how the volitive faculty having been transformed into a corporeal woman, the physical hindrances opposed to the exercise of the will, have been no more than the pains which accompany childbirth. But one cannot accuse the Hellenists entirely of this change. It was an inevitable consequence of the corruption of the Hebraic tongue, of its total loss and of the wretched inclination of the Jews to bend everything to their gross ideas. Moreover the vulgar translation seems to offer at first some appearance of reason. Only a moment of reflection, nevertheless, is necessary to discover the error, as I hope to show in a few words.

In the first place, it is not true that Moses made the Being of beings say, that he will multiply *the sorrows and the conceptions* as the Hellenists translate it, λύπας καὶ ζεναγμοῖς ; but that he will multiply the number of *the obstacles and the conceptions*, as Saint Jerome has not been prevented from seeing, "ærumnas et conceptus". The Hellenists have followed, in this instance, a poor phrasing of the Samaritans: ᙓᙏᙢᗡᙅᙅ·ᙓᙏᙌᙆᙉᙍᙄᙍ: whereas Saint Jerome adhered to the Chaldaic targum as more conformable with the Hebrew: צַעֲרִיךְ וְעֵדוּאִיךְ .

16. Unto-the-volitive-faculty, he-said: the-number I-shall-multiply of-the-woeful-natural-hindrances-t h i n e, and - of-the-conceits-of-thee; in-panging-l a b o u r thou-shalt-bring-forth products: and-toward-the-intellectual principle-thine, the-desire-thou-shalt-lean of-thee; and-he will-rule in-thee (symbolical acting).

16. À-la-faculté-volitive, il-dit: le-nombre je-multiplierai des-obstacles-physiques-de-toute-sorte-à-toi, et-des-conceptions-tienne: en-travail-angoisseux tu-enfanteras des-produits; et-vers-le-principe-intellectuel-à-toi le-penchant-tu-a u r a s-tien; et-lui il-dominera en-toi (s'y représentera symboliquement).

Now, I ask, in the second place, how the Being-of-beings could have said to the corporeal woman that he would multiply the number of her conceptions or her *pregnancies*, as one understands it, since it would in such a manner shorten her life? Would he not rather have said that he would diminish the number, by rendering them more and more painful and laborious? But the Hebraic text is clear as the day. There is strong evidence that the Hellenists only abandoned it to follow the Samaritan version, because they saw plainly that it exposed the spiritual meaning, as indeed it does. For, while it is in accordance with reason and experience, to think that the volitive conceptions increase in proportion to the obstacles which are opposed to their realization and which force them to be divided, it is absurd and contradictory to affirm it of the pregnancies of physical woman, which are necessarily diminished with the pains, maladies and sufferings which accompany and follow them.

תלרי בנים, *thou-shalt-bring-forth products....* The compound radical verb ילור comes from the root לר, which, formed by the union of the signs of directive movement and of natural abundance, expresses all propagation, all generation, all extension of being. This verb is employed in Hebrew, literally as well as figuratively, as much in relation to the generation of spirit, as to that of substance, without any distinction of sex: so that it is wrong when one has wished to restrict the meaning to a corporeal childbirth. The word which follows בנים, is also very far from signifying simply *children*. It characterizes, in general, the analogous creations of a creative being, whatever it may be.

17. W'l'Adam, âmar, èhi-shamahetha l'kôl Aisheth-èha, wa-thâoèhal min-ha-hetz âsher tziwîthîèha l'-æmor loâ-thâoèhal mi-men-noû; ârrourah ha-âdamah bahabour èha, b'hitzabôn thoâèhelnah èhol-îemei haîî-èha.

וּלְאָדָם אָמַר כִּי שָׁמַעְתָּ לְקוֹל
אִשְׁתְּךָ וַתֹּאכַל מִן־הָעֵץ אֲשֶׁר
צִוִּיתִיךָ לֵאמֹר לֹא־תֹאכַל מִמֶּנּוּ
אֲרוּרָה הָאֲדָמָה בַּעֲבוּרֶךָ
בְּעִצָּבוֹן תֹּאכֲלֶנָּה כֹּל יְמֵי חַיֶּיךָ :

הַשׁוּקְתֶךָ, *the-desire-thou-shalt-lean of-thee*.... This is an ellipsis of such boldness that the Hebrew tongue is the only one that permits it. The verb שׁוּק signifies to have a movement, a tendency toward a determined end, as water, for example. Now, in what manner does Moses express the tendency which the volitive faculty shall submit to its intellectual principle? He takes this verb, and after having employed it according to the positive form of the second person future, feminine singular, he makes abruptly a constructive noun of it, by means of the sign ת, which he adds to it; in this state he joins the nominal affix ךְ, as if to say in an hieroglyphic manner, that the dependence in which the will shall be with regard to its principle, shall take away nothing of its liberty and shall be as a result of its own tendency. I know of no other tongue in the world where this ellipsis could be rendered.

יִמְשֹׁל, *he-will-rule*.... The verb מָשֹׁל, which means equally *to rule*, and *to be represented, to be expressed by symbols*, is used with purpose in this passage, to conceal no doubt a mystery which is not my purpose to penetrate; for I translate Moses and do not comment. One can see what I have said in v. 16 ch. 1. The Samaritan makes use of the same verb ᙡ2ᙨᙨ.

v. 17. There are no difficult terms here.

v. 18. וְקוֹץ, *and-harsh-and-rough-productions*.... The root קוּץ expresses the action of *cutting, cutting off, tearing*. It is impossible not to feel here, the effect of the compressive and cutting sign ק united to the terminative sign ץ.

וְדַרְדַּר, *and-the-uncultivated-and-unruly-productions*.... The root דַר furnishes the idea of circuit, of order, period, age and circular habitation; but in doubling the last character, which is that of movement proper, one opens, as it were, the circle, and obtains the intensive root דָרַר, which signifies *license, a rupture of order, an invasion*. It is

17. And-unto-*Adam* (col·lective man) he-said: because thou-hast-listened t o t h e-v o i c e of-the-intellectual-mate-thine (thy volitive faculty) and-hast-fed-u p o n t h e-e l e m e n t a r y-growth w h i c h I-did-prescribe-to-t h e e by-saying: not-shalt t h o u-feed-upon any-of-it: cursed! be-the-adamic (homogeneal, universal ground) f o r-t h e-s a k e-thine: with-panging-labour shalt-thou-feed-u p o n-i t all-the-days (manifesting lights) of-the-lives-thine-own.

17. Et-à-*Adam* (l'homme universel) il-dit: puisque tu-as-écouté à-la-voix de l'-é p o u s e-intellectuelle-à-toi (ta faculté volitive) et-que-tu-t'es-alimenté de-cette sub-stance, laquelle j'avais-forte-ment-recommandé à-toi, se-lon-ce-dire: non-pas-tu-t'ali-menteras d e-q u o i-d'elle: maudite! soit-la-terre-ada-mique (homogène et simi-laire à toi) dans-le-rapport -tien: en-travail-angoisseux tu-t'alimenteras-d'elle tous-les-jours (les manifestations phénoméniques) des-vies-à-toi.

---

this last word that is derived from the one which makes the subject of this note, and by which one expresses, in general, all unruly pro-ductions, whether literal or figurative. The Hebraic genius derives *liberty*, in the good sense, from the word דרר, which is *license* or evil liberty, by simply inserting the intellectual sign ו, as is seen in the word דרור.

עשב, *upon-the-most-sharp-and-wasted-fruits-of-nature....* We know that the primitive root אש is applied, in general, to the elementary principle of things, and in particular, to *fire*. We also know that by reinforcing the initial vowel א, it suffices to increase progressively its force. Now, if the word which is the subject of this note, is composed of the contracted roots עש-אב, of which there is no doubt, it will signify not simply χορτός, *dried grass, herb of the field*, following the interpretation of the Hellenists, weakened by Saint Jerome; but indeed, *a sharp and wasted fructification*. For this is the true meaning of the word עשב. The Arabic عشب is explicit.

v. 19. בזעת עפיך, *in-a-tossing-motion of-the-mind-thine....* When the Hellenists said, ἐν ἱδρωτι τοῦ προσώπου σου: *in the sweat of thy face*, the natural inference is, that this phrase was in the Hebrew text, but it is not there. The face of Adam has never sweat physically except in the mind of the translators of Moses. The hierographic

18.   W'kôtz w'dareddar thatzemîha la-čha w'âčha-leth æth-hesheh ha-shadeh.

וְקוֹץ וְדַרְדַּר תַּצְמִיחַ לָךְ וְאָכַלְתָּ אֶת־עֵשֶׂב הַשָּׂדֶה :

19 B'zewhath âpphei-čha thoâčhal lehem, had shoûb-čha æel-ha-Adamah, čhî-mi-men-nah lukkahetha čhi-haphar âthah w'æl-haphar thashoûb.

בְּזֵעַת אַפֶּיךָ תֹּאכַל לֶחֶם עַד שׁוּבְךָ אֶל־הָאֲדָמָה כִּי מִמֶּנָּה לֻקָּחְתָּ כִּי־עָפָר אַתָּה וְאֶל־עָפָר תָּשׁוּב :

---

writer did not have such ideas. The word זֵעַת comes from the root זוּע which develops the idea of a restless agitation, an anxiety, a movement of fear for the future. The word which follows אַף can, in truth, signify *the nose*, in a very restricted sense, but it expresses much more generally, not *the face*, but the irascible part of the soul which constitutes the animistic mind, or the understanding.

עַד שׁוּב, *till-the-restoring-thine....*   The verb שׁוּב, being formed of the root שׁב, expressing every idea of restitution, of return toward a point of departure, and this root being itself composed of the sign of relative duration, and of the paternal and central sign, it is evident that this verb must be applied to every moral or physical revolution, which brings the being back to its primitive state. See Rad. Vocab. roots שׁב, אוֹב and שׁוּ.

עָפָר, *spiritual-element....*   Although I have already spoken several times of this important word, I cannot refrain from referring to it again here, because it is to the wrong interpretation of the translators, that one must impute the accusation of materialism brought against Moses; an accusation from which it was impossible to clear him as long as one had only the version of the Hellenists, or that of their imitators. For, if man is drawn from the dust, and if he must return to the dust, as they make him say, where is his immortality? What becomes of his spiritual part? Moses says nothing of it, according to them. But if they had taken the trouble to examine the verb שׁוּב they would have seen that it expressed not a material return, but a

18. And-harsh and-rough productions (thorns a n d thistles) shall-plentifully-g r o w for-thee; and-thou-shalt-feed upon-the-m o s t-sharp-and-wasted-fruits of-nature.

18. E t-l e s-productions-tranchantes, et-les-product-ions-i n c u l t e s-et-désordon-nées germeront-abondam-ment pour-toi; et-tu-t'ali-menteras des-fruits-âcres-et-desséchés de-la-nature-élé-mentaire.

19. In-a-tossing motion of-the-mind-thine shalt-thou-eat-f o o d till-the-restoring thine (rising again) toward-the-a d a m i c (homogeneal l a n d); for-such-as f r o m some-of-it wast-thou-taken, such-spiritual-element art-thou and-toward-the-spirit-ual-element wilt-thou-rise-again.

19. En-agitation-contin-uelle de-l'esprit-tien, tu-t'ali-menteras de-nourriture jus-qu'au-restituer (au réinté-grer, au ressusciter)-tien à-la-terre-adamique (homogè-ne et similaire à toi)car-tel-de-quoi-d'elle tu-as-été-tiré, tel-esprit-élémentaire tu-es; et-à-l'élément-spiritueux tu-dois-être-restitué.

---

restitution to a place, to a primordial state, *a resurrection*, in the sense that we give today to this word; they would have seen that this place was, not the earth, properly speaking, אֶרֶץ; but the similitude of man, his original, homogeneous country, אֲדָמָה, and they would have seen finally, that this was neither *the dust* of the one, nor *the mire* of the other, to which he must return; but the spiritual element, principle of his being.

v. 20. חוה, *Hewah*.... Here is a name where the changing of the vowel into consonant has caused a strange metamorphosis. This name which, according to the allusion that Moses makes, ought to signify, and signify effectively, *elementary existence*, being derived from the absolute verb הוֹה *to be-being*, by the sole reinforcement of the initial vowel ה into ח, has come to designate no more than a formless heap of matter, its aggregation, its mass; and by the harden-ing of the convertible sign ו sanctioned by the Chaldaic punctuation, serves as verb only to indicate the inert and passive existence of things. The change brought about in the derivative verb הוה, has been even more terrible in the absolute verb, חוֹה; for this verb, des-tined to represent the Immutable Being, expresses only an endless cal-

20. Wa-îkerâ ha-A d a m
shem Aisheth-ô hawah c̀hî-
hiwâ haîth æn-c̀hol-haî.

וַיִּקְרָא הָאָדָם שֵׁם אִשְׁתּוֹ חַוָּה
כִּי הוּא הָיְתָה אֵם כָּל־חָי ׃

21. Wa-îahash I H O A H
Ælohîm l' Adam w'l'âisheth-
ô-c̀hi-thenôth hôr wa-îaleb-
bish'em.

וַיַּעַשׂ יְהוָֹה אֱלֹהִים לְאָדָם
וּלְאִשְׁתּוֹ כָּתְנוֹת עוֹר וַיַּלְבִּשֵׁם ׃

22. Wa-îâomer I H O A H
Ælohîm hen ha-Adam haîah
c̀hi-ahad mi-mennoû, la-da-
hath tôb wa-rawh, w'hatthah
phen-îshelah îad-ô w'lakah
gam me-hetz ha-haîîm, w'-
âc̀hal, w'a-haî l'holam.

וַיֹּאמֶר יְהוָֹה אֱלֹהִים הֵן הָאָדָם
הָיָה כְּאַחַד מִמֶּנּוּ לָדַעַת טוֹב
וָרָע וְעַתָּה פֶּן־יִשְׁלַח יָדוֹ וְלָקַח
גַּם מֵעֵץ הַחַיִּים וְאָכַל וָחַי
לְעֹלָם ׃

---

amity, as I have explained in speaking of the Sacred Name יהוה, in
v. 4. ch. II. As to the reasons for the alterations undergone by this
proper noun I can only refer the reader to the name of the volitive
faculty, אשה which, as we have seen, had preceded that of elementary
existence חוה. See v. 22, ch. II and v. 12 of this chapter.

   v. 21. כתנות, *body-like*.... It is because they have not wished
to recognize the assimilative article כ that the Hellenists have interpreted *garments*, χιτῶνας instead of body. The root תן, from which
the plural substantive here referred to is derived, develops every idea
of added substance, or of corporeity increasing more and more.

   עור, *sheltering-shapes*.... It is from this badly understood root
that the verb עור *to watch over the defence, to guard*, is derived, and
the substantive עיר, *a city*; that is to say, a fortified enclosure. Thence
urbs, in Latin; *ward*, in Saxon; *gare, garde*, and even *boule-vard*, in
French: all these words express the same idea of a place destined
to guard and to defend. I beg the reader to consider that this new
envelope עור, in which dominates the sign of material sense ע, is substituted for the ancient גן, which has been ridiculously taken for a
garden.

   v. 22. כאחר, *such-as-one*.... I only mention this word to show
the use of the assimilative article כ, an important article often misunderstood by the translators.

20. A n d-h e-designated, *Adam*, for-name to-the intellectual-mate-of-him (his volitive faculty) *H e w a h* (elementary existence) because it-was the-mother of-all-existence.

21. And-he-made, IHOAH the-Being-of beings, unto-*Adam* (collective man) and-unto - the-intellectual - mate-of-him, body-like sheltering-shapes; and-he-involved (incrusted)-them-carefully.

22. And-he-said, IHOAH, HE-the-Gods, B e h o l d ! *Adam* being such-a s-o n e from-those-of-us, by-knowing good and-evil: and-now lest-he-should put-forth the-hand-his-own and-take also from-the-elementary-growth of-lives and-feed-upon, and-l i v e for-an-infinite-period (forever):

20. Et-il-assigna, *Adam*, nom-à l'épouse-intellectuelle-sienne (sa faculté volitive) *Hewah* (existence élémentaire) à-c a u s e-qu'elle-était la-mère de-toute-existence.

21. Et-il-fit, IHOAH, l'-Être-des êtres à-*Adam* (l'-h o m m e-universel) et-à-l' épouse-intellectuelle-sienne, tels-que-des-corps de-défense (des remparts) et-il-les-enveloppa-avec-soin.

22. Et-il-dit, IHOAH, LUI-les-Dieux, V o i c i ! *A d a m* étant tel-qu'un de-l'espèce-à-nous, selon la-connaisance du-bien et-du-mal: et-à-ce-temps, de-peur-qu'il-étendra la-main-s i e n n e et-prendra a u s s i de-la-substance-élémentaire des-vies, et-qu'il-s'alimentera et-vivra selon-la-période-infinie (l'éternité):

מעץ החיים, *from-the-elementary-growth-of-lives....* I think I have made the signification of the word עץ sufficiently clear, so that I can dispense with any further detail to prove that it signifies neither *wood*, nor even *tree;* as the translators, either through ignorance or intent of purpose, had said: but what I believe should be added, is, that the text here reads החיים of *lives*, and not החיה, of *life*, as they have translated it in their versions. This difference is very essential. The Samaritan says 𐤀𐤍𐤕𐤉𐤌. 𐤏𐤌𐤑𐤁 : *the growth*, or *the natural substance of lives*, exactly as the Hebrew. I trust that the etymologist will find pleasure in seeing that the word רע, by which the Hebrew text ex-

23.   Wa-î s h a l l e h-hoû
IHÔAH Ælohîm mi-gan-he-
den la-habod æth-ha-âdamah
âsher lukkah mi-sham.

וַיְשַׁלְּחֵהוּ יְהֹוָה אֱלֹהִים מִגַּן־עֵדֶן לַעֲבֹד אֶת־הָאֲדָמָה אֲשֶׁר לֻקַּח מִשָּׁם ׃

24.   Wa-îgaresh æth-ha-
Adam, wa-iashe-chen mi-kedem l'gan-heden æth-ha-che-
r u b b î m, w'æth-lahat ha-
hereb ha-mithehapphecheth
li-shemôr æth-derech hetz
ha-haîîm.

וַיְגָרֶשׁ אֶת הָאָדָם וַיַּשְׁכֵּן מִקֶּדֶם לְגַן־עֵדֶן אֶת־הַכְּרֻבִים וְאֵת־לַהַט הַחֶרֶב הַמִּתְהַפֶּכֶת לִשְׁמֹר אֶת־דֶּרֶךְ עֵץ הַחַיִּים ׃

---

presses *evil*, in this phrase, לדעת טוב ורע, *by-knowing good and-evil*, is rendered in the Samaritan text by the word ᛘᛗᛒ . Now this word, pronounced *bish* or *vish* is very certainly the one whence is derived the Latin *vitium*, from which we have made *vice*. This derivation merits observation for many reasons. The Teutonic and Saxon have preserved this word with slight alteration, the one, in *bös*, and the other, in *bad*. The Chaldaic and Syriac agree in the sense of the word ביש and ﺤﻤ : the Arabic alone differs.

v. 23.   לוּקַּח, *he-had-been-taken from*.... It is the verb לקח *to take*, *to draw*, *to extract*, used here after the intensive form, passive movement, third person singular. I make this remark only to show that the median character ק, should be doubled if the interior point does not take the place of the second. This verb which is written without the Chaldaic *kibbuz*, has need of the character ו to indicate the passive movement.

v. 24.   מקדם, *from-the-foregone-principle-of-times*.... See v. 8. ch. II.

הכרבים, *that-self-same-Cherubim*.... The root רב, which contains the idea of all multiplication, of all infinite number, has already been explained. It is used in the plural and governed by the assimilative sign כ.

23. Then-he-parted-him, IHOAH, the Being-of beings, f r o m-t h e-enclosing-sphere of-sensible-times; for-working that-same-adamic (homogeneal ground), which he-had-been-taken-from.

24. And-he-p u t-f o r t h that-same *Adam* (collective man) and-he-c a u s e d-t o-abide from-the-f o r e g o n e-principle-of-times near-the-organic-sphere of-temporal-sensibleness that-selfsame-Cherubim (innumerable legions like) and-that-self-s a m e-flaming of-wild-destruction, whirling-round-on-itself to-keep the-way of-t h e-elementary-growth of-lives.

23. Alors-il-detacha-lui-IHOAH, l'Être-des-êtres, de-la-sphère-organique d e-l a-sensibilité-temporelle; afin-de-travailler cette-m ê m e-substance-adamique, de-la-quelle il-avait-été-pris-hors.

24. Et-il-éloigna ce-mê-me-*Adam* (l'homme univer-sel), et-il-fit-résider de-l'an-tériorité-universelle _ des temps, à-la-sphère-tempor-elle-et-sensible, ce-m ê m e,-Cherubim (un être sem-blable aux innombrables lé-gions) et-cette-même-flam-me-in c an d e s c e n t e de-l'ar-deur-dévastatrice tourbil-lonnant-sans-cesse-sur _ elle-même, pour garder la-route de_la-substance-élémentaire des_vies.

הַחֶרֶב, *of-wild-destruction*.... The Hellenists who sought to restrict everything and to materialize everything, have rendered this word by that of ρομφαία, *a sort of waving sword*. It can be remarked that the most petty images are always the ones that they have chosen. They took pains not to see here the root חֵר, expressing every wild destruction, every igneous, wrathful force, modified by the active and central sign ב : a single word badly veiled would have sufficed to betray the spiritual sense that they wished to hide.

הַמִתְהַפֶּכֶת, *whirling-round-on-itself*.... This is the verb חָפֹךְ, *to turn*, used according to the reflexive form, as feminine, continued facultative. This facultative is preceded by the emphatic article ה, in order to take for it, the place of the modificative, and to increase its force.

SEPHER BERÆSHITH
D.

סֵפֶר בְּרֵאשִׁית ד׃

---

1. W'ha-Adam î a d a h æth-Hewah Aisheth-ô, wa-thahar, wa-theled æth-Kaîn, wa-thâomer kanîthî a î s h æth-IHÔAH.

וְהָאָדָם יָדַע אֶת־חַוָּה אִשְׁתּוֹ וַתַּהַר וַתֵּלֶד אֶת־קַיִן וַתֹּאמֶר קָנִיתִי אִישׁ אֶת־יְהֹוָה׃

---

v. 1. את־קין, *the-self-sameness of-Kain....* Need I speak of the importance that the peoples of the Orient have attached to proper names, and of what deep mysteries their sages have often hidden beneath these names? Had I space here to express myself in this subject, my only perplexity would be making a choice among the numberless proofs. But the time is short and these notes are already too voluminous. The intellectual reader has no need of a vain display of useless erudition, to be taught what he already knows. Let it suffice therefore, for me to say that Moses is the one, of the writers of antiquity, who has developed most subtly the art of composing proper names. I have endeavoured to give an idea of his talent, or that of his instructors in this respect, by developing the name of universal man אדם, *collective unity, eternal similitude,* and that of the Supreme Divinity יהוה, *the Being who is, who was, and who will be.* But I must make it clear that these two names, and some others, were sufficiently elevated by their nature to be translatable without danger. The names which follow will be, almost all, a very different matter. Moses has been often obliged to throw over them a veil, that I ought and wish to respect. Although I might perhaps give the literal word, I shall not do so. I inform my reader of this in order that he may be watchful: for if he desire it, nothing shall prevent him from knowing.

The root of the name *Kain,* is קן, which is composed of the eminently compressive and trenchant sign ק, and that of produced being ן. It develops the idea of strongest compression and of most centralized existence. In the proper name under consideration, it is presented animated by the sign of manifested power: thus קין, can signify *the strong, the powerful, the rigid, the vehement,* and also

GENESIS IV.

1. And-he-*A d a m* (collective man) knew-that-self-same-*H e w a* (elementary l i f e) intellectual-mate-of-h i m (his-volitive-faculty) and-she-conceived, and-she-bare the-selfsameness of-*Kain* (the strong, the mighty one; he who lies in the centre, who assumes and assimilates to himself) and-she-s a i d, I-d i d-c e n t r e (framed by centering) an-intellectual-being selfsame-ness of-IHOAH.

COSMOGONIE IV.

1. Et-lui-*Adam* (l'homme universel) connut-cette-même-*Hewa* (l'existence-élémentaire) l'épouse-intellect-uelle-sienne (sa faculté voli-tive) et-elle conçut, et-elle-enfanta l'existence-de-*Kain* (le forte, le puissant; celui qui tire au centre, qui saisit, qui agglomère, qui assimile à soi); et-elle-dit, j'ai-cen-tralisé (formé par centralisation) un-être-intellectuel de-l'essence-même-à-IHOAH.

---

the central, that which serves as basis, rule, measure; that which agglomerates, appropriates, seizes, comprehends, assimilates with itself. It is in this last sense that Moses appears to have represented it in the verb which follows.

קניתי, *I-did-centre....* This is the verb קנה, used according to the positive form, active movement, first person, past tense. The Hellenist translators who have made it signify *to get*, have chosen, as is their habit, the most restricted sense. The Arabic words قين and قان which have the same root, signify *to forge, to agglomerate, to equalize, to form.*

The Samaritan translator has rendered this same verb קנה, by which Moses explains the name of *Kain*, by 𐤒𐤍 *to rule*, to display the power of a king; so as to have good cause for saying that, in a multitude of tongues, the idea of power and of royalty has come from the root *Kan, Kin*, or *Kain*. See Rad. Vocab.

את־יהוה, *selfsameness-of* IHOAH.... The savants who know the lively quarrels that this expression has caused, particularly since Luther asserted that it should be translated: *I have acquired a man who is the Lord*, will perhaps be interested in seeing what the prin-

2. Wa-thosseph la-ledeth æth-âhî-ô æth-Habel, wa-îhî hebel roheh tzoâm, w'Kain haîah hobed âdamah.

וַתֹּסֶף לָלֶדֶת אֶת־אָחִיו אֶת־הֶבֶל וַיְהִי הֶבֶל רֹעֵה צֹאן וְקַיִן הָיָה עֹבֵד אֲדָמָה ׃

---

cipal translators have thought. I am about to satisfy them by quoting successively the Samaritan, Chaldaic, Hellenist and Latin phrase.

𐤟𐤟𐤟·𐤟𐤟𐤟·𐤟𐤟𐤟

I have-sovereignly-typified a-hero from-Ihoah.

קָנִיתִי גֶּבֶר קֶדֶם ייי ׃

I have-acquired-in-central-force a-hero in-principle from-the Eternal.

'Εκτήσαμην ἀνθρώπον διὰ τοῦ Θέος.

I have-gotten a-man through God.

Possedi hominem per Dominum.

I have-gotten a-man through the-Lord.

The Hebrew is understood. The hieroglyphic mystery consists of the way in which Moses has employed the designative proposition את, which indicates the selfsameness or the objectivity of things, as constructive substantive, with the Sacred Name of the Divinity יהוה.

v. 2. את־הבל, *the-selfsameness-of-Habel....* Moses, for reasons which were doubtless particular ones, has given no ostensible explanation of this name. We can, to a degree, make up for this silence by an examination of the root from which it is derived. This root is בל, which, composed of the sign of interior action ב, joined to that of expansive movement ל, expresses all ideas of expansion, dilation and tenuity. Therefore, if we have understood that the compressive force could be characterized by the root קן, we shall understand now that the expansive force can be characterized by the root בל; consequently, every time one has seen strength, power, density, possession, in the name of *Kain*, one has also seen weakness, rarity, surrender, in that of *Habel*.

But it must not be believed that this force and this power, which the name of *Kain* characterizes, have always been taken in the good sense. Very far from it: for the majority of the peoples have attached to it only a blind fatality, and *Kain* has been for them only the

2. And-she-added by-the bringing-forth the-brotherly-self-of-h i m, t he -selfsame-ness-of-*H a b e l*, and-he-was, *Habel*, a-leader (overseer) of-the-indefinite-being (elementary corporeal world) and *Kain*, was-a-servant (a tiller) of-the-adamic (homogeneal ground).

2. Et-elle-ajouta p a r-l' action-d'enfanter l'ipséité-fraternelle-à-lui, l'existence-·d'*Habel*; et-il-fut *Habel*, conducteur (surveillant) de-l' être-indéfini, (le monde corporel) et-*Kain*-fut serviteur, (ellaborateur) de-l'élément-adamique.

---

genius of Evil. In this case, the contrary attributes contained in the name of *Habel*, are adorned with more favourable shades: the weakness has become gentleness and grace; the rarity, spiritual essence; surrender, magnanimity: *Habel*, in short, has been the genius of Good. These singular contrasts exist in the tongues of the Hebrews and of the Chaldeans; for if the word בל signifies *the mind*, and *the soul* which is its source; this same word also offers the negative relation, *no*: and if one finds יכול, to express ideas of abundance, profusion and even of inundation, one finds also the word בלי, to express those of lack, want, absolute nothingness. The emphatic sign ה, added to this singular root, can be likewise, in the name of *Habel*, the emblem of that which is noblest in man: thought and meditation; or of that which is vainglorious, the illusions of pride, and vanity itself.

It is the same with the qualities expressed in the name of *Kain*, which become good or bad, according to the manner in which they are considered.

צאן, *the-indefinite-Being*.... The root of this word, as the one of which I have just spoken, has the singular property of the same contradictory ideas. Also, it is not without reason that Moses, who did not wish to explain the name of *Habel*, has employed the word צאן, as synonym in hieroglyphic style. I believe it to be useless to explain here, how it is that אין, whose proper meaning is *indefinite-being, world, time*, as can be recognized in the Greek word αἰών which is derived from it, has characterized at the same time, in Hebrew, *being* and *nothingness, weakness* and *virtue, riches* and *poverty;* because this is again a consequence of the degradation of its vocal sound of

3. Wa-îehî mi-ketz îam-
îm wa-îabæ Kaîn mi-pherî
ha-âdamah   m i n e h h   la-
IHÔAH.

וַיְהִי מִקֵּץ יָמִים וַיָּבֵא קַיִן מִפְּרִי
הָאֲדָמָה מִנְחָה לַיהוָה :

4. W'Habel hebîa gam-
houâ mi-bechorôth tzoân-
ô, w'me-heleb-be-hen, wa-
îshah, IHÔAH, æl-Habel w'
æl-minehath-ô.

וְהֶבֶל הֵבִיא גַם־הוּא מִבְּכֹרוֹת
צֹאנוֹ וּמֵחֶלְבֵהֶן וַיִּשַׁע יְהוָה אֶל־
הֶבֶל וְאֶל־מִנְחָתוֹ :

---

which I have spoken sufficiently. All that I believe necessary to add
is, that the Hellenists have rendered the word צֹאן by πρόβατον, *a flock
of sheep*, because they have taken it, following their habit, in the
most restricted sense. For the sign of final movement צ, being united
with the root אֵן or אִין, *produced being*, has made it in general צֹאן,
indefinite being; in particular, *a body*. Now it is very easy to perceive
that this word צֹאן signifying *a body*, needs only a simple abstraction
of thought, to make it signify *a troop* or *a flock*. The Hebrews have
said *a corps of sheep*, and simply *a corps*, to express *a flock;* as we
say *a corps of soldiers*, and simply *a corps*, to signify *a troop*.

The Samaritan renders the word צֹאן by that of ᘔ᙭Ⴃ, which
contains the several significations of *tabernacle, temporal dwelling,
time, corporeal aggregation, corps,* etc. It is the analogue of the
Hebraic root עוֹן, as can be seen in the Radical Vocabulary.

v. 3. מִקֵּץ יָמִים, *from-the-end-of-the-seas*.... The translators of
Moses, either accustomed to see in *Adam*, a material and limited man,
or conforming in this to the vulgar ideas of their time, have been
forced either to see men of blood, flesh and bones, in *Kain* and *Habel*,
or feign to see them, making it impossible to render the clear and
simple signification of this verse. For how could it be said that a
man, such as they conceived him in *Kain*, made an offering to IHOAH
from the end of the seas? They have easily substituted the expression
of *days* for that of *seas*, because the Hebraic word does not differ;
but what could they do with מִקֵּץ which can absolutely signify only
from the end, the extremity, the summit? Some, as the Samaritan
and the Chaldaic translators, were content to be unintelligible; the

3. Now-it-was from-the-end of-the-seas, t h a t-h e-caused-to-go, *Kain*, from-the-product of-the-adamic (elementary ground) an-offering unto-IHOAH.

4. And-*Habel* caused-to-go, also-he, from-the-first-lings of-the-w o r l d of him, a n d - from-the-quintessence (the best, over-t o p p i n g qualities)-of-them: and-he-proved-a-saviour, I H O A H, unto-*Habel*, and-u n t o-the-offering-of-him.

3. Or-ce-fut de-la-cime d e s-m e r s, qu'il-fit-a l l e r, *Kain*, du-produit de-l'élé-ment-adamique, (homogène) un-oblation à IHOAH.

4. Et-*Habel* fit-a l l e r, aussi-lui, des-prémices du-monde-à-lui; et-de-la-quin-tessence (de la qualité émi-nente)-à-eux: et-il-se-mon-tra-sauveur, IHOAH, envers-*Habel*, et-envers-l'offrande sienne.

Hellenists have changed the text, in which they have been followed by Saint Jerome. They have said: καὶ ἐγεντο μέθ' ἡμέρας, "factum est autem post multos dies." *It came to pass after many days....* Now according to the thought of the hierographic writer, *Kain*, being a cosmological being, very different from a man properly so-called, can, without the least incongruity, cause to ascend to IHOAH, an offering from the end of the seas, or from the superficies of phenomenal manifestations, if one would fathom the hieroglyphic meaning of the word ימים.

v. 4. מבכרות צאנו, *from-the-firstlings of-the-world-of-him....* The word בכר comes from the two roots בא־כר of which the first בא develops every idea of progression, of gradual progress, of generative development; the second כר, designates all apparent, eminent things which serve as monument, as distinctive mark; so that, by בכר, should be understood, that which, in a series of beings, takes precedence, dominates, characterizes, announces, presages, etc. This word has important relations with בכר, of which I have spoken in v. 5, ch. I. The Arabic كَر signifies literally, *to be early;* figuratively, *to prosper, to surpass, to take precedence with brilliance, with glory.* Thence باكر or بكر; *a virgin.*

5. Wæl Kaîn w'æl-mine-
hath-ô loâ-shahah, wa'îhar
l'Kaîn m â o d   wa-îpheloû
phanaî-ô.

וְאֶל ־ קַיִן וְאֶל מִנְחָתוֹ לֹא שָׁעָה
נִיחַר לְקַיִן מְאֹד וַיִּפְּלוּ פָּנָיו :

6. Wa-iâomer IHÔAH æl-
Kaîn, lammah harah le-čha,
w'lammah napheloû phaneî-
čha.

וַיֹּאמֶר יְהֹוָה אֶל־קַיִן לָמָּה חָרָה
לָךְ וְלָמָּה נָפְלוּ פָנֶיךָ :

וּמֵחֶלְבֵהֶן, *and-from-the-quintessence-of-them....* The Hellenists having interpreted *a flock*, for *a world*, have been obliged necessarily, in
order to be consistent, to interpret *first-born* instead of *firstlings*, and
the *eminent qualities* of these same firstlings, as *fat*. Such was the
force of a first violation of the text. All of these base and ridiculous
ideas spring one from another. Either they have purposely remained
silent or else they were ignorant of the first elements of the Hebraic
tongue, not to feel that the word חֶלֶב signifies *fat*, only by an evident
abuse made by the vulgar, and that the two roots חַל and לֵב, of which
it is composed, being applied, the one, to every superior effort, and
the other, to every quality, to every faculty, resulting from this effort,
the word חֶלֶב, ought to characterize every extraction of essential
things: which is proved by the meaning attached to it by the Chaldeans
and the Hebrews themselves; taking the substantive, for milk or
cream; and the verb, for the action of milking, extracting, making
emanate. Thence innumerable relative expressions. ܚܠܒ is taken in
Syriac for *cream, foam, sperm*, etc.; the Ethiopian word ሐለብ (*he-
leb*), offers as does the Arabic حلب the ideas of *emulsion; derivation,
emanation, distillation*, etc

וַיִּשַׁע, *and-he-proved-a-saviour* .... The verb שָׁעָה has been taken
by all translators in the sense of *having regard*, of *respecting;* but it
should here be in the sense of *redeeming*, of *saving*, of *leading to
salvation.* It is from the root שַׁע, containing in itself all ideas of
preservation, salvation and redemption, which come, on the one hand,
from the compound radical verb יָשַׁע and on the other, from the compound שָׁעָה, whose signification is the same. When this latter verb

5. And-unto-*Kain*, and-unto-the-offering-h i s-o w n, n o t-to-prove-a-a-s a v i o u r: which-raised-up-the-w r a t h of-*Kain* quite-thoroughly; a n d-w e r e-cast-down the-faces-of-him.

6. And-he-said, IHOAH, unto-*Kain;*•why the-raising-up-t h e-fiery-wrath-to-thee? and-w h y the-casting-down of-the-faces thine?

5. Et-envers-*Kain*, e t-envers-l'o b l a t i o n-sienne, non-pas-se-montrer-sauveur: c e-qui-causa-l'embrasement à-*Kain* tout-à-fait; et-fur-ent-abattues les-faces-sien-nes.

6. Et-il-dit, I H O A H, à-*Kain;* pourquoi le-soulève-ment-e m b r a s é-à-toi? et-pourquoi la-chute (la dé-pression) de-la-face-tienne?

---

expresses the action of having regard or respect, it is composed of the root עו, which is related to exterior and sentient forms of objects, governed by the sign of relative movement ש.

v. 5 and 6. There is nothing difficult in these terms: the meaning itself need not perplex, only so far as the nature of *Kain* and *Habel* is not clearly understood. I would call attention to the fact, that from the beginning of this chapter, Moses, employs only the sole Sacred Name of IHOAH, to designate the Divinity. It seems that he may have omitted the plural surname אלהים *Ælohim*, HE-the-Gods, to make it understood that GOD no longer acts toward the two broth-ers, only in his primitive unity.

v. 7. הלוא, *the-not-being*.... The bold and numerous ellipses with which this verse abounds, render it very difficult to be understood. It is generally the manner of Moses, to be lavish with ellipses when making the Divinity speak. At first, it is here the negative relation לוא, *not*, which, animated by means of the sign ו, and inflected sub-stantively by means of the determinative article ה, makes the entire phrase a single word issuing simultaneously from the mouth of GOD. It seems, by an effect of this boldness, that the divine thought is substantialized, as it were, so as to be grasped by man.

שאת, *that-the-sign*.... What then could be more rapid than this figure? The pronominal article ש, united without intermediary to

7. Ha-lôâ-âim-theîtîb sh'-æth w'aîm loâ-theîtîb-la-phethah ha-tâth robetz, w' æleî-čha theshoûkath-ô w' athah thimeshal-b'ô.

הֲלוֹא אִם־תֵּיטִיב שְׂאֵת וְאִם לֹא תֵּיטִיב לַפֶּסַח חַטָּאת רֹבֵץ וְאֵלֶיךָ תְּשׁוּקָתוֹ וְאַתָּה תִּמְשָׁל־בּוֹ :

8. Wa-îâomer Kaîn æl-Habel âhî-ô, wa-îhî bi-hei-ôth'am be-shadeh, wa-îakam Kaîn æl-Habel âhî-ô, wa-îahareg-hoû.

וַיֹּאמֶר קַיִן אֶל־הֶבֶל אָחִיו וַיְהִי בִּהְיוֹתָם בַּשָּׂדֶה וַיָּקָם קַיִן אֶל־הֶבֶל אָחִיו וַיַּהַרְגֵהוּ :

---

the designative preposition את, does it not depict with an inimitable energy, the rapidity with which the good that man does, leaves its imprint in his soul? This is the seal of Moses. The translation of the Hellenists here is wholly amphibological. These are words which are related one with another without forming any meaning.

v. 8. ויהי בהיותם, *and-it-was by-the-being-both in-the-begetting-nature....* All the translators have believed that there existed before this word, a lacuna which they felt obliged to fill, by inserting as in the Samaritan text, copied by the Hellenists and by Saint Jerome:

ᚦᛈ᛫᛫ᚦ · ᚦᚴ2ᛕ: διέλθωμεν εἰς τὸ πεδικῶν: "egrediamur foras." *Let us go into the field,* or *outside.*

But they have not noticed that the verb אמֹר which signifies not simply *to say,* but *to declare one's thought, to express one's will,* has no need, in Hebrew, of this indifferent course. *Kain* and *Habel,* I repeat, are not men of blood, of flesh and bones; they are cosmogonical beings. Moses makes it felt here in an expressive manner, by saying, that at this epoch they existed together in nature. They existed thus no longer from the moment that the one rising in rebellion against the other, had conquered its forces.

ויהרגהו, *and-he-slew-him....* This verb comes from the two contracted roots הר־רג. The first, which is an intensifying of the

7. The-not-being, if-thou-shalt-do-well, that-the-sign (the token in thee)? and-if not-thou-wilt-do-well, at-the-door the-sin-lying; and-unto-thee the-mutual-proneness-its own, and-thou! the-symbolical-sympathetic-acting unto it?

8. And-now-he-declared-his thought, *Kain,* unto *Habel* the brother-his-own: and-it-was by-the-being-both in-the-begetting-nature: then-he-rose-up (stood up substantially) against-*Habel* the-brother-his-own; and-he-slew-him.

7. Le-non-pas-être, si-tu-feras-bien, que-le-sign (l'image du bien en toi)? et-si non-pas-être, tu-feras-bien, à-l'entrée le-péché reposant, et-envers-toi le-desir-mutuel-sien, et-toi! la représentation-mutuelle dans-lui?

8. Et-ensuite, il-déclara-sa-pensée, *Kain,* à-*Habel* le-frère-sien: et c'était durant-l'action-d'exister - ensemble-dans-la-nature-productrice: or il-s'insurgea (s'éleva en substance, se matérialisa) contre-*Habel*, le-frère-sien, et-il-immola-lui.

---

primitive אר, designates in general, *an exaltation, an height;* it is literally, *a mountain,* and figuratively, that which is strong, robust, powerful; the second root רז, characterizes a disorganizing movement. Thus *Kain* displays against *Habel,* only the power of which he is possessor, that which results from physical force.

This same allegory is found in the Pouranas of the Hindus, under the names of *Maha-dewa,* in place of *Kain,* and of *Daksha* in place of *Habel. Maha-dewa* is the same as *Siwa,* and *Daksha* is a surname of *Brahma,* which can be translated by *Ethereal.* The Egyptians gave to *Kronos* of the Greeks, whom we call *Saturn,* after the Latins, the name of *Chivan* or *Kiwan;* this same *Kiwan* was, from most ancient times, adored by the Arabs of Mecca under the figure of a black stone. The Jews themselves gave to Saturn this same name of כיון; and one can read, in a Persian book cited in the English Asiatic Researches,

9. Wa-îâomer IHÔAH æl-
Kaîn, æî-Hebel âhî-ċha, wa-
îâomer loâ-îadahethî, ha-
shomer âhî ânoċhî.

וַיֹּאמֶר יְהוָֹה אֶל־קַיִן אֵי הֶבֶל
אָחִיךָ וַיֹּאמֶר לֹא יָדַעְתִּי הֲשֹׁמֵר
אָחִי אָנֹכִי :

10. Wa-îâomer meh has-
hîtha kôl dhemæi âhî-ċha
tzohakîm æloî min-ha-âda-
mah.

וַיֹּאמֶר מֶה עָשִׂיתָ קוֹל דְּמֵי
אָחִיךָ צֹעֲקִים אֵלַי מִן־הָאֲדָמָה :

11. W'hatthah, â r o u r
âthah min-ha-âdamah âsher
phatzethah æth-phî-ha la-
kahath æth-dhemeî âhî-ċha
mi-îade-ċha.

וְעַתָּה אָרוּר אָתָּה מִן־הָאֲדָמָה
אֲשֶׁר פָּצְתָה אֶת־פִּיהָ לָקַחַת
אֶת־דְּמֵי אָחִיךָ מִיָּדֶךָ :

12. Chi thahabod æth-
ha-âdamah, l o â thosseph
theth-ċhoh-ha, la-ċha nawh
wa-nad thiheîeh b'âretz.

כִּי תַעֲבֹד אֶת־הָאֲדָמָה לֹא־
תֹסֵף תֵּת־כֹּחָהּ לָךְ נָע וָנָד תִּהְיֶה
בָאָרֶץ :

---

that the Hindus had formerly many sacred places, dedicated to *Kywan*,
who was no other than their *Siwa* or *Siwan*, of which I have spoken
above.

v. 9. Contains no difficulty.

v. 10. רְמִי, *the-likenesses*.... The Hellenists seeing, or feigning
to see in *Habel*, a corporeal man, could not avoid seeing a man of
blood in the word רמי: but this word, in the constructive plural, and
agreeing with the facultative צעקים, should have caused Saint Jerome

9. And-he-said, IHOAH, unto-*Kain*, where-is *Habel*, the-brother-thine? and-he-said (answering *Kain*) not-did-I-know: the-keeper of-the-brother-mine am-I?

10. And-he-said, IHOAH, what-hast-thou-done? t h e-voice of-the-l i k e n e s s e s (identic future progenies) of-the-brother-thine, groan-ing-rise t o w a r d-m e from-the-a d a m i c (elementary ground).

11. And-this-time, cursed b e-thóu! from-the-adamic, which did-open the-mouth-its-own for-receiving those-likenesses (future progen-ies) of-the-brother-thine, by-the-hand-thine-own.

12. Then-whilst thou-shalt-work t h a t-a d a m i c (elementary ground) not-will-it-yield the-strength its-own unto-thee: staggering a n d-r o v i n g (wandering with fright) thou-shalt-be in-the-earth.

9. Et-il-dit I H O A H, à *Kain*, où-est *Habel*, le-frère-tien? et-il-dit (répondant *Kain*): non pas-savais-je; le-gardant du-frère-m i e n suis-je.

10. Et-il-dit, IHOAH, que-fis-tu? la-voix des-homogèn-éités (des générations iden-tiques) du-frère-tien plai-gnantes, s'élève-vers-moi de l'élément-adamique.

11. Et-à-ce-temps, mau-d i t sois-tu! de-l'élément-adamique, lequel ouvrit la-bouche-sienne pour-recevoir ces-homogénéités (ces gé-nérations futures) du-frère-tien, par-la-main-à-toi.

12. Ainsi-quand tu-tra-vailleras cet-élément-ada-m i q u e; non-pas-il-joindra don-de-force-virtuelle-sienne à-toi: vacillant (agité d'un mouvement incertain) et-vaguant (agité d'un mouve-ment d'effroi) tu-seras en-la-terre.

---

to think that Moses meant something else. The Chaldean paraphrast had perceived it in writing this phrase thus:

רב־זרעין דעתירין למפק *The-like-generations which-future-progenies were-*
מן אחוך קבלן קרמי.... *to-proceed of-the-brother-thine, groaning-are be-fore-me....*

v. 11. These terms are understood.

v. 12. נע, *staggering....* A very remarkable root which, with

13.   Wa-îâomer Kaîn æl-
IHÒAH gadôl haôn-î mi-nes-
hoâ.

וַיֹּאמֶר קַיִן אֶל ־ יְהוָֹה גָּדוֹל עֲוֹנִי
מִנְּשׂוֹא :

14.   H e n , gherashetha
âoth-î ha-iôm me-hal phenî
ha-â d a m a h , w'mi-phanî-
cha æs-s a t h e r, w'haîîthî
nawh wa-nad ba-âretz, w'
haîah chol-mot-zeâ-î îahe-
regnî.

הֵן גֵּרַשְׁתָּ אֹתִי הַיּוֹם מֵעַל פְּנֵי
הָאֲדָמָה וּמִפָּנֶיךָ אֶסָּתֵר וְהָיִיתִי
נָע וָנָד בָּאָרֶץ וְהָיָה כָל ־ מֹצְאִי
יַהַרְגֵנִי :

---

the one following, assists in penetrating the nature of *Kain*: mysterious nature, the understanding of which would lead very far. This
root is used here in the continued facultative, active movement and
should be written נוע. The radical verb which is formed from it,
נוע, signifies *to be moved about, to stagger, to wander aimlessly*. One
must remark here that the sign of produced being נ, is arrested by
the sign ע, which is that of material sense.

נר, *roving....* Another facultative **which** should be written נור.
The radical verb נור, which is derived from it, expresses a movement
of flight, of exile; a painful agitation. The **sign** of division ר, replaces
in this **root**, the sign of material sense, with which the preceding one
is terminated.

v. 13.   עוֹנִי, *the-perverseness-mine....* Let us consider a moment
this word, whose whole force comes from the sign ע. We have seen
in v. 2 of this chapter, **that** the root אִין, which characterizes in general,
the produced being, time, the world, developed the most contrary
ideas following the inflection given to the vocal sound: expressing
sometimes being, sometimes nothingness; sometimes strength, sometimes weakness: this same root, inclined toward the bad sense by the
sign ע, is now fixed there and no longer signifies anything but what
is perverse. It is, as it were, the opposite of being: it is vice, the
opposite of that which is good.

And let us notice its origin: it is worthy of attention. הוֹר is, as
we well know, the verb *par excellence*, to be-being. But this verb,
ceasing to be absolute in particularizing itself in speech, can be corrupted: that is to say, the vocal sounds which constitute it can be
materialized in passing into consonants. This is what happens in the
word הֹוֶה, where the intellectual sign ו. becoming extinct, indicates

13. And-he-said, *K a i n,* unto-IHOAH, great-is the-perverseness-mine b y-t h e-cleansing.

14. Lo! thou-hast-driven-out mine-own-self this-day, from-over-the-face o f-t h e-adamic: then-from-the-face-thine shall-I-be-hid, and-I-shall-be-staggering and-rov-ing in-the-earth: and-he-shall-be, every-one finding-me, he-who-shall-slay-me.

13. Et-il-dit, *Kain,* à-IHOAH, grande-est la-per-versité-mienne par-la-puri-fication.

14. Voici! tu-as-chassé l' ipséité-mienne ce-jour, de-dessus-la-face de-l'élément-adamique: donc-de-la-face-à-toi je-me-cacherai-avec-soin, et-j'existerai tremblant et-vaguant-en-la-terre: et-il-sera, tout-trouvant-moi, le-qui-accablera-moi.

---

thenceforth, only *a calamity.* Nevertheless, the root of life חה, remains there still, and this word receives from it enough force to designate sometimes *desire,* and the *substance* which is its object: but if this root is altered entirely, as in עוה then nothing good subsists: it is *perversity, the absolute depravation of being.*

Now, from the verb חוה, *to be-being,* was formed the root און or הון, by the addition of the final character ן, image of every increase and sign of produced being: we have seen its several acceptations. It is in the same manner that, from the verb, עוה *to be depraved, perverted,* is formed the substantive עון or עוון, whose signification and origin I have just explained.

v. 14. יהרגני, *he-who-shall-slay-me....* Here, by the effect of an ellipsis of another kind, is a verb, employed according to the positive form, active movement, third person future, which is transformed into a qualificative noun, in order to become the epithet of every being who finding *Kain,* shall slay him.

v. 15. לכן, *thus-saying....* This is the assimilative preposition כן inflected by the directive article ל. The Hellenist translators who have seen the negation לא are evidently mistaken, as is proved by the Samaritan and Chaldaic paraphrasts who read it as I have.

יקם, *he-shall-be-caused-to-raise....* This expression is remarkable for the manner in which it has been misinterpreted by nearly all the translators. Moses did not say, as he has been made to say, that he

15. Wa-îâomer l'ô
IHÔAH, la-chen chol-horeg
Kaîn shibehathîm îukkam
waîashem I H Ô A H l'Kaîn
âôth l'billethî hacchoth âôth-
ô chol motzæ-ô.

וַיֹּאמֶר לוֹ יְהֹוָה לָכֵן כָּל־הֹרֵג קַיִן
שִׁבְעָתַיִם יֻקָּם וַיָּשֶׂם יְהֹוָה לְקַיִן
אוֹת לְבִלְתִּי הַכּוֹת־אֹתוֹ כָּל־
מֹצְאוֹ :

16. Wa-îetzæ Kaîn mi-
l'pheneî IHÔAH wa-îesheb b'
æretz-nôd kidemath heden.

וַיֵּצֵא קַיִן מִלִּפְנֵי יְהֹוָה וַיֵּשֶׁב
בְּאֶרֶץ־נוֹד קִדְמַת־עֵדֶן :

17. Wa-îedah Kaîn æth-
âisheth-ô, wa-thahar wa-
theled æth-Hanôch, wa-îhî-
boneh whîr, wa-îkerâshem
h a-w h î r che-shem b e n-ô
Hanôch.

וַיֵּדַע קַיִן אֶת־אִשְׁתּוֹ וַתַּהַר וַתֵּלֶד
אֶת־חֲנוֹךְ וַיְהִי בֹּנֶה עִיר וַיִּקְרָא
שֵׁם הָעִיר כְּשֵׁם בְּנוֹ חֲנוֹךְ :

---

who shall kill *Kain* shall be punished seven-fold; but that he who shall
slay him shall give him seven times more strength. The verb קוֹם,
which is used in this instance, is the same as the one used in v. 8. of
this chapter, to depict the action of *Kain* being raised against his
brother. This must not be forgotten, for this verb is purposely repeated here. Moses has employed it according to the excitative form,
passive movement, future tense. He would have it understood by
this, that *Kain* shall influence in such a manner the being who would
slay him, that this being shall himself receive the blows which he
believes will fall upon *Kain*, and increase sevenfold his strength in
thinking to annihilate it.

v. 16. All these terms have been explained.

15. And-he-declared-his-will unto-him, IHOAH, thus saying; e v e r y-one-slaying *Kain,* seven-fold he-shall-be-caused-to-raise (*Kain*): and-he-put, IHOAH, unto-*Kain,* a-token, in-order-that-not-at-all could-strike-him, everyone-finding-him.

16. A n d - h e-withdrew, *Kain,* from-over-against the-face of-IHOAH, and-dwelt in-the-land of-the-banishment, (of the staggering w i t h fright) t h e-foregone-principle of-temporal-sensibleness.

17. And-he-knew, *Kain,* the-intellectual-m a t e-h i s-own (his volitive faculty): and-she-conceived a n d-she bare the-selfsameness of-*Henoch,* (the founder, the central might): then-he-builded a-sheltering-w a r d, and-he-designated-the-name-of-that-ward by-the-name of-the-son-his-own *Henoch.*

15. Et-il-déclara sa-volonté à-lui IHOAH, ainsi disant; tout-accablant *Kain* les-sept-fois il-fera-exalter *Kain*: et-il-mit, IHOAH, à-*Kain* un-signe afin-de-nullement-pouvoir frapper-l u i, tout-trouvant-lui.

16. Et-il-se-retira, *Kain,* de-devant le-face de-IHOAH; et-il-alla habiter dans-la-terre d'exil (de la dissension de l'effroi), l'antériorité temporelle de-la-sensibilité-élémentaire.

17. Et-il-connut, *Kain* la-femme-intellectuelle-sienne (sa faculté volitive): et-elle-conçut et-elle-enfanta l'-existence-de-*H e n o c h* (la force centrale, c e l u i qui fonde): ensuite-il-f u t-édifiant un-circuit-de-retraite, (un lieu fort) et-il-désigna-le-nom-de-ce-circuit par-le-nom-du-fils-à-lui, *Henoch.*

---

v. 17. חֲנוֹךְ, *Henoch*.... Again I urge the reader to give close attention to the proper names; for to them Moses attaches great importance. The greater part of the hieroglyphic mysteries are now in the form of these names. The one referred to in this passage, is composed of the two roots חן and אךְ. The first חן, characterizes proper, elementary existence: it is a kind of strengthening of the analogous root הן, more used, and which designates *things* in general. The second אךְ, contains the idea of every compression, of every effort that the being makes upon itself, or upon another, for the

18. Wa-îwaled la-Hanôċh æth-Whirad, w'Whirad îalad æth-Mehoûjaæl w'Mehoûjaæl îalad æth-Methoûshaæl îalad æth-Lameċh.

וַיִּוָּלֵד לַחֲנוֹךְ אֶת־עִירָד וְעִירָד יָלַד אֶת־מְחוּיָאֵל וּמְחוּיָאֵל יָלַד אֶת־מְתוּשָׁאֵל וּמְתוּשָׁאֵל יָלַד אֶת־לָמֶךְ :

19. Wa-îkkah-lô Lameċh shethî nashîm, shem haâhath Whadah, w'shem hashenith Tzillah.

וַיִּקַּח־לוֹ לֶמֶךְ שְׁתֵּי נָשִׁים שֵׁם הָאַחַת עָדָה וְשֵׁם הַשֵּׁנִית צִלָּה :

---

purpose of fixing itself or another. The verb which comes from these two roots, חָנוֹךְ signifies *to fix, to found, to institute, to arrest any existence whatsoever.*

It is from a composition quite similar, that the personal pronoun אָנוֹכִי, *myself,* in Hebrew, results; that is to say אָן or הֵן, *the finished, corporeal being,* אוּךְ, *founded,* י, *in me.*

v. 18. עִירָד, *Whirad....* This noun is formed from two roots עוּר and רד: the first עוּר, offers the idea of all excitation, ardour, interior passion: the second רד, depicts proper, indefinite movement, as that of *a wheel,* for example. For the rest, consult Radical Vocabulary for these roots and those which follow.

מְחוּיָאֵל, *Mehoujael....* This is the verb חוּי, *to manifest, to announce, to demonstrate,* employed as facultative, according to the intensive form, by means of the initial character מ and terminated by the root אל, which adds the idea of strength and unfoldment.

מְתוּשָׁאֵל, *Methoushael....* This noun comes from two distinct roots. The first מוּת, designates *death:* the second שאה, characterizes every emptiness, every yawning void, every gulf opened to swallow up. In the hieroglyphic formation of the word מְתוּשָׁאֵל, the con-

18. A n d-it-was-caused-to-beget unto *Henoch* the-selfsameness-o f-*W h i r a d ,* (stirring-up motion, self-leading p a s s i o n): and *W h i r a d* begat *Mehujael* (elemental manifestation of existence) and-*Mehujael* begat *Methushael,* (d e a t h ' s fathomless pit): and-*Meth-ushael* begat *Lamech* (the tie of what tends to dissolution, thing's pliant bond).

19. And-he-took - u n t o-him, *Lamech,* two corporeal-wives (two natural facul-ties); the-name of-the-one-was *Whadah,* (the periodic, the testifying) and-the-name of-the-second, *Tzillah* (the deep, the dark).

18. E t-i l f u t-faire-pro-duire à-*Henoch* l'existence-de-*Whirad,* (le mouvement excitateur, la passion, la vo-lonté c o n d u c t r i c e); et-*Whirad* produisit celle-de-*Mehoujael* (la manifestation de l'existence) et *Mehou-jael* produisit celle-de-*Me-thoushael,* (le gouffre de la mort), et-*Methoushael* pro-duisit-celle-de-*Lamech* (l e nœud qui saisit la dissolu-tion et l'arrête; le lien flex-ible des choses).

19. Et-il-prit-p o u r-l u i, *Lamech,* deux épouses-cor-porelles, (deux facultés phy-siques): le-nom de-la-pre-mière était-*Whadah* (la périodique, l'évidente): et-le-nom de-la-seconde, *Tzillah* (la profonde, l'obscure, la voilée).

---

vertible sign of the first root ו, has been transposed to serve as liaison with the second, to which has been joined by contraction, the syllable אל whose signification I have given.

למך, *Lamech*.... The roots of this name are clear and simple. It is, on the one part, לֹ, which contains all ideas of cohesion and agglutination, and on the other מוך, which develops all those of lique-faction, dissolution, prostration, submission, etc. Therefore, this name characterizes the kind of bond which prevents a thing, at first vehem-ent, violent, and now subdued, softened, cast down, ready to be dis-solved, from being dissolved and from being wholly dissipated.

The reader can observe that *Lamech* is here the descendant of *Adam,* by *Kain* in the sixth generation, because we shall see reappear another who shall be by *Seth,* in the eighth.

v. 19. שתי נשים, *two-corporeal-wives*.... I beg the attentive

20. Wa-theled Whadah æth-Jabal, houâ haîah âbî îsheb âohel w'mikeneh.

וַתֵּלֶד עָדָה אֶת־יָבָל הוּא הָיָה אֲבִי יֹשֵׁב אֹהֶל וּמִקְנֶה :

21. W'shem âhî-ô Joubal, houâ haîah âbî cholthophesh chi-nor w'hoûgab.

וְשֵׁם אָחִיו יוּבָל הוּא הָיָה אֲבִי כָל־תֹּפֵשׂ כִּנּוֹר וְעוּגָב :

---

reader to remember that intellectual man אִישׁ, *Aish*, had not yet appeared upon the cosmogonical scene, and that Moses had only named universal man אָדָם, *Adam*, when he mentioned for the first time intellectual woman אשה, **Aishah,** volitive faculty of universal man. Thus it is, that the name of the Adamic element אדמה, had preceded the name itself of *Adam*. The hierographic writer follows still the same course. Corporeal man אֱנוֹשׁ, *Ænosh*, is not born, and behold already corporeal woman who appears as the double physical faculty of the cosmogonic being, designated by the name of *Lamech*, descendant of *Kain*.

I shall not dwell now upon the radical etymology of the word which Moses uses on this occasion. I shall wait until making the analysis of the name itself of corporeal man אֱנוֹשׁ, from which it is derived. For the moment, I shall only observe that corporeal woman is not presented as such, but as divided in two physical faculties, *Whadah* and *Tzillah*, the evident and the veiled, whose productions we are about to see.

עדה, *Whadah*.... In this proper name should be seen the root עוד, which characterizes the periodic return of the same thing, its evidence and the testimony rendered.

צלה, *Tzillah*.... This name is attached to the root צול, which

20. And-she-bare, *Whadah,* the-selfsameness of-*Jabal,* (the over flowing, the waterish, the plenty of nature)he-who was the-father (founder) of-the abode-aloft, (repairing distinguished place) and-of-the-own-making-might, (lawful property).

20. Et-elle-enfanta *Whadah* ce-qui-concerne-*Jabal,* (le flux des eaux, l'abondance naturelle, la fertilité), lui-qui fut le-père-(le créateur) de l'habitation-élevée (lieu de retour fixe et remarquable,) et-de-la-force-concentrante et- appropriatrice, (la propriété).

21. And-the-name-of-the-brother-of-him was-*J u b a l,* (universal effluence, principle of sound, jubilation, thriving) he-who was the-father (founder) of-every conception, hint-brightness-like and-love-worthy (useful and pleasing arts).

21. Et-le-nom du-frère-à-lui était-*Joubal,* (le fluide universel, le-principe du son celui qui communique la joie et la prospérité), lui-qui fut le-père de-toute-conception-lumineuse et-digne-d'amour (de toutes les sciences et de tous les arts utiles et agréables).

---

designates a depth to which the light cannot penetrate, a dark, gloomy place; a shadowy, veiled thing, etc.

v. 20. יבל, *Jabal....* This is the root בל or בול spoken of in v. 2 of this chapter, verbalized by the initial adjunction י.

ומקנה, *and-of-the-own-making-might....* I refer the reader to v. 1 and 2 of this chapter, wherein I have spoken of the root קן, and of the verbs קון and קנה, which are drawn from it. This root, which develops here the idea of taking possession, of property, is governed by the plastic sign of exterior action מ.

v. 21. יובל, *Jubal....* This name is attached to the same root as that of *Jabal,* but it is taken in a loftier sense, by means of the sign ו, which makes it a continued facultative. The Hellenists have seen in this *Jubal,* a player upon the psaltery and harp; and Saint Jerome, a master of song upon the harp and upon the organ ! this latter translator has only followed the Chaldaic targum.

22. W'Tzillah gam-hîa
îaledah   æth-Thoûbal-Kaîn
lotesh čhol-horesh nehosheth
w'barzel, w'âhôth Thoûbal-
Kaîn Nahomah.

וְצִלָּה גַם־הִיא יָלְדָה אֶת־תּוּבַל
קַיִן לֹטֵשׁ כָּל־חֹרֵשׁ נְחֹשֶׁת וּבַרְזֶל
וַאֲחוֹת תּוּבַל־קַיִן נַעֲמָה :

23. Wa-îâomer Lemečh l'
nashaî-ô Whadah w'Tzillah,
shemahan kôl-î noshei Le-
mečh, ha-âzennah âmerath-
î čhi aîshharagthî l'phitzehî
w'îeled l'habburath-î.

וַיֹּאמֶר לֶמֶךְ לְנָשָׁיו עָדָה וְצִלָּה
שְׁמַעַן קוֹלִי נְשֵׁי לֶמֶךְ הַאֲזֵנָּה
אִמְרָתִי כִּי אִישׁ הָרַגְתִּי לְפִצְעִי
וְיֶלֶד לְחַבֻּרָתִי :

כנור, *brightness*.... This word which these same interpreters
have made to signify a harp, is only the word נור *light*, or *glory*,
inflected by the assimilative article כ. The reader has observed a
great number of blunders which have no other source than the oversight of this important article.

ועוגב, *and-worthy-of-love*.... I cannot conceive how one has seen
here a psaltery or an organ, since it is known that the Hebrew word
עגב signifies loving attention, and that its Arabic analogue عجب expresses
that which leads to admiration, joy and happiness. All these errors
proceed from having taken the facultative הׂשֵׂפ, *to be comprehending*,
seizing, in the material sense, instead of the spiritual; that instead
of seeing an effect of the intelligence, one has seen a movement of the
hand.

v. 22. תובל־קין, *Thubal-Kain*.... It is always the same root בל,
from which are formed the names of Jabal and Jubal; but ruled on
this occasion by the sign of reciprocity ת. The name of *Kain*, which
is added to it, has been explained as much as it could be, in v. 1, of
this chapter.

נעמה, *Nawhomah*.... The root עם contains all ideas of union,
junction, bringing together: it is, on the one part, the sign of material
sense and on the other, the plastic sign of exterior action, which, as

22. And *Tzillah* also, she-b a r e w h a t-relates-to-*Thu-bal-Kain* (mutual yielding of the central might), whetting e v e r y-cutting-b r a s s and-iron: and-the-kindred-of-*Thubal-Kain* was *Naw-homah* (meeting might, sociableness).

23. And-he-said, *Lamech*, u n t o-t h e-corporeal - wives-his-own, his bodily faculties) *Whadah*, and-*Tzillah*: hearken-to the-voice-m i n e, ye-wives of-*Lamech;* listen-to-the-speech-mine: f o r-a s the-intellectual-man (that is to say, man individuated by his own will) I-have-slain-for-the-stretching (solution, freedom)-mine; and-the-p r o g e n y (particular stock) for-the framing-mine (in society):

22. Et-*Tzillah* aussi, elle-e n f a n t a ce-qui-concerne-*Thoubal-Kain* (la diffusion abondante de la force central), aiguisant tout-coupant d'airain et-de-fer: et-la-parenté de *Thoubal-Kain* fut *Nawhomah* (la sociation, l'-aggrégation).

23. Et-il-d i t, *Lamech*, aux é p o u s e s corporelles-siennes (ses facultés physiques) *Whadah* et-*Tzillah*: é c o u t e z l a-voix-mienne, épouses de-*Lamech;* prêtez l'oreille-à la-parole-à-m o i: car comme l'homme-intellectuel (l'homme individualisé par sa propre volonté) j'ai-accablé (détruit) pour-la-dilatation (la solution, la libre extension)-mienne, et-la-progéniture (la lignée, la famille particulière), pour-la-formation-à-moi:

final character, offers the image of generalization. Taken as noun, this root designates *a people;* as relation, it acquires a copulative force and signifies *with.* In this instance it is employed as continued facultative, passive movement, feminine, and signifies literally, *the-becoming-united, assembled, formed by aggregation.*

v. 23.... This is one of the verses of the Cosmogony of Moses, that its translators have mutilated the most. I beg the reader to examine this Latin which is the exact translation of the Greek: "Dixitque Lamech uxoribus suis Adæ et Sellæ: audite vocem meam, uxores Lamech, ausculate sermonem meum; quoniam occidi virum in vulnus meum et adolescentulum in livorem meum." This is to say, that after

24. Chi shibehathaîm îuk-   כִּי שִׁבְעָתַיִם יֻקַּם קָיִן וְלֶמֶךְ
kam Kaîn, w'Lemeĉh shibe-
haîm w'shibehah.   שִׁבְעִים וְשִׁבְעָה :

---

all the emphasis that Lamech has given to make his wives listen, he ridiculously tells them that he has killed a man to his wounding, and a young man to his hurt. Let us examine the real meaning of this phrase.

אִישׁ, *the-intellectual-man*.... As I have had occasion to state several times, the Hebraic tongue possesses many expressions to designate *man*. These expressions, formed with high wisdom, all contain a figurative and hieroglyphic sense beyond the literal one. I have taken care to make an exact analysis of them according as they present themselves to me. I have already explained the name of *Adam*, universal man, and that of *Aish*, intellectual man, and made clear the difference. The reader can review what I have said upon this subject in v. 6, ch. 1, and in v. 23, ch. II. The name of *Ænosh*, corporeal man, has not yet been presented for our examination; but we have already seen the physical faculties which lead to it. These several expressions for designating *man*, are very far from being synonyms. Moses who carefully distinguishes them, places and uses them with an infinite art. The one referred to here, is not corporeal man, as its trans- lators would believe, but intellectual man; that is to say, man individualized by his efficient will. Therefore it is not a man, properly so-called, that *Lamech* kills, but the moral individuality of man which he causes to disappear. He does not kill it "in vulnus", to his wound- ing, to Lamech's, which has no sense.

לְפִצְעִי, *for-the-stretching-mine*.... That is to say for my extension, for the free exercise of my forces. This is proved beyond question, by the root פּוּץ, whence this word is derived, and which is related to all ideas of diffusion, of loosening, of setting at liberty. The Chaldaic פצה, the Syriac ڢڡ, the Samaritan , the Arabic فصيه all give evidence in favour of this meaning.

וִילֶד, *and-the-progeny*.... This is not a young man, "adolescen- tulum" which Lamech kills or destroys, it is the spirit of the race,

24. So-seven-fold it-shall-be - caused - to - raise *Kain*, and *Lamech* seventy and-seven-fold.	24. Ainsi les-sept-fois il-sera-fait-exalter *Kain*, et-*Lamech* septante et-s e p t-fois.

---

the lineage, the filiation, which he sacrifices with אִישׁ, individualized man, by his will, and this is why:

לְחַבְּרתִי, *for-the-framing-mine....* The term is clear as daylight. Not only the root בַּר, *a son*, and the verb בָּרוֹא *to create*, whence this word is derived, lead to this meaning, but also the analogous verbs used in Chaldaic, Syriac, Ethiopic, etc., leave no doubt in this regard. Now, let the reader consider whether there is anything more just than this phrase, wherein Lamech, considered as a certain bond destined to arrest the dissolution of things, as a legislative force, announces, that to extend general liberty, he has destroyed the moral individuality of man; and that, to form the great family of peoples, he has destroyed the spirit of the particular family, which is opposed to him.

Whatever Lamech may be, and neither can I, nor do I wish to explain his origin, he is, as we have seen, the bond of that which is subdued in his passion: for, he has two corporeal wives, or rather two physical faculties which give him; *Jabal*, principle of aqueous effusion, whence come terrestrial fertility, the settling of wandering tribes and property; *Jubal*, principle of ethereal effusion, source of moral affections and of happiness: *Thubal-Kain*, principle of central or mercurial effusion, whence result physical power, metals, and the instruments that they furnish; and finally, *Nawhomah*, principle of union in society. This is a chain of ideas which leaves nothing to be desired and which throws upon the phrase alluded to, a light that I believe irresistible.

v. 24. יֻקַּם, *it-shall-be-caused-to-raise....* What I have said concerning this word, can be reviewed in v. 15 of this chapter. That which was applicable then to *Kain*, has become so for *Lamech*, but in a much more eminent degree.

25. Wa-îedah Adam hôd æth-âisheth-ô wa-theled ben, w a-t h i k e r â   æth-shem-ô Sheth, chi-shath lî Ælohîm, zerah aher thahath Hebel chi harag-ô Kaîn.

יֵּדַע אָדָם עוֹד אֶת־אִשְׁתּוֹ וַתֵּלֶד בֵּן וַתִּקְרָא אֶת־שְׁמוֹ שֵׁת כִּי שָׁת־לִי אֱלֹהִים זֶרַע אַחֵר תַּחַת הֶבֶל כִּי הֲרָגוֹ קָיִן :

---

v. 25.   שֵׁת, *Sheth*.... The signification of this name is of the utmost importance for those seeking to penetrate the essence of things. This name, as mysterious as those of *Kain* and *Habel* could never be translated exactly. All that I can do is to furnish the means necessary for unveiling the hieroglyphic depth. First let us examine the root. The two signs which compose it are שׁ, sign of relative duration and of movement, and that of reciprocity, of mutual tendency, of the liaison of things, ת. United by the universal, convertible sign, they form the verbal root שׁוּת, which is related to every action of placing, dis- posing, setting, founding. Considered as noun, the root שׁת, signifies *foundation*, in all of the acceptations of this word, and depicts the good, as well as the bad, the highest, as well as the lowest of things. It can signify also, every kind of beverage, and provides the verb שׁתֹה *to drink;* because it is water, which, by its determined movement, in- dicates always the deepest place, that upon which is placed the found- ation.

But not only does the word שׁת express at once, the foundation of things, and the element which inclines to it, but it also serves in Hebrew, to designate the number *two*, in its feminine acceptation, and in Chaldaic, the number *six*. I shall not speak now concerning the signification of these numbers, because it would engage me in details that I wish to avoid: later on I shall do so. Suffice to say here, that the name of *Sheth*, or *Seth*, presents itself, as those of *Kain* and of *Habel*, under two acceptations wholly opposed. We have seen in treat- ing of the latter two, that if *Kain* was the emblem of force and power, he was also that of rage and usurpation; we have seen that if one considered *Habel* as the emblem of thought and of the universal soul,

25. And-he-knew, *Adam,* again, the-intellectual-mate-his-own (his efficient volitive faculty): and-she-bare a-son; and-she-assigned for-name-to-him *Sheth* (the bottom, the site): for-thus (said she) he-has-settled-for-me, ʜᴇ-the-Gods, a-seed other of-t h e-a b a t e m e n t (falling-down) of *H a b e l,* whilst he-slew-him, *Kain.*

25. Et-il-connut, *Adam,* encore, l'épouse-intellectu-elle-sienne (sa faculté volitive efficiente): et-elle-en-fanta un-fils; et-elle-assigna c e-n o m-à-l u i *S h e t h* (l a base, le fondement): parce-qu'ainsi il-a-fondé pour-moi, (dit - elle) ʟᴜɪ - les Dieux, une-semence autre de-l'abattement d'*H a b e l,* lorsqu'il-accabla-lui, *Kaiн.*

---

he was also regarded as that of nothingness and of absolute void: now, *Sheth* is the object of a contrast no less striking. The Hebrews, it is true, have represented him as the type of a chosen family; the historian Josephus has attributed to him the erection of those famous columns, upon which was carved the history of mankind and the principles of universal morals; certain oriental peoples and particularly those who make profession of sabæanism, have revered him as prophet; indeed many of the gnostics called themselves *Sethians*: but it is known, on the other hand, that the Egyptians confusing him with *Typhon*, called him *the violent, the destructor*, and gave him the odious surnames of *Bubon* and of *Smou*: it is also known that the Arabs considering him as the genius of evil, called him *Shathan*, by adding to his primitive name שׁת the augmentative final ן. This terrible name, given to the infernal adversary, *Satan,* in passing into the Hebraic tongue with the poems of *Job*, has brought there all the unfavourable ideas which the Arabs and the Egyptians attached to the name of *Seth, Sath* or *Soth*, without harming, nevertheless, the posterity of this same *Sheth*, whom the Hebrews have continued to regard as the one from whom men, in general, and their patriarch, in particular, drew their origin.

תחת, *of-the-abatement....* This word is one of extreme importance for the understanding of this verse. It indicates clearly, the source of this new seed from which *Sheth* has been formed. The Hellenists and Saint Jerome, took care not to see nor render it. The Samaritan translator is the only one who has given it attention. He has rendered it by ᴧᴊᴧ2ᴴ . *transition, mutation, misfortune.*

26. W'l'Sheth gam-houâ
îullad-ben, wa-îkerâ æ t h-
shem-ô Ænôsh âz hoûhal li-
keroâ b'shem IHÔAH.

וּלְשֵׁת גַּם - הוּא יֻלַּד - בֶּן וַיִּקְרָא
אֶת־שְׁמוֹ אֱנוֹשׁ אָז הוּחַל לִקְרֹא
בְּשֵׁם יְהֹוָה :

---

v. 26. אֱנוֹשׁ, *corporeal man*.... This is the third name which
Moses has employed to designate man. By the first, אָדַם, he designated universal man, divine similitude; by the second, אִישׁ, he characterized intellectual man, considered relative to the volitive faculty,
free and efficient, which individualizes him and makes him a particular
being; now he considers man in relation to his physical faculties,
and he calls him אֱנוֹשׁ *corporeal man*.

Let us examine the inner composition of this third name. Two
roots are found here contracted, אוּן־נוֹשׁ. The first אוּן develops, as I
have already said, the contradictory ideas of being and nothingness,
of strength and weakness, of virtue and vice. The second נוֹשׁ, expresses the instability of temporal things, their caducity, their infirm-
ity. This last root is found in the Arabic ﻧﺶ , in the Syriac ﻧﻮ ,
and is recognized easily in the Greek νοσεῖν, which is derived from it.

Thus constituted, the word אֱנוֹשׁ produces its feminine נשה: but
here the hieroglyphic meaning is discovered. I have already remarked
that Moses or his instructors, wishing to draw from the intellectual
principle אִישׁ, the volitive faculty אשה, makes the sign of manifestation disappear. Now, in order to deduce the physical faculties of
the corporeal being אֱנוֹשׁ they suppress the initial sign of power א,
and that of light י , and put the word נש thus restricted, in the
masculine plural נשׁים, a number which, as we have learned by the
Grammar is confounded with the dual feminine.

Here already are three different names given to man, considered
as universal, intellectual or corporeal, of which the translators have
made no distinction. Further on we shall find a fourth. I urge the
reader to reflect upon the gradation that Moses has kept in the
employment of these terms. At first, it is the Divinity who creates אדם
Adam, universal man, and who gives him for companion אשה, efficient
volitive faculty. This faculty, become חוּרה *Hewah*, elementary life,
creates in its turn אִישׁ, intelligent being, man individualized by his
will. Afterward, it is the intellectual being, who, under the name of
Sheth, son of *Adam*, brings forth corporeal man אֱנוֹשׁ, *Ænosh*, but
already the physical faculties נשׁים *Noshim*, had been named as wives
of *Lamech*, descendant of *Adam*, by *Kain* in the sixth generation.

I beg the reader also, to compare carefully *Kain* and *Sheth*, and
the posterity of the one, with the posterity of the other. If he recalls

26. And-unto-*Sheth*,-also-him, it-was-caused-to beget a-son; and-he-assigned for-name-to-him *Æ n o s h* (corporeal man), then it-was-caused-to-hope by-the-calling-u p o n in-the-name of-IHOAH.

26. Et-à-*Sheth*, aussi-lui, il-fut-fait-engendrer un-fils: et-il-assigna ce-n o m-à-l u i *Ænosh* (l'homme corporel), alors il-fut-espérer, selon-l' action d'invoquer au-nom de-IHOAH.

---

that *Kain* produced *Henoch* and if he examines now the one which produces *Sheth*, he will find that the name of *Ænosh*, here referred to, differs only from the former by a certain softening in the characters of which both are composed. The vowel ח, which begins the name of *Henoch*, indicates a painful effort; the consonant כ, which terminates it, a sharp compression: on the contrary, the vowel א which begins that of *Ænosh*, announces a tranquil power, and the consonant ש, which terminates it, a gentle movement relative to a transient duration. *Henoch* arrests, fixes, centralizes: *Ænosh* lets go, relaxes, carries to the circumference.

הוֹחֶל, *it-was-caused-to-hope*.... The verb הוּל, in question here, springs from the root חל, which presents the idea of a persevering effort, of a sharp tension. As verb, it would mean in this instance, for it contains besides a great number of acceptations, *to suffer with patience one's misfortunes, to hope, to place faith in something*. It is employed according to the excitative form, passive movement, third person, past tense. I urge the reader to note with what adroitness, Moses, producing upon the scene of the world corporeal and suffering man, gives him the necessary firmness to support his sorrow courageously, by putting his hope in the invocation of the Sacred Name of the Divinity.

I urge the reader to refer constantly to the Radical Vocabulary to obtain a more ample account of the roots that I have often only indicated. This research will be especially useful in the chapter which follows.

SEPHER BERÆSHITH
H.

סֵפֶר בְּרֵאשִׁית ח׳

1. Zeh Sepher thô-ledoth Adam b'iôm beroà Ælohîm Adam bi-demoûth Ælohîm hashah âoth-ô.

זֶה סֵפֶר תּוֹ־לְדֹת אָדָם בְּיוֹם בְּרֹא אֱלֹהִים אָדָם בִּדְמוּת אֱלֹהִים עָשָׂה אֹתוֹ :

2. Zaċher w-nekębah bherâ am wa-îbareċh âoth-am, wa-îkerâ æth-shemam Adam b'iôm bi-barâm.

זָכָר וּנְקֵבָה בְּרָאָם וַיְבָרֶךְ אֹתָם וַיִּקְרָא אֶת־שְׁמָם אָדָם בְּיוֹם הִבָּרְאָם :

3. Wa-îhî Adam shelos-hîm w-mâth shanah wa-iôled bi-demouth-ô b'tzalem-ô wa-îkerâ æth-shem-ô Sheth.

וַיְחִי אָדָם שְׁלֹשִׁים וּמְאַת שָׁנָה וַיּוֹלֶד בִּדְמוּתוֹ בְּצַלְמוֹ וַיִּקְרָא אֶת־שְׁמוֹ שֵׁת :

---

v. 1. All these terms have been previously explained.

v. 2. שמם, *universal-name*.... This is the substantive שם, to which Moses here adds the final collective sign ם, to leave no doubt as to the universal signification which he gives to *Adam*. I wish to call particular attention to this sign, as I shall refer to it again upon a very important occasion.

v. 3. שנה, *of-being's-temporal-revolving-change*.... Before explaining this word, I believe it advisable to give the etymology of the names of the numbers about to be presented in this chapter. These names are not placed undesignedly or simply introduced in chronological order, as has been supposed. Those who have understood them in their strict acceptations, and who have taken them literally as

GENESIS V.

COSMOGONIE V.

1. This-is the-book of-the symbolical-progenies o f - *Adam,* at-the-day that-creating, HE-the-Gods, *A d a m* (collective man) in-the-like-making-like HIM-the-Gods, he-made the-selfsameness-his.

2. Male and-female, he-c r e a t e d-t h e m; and-he-blessed-them, and-he-assigned this-u n i v e r s a l-n a m e *Adam,* at-the-day, of-the-being-created-them - universal-ly.

3. And-he-was-b e i n g, *Adam,* three-tens and-one-hundred (extension, ' stretching), of-being's temporal-revolving-change; a n d-he-b e g a t by-the-like-making-like-himself, in-the-shadow-his-own (an i s s u e d off-spring) a n d-h e-assigned this-name-to-him, *Sheth.*

1. Ceci-est le-livre des-caractéristiques-générations d'*A d a m,* dès-le-jour que-créant, LUI-les-Dieux, *Adam* (l'homme universel) selon-l'action-assimilante de-LUI-les-Dieux, il-fit l a-s é i t é-sienne.

2. Mâle et-femelle il-créa-eux; et-il-bénit-eux; et-il-a s s i g n a ce-nom-universel *A d a m,* dès-le-jour d'être-créés-eux-universellement.

3. Et-il-exista, *A d a m,* trois-décuples et-une-centaine (une extension), de-mutation-temporelle-ontolo-gique; et-il-généra selon-l'action-d'assimiler-à-lui, en-ombre-s i e n n e (u n ê t r e émané) et-il-assigna-ce-nom-à-lui, *Sheth.*

---

being applied to days, months or years, have proved their ignorance or their bad faith. To believe that Moses has really restricted to a duration of six days, such as we understand them today, the act of universal creation, or that he here restricts the lives of the cosmogonic beings of which he speaks, to a certain number of years such as we calculate them, is to do him gratuitous injury, and treat him in this respect, as one would treat an orator whose eloquence one condemns before learning the tongue in which the orator is expressing himself.

4. Wa-îhîou îmeî-Adam
ahareî. hôlid-ô æth-Sheth
shemoneh mâoth shanah,
wa-iôled banîm w'banôth.

וַיִּהְיוּ יְמֵי־אָדָם אַחֲרֵי הוֹלִידוֹ
אֶת־שֵׁת שְׁמֹנֶה מֵאֹת שָׁנָה וַיּוֹלֶד
בָּנִים וּבָנוֹת :

I believe I have made it sufficiently understood that the word יוֹם
day, by which Moses designates the phenomenal manifestations of the
act of the creation, should be applied to a certain revolution of light,
which the genius of this wonderful man, or of his instructors, had
foreseen. In the note which follows I shall explain, that the word
שנה, which has been translated by *year*, signifies an ontological, temporal duration; that is to say, relative to the diverse mutations of
the being to which it is applied. I shall omit in the following, the
ontological epithet, in order to avoid delays, but it is implied. Here
are the names of numbers.

I. אחד, *one*. The root חד, from which this word is formed, and
which is sometimes taken for unity itself, particularly in Chaldaic,
signifies literally, *a point, a summit, the sharpest part of a thing; the
top of a pyramid.* It is division arrested, subjugated by a sort of
effort; as the two signs ד and ח which compose it, indicate. In the
feminine it is written אחת.

II. שן, שני or שנים, *two*. The root שן, composed of the sign of
relative duration ש, and that of produced being or growth ן, contains
all ideas of mutation, of transition, of passing from one state to another, of redundancy. Thus the name of this number in bringing
diversity, change and variation, is the opposite in everything from the
preceding number, which, as we have seen, arrests division and tends
to immutability. The feminine is שת, שתי and שתים.

III. שלוֹש, *three*. This word is formed from the two contracted
roots של־לוש, as opposed in their significations as in the arrangement
of their characters. By the first של, is understood every extraction
or subtraction; by the second לוש, on the contrary, every amalgamation, every kneading together, if I may use this word. Thus the name
of number *three*, presents therefore, in Hebrew, under a new form,
the opposed ideas contained in *one* and *two;* that is, the extraction,

4. **And-they-were the-days** (the manifested lights) of-*A d a m,* a f t e r-the-causing-him-to-beget the-selfsame-ness-of-*Sheth,* eight hundreds of-revolving-change: a n d-he-t e e m e d sons and-daughters (many issued beings).

4. Et-ils-furent les-jours (les manifestations phénoméniques) d'*Adam* après-le-faire-enfanter-à-lui l'ipséité-de-*Sheth,* huit centaines de-mutation-temporelle: et-il-généra fils et-filles (une foule d'êtres emanés).

---

consequence of the division, becomes a kind of relative unity. This new unity is represented in a great many words under the idea of peace, welfare, perfection, eternal happiness, etc.

IV. ארבע, *four.* I have spoken of this word in v. 10 of chapter II; it is needless to repeat. Its root רב involves every idea of strength, of solidity, of greatness, resulting from extent and numerical multiplication.

v. חמש, *five.* This word expresses a movement of contraction and of apprehension, as that which results from the five fingers of the hand grasping a thing, pressing tightly and warming it. Its root is double. חם, the first, designates the effect of the second, מש, that is to say, the former depicts the general envelopment, the heat which results and the effect of the contractile movement impressed by the latter.

VI. שש, *six.* The root שו contains all ideas of equality, of equilibrium, of fitness, of proportion in things. United to the sign of relative duration ש in order to form the name of this number, it becomes the symbol of every proportional and relative measure. It is quite well known that the number *six* is applied in particular, to the measure of the circle, and in general, to all proportional measures. One finds in the feminine, ששת, and the Chaldaic reads שרת: which is not unlike the name of number *two;* furthermore, between these there exist great analogies, since *six* is to *three*, what *two* is to *one;* and since we have seen that *three* represented a sort of unity.

VII. שבע, *seven.* One can review v. 3, chapter II, wherein I have given the origin of this word and stated why I attach to it ideas of complement, of accomplishment, and of the consummation of things and of times.

VIII. שמנה, *eight.* This word springs from the double root שום and מון. By the first שום, is understood the action of placing,

5. Wa-îhîou   ċhol-îmeî   וַיִּֽהְיוּ כָּל־יְמֵי אֲשֶׁר־חַי
Adam   âsher-haî   theoshah   תְּשַׁע מֵאוֹת שָׁנָה וּשְׁלֹשִׁים שָׁנָה
mæôth shanah w-sheloshîm
shanah, wa-îamoth.   וַיָּמֹת :

---

of putting one thing upon another; by the second מוּן that of specifying, of distinguishing by forms. It is therefore, the accumulation of forms that should be understood by this number. This signification is made obvious by that of the verb שָׁמוּן, which means literally, *to fatten, to make larger*.

IX. הֵשַׁע, *nine*. The root שַׁע, which signifies literally, *lime, cement*, draws with it all ideas of cementation, consolidation, restoration, conservation, etc. The verb שׁוּע, which comes from it, expresses the action of cementing, plastering, closing carefully. Therefore the name of this number, being visibly composed of this root שַׁע, governed by the sign of reciprocity ה, should be understood as cementation, as mutual consolidation. It maintains with number *three*, a very intimate relation, containing like it, ideas of preservation and salvation.

X. עֶשֶׂר, *ten*. This is to say, *the congregation of power proper, of elementary motive force*. This meaning results from the two contracted roots עֶשׂ־שַׂר. By the first עֶשׂ, is understood, every formation by aggregation; thence, the verb עָשֹׂה *to make;* by the second, שַׂר, every motive principle; thence, the verb שׁוּר *to direct, to govern*.

In going back now over these explanations, the general significations of the Hebraic decade can be given as follows:

1, principiation and stability: 2, distinction and transition: 3, extraction and liberation: 4, multiplication: 5, comprehension: 6, proportional measurement: 7, consummation, return: 8, accumulation of forms: 9, cementation, restoration: 10 aggregation, reforming power.

Excepting number twenty, which is drawn from number ten by the dual עֶשְׂרִים, 20, all decuple numbers, from 30 to 90 are formed from the plural of the primitive number; in this manner: 30, שְׁלֹשִׁים: 40, אַרְבָעִים: 50, חֲמִשִּׁים: 60, שִׁשִּׁים: 70,שִׁבְעִים: 80, שְׁמֹנִים: 90, תִּשְׁעִים. So that each decuple number is only the complement of its radical number.

מֵאת or מֵאָה, *one hundred*. The name of this number indicates an extension produced by the desire to be extended, to be manifested.

5. And-they-were all-the-days (manifested lights) of *A d a m* (collective man) which-he-lived-in, nine hundreds of revolving-change; and-thirty of-r e v o l v i n g change; and-he-deceased.

5. Et-ils-furent tous-les-jours (les manifestations phénoméniques) d'*A d a m* (l'homme universel) qu'il-exista, neuf centaines de-m u t a t i o n-temporelle, et-trois-décuple de-mutation; et-il-passa.

The root of this word אוה, literally *desire*, is here governed by the sign of exterior action מ. One finds the Arabic الا expressing *to extend* and *to dilate*. In nearly all the tongues of Asia, *mah* signifies *great*.

אלף, *one thousand*. That is to say, a very high, very strong and very powerful principle. It is the name of the first letter of the alphabet, א.

v. 4. שנה, *revolving-change*.... I now return to this word which the length of the preceding note forced me to slight. The Hellenists, and Saint Jerome following these unreliable masters, have rendered it by ἔτος, "annus", *a year*. But they have, as is their custom, restricted what was taken in a broad sense, and applied to a particular revolution, that which was applicable to an universal, ontological revolution. I have already spoken of this word in v. 14. Ch. I. Its root is שן which we have just now seen to be that of number *two* and containing every idea of mutation, of variation, of passing from one state to another. Thus the word שנה, expresses a temporal mutation, relative to the being which is its object. The Hebraic tongue has several terms for expressing the idea of temporal duration. עוד characterizes the same state continued, an actual duration; as relation, we translate it by *still;* חרש, carries the idea of a beginning of existence, either in the order of things, or in the order of time: in its most restricted sense, it means a monthly duration: שנה is applied to the transition of this same existence, to a mutation of the being: that is to say, that the being which is its object, is not found at the end of the period which it expresses, at the same point or in the same state that it was at its beginning: in the more restricted sense, it is the space of a year: finally, the last of these terms is שוב, which should mean every revolution which replaces the being in its original state. These divers periods, always relative to the being to which they are applied, can mean the most limited dura-

6. Wa-îhî-Sheth hamesh shanîm w-mâth shanah wa-iôled Ænosh.

וַיְחִי־שֵׁם חָמֵשׁ שָׁנִים וּמְאַת שָׁנָה וַיּוֹלֶד אֱנוֹשׁ:

7. Wa-îhî Sheth âhareî hôlîd-ô-æth-Ænôsh shebah shanîm w'shemoneh mæôth shanah wa-iôled banîm w-banôth.

וַיְחִי־שֵׁת אַחֲרֵי הוֹלִידוֹ אֶת־אֱנוֹשׁ שֶׁבַע שָׁנִים וּשְׁמֹנֶה מֵאוֹת שָׁנָה וַיּוֹלֶד בָּנִים וּבָנוֹת:

8. Wa-îhîou chol-î m e î Sheth s h e t h î m heshereh shanah, w-theshah mæôth shanah, wa-iamoth.

וַיִּהְיוּ כָּל־יְמֵי־שֵׁת שְׁתֵּים עֶשְׂרֵה שָׁנָה וּתְשַׁע מֵאוֹת שָׁנָה וַיָּמֹת:

9. Wa-îhî Ænosh thishe-hîm shanah wa-iôled æth-Keînan.

וַיְחִי אֱנוֹשׁ תִּשְׁעִים שָׁנָה וַיּוֹלֶד אֶת־קֵינָן:

---

tion, as well as that whose limits escape the human understanding. The numbers *one*, *two* and *seven* take their roots from this.

It is because the ancient periods have been restricted and particularized, that one has so badly understood the *Sethites* of the Egyptians, the *Saros* of the Chaldeans, the *Yogas* of the Brahmans, etc.

בנים ובנות, *sons and-daughters*.... One ought not to think that the root בן, from which these two words are derived, is limited to expressing *a son*. It is *an emanation*, literally as well as figuratively, *a generative extension*, *a formation of any sort whatever*.

v. 5. וימת, *and-he-deceased*.... This is the verb מות, in which the

6. And-he-lived, *Sheth,* five revolving-changes and-o n e-hundred of-revolving-c h a n g e ; a n d-h e-begat *Ænosh* (corporeal man).

7. And-he-lived, *S h e t h,* after - the-causing-him-to-beget that-same *Ænosh,* seven revolving-changes, and-eight h u n d r e d ʂ o f-revolving-change; and he-begat sons and-daughters (a flocking throng of issued beings).

8. And-they-were all-the-days (manifested lights) of-*Sheth,* two and-one-ten of-revolving-change, and-nine h u n d r e d s o f revolving-change; and-he-deceased.

9. And-he-lived, *Ænosh,* n i n e-t e n s o f-revolving-change; and-he-begat the-selfsameness - o f - *K a i n a n* (general invading).

6. Et-il exista, *S h e t h,* cinq mutations et-une-cen-taine d e-mutation-tempor-elle; et-il-généra *Ænosh,* (l' homme corporel).

7. Et-il-exista, *S h e t h,* après-le-faire - enfanter-à-lui ce-même-*Ænosh,* sept mu-tations, et-huit-centaines de-mutation-temporelle; e t-i l généra fils et-filles (u n e foule d'êtres émanés).

8. Et-ils-furent tous-les-j o u r s (les manifestations phénoméniques) d e-*Sheth,* deux et-un-décuple de-mu-tation-temporelle, e t-neuf-centaines de-mutation; et-il-passa.

9. E t-i l-exista, *Ænosh* neuf-décuples de-mutation-temporelle; et-il produisit l' existence-de-*Kainan* (l'en-vahissement général).

Chaldaic punctuation has suppressed the sign י, used in the future tense, made past by the convertible sign ו. This verb which has or-dinarily been translated by *to die,* expresses, as I have said, a sym-pathetic movement, a passing, a return to universal seity. Refer to Radical Vocabulary, root מת.

v. 6, 7 and 8. Nothing more to explain relative to these terms.

v. 9. קינן, *Kainan....* I have explained as much as possible, *Kain* and his brother *Sheth,* and the son of *Sheth, Ænosh:* here now is this same *Ænosh* who reproduces another *Kain;* but by extending, and as it were, by diluting its primitive forces; for although *Kainan*

10.   Wa-îhî Ænôsh âhoreî hôlid-ô æth-Keînan hamesh heshereh shanah w'shemoneh mæôth shanah: wa-iôled banîm w-banôth.

וַיְחִי אֱנוֹש אַחֲרֵי הוֹלִידוֹ אֶת־קֵינָן חֲמֵש עֶשְׂרֵה שָׁנָה וּשְׁמֹנֶה מֵאוֹת שָׁנָה וַיּוֹלֶד בָּנִים וּבָנוֹת :

11.   Wa-î h î o u chol-îmeî Ænôsh hamesh shanîm w-theshah mæôth shanah; wa-îamoth.

וַיִּהְיוּ כָּל־יְמֵי אֱנוֹש חָמֵש שָׁנִים וּתְשַׁע מֵאוֹת שָׁנָה וַיָּמֹת :

12.   Wa-îhî Keînan shibehim shanah, wa-iôled æth-Maholalæl.

וַיְחִי קֵינָן שִׁבְעִים שָׁנָה וַיּוֹלֶד אֶת־מַהֲלַלְאֵל :

13.   Wa-îhî Keînan ahorei holid-o æth-Maholalæl ârbahîm shanah w-shemoneh mæôth s h a n a h, w-i ô l e d banîm w-banôth.

וַיְחִי קֵינָן אַחֲרֵי הוֹלִידוֹ אֶת־מַהֲלַלְאֵל אַרְבָּעִים שָׁנָה וּשְׁמֹנֶה מֵאוֹת שָׁנָה וַיּוֹלֶד בָּנִים וּבָנוֹת :

---

may be only the word *Kain* to which Moses has added the augmentative final יָן, it is very necessary that there should be preserved in the posterity of *Sheth*, the same nature that he has in his own. It is extended, it is diluted, as I have said, and its force which consisted in a violent centralization, has diminished in proportion to its extent. We have already observed this difference between *Henoch* and *Ænosh*, in v. 26 of the preceding chapter.

v. 10 and 11.   These terms are all understood.

v. 12. מהללאל, *Mahollael*.... That is to say, potential exaltation,

10. And-he-lived, *Ænosh* after-the-causing-him-t o-be-g e t t h e-selfsameness-of-*Kainan,* five and-one-tens of-revolving-change, and-eight-hundreds of-revolution; and-he-begat sons and-daughters (many issued offspring).

10. Et-il-exista, *Ænosh.* après-le-faire-enfanter-à-l u i ce même *Kainan,* cinq et-un-d é c u p l e de-mutation, et-huit-centaines de-mutation-temporelle; et-il-généra fils-et-filles (une foule d'êtres émanés).

11. And-they-were a l l-the-days (manifested lights) of-*Ænosh,* five revolving-changes, and-nine hundreds of revolution: a n d-he-de-ceased.

11. Et-ils-furent t o u s-les-jours (les manifestations phénoméniques) d'*Ænosh,* cinq mutations, et neuf-cen-taines de-mutation-tempor-elle et-il-passa.

12. And-he-lived, *Kainan,* s e v e n tens of-revolving-change; and-he-begat the-selfsameness o f-*Mahollael* (mighty rising up, bright-ness).

12. Et-il-exista, *Kainan,* sept décuples de-mutation-temporelle; et-il-généra l'ip-séité-de-*Mahollael* (l'exalta-tion puissance, l a splen-deur).

13. And-he-lived, *Kain-an,* after-the-causing-h i m-to-beget that-same-*Maholl-ael,* four-tens of-revolving-change, and-eight hundreds of-revolution; and-he-begat sons and-daughters (many issued offspring).

13. Et-il-exista, *Kainan,* après-le-faire e n f a n t e r-à-lui ce-même *M a h o l l a e l* quatre-décuples de-mutation et-huit-centaines d e-muta-tion-temporelle; et-il-généra fils et-filles (une foule d' êtres émanés).

---

splendour, glory. The root הל, containing in itself all ideas of ex-altation, is again strengthened by doubling the final character ל, and by the addition of the root אל, which expresses the force of exhaling movement. The plastic sign מ. is only there to coöperate with the formation of the proper name.

v. 13 and 14. These terms are understood.

14.   Wa-îhîou chol-îmeî
Keînan hesher shanîm w-
theshah mæôth shanah: wa-
îamoth.

וַיִּהְיוּ כָּל־יְמֵי קֵינָן עֶשֶׂר שָׁנִים
וּתְשַׁע מֵאוֹת שָׁנָה וַיָּמֹת :

15.   W a-î h î Maholalæl
hamesh shanîm w-shishîm
shanah wa-iôled æth-Iared.

וַיְחִי מַהֲלַלְאֵל חָמֵשׁ שָׁנִים
וְשִׁשִּׁים שָׁנָה וַיּוֹלֶד אֶת־יָרָד :

16.   W a-î h î Maholalæl
âhoreî hôlid-ô æth-I a r e d
sheloshîm s h a n a h w-shemoneh mæôth shanah: wa-
iôled banîm w'banôth.

וַיְחִי מַהֲלַלְאֵל אַחֲרֵי הוֹלִידוֹ
אֶת־יֶרֶד שְׁלֹשִׁים שָׁנָה וּשְׁמֹנֶה
מֵאוֹת שָׁנָה וַיּוֹלֶד בָּנִים וּבָנוֹת :

17.   Wa-îhîou chol îmeî
Maholalæl hamesh w-thisha-
hîm s h a n a h w'shemoneh
mæôth shanah: wa-îamoth.

וַיִּהְיוּ כָּל־יְמֵי . מַהֲלַלְאֵל חָמֵשׁ
וְתִשְׁעִים שָׁנָה וּשְׁמֹנֶה מֵאוֹת
שָׁנָה וַיָּמֹת :

18.   Wa-îhî Iared shethaîm w'shishîm shanah w'
mæôth s h a n a h: wa-iôled
æth-Hanoch.

וַיְחִי־יֶרֶד שְׁתַּיִם וְשִׁשִּׁים שָׁנָה
וּמְאַת שָׁנָה וַיּוֹלֶד אֶת־חֲנוֹךְ :

---

v. 15. ירד, *Ired*.... Here among the descendants of *Sheth* is this
same *Whirad*, that we have seen figuring among those of *Kain;* but
who is presented now under a form more softened. In losing its
initial sign ע, which is that of material sense, it has left its passionate and excitative ardour. The natural sense which it contains

14. And-they-were, all-the-days, (m a n i f e s t e d lights) of-*Kainan,* ten revolving-changes, and-nine hundreds of-revolution; and-he-deceased.

15. And-he-lived, *Mahollael,* five revolving-changes, and-six-tens of-revolution; and-he-begat the-selfsameness-of *Ired* (the steadfast one).

16. And-he-lived, *Mahollael,* after the-causing-him-t o-b e g e t that-same-*Ired,* t h r e e-t e n s of-revolving-change and-eight hundreds of-revolution; and-he-begat sons and-daughters (many issued offspring).

17. And-they-were, all-the-days, (m a n i f e s t e d lights) of *Mahollael,* f i v e and-nine-tens of-revolving-change and eight hundreds of revolution: and-he-deceased.

18. And-he-lived, *I r e d,* two and-six-tens of-revolving change, and-one-hundred of-revolution; and he-begat the-selfsameness-of-*Henoch* (the central might, and-also-the-panging one).

14. Et-ils-furent, t o u s-les-jours, (les manifestations phénoméniques) de-*Kainan,* dix-mutations et neuf centaines de-mutation-temporelle; et-il-passa.

15. Et-il-exista, *Mohollael,* cinq mutations et-six-décuples de-mutation-temporelle; et-il-produisit l'existence-d'*Ired* (ce qui est persévérant dans son mouvement).

16. Et-il-exista, *Mahollael,* après le-faire-enfanter-à-lui ce-même-*I r e d,* trois-décuples de-mutation et-huit-centaines de-mutation-temporelle; et-il-généra fils et filles (une foule d'êtres émanés).

17. Et-il-furent, tous-les-jours (les manifestations phénoméniques) d e-*Mahollael,* cinq-et-neuf-décuples de-mutation, e t-h u i t-centaines de-mutation-temporelle; et-il-passa.

18. Et-il-exista, *I r e d,* deux et-six-décuples de-mutation, et-une-centaine de-mutation-temporelle; et-il-produisit l ' existence - de-*Henoch* (la puissance centrale, et aussi le souffrant, l'angoisseux).

---

is now that of perseverance, of steadfastness to follow an imparted movement. It is true that this movement can be good or evil, ascend-

19.   Wa-îhî Iared âhoreî hôlid-ô æth-H a n ô c h she-moneh mæôth shanah: wa-îôled banîm w-banôth.

וַיְחִי־יֶרֶד אַחֲרֵי הוֹלִידוֹ אֶת־חֲנוֹךְ שְׁמֹנֶה מֵאוֹת שָׁנָה וַיּוֹלֶד בָּנִים וּבָנוֹת :

20.   Wa-îhîou chol-îemeî-I a r e d shethîm w-shishîm shanah   w-theshah   mæôth shanah: wa-îamoth.

וַיִּהְיוּ כָּל־יְמֵי־יֶרֶד שְׁתַּיִם וְשִׁשִׁים שָׁנָה וּתְשַׁע מֵאוֹת שָׁנָה וַיָּמֹת :

21.   Wa-îhî Hanôch ha-mesh w'shishîm shanah : wa-îôled æth-Methoûshalah.

וַיְחִי חֲנוֹךְ חָמֵשׁ וְשִׁשִׁים שָׁנָה וַיּוֹלֶד אֶת־מְתוּשָׁלַח :

22.   Wa-îthehallech Ha-nôch æth-ha-Ælohîm âhoreî hôlid-ô   æth-Methoûshalah, shelosh mæôth shanah; wa-îôled banîm w-banôth.

וַיִּתְהַלֵּךְ חֲנוֹךְ אֶת־הָאֱלֹהִים אַחֲרֵי הוֹלִידוֹ אֶת־מְתוּשֶׁלַח שְׁלֹשׁ מֵאוֹת שָׁנָה וַיּוֹלֶד בָּנִים וּבָנוֹת :

---

ing or descending; as is proved by the two verbs springing from the root יָרֹד: the one, רָדֹה means *to govern, to dominate;* the other, יָרֹד, signifies *to sink, to descend.*

v. 16 and 17.   These terms are understood.

v. 18. חֲנוֹךְ, *Henoch....* This name is presented here with all the force which it has in the posterity of Kain. It is the same central power, the same corporate force: but the posterity of *Sheth* influenc-ing the moral idea which it contains, can be considered now under the relation of repentance and contrition; that is to say, that the pressure, the shock, which it expresses literally, can be taken figur-atively and become *a pang.*

19. And-he-lived, *I r e d,* after the-causing-him-to-beget that-same-*Henoch,* eight hundreds o f-r e v o l v i n g-change; and-he-begat sons and-daughters (m a n y issued offspring).

20. And-they were, all-the-days, (m a n i f e s t e d lights) of-*Ired,* two and-six-tens-of-revolving-c h a n g e, and-nine hundreds of revolution; and-he-deceased.

21. And-he-endured, *He-noch,* five and-six-tens of revolving-change, and-he-begat *Methushalah,* (e a g e r shaft of death).

22. And-he-trod, *Henoch,* (in the steps) of-HIM-the-Gods, after the causing-him-to-beget that-same *Methushalah,* three hundreds of-revolving change; and-he-begat s o n s a n d-daughters (many issued offspring).

19. Et-il-exista, *I r e d,* après le-faire enfanter-à-lui ce-même-*Henoch,* huit cen-t a i n e s de-révolution temporelle; et-il-généra fils et-filles (une f o u l e d'êtres émanés).

20. Et-ils-furent, tous-les-j o u r s (les manifesta-tions phénoméniques) d' *Ired,* deux et-six-décuples de-mutation, et-neuf cen-taines de-mutation-tempor-elle; et-il-passa.

21. Et-il-exista, *Henoch,* cinq-et-six-décuples de- mu-tation-temporelle et-il-pro-duisit l'existence-de-*Methou-shalah,* (l'émission de la mort).

22. Et-il-suivit, *Henoch,* (les traces) mêmes-de-LUI-les-Dieux, après-le-faire-en-f a n t e r-à-lui ce-même-*Me-thoushalah,* trois centaines de-mutation-temporelle; et-il-généra fils et-filles (une foule d'êtres émanés).

---

v. 19 and 20. The terms of these are understood.

v. 21. מתושלח, *Methushalah*... It is no longer *Whirad* who is be-gotten by *Henoch;* for, in this generation, this same *Whirad,* changed to *Ired,* has become the father of *Henoch: Methushalah,* whom we have seen in the posterity of *Kain,* is likewise the grandson of *Whirad.* The change brought into this name is hardly perceptible. It is always the root מות, *death,* which constitutes its foundation. The word שלח, which is added, signifies literally *a dart.* In the posterity

23.   Wa-îhîou čhol îmeî
Hanôčh hamesh w'shishîm
shanah   w-shelosh mæôth
shanah.

וַיְהִיוּ כָּל־יְמֵי חֲנוֹךְ חָמֵשׁ וְשִׁשִּׁים שָׁנָה וּשְׁלֹשׁ מֵאוֹת שָׁנָה :

24.   Wa-îthehallečh Ha-
nôčh æth-ha-Ælohîm w'-
æine-nou čhi-lakah âoth-ô
Ælohîm.

וַיִּתְהַלֵּךְ חֲנוֹךְ אֶת־הָאֱלֹהִים וְאֵינֶנּוּ כִּי־לָקַח אֹתוֹ אֱלֹהִים :

---

of *Kain*, מתושאל symbolizes *the gulf of death*, that is to say, a death
which precipitates and devours; whereas in that of *Sheth*, מתושלח
characterizes *the dart of death*, that is, a death which hurls toward
the eternity of existence. Thus Moses admits two kinds of death:
this is worthy of notice.

v. 22 and 23, ויתהלך, *and-he-trod*.... This is the verb הלך of which
I have already spoken in v. 8. ch. III. It is used here according to
the reciprocal form and signifies literally to be carried in every
sense; to go and come.

This action, which Moses attributes to *Henoch*, proves, as I
have insinuated, that it ought to be taken in a more moral sense, as
descendant of Sheth, rather than as descendant of Kain. The number 365, which is that of its temporal and ontological mutations, has
been noticed by all allegorists.

v. 24. ואיננו, *and nought of-him*.... I have spoken several times
of the root אין, and I have also shown the singular peculiarity that
it has of developing ideas most opposed in appearance, such as being
and nothingness, of strength and weakness; etc. But I think that
here is the occasion to state, that this surprising peculiarity rests
less in the root itself, than in the object to which it is opposed.
Thus, for example, whatever the thing that one admits as existing,
good or evil, strong or weak, this root, manifested by the adverbial

23. And-they-were, all-the days (m a n i f e s t e d lights) of-*Henoch*, five and-six-tens of-revolving-change and three-hundreds of-re-volution.

24. And-he-applied-him-self-to-tread, *Henoch* (in the s t e p s) of-H I M-*the-Gods*, and nought (no substance) of-him; for-he-resumed-him, HE-the-Being-of-beings.

23. Et-ils-furent, tous-les-jours (les manifestations phénoméniques) de-*Henoch*, cinq et-six-décuples de-mu-tation, et-trois centaines de-mutation-temporelle.

24. E t-i l-s'excita-à-sui-vre, *Henoch* (les traces) de-L U I-les-Dieux; et-non-être-substance-de-l u i, car-il-re-tira-lui, L U I l'Ê t r e-d e s-êtres.

---

relation יִן, will be its absolute opposite. If the substance is granted as *all*, יִן is the symbol of *nothing*. If the substance is considered as *nothing*, יִן is the symbol of *all*. In a word, יִן characterizes the absence of the substance. It is an abstraction, good or evil, of spir-ituality. This is the origin of the syllable *in*, which we sometimes use to change the signification of words.

In the case referred to, the adverbial relation יִן, indicates a transmutation in the mode of existence of *Henoch* and not a simple change of place, a removal, as the translators understand it. If *Henoch* was substance, he ceased being this to become spirit. He was אֵינֶנּוּ , *in-him*, that is to say, *insubstantial*.

I should state here that, at the very time of the Samaritan ver-sion, the most ancient of all, and shortly after the captivity of Baby-lon, this expression, so vital, was not understood. The author of this version substituted for the Hebrew אֵינֶנּוּ, the word ᘓᙀᙏ12ᖾ , *and-no-sign-of-him;* adding: ᙇᙈᙆᙀ2ᙆ ᙇᙏᙈᖾ ᗤ2ᙅ , *for-they-carried-him away, the angels.* The Chaldaic uses the same word וליתיהי *and-no-sign-of-him.* The Hellenists take a turn still more curious: καὶ οὐχ εὑρίσκετο, *and he was not found.* And Saint Jerome takes a middle course in saying "et non apparuit" *and he appeared not.*

25. Wa-îhî Methoûshelah shebah w-shemonîm shanah w'mâth s h a n a h: wa-îôled æth-Lamech.

וַיְחִי מְתוּשֶׁלַח שֶׁבַע וּשְׁמוֹנִים שָׁנָה וּמְאַת שָׁנָה וַיּוֹלֶד אֶת־ לָמֶךְ :

26. Wa-îhî Methoûshelah âhoreî hôlîd-ô æth-Lamech, shethaîm w-shemonîm sha-nah, w-shebah mæôth sha-nah: wa-îôled b a n î m w-banôth.

וַיְחִי מְתוּשֶׁלַח אַחֲרֵי הוֹלִידוֹ אֶת־לֶמֶךְ שְׁתַּיִם וּשְׁמוֹנִים שָׁנָה וּשְׁבַע מֵאוֹת שָׁנָה וַיּוֹלֶד בָּנִים וּבָנוֹת :

27. Wa-îhîou chol-îemeî Methoûshelah theshah w-shishîm shanah, w-theshah mæôth shanah: wa-îamoth.

וַיִּהְיוּ כָּל־יְמֵי מְתוּשֶׁלַח תֵּשַׁע וְשִׁשִּׁים שָׁנָה וּתְשַׁע מֵאוֹת שָׁנָה וַיָּמֹת :

28. Wa-îhî Lamech she-thîm w-shemonîm shanah w-mâth shanah: wa-îôled ben.

וַיְחִי־לֶמֶךְ שְׁתַּיִם וּשְׁמוֹנִים שָׁנָה וּמְאַת שָׁנָה וַיּוֹלֶד בֵּן :

---

v. 25. לֶמֶךְ. Lamech.... What I have said concerning this per-sonage can be seen in v. 18, ch. IV. This Lamech differs from the former Lamech only by the generation to which he belongs. He has the same character, but in another nature. The former, which issued from the generation of Kain, is the sixth descendant from Adam; the latter, which belongs to that of Sheth, is the eighth. The one has two corporeal wives, that is to say, two physical faculties which give him three sons; or rather three cosmogonic principles, source of all

25.   And-he-was-in-being, *Methushalah,* s e v e n and-e i g h t-t e n s o f-revolving-change, and-one-hundred of-revolution: and-he-begat *Lamech* (the tie of dissolution).

26.   And-he-lived, *Methushalah* a f t e r the-causing-him-to-beget that-same-*Lamech,* two and-eight-tens of-revolving-change, and-seven hundreds of-revolution, and-he-begat sons and-daughters (many issued offspring).

27.   And-they-were, a l l-the days, (m a n i f e s t e d l i g h t s) o f-*Methushalah,* nine and-six-tens of-revolving-change, and-nine hundreds of-revolution: and-he-ceased (to be in being).

28.   A n d-h e-lived, *Lamech,* two and-eight-tens of-revolving-change, and-o n e-hundred of-revolution: and-he-begat a-son (an issued offspring).

25.   Et-il-exista, *Methoushalah,* sept et-huit-décuples de-mutation, et-une-centaine de-mutation-temporelle; et-il-produisit l'existence de-*Lamech* (le nœud qui arrête la dissolution).

26.   Et-il-exista, *Methoushalah,* après-le-faire-enfanter-à-lui ce-m ê m e-*Lamech,* deux et-huit-décuples de-mutation, et-sept centaines de-mutation-temporelle, e t-i l-généra fils e t-f i l l e s (une foule d'êtres émanés).

27.   Et-ils-furent, tous-les-jours, (les manifestations phénoméniques) de *Methoushalah,* neuf et-six-décuples de-mutation; et-n e u f centaines de-mutation-temporelle: et-il-passa.

28.   Et-il-exista, *Lamech,* deux et-huit-décuples de-mutation, et-une-centaine de-mutation-temporelle: et-il-g é n é r a un-fils (un être émané).

---

fertility, of all prosperity, of all power upon the earth: the other, left only one son, who saw mankind finish and begin again.

v. 26, 27 and 28.   These terms are understood.

v. 29.   נֹחַ, *Noah....* or *Noe,* as it has been vulgarly written following the orthography of the Hellenist translators.   The root from

29.   Wa-îkkerâ æth-sham-
ô Noah, l'æmor zeh înahome-
nou mi-mahoshenou, w-me-
whitzebôn îadeînou min-ha-
âd a m a h   â s h e r   ærorha
IHOAH.

וַיִּקְרָא אֶת־שְׁמוֹ נֹחַ לֵאמֹר זֶה
יְנַחֲמֵנוּ מִמַּעֲשֵׂנוּ וּמֵעִצְּבוֹן יָדֵינוּ
מִן־הָאֲדָמָה אֲשֶׁר אֵרֲרָהּ יְהֹוָה :

30.   Wa-îhî Lamec̀h âhoreî hôlîd-ô æth-ben, hamesh
w-thishehîm shanah wa-ha-
mesh mæôth shanah: wa-
îôled banîm w-banôth.

וַיְחִי־לֶמֶךְ אַחֲרֵי הוֹלִידוֹ אֶת־בֶּן
חָמֵשׁ וְתִשְׁעִים שָׁנָה וַחֲמֵשׁ
מֵאוֹת שָׁנָה וַיּוֹלֶד בָּנִים וּבָנוֹת :

---

which this important name comes, is composed of the sign of produced being ב, image of reflected existence, and the sign of the effort
of Nature ה, which gives birth to vital equilibrium, to *existence*. This
root offers the idea of that perfect repose, which, for a thing long
agitated in opposed directions, results in that state of equilibrium
where it dwells immobile.

Nearly all the tongues of the Orient understood this mysterious
expression.   The Hebrew and the Chaldaic draw from it two verbs.
By the first נהה, one understands, *to lead to the end, to guide toward
the place of repose;* by the second, נוא, *to repose, to rest tranquil, to
be in a state of peace, of calm, of perfect bliss.*   It is from the latter,
that the name of the cosmogonic personage who saw the end of the
world and its renewal, is derived.   It is the emblem of the repose of
elementary existence, the sleep of Nature.

זה ינחמנו, *this will-release us*....   Moses rarely forgets to explain
the substantive by the verb, or the verb by the substantive: this cannot be repeated too often, for it is the seal of his style.   The Samaritan translator, far from seeking to follow this course, so simple and
so expressive, nearly always swerves from it.   In this instance for

29. And-he-assigned-f o r name-to-him, *Noah;* thus-declaring-his-thought: t h i s will release-us (will lessen, relieve us) from-the-hardworking-our, and-from-thegreat-natural-hindrance of-the-hands-ours, because-of-t h e-a d a m i c (elementary g r o u n d) which he-has-cursed-it, IHOAH.

29. Et-il-assigna ce-nom-même-à-lui, *Noah,* pour-déclarer-sa-pensée (disant): celui-ci reposera-nous (nous allégera, nous soulagera) de-ce-qui-constitue l'œuvre-notre et-de-ce-qui-fait-l'obstacle-physique des-mains-à nous, à-cause de-la terre-adamique, laquelle il-a-maudite-elle, IHOAH.

30. A n d-h e-lived, *La-mech,* a f t e r-t h e-causing-him-to-beget a-son, five and-nine-t e n s of-r e v o l v i n g-change, and-five hundreds of-revolution, and-he-begat sons and-daughters (many issued offspring).

30. Et-il-exista, *Lamech,* après-le-faire-enfanter-à-lui ce-fils cinq et-neuf-décuples-de-mutation-temporelle, et-cinq centaines de-mutation, et-il-généra f i l s et-filles (une foule d'êtres émanés).

---

example, instead of the verb נֹחַם, which Moses uses to explain the meaning that he wishes to give to the name of *Noah,* and which the Samaritan could very well render by the analogue **נֵאצֵל**, one finds **יֹצֵל**, which signifies *to support, to moderate, to temper.*

This proves how little the Hebraic text was already felt at this remote time, and how the meaning of the words was altered.

v. 30 and 31. These terms are understood.

v. 32. בֶּן־חֲמֵשׁ, *a-son of-five....* This should be observed. In v. 28, Moses says that *Lamech* begat a son, בֵּן; that is, produced an *offspring;* for we shall see later on that the veritable signification of this word is here; in v. 29, he names this son נֹחַ, *Noah,* that is to say, *the sleep of nature, the repose of existence;* and now he says that he was *a-son of-five hundred-fold of-revolving-change.* To believe that Moses had wished to indicate by that, simply the age of *Noah,* is to misinterpret his genius.

I invite the reader to observe that *Adam,* universal man, in the beginning of things, begat three sons: *Kain, Habel and Sheth;* that

31.   W-îhî ċhol-îmeî-Le-
meċh s h e b a h w-shibehîm
shanah, w-s h e b a h mæôth
shanah: wa-îamoth.

וַיְהִי כָּל־יְמֵי־לֶמֶךְ שֶׁבַע וְשִׁבְעִים
שָׁנָה וּשְׁבַע מֵאוֹת שָׁנָה וַיָּמֹת :

---

now, *Noah*, who represents the repose of existence, in the waning of
things, begat *Shem, Ham* and *Japheth.* I have earnestly endeavoured
to make the true signification of the names of the children of *Adam*
understood; I shall now make the same efforts with respect to those
of *Noah.*

שׁם, *Shem....* The sign of relative duration and movement which
is connected here, and the sign of exterior action used as final collective sign, compose a root which produces the idea of that which
is distinguished exteriorly by its elevation, its splendour, its own
dignity. It is, in its most restricted acceptation, the proper name of
a thing, the particular designation of a remarkable place, or of a
remote time; it is the mark, the sign by which they are recognized;
it is the renown, the splendour, the glory which is attached to them.
In its broadest acceptation, it is ethereal space, the empyrean, the
heavens, and even GOD, that one finds designated by this singular
word, in Hebrew, as well as in Samaritan, in Chaldaic or in Syriac.

It is extremely difficult to choose, among so many significations,
that which is most consistent with the son of *Noah.* Nevertheless
one can without erring, translate it by the words, *the sublime, the
splendid, the radiant, etc.*

חם, *Ham....*   This name is on the whole, the opposite of that
of *Shem.* The sign ח which constitutes it, recalls all ideas of effort,
of obstacle, of fatigue, of travail. The root which results from its
union with the sign of exterior action, employed as collective, presents a bending, a dejection, a thing which inclines toward the lower
parts: it is the heat which follows a sharp compression: it is the hidden fire of nature: it is the warmth which accompanies the rays of
the sun; it is the dark colour, the blackness, which results from their
action; it is finally, in the broadest sense, *the sun* itself considered as
the cause of heat and of torrefaction.

When the name of *Ham* is presented alone and in an absolute
sense, it can, to a certain point, be taken in a good sense, since it

31. And-they-were, a l l-the-days (periodical lights) of-*Lamech*, seven and-seven-t e n s   o f-revolving-change, and-seven hundreds of-revolution : and-he-ceased.

31. Et-ils-furent, t o u s-les-jours, (l e s manifestations phénoméniques) d e-*Lamech*, sept et-sept-décuples de-mutation-temporelle; et-sept centuples de-mutation : et-il-passa.

---

expresses the effect of the sun upon inferior bodies; but if one only sees in it the opposite of *Shem*, it offers only sinister ideas. If *Shem* is the sublime, the superior, *Ham* is the abased, the inferior; so if the former is the radiant, the exalted, the infinite; the latter is the obscure, the bending, the limited, etc.

יפת, *Japheth*.... This name holds a sort of medium between those of *Shem* and *Ham*, and partakes of their good or evil qualities without, having them in itself. It signifies, in a generic sense, material extent, indefinite space: in a more restricted sense, latitude. The root פה, from which it comes, contains every idea of expansion, of facility to extend, to allow itself to be penetrated; every solution, every divisibility, every simplification. It is governed by the sign of potential manifestation ׳, which adds to its force and universalizes it.

This is all that I can say at this moment, pertaining to the three symbolic personages, who, emanated from *Noah*, the repose of Nature, survive the ruin of the world through the inaccessible shelter which their father gives them, the narrative of which we shall hear presently. It is possible, notwithstanding all the etymological light which I have tried to throw upon them, that the reader may still find many obscurities in the hieroglyphic sense of their names: I do not deny that they are there and many of them; but if he is sincerely earnest in penetrating these ancient mysteries, toward which Moses has traced sure routes, although ignorance and prejudice even more than time, have covered them with obstacles, he must not become discouraged. Let him compare diligently, the three sons of *Adam* with those of *Noah*, and he will find in the comparison, analogies which will serve to fix his ideas.

The first production of *Adam*, after his fall, is *Kain;* the second, *Habel;* the third, *Sheth*.

32. Wa-îhî Noah ben-ha-
mesh mæôth shanah, wa-
îôled Noah æth-Shem, æth-
Ham w'æth-Japheth.

וַיְהִי נֹחַ בֶּן־חֲמֵשׁ מֵאוֹת שָׁנָה
וַיּוֹלֶד נֹחַ אֶת־שֵׁם אֶת־חָם וְאֶת־
יָפֶת :

Moses, for very strong reasons, inverted the order of similitudes of the productions of Noah. *Shem*, whom he names the first, in this instance, corresponds with *Habel* whom he has named second in the other; *Ham*, whom he names second, corresponds with *Kain*, whom he has named first; *Japheth*, who corresponds with *Sheth* preserves with him the same rank.

It is without doubt very difficult to know what Moses has concealed under the symbolic names of *Kain*, *Habel* and *Sheth*: but if one wishes to admit that this may be the three constituent principles of the being called *Adam*, that is to say, the developed, or decomposed triad of that collective unity, he will soon perceive that the symbolic names of *Ham*, *Shem* and *Japheth*, are the constituted principles of the being called *Noah*, and that these cosmogonic per-

32.   And-he-was, *Noah,*
(nature's rest) a-son of-five
hundred-fold o f-revolving-
change : a n d-he-begat, he-
Noah,   the-selfsameness-of-
Shem, of-*Ham,* and-of-*Japheth* (that is to say, the
self-existing of what is lofty
and   bright,   of   what   is
gloomy, curved and warm,
and of what is extended and
wide).

32.   Et-il-fut *Noah* (le repos de la nature élémentaire) fils de-cinq centuples
de-mutation-temporelle : et-
il-produisit, lui-*Noah,* l'existence de-*Shem,* celle-de-*Ham*
et-celle-de-*Japheth* (c'est-à-
dire, l'ipséité de ce qui est
élevé et brillant, de ce qui
est courbe et chaud, et de ce
qui est étendu).

---

sonages are related one to the other, in the same manner as the
effect is related to its cause.

One ought not to forget besides, what I have said pertaining to
the extreme importance that the ancients attach to *proper names;* it
cannot be given too great attention. Notwithstanding the length of
my notes and even the numerous repetitions into which I purposely
fall, it will always be well for the reader to consult the Radical
Vocabulary for the signification of their roots.

SEPHER BERÆSHITH   ‏סֵפֶר בְּרֵאשִׁית ו. ‏
W.

1. Wa-îhî chi-hehel ha-   ‏וַיְהִי כִּי־הֵחֵל הָאָדָם לָרֹב עַל־‏
Adam larob hal-pheneî ha-   ‏פְּנֵי הָאֲדָמָה וּבָנוֹת יֻלְּדוּ לָהֶם : ‏
âdamah w-banôth îulledou
la-hem.

---

v. 1. ‏כִּי־הֵחֵל‏, *because-of-being-dissolved*.... The beginning of this
chapter is difficult and profoundly mysterious. The Hellenists for
fear no doubt of saying too much, say nothing about it; for it would
otherwise be inconceivable, that they should have forgotten so soon
the collusion of *Adam*, to which *Moses* makes so direct a reference.
However it may be, these translators render the radical verb ‏חוּל‏,
which the hierographic writer uses on this occasion by the nominal
passive ‏הֵחֵל‏, as ἤρξαντο, *they began;* not understanding, or not wishing
to understand, what connection the fall of Adam can have with the
generation of *daughters*, referred to hereafter.

But the verb ‏חוּל‏, has never signified precisely *to begin*: it is
always, in what ever relation one considers it, the expression of
violent effort, of distention, of writhing, which brings about solution
or dissolution. The root ‏חל‏ from which it comes, contains the idea
of an unknown force which destroys the ties of the body, by stretching them, breaking them, reducing them to shreds, or dissolving and
loosening them to excess. It is true that the verb in question can
present sometimes the idea of *an opening*, by extension of the idea of
solution, but it is in the same manner that it has also expressed the
idea of wound, of weakness, of laceration, of pain in bringing forth,
etc.

It is in taking figuratively the idea of dissolution, or of relaxation, that one has drawn from this root the idea of profanation and
of prostitution, to which Moses appears to make allusion in this
instance.

‏וּבָנוֹת‏, *that-daughters*.... The conjunctive article ‏ו‏, when it joins
the noun or the verb which it inflects, to the antecedent member of
the phrase, is perfectly expressed by the conjunction *that*.

GENESIS VI.

1. Now-it-was (it came to pass) because-of-being-dissolved (dissolute, loose) *Adam* (collective man) by-multiplying on-the-face of-the-adamic, that-daughters (corporeities) were-plenti-f u l l y-begotten unto-them (*Adam*).

COSMOGONIE VI.

1. Or-il-fut (il advint) à-cause-de s'être- dissous (dissolu, profané) *Adam* (l' homme universel) selon-l' action-de-multiplier sur-la-terre-adamique, que-des-fil-les (des formes corporelles) furent-abondamment-engen-drées à-eux (*Adam*).

The root בֵן, from which comes the word בַת, irregular feminine of the masculine בֵן *a son*, signifies in general, *an emanation, a forma-tion, any edification whatsoever*. The paternal sign בּ, hieroglyphic symbol of creative action, united to that of produced being ן, leaves no doubt in this respect. Thus the plural word בנות, which in a restricted sense would mean simply, *daughters*, taken in a figurative sense designates *corporations, assemblages, corporeal forms, corpore-ities*, etc.

ילדוּ, *were-plentifully-begotten*.... This is the compound ra-dical verb ילוד or לרת, used in the intensive form, passive movement, past tense. The Hellenists have evaded its force, which could not agree with the insignificant meaning that they had given to the word החל. Furthermore, I must say, as much for their exoneration as for that of Saint Jerome who copied them, that already at the time when the Hebrew text was translated into Samaritan, the beginning of this chapter experienced great difficulties. What proves this is, that not only in this instance, has the nominal passive החל been replaced by the active 𐤔𐤓𐤀, which, being derived from the verb שרה, signifies only *to reach out, to take possession of;* but, for the important words ארם and אדמה *Adam*, universal man, and *Adamah*, elementary earth, were substituted 𐤀𐤍𐤔 , *Ænosh*, corporeal man, and 𐤀𐤓𐤅𐤄 *Arwhah*, earth, properly so-called.

All these oversights conform more and more with· what I have

2. Wa-îrâoû beneî ha-
Ælohîm æth-benôth ha-
Adam chi-toboth hennah,
wa-îkkehoû la-hem nashîm
michol âsher bhaharoû.

וַיִּרְאוּ בְנֵי הָאֱלֹהִים אֶת־בְּנוֹת
הָאָדָם כִּי־טֹבֹת הֵנָּה וַיִּקְחוּ לָהֶם
נָשִׁים מִכֹּל אֲשֶׁר בָּחָרוּ :

---

always advanced regarding the loss of the Hebraic tongue. There
was no means for anyone to doubt that the words אדם and אנוש were
synonyms in the idiom of Moses, unless to pretend against all reason
and all likelihood.

v. 2. בני, *the-sons*.... I have just explained the root of this
word. These sons of the Divinity, that have so perplexed the savants,
are what the gnostics understood by their *Æons*: that is to say,
emanated beings. The root אן, of which I have already spoken several times and from which come, without any addition, the *Æons* of
the gnostics, exists in the Hebrew word בן, but contracted and ruled
by the paternal sign ב, in this manner ב־אן.

האלהים, *of* HIM-*the-Gods*.... This expression of Moses, upon which
many commentaries have been written, had already alarmed the
Samaritan translator, who, no longer understanding the moral sense
of the word בני, and not wishing to give *children* to the Being of beings, had distorted the text and replaced אלהים by 𐤔𐤋𐤈𐤍2.
Now, this word which is derived from the verb שלט, *to dominate*,
instead of having any bearing upon the Divinity, designates only
potentates or *sultans*. It was getting around the difficulty and not
solving it; for, how can one imagine that Moses had abruptly changed
the meaning of a Sacred Name which he had constantly given to
GOD, to apply it to *sultans?*

The author of the Chaldaic targum has fallen into the same error
and seems to have gone to extremes. Here is its entire phrase:

וחזו בני רברביא ית בנת אנשא :   And-they-looked-upon, the-sons of-the
-chiefs-of-the-multitudes, those-daught-
ers of-*Anosha* (corporeal man).

In consideration of this it is obvious that the Hellenists had no
need of efforts to veil the spiritual meaning of the Sepher; they
had only to follow the path which was traced for them. An astonishing thing is, that they dared not however, insult the text in this
passage, they say: οἱ υἱοὶ τοῦ Θεοῦ, *the sons of* GOD.

2. And-they-did-observe, the-sons, (spiritual off-spring) of-H I M-the-G o d s, those-daughters (corporeities) of-*Adam;* that fair they-were: and-they took for-them corporeal-mates (natural faculties) from-every-one whom they-liked-the-best.

2. Et-ils-considérèrent, les-fils-(émanations spirituel-les) de-LUI-les-Dieux, ces-filles (ces mêmes formes corporelles) d'*A d a m,* que bonnes elles-étaient: et-ils-prirent pour-eux des-épou-ses-corporelles (des facul-tés physiques) de-toutes cel-les qu'ils chérirent-le-plus.

נשים , *corporeal-mates*.... Moses does not here use the word אשה, which being derived as we have seen from the substantive איש *in-tellectual man*, should characterize figuratively, *intellectual faculties,* but the word נשים, which, formed by ellipsis of the word אנוש, *cor-poreal man*, indicates *physical faculties*. These are the modifications which must be grasped in reading a writer so precise, so exact as Moses. The more one studies him the more one is assured that he possessed to an eminent degree, the Egyptian tongue in which he had been brought up. It is incredible with what infinite art, he re-conciles the three meanings in his narration, with what force he at-taches the literal to the figurative, and the hieroglyphic to the literal. The tongues in which I can make myself understood, are wholly in-capable of rendering this profound calculation, this extraordinary labour by means of which he triples the thought, by vesting it with an expression which, although unique, is presented under three forms.

אשר בחרו, *whom-they-liked-the-best*.... This verb comes from the root חר, which depicts a focus from which the heat escapes by ra-diation. The sign of interior action ב, which governs this root gives it the figurative expression of a vehement passion which is fixed upon an object.

v. 3. לא־ירון, *shall-not-diffuse*.... This verb is derived from the root רן, which is related to every idea of abundance and division, as is proved by its derivatives ירוה, *to emit, to spread, to divulge;* נרה *a profusion, a prostitution;* נרן *a prodigality*, etc.

בשגם, *by-his-decaying-quite*.... This important word has not been

3. Wa-îâomer I н ô а н
loâ-îadôn rouh-î b'Adam, l'
holam b'shaggam houâ bas-
har w'haîou îamaî-ô meâh
w'hesherîm shanah.

וַיֹּאמֶר יְהֹוָה לֹא־יָדוֹן רוּחִי בָאָדָם
לְעֹלָם בְּשַׁגָּם הוּא בָשָׂר וְהָיוּ
יָמָיו מֵאָה וְעֶשְׂרִים שָׁנָה :

4. Ha-Nephilîm haîou b'
âretz b'îamîm ha-hem, w'
gam âhoreî-chen asher îaboâou beneî ha-Ælohîm æl-
benôth ha-Adam, w'îalodou
la-hem hemmah ha-ghibbo-
rîm âsher me-hôlam ânosheî
ha-shem.

הַנְּפִלִים הָיוּ בָאָרֶץ בַּיָּמִים הָהֵם
וְגַם אַחֲרֵי־כֵן אֲשֶׁר יָבֹאוּ בְּנֵי
הָאֱלֹהִים אֶל־בְּנוֹת הָאָדָם וְיָלְדוּ
לָהֶם הֵמָּה הַגִּבֹּרִים אֲשֶׁר מֵעוֹלָם
אַנְשֵׁי הַשֵּׁם :

---

comprehended by any of the translators, who, forgetting always the
collusion of Adam, to which Moses continually alludes, have seen here
only corporeal man. The Samaritan has even gone to the point of
suppressing the word אדם *universal man*, which embarrasses him in
this verse, substituting that of Ænosh, אַנַש , *corporeal man*, as
he has done in other instances. The Chaldean has overthrown all the
ideas. Besides, the verb שׁוּג or שָׁגָה signifies equally *to decline, to
err, to degenerate*. It is the latter which, on this occasion, is used
as nominal active, inflected by the mediative article בּ, and generalized by the collective sign ם.

v. 4. הַנְּפִלִים, *then-the-Nephilites*.... That is to say, men distinguished from others by their power or their strength; for the
giants, γιγάντες, "gigantes", that the Hellenists and Saint Jerome have
seen here, have existed only in their imagination, at least if these
translators have understood by this, what the vulgar ordinarily understands, that is, men of greater stature than others. If the Hel-

3. And-he-said, IHOAH, shall-not-diffuse (lavish it-self) the-breath-mine (my-vivifical spirit) unto *Adam* (collective man), forever by-his-decaying-quite: since-he-is b o d i l y-shape, they s h a l l-be, the-days (manifested lights) of-him, one-hundred-fold and-two-tens of-revolving-change.

4. T h e n-the-*Nephilites* (distinguished, illustrious, noble men) were in-the-earth by-the-days those: and-also, a f t e r-that-so (happened) that t h e y-were-c o m e, the-sons (spiritual offspring) of-HIM-the-Gods, near-the-daughters (corporeal faculties) of-*Adam* (collective man) and-that-they-had-begotten-through-t h e m t h o s e-very-*G h i b o r i t e s* (mighty men, lords) who-were of-old-old, corporeal-men of-renown.

3. Et-il-dit, IHOAH, non-pas-s'épandra (s e prodiguera) le-souffle-mien (mon esprit vivifiant) chez-*Adam* (l'homme universel) pour-l' immensité-temporelle, dans-l'a c t e-d e-décliner-entière-ment: puisqu' il-est forme-corporelle, ils-seront, les-jours (les manifestations lu-m i n e u s e s) à-lui, un-cen-t u p l e et-deux-décuples de-mutation-temporelle.

4. O r, l e s-*Néphiléens* (les-hommes distingués, les nobles) étaient en-la-terre par-les-j o u r s ceux-là: et-aussi, après-qu'ainsi (cela fut a r r i v é) qu'ils-furent-venus les-fils (émanations spirituelles) d e-L U I-l e s Dieux auprès-des-filles (formes corporelles) d'*Adam* (l' homme universel) et-qu'ils-eurent-généré s e l o n-e u x ceux-là-mêmes, les *Ghibo-réens* (les hommes supér-ieurs, les heros, les Hyper-boréens) l e s q u e l s-furent dans-l'immensité-temporelle, les-hommes-corporels de-re-nom.

---

lenists, who, in other instances, have copied the Samaritan transla-tion, had given attention to this one, they would have seen that the word by which this translation renders נפלים, is 𐤀𐤌𐤐𐤒𐤕, used alike in the Hebrew גברים, and which is placed precisely at the end of the same verse, as synonymous epithet; for this word is nearer

5. Wa-îaræ, IHôAH, ĉhi rabbah rahath ha-Adam b' âretz, w'ĉhol-îetzer mahesheboth lib-ô rak rah ĉhol-ha-îôm.

וַיַּרְא יְהֹוָה כִּי רַבָּה רָעַת הָאָדָם בָּאָרֶץ וְכָל־יֵצֶר מַחְשְׁבֹת לִבּוֹ רַק רַע כָּל־הַיּוֹם:

---

than one imagines to the epithet which the 'Τπερβορέοι bear: those famous *Hyperboreans*, whose origin has so troubled the savants.

These savants had before them, the Latin word *nobilis*, which comes from the same root as the Hebrew נפלים, and presents the same characters with the sole difference of the *b*, which, as in numerous derivative words, has taken the place of *p*, or of *ph*. They have not seen that the Latin word *nobilis*, having passed from Asia into Europe, was the real translation of the word נפלים; and that consequently, in the *Nephilites* of Moses must be seen, not *giants*, nor men of colossal stature, but *Great Ones;* illustrious, distinguished men, *Nobles*, in fact.

Now what is the root of this word? It is פל which always develops the idea of a thing apart, distinguished, raised above the others. Thence the two verbs פלא or פלה, used only in the passive movement הפלא or הפלה, *to be distinguished, illustrious;* of which the continued facultative נפלא or נפלה, *becoming distinguished, illustrious,* gives us the plural נפלים which is the subject of this note.

Those of my readers who know how much the word נפלים has involved the commentators, and who doubt the justice of my etymology, not conceiving how the analogues which I have cited could have escaped the sagacity of the savants, have only to open any Hebrew dictionary to the articles פלא or פלה, and they will see among others, נפלאים *marvelous, wonderful things;* נפלאות, *unheard-of exploits, astonishing things, miracles;* נפלאת, *a profound mystery,* etc.

בימים, *by-the-days....* I have followed here the vulgar interpretation, having no adequate reason for changing it; but, as I have already said, the word ימים, from which the Chaldaic punctuation has suppressed the sign י, can mean equally *days* or *seas:* so that if one admits this last signification, the text will bear, that the *Nephilites*, that is, the *Nobles*, the distinguished among men, subdued at the same time the land and the seas.

5. And-he-did-ken, I H O A H, that increased-it-self-eagerly the-wickedness o f-*Adam* (collective m a n, mankind) in-the-earth, and-t h a t-every-conceit (intellectual operating) from-the-thoughts-out of-the-heart-of-him, diffused evil all-that-day (that whole light's manifestation).

5. Et-il-considera, IHOAH, que se multipliait-avec-violence la méchanceté d'*Adam* (de l'homme universel, règne hominal) en-la-terre, et-que-toute conception (production intellectuelle)des-pensées selon-l e-cœur-à-lui, épandait le-mal (en remplissait) t o u t-ce-jour (toute c e t t e manifestation phénoménique).

הגברים, *the Ghiborites....* This important word is composed of two roots which usage has contracted, גב-בור. The first גב, develops literally the idea of a thing placed or happening above another, as a boss, an eminence, a protuberance. Figuratively, it is an increase of glory, strength, honour. The second בור, contains the idea of distinction, of splendour, of purification. It must not be confused with the root spoken of in v. I ch. I, and from which comes the verb ברא *to create.* This latter is composed, as I have stated, of the signs of interior action ב, and the elementary root אר: the one now under consideration, unites to the same generative sign ב, the modified root אור , which, applied particularly to *fire,* develops all ideas attached to that element. It is from this that the following words are derived. בר *wheat,* the grain *par excellence;* בורר *to elect, to choose, to distinguish;* בהיר, *that which is white and pure;* בחור *that which is selected, put aside, preferred,* etc.

Let us observe that the vowel which constitutes this root, undergoing the degradation of which I have already spoken so often, forms the verb בעור, *to inflame, to fill with burning ardour; to make passionate, furious,* etc.

We can infer from this etymological knowledge, that the word גברים , by which Moses explains that of נפלים, and which perhaps in his own time had begun to be obsolete, is the exact translation of it, and that it signifies *very distinguished, very remarkable, very noble men.* The first root גב, which I have rendered in this instance by the superlative *very,* has been rendered by the ancient Greeks by the adverbial relation ὑπερ *above;* the second root בור, has been pre-

6. Wa-înnahem, IHOAH, ǒhi-hashah æth-ha-Adam, b' âretz wa-îthe-hatzeb æl-lib-ô.

וַיִּנָּחֶם יְהֹוָה כִּי־עָשָׂה אֶת־הָאָרָם בָּאָרֶץ וַיִּתְעַצֵּב אֶל־לִבּוֹ :

---

served in the plural Βόρεοι, *Boreans*: that is to say, *the illustrious, the powerful, the strong*, in short, *the Barons*: for the Celtic word *baron*, is the analogue of the Hebrew גברון, written with the extensive final וֹן; the Greek word Ὑπερβόρεοι, of which the savants have said so much, is no other than *the high, arch-barons*. And thus, confusing constantly the name of a caste with the name of a people, as they have done with regard to the Chaldeans, these same savants have been greatly troubled to find the fixed abode of the Hyperborean nation.

Before terminating this already very lengthy article, I cannot dispense with stating two things. The first, that the word גבור, here referred to, constitutes the fourth name that Moses gives to man: the second, that this hierographic writer, makes this superior man descend, by the union of divine emanations with natural forms, that is to say, in other terms, spiritual faculties joined to physical faculties.

Adam, universal man, the kingdom of man, issues in principle from the hands of the Divinity, in principle male and female.

The element from which he must draw his passive nature substance, is named after him, *adamah*. Soon the divine spirit is united to his elementary spirit: he passes from power into action. The Being of beings individualizes him by detaching from him his efficient volitive faculty and makes him thus, free, susceptible of realizing his own conceptions. Then intellectual man, *Aish*, exists.

The covetous passion, universal incentive of elementary nature, inevitably attacks thenceforth this volitive faculty, now isolated and free. *Aisha*, seduced and believing to take possession of his active nature principle, gives way to the natural principle. Intellectual man is corrupted. His volitive faculty is changed into elementary existence, *Hewah*. Universal man, *Adam*, is decomposed and divided. His unity, passed first to number three in *Kain, Habel*, and *Sheth*,

6. And-h e-withdrew-in-h i m s e l f (he forsook the care), IHOAH, t h r o u g h-which he-had-made *Adam,* (collective man) and-he re-pressed (he r e s t r a i n e d, proved himself severe) unto-the-heart-his-own-self.

6. Et-il renonça-entière-ment (il se reposa du soin) IHOAH, à-cause-de-quoi il-avait-fait l'ipséité d'*Adam* (l'homme universel) en-la-t e r r e, et-il-se-réprima (se comprima, se rendit sévère) au cœur sien.

---

goes to number six through *Kain*, and to number nine through *Sheth*. The corporeal faculties succeed to elementary existence. Corporeal man, *Ænosh*, appears upon the cosmogonic scene.

In the meantime, the divine emanations are united to the cor-poreities born of the dissolution of *Adam*, and corporeal man gives place directly to superior man, *Ghibor*, hero, demi-god. Very soon this *Ghibor*, this superior man, abandons himself to evil, and his inevitable downfall brings about the repose of Nature.

Thus, in the profound thought of Moses, these four hieroglyphic names succeed one another: אָדָם, *universal man,* אִישׁ, *intellectual man,* אֱנוֹשׁ *corporeal man,* גִּבּוֹר *superior man.* And these four names, so different in form and in signification, employed by Moses with an art more than human, have been rendered by the same word as synonyms!

v. 5. יֵצֶר, *conceit....* I have already explained the forma-tion of this difficult and important word v. 7. ch. II. It is used here as substantive.

רַק, *diffused....* While explaining the word רָקִיעַ, rarefaction, ethereal expansion, v. 6. ch. I, I stated that the root רַק contained the idea of expansion, of diffusion. Moses in using it here as verb, gives it no other meaning.

v. 6. וַיִּנָּחֶם, *And-he-withdrew-in-himself....* The Christian here-siarchs who have rejected the Books of Moses as unjust to the Divin-ity, in claiming them to be inspired by the genius of evil, or at least by an intermediary being, an Æon, very different from the

7. Wa-îâomer I H Ô A H
æmeheh æth-ha-Adam âsher
barâthî me-hal pheneî ha-
âdamah, me-Adam had-be-
h e m a h had-remesh w'had-
hôph ha-shamaîm ĉhi-niha-
methî ĉhi-hashithîm.

וַיֹּאמֶר יְהֹוָה אֶמְחֶה אֶת־הָאָדָם
אֲשֶׁר בָּרָאתִי מֵעַל פְּנֵי הָאֲדָמָה
מֵאָדָם עַד־בְּהֵמָה עַד־רֶמֶשׂ
וְעַד־עוֹף הַשָּׁמָיִם כִּי־נִחַמְתִּי
כִּי עֲשִׂיתִם :

Supreme Being, have all relied upon this verse, thus translated by
Saint Jerome: "Poenituit eum quod hominem fecisset in terra; et
tactus delore cordis intrinsecus."

These heresiarchs found that it was not consistent to say of the
Most High, of the Immutable Being, infinitely perfect, that he re-
pented of a thing that he had done, or that his heart had been
grieved.

It would appear that the Hellenists, having felt this very great
inconsistency, wished to palliate it: they say in their version, that
GOD considered the creation which he had made of man upon the
earth, and he reflected, καὶ ἐνεθυμήθη ὁ θεὸς, ὅτι ἐποίησεν τὸν ἄνθρωπον ἐπὶ τῆς
γῆς καὶ διενόηθη. But besides, the Hebraic terms do not in the least
present this meaning, the most ancient translations which have been
made from the Greek, and which are in accord with the Latin, make
one suspect that the version of the Hellenists has been mutilated in
this place as in some others.

The Chaldaic paraphrast takes this curious turn.

והב ייי במימריה ארי עבד ית
אינשא בארעא ואמר במימריה
למתבר תוקפיהון ברעותיה

And-he-returned, the Eternal Jaii, in-
his-word, because-he-had-made sub-
stantial-man upon-the-earth: and-he-
declared-in-his-word, for-the-action-be-
ing-broken (that he would break) the-
pride-of-them, conformable-to-his-sover-
eign-will.

As to the Samaritan, the terms that it employs are so obscure
that it is fitting before explaining them, to give the reasons for my
translation. Indeed how is it that so many savants who have studied
the Hebraic tongue, and whose piety must be shocked by the mislead-

7. And-he-said, IHOAH, I-shall wash-off the-selfsame-ness of-*A d a m* (collective man) which-I-have-created, from-above the-face of-the-adamic: from *Adam* (man-kind) to-the-quadruped, the creeping-kind, the fowl of-heavens: for-I withdrew- (I forsook the care) through-which I-made-them.

7. Et-il-dit, IHOAH, je-laverai (j'effacerai au mo-yen de l'eau) cette-exis-tence-objective-d'*A d a m* (l' homme universel) que j'ai-créé, de-dessus-la-face de-la-terre-a d a m i q u e; depuis-*Adam* (le règne hominal) j u s q u'au-quadrupède, au-rampant, au-volatile des-cieux; car j'ai-renoncé-tout-à-fait (au soin) à-cause-de-quoi j'avais-fait-eux.

ing meaning given to this verse by the Vulgate, have not sought to reéstablish the thought of Moses in its purity? What was the mat-ter? It was only necessary to recognize the collective sign ם, which this hierographic writer has added to the verb, to give it, accord-ing to the intensive form, a meaning stronger and more general which it would not have had otherwise. The addition of this final sign is sufficiently common in Hebrew for it to have been noticed; but, as I have already observed, the folly of those who believe them-selves savants, is seeking afar the truth which is before them.

The final character ם, whether alone, or accompanied by the vowel ה, is added not only to nouns, but also to relations and to verbs, to generalize their expression: the genius of the Hebraic tongue, goes so far even as to tolerate its addition to the temporal modifications of verbs, as I shall have occasion to state in v. 13 of this chapter.

Now, the verb נוה thus generalized by the collective sign ם signifies literally, *to renounce wholly, to cease entirely, to desist, to lay aside care, to abandon an action, a sentiment,* etc. The mean-ing that should be attached to this verb, depends therefore upon the care, the sentiment, the action, whose suspension it indicates. If it is an evil act, a sin, it can indeed signify *to repent,* as it can also signify *to be consoled,* if it is a pain, an affliction; but neither sin nor pain can be attributed to GOD; this verb could never involve

8. W-Noah matzâ hen b' heînei Ihôah.

וְנֹחַ מָצָא חֵן בְּעֵינֵי יְהֹוָה :

9. Æleh thô-le d o t h Noah: Noah aîsh tzaddîk thamîm haîah b'dorothaî-ô: æth-ha-Ælohîm hithhallech-Noah.

אֵלֶּה תּוֹלְדֹת נֹחַ נֹחַ אִישׁ צַדִּיק תָּמִים הָיָה בְּדֹרֹתָיו אֶת־הָאֱלֹהִים הִתְהַלֶּךְ־נֹחַ :

10. Wa-ioled Noah she-loshah b a n i m : æth-Shem, æth-Ham wæth-Japheth.

וַיּוֹלֶד נֹחַ שְׁלֹשָׁה בָנִים אֶת־שֵׁם אֶת־חָם וְאֶת־יָפֶת :

---

this meaning relative to him. If God renounces a sentiment, if he ceases entirely from making a thing, as the verb נוחם, expresses it, this sentiment can be only love, this action can be only the conservation of his work. Therefore, he does not *repent*, as Saint Jerome says; but he *renounces*, he *forsakes;* and at the most *is angry*. This last meaning which is the strongest that can be given to the verb נוחם, has been quite generally followed by the Hebrew writers subsequent to Moses. But one must observe that when they use it, it is only as a sequence of the suspension of the love and of the conservative action of the Divinity; for this meaning is not inherent in the verb in question.

Now let us turn to the Samaritan translator. If any one had taken the trouble to investigate the obscurity of his expressions, he would see that it is not very unlike the meaning that I have given this verse.

ᴙᛉ·ᏕᏕᏙ·Ꮥᛉ·ᏕᛉᏕᛞᚠᚷ·ᛉᎫᎫᎪᛉᛉᛉ

ᛉᏕ·ᎤᛗᛞᎤᛉᛉᛉ·ᏕᏙᎤᛉᏕ·ᛉ2ᏕᏙ

ᏕᎤᛉ

And-he-withdrew-to-him-the-breath, Ihoah, by-which he-had-made the Universal in-the-earth: and-he-shut-up (contracted exceedingly) un-to-the-heart-his-own.

8. But-*N o a h* (nature's rest), found grace in-the-eyes of-IHOAH.

9. These-are the-symbolical-p r o g e n i e s of-*Noah*; *Noah*, intellectual- principle right-proving of-universal-accomplishments was-he, in-the-p e r i o d s-his-own: together·with HIM - the - Gods, h e-applied-himself-t o-walk, *Noah*.

10. A n d-h e-d i d-beget, *Noah* (nature's rest) three sons (spiritual offspring): t h e-selfsameness-o f-*S h e m* (the lofty, the bright one) of-*Ham* (the down bent, the gloomy one) and-of-*Japheth* (the extended and wide).

8. Mais-*Noah* (le repos de la nature) trouva grâce aux-yeux de-IHOAH.

9. Celles-ci-sont les-symboliques - générations d e- *Noah*; *Noah*, principe-intellectual manifestant-la-justice des-vertus-universelles il-était, dans-les-âges-siens: les-traces-mêmes de-LUI-les-Dieux, il-s'appliquait-à-suivre, *Noah*.

10. Et-il engendra, *Noah*, (le repos de la nature) trois fils (trois émanations): la-séité-de-*S h e m* (l'élevé, l' éclatant) de-*Ham* (le courbe, le chaud) et-de-*Japheth* (l'étendu).

ויתעצב, *And-he-repressed-himself*.... This is to say, that the Being of beings withdrew into his own heart. The Samaritan translator is the only one who seems to have felt the force of this expression. The compound עצב, springs as I have already said, from the two contracted roots עץ-צב. It is used in this case as verb according to the reflexive form.

v. 7. After the explanations that I have just given, there is nothing more to dwell upon in this verse.

v. 8. ונח *but-Noah*.... For the interpretation of this word, see v. 29, ch. V.

v. 9. בדרותיו, *in-the-periods-his-own*.... Several ideas are attached to the root דור which forms the basis of this word. By the first, should be understood a circle, an orb; by the second, any cir-

11. Wa-th i s h h e t h ha-âretz li-pheneî ha-Ælohîm wa-thimmalæ ha-âretz hamass.

וַתִּשָּׁחֵת הָאָרֶץ לִפְנֵי הָאֱלֹהִים וַתִּמָּלֵא הָאָרֶץ חָמָס :

12. Wa-îaræ Ælohîm æth-ha-âretz, w'hinneh ni-s h e h a t h a t čhi-hisheheth čhol-basher æth-darčh-ô hal-ha-âretz.

וַיַּרְא אֱלֹהִים אֶת־הָאָרֶץ וְהִנֵּה נִשְׁחָתָה כִּי־הִשְׁחִית כָּל־בָּשָׂר אֶת־דַּרְכּוֹ עַל־הָאָרֶץ :

13. Wa-îâomer Ælohîm l'Noah: ketz čhol-bashar bâ l'phana-î čhi-malâh ha-âretz hamass mi-pheneihem: w' hin-nî mashehitham æth-ha-âretz .

וַיֹּאמֶר אֱלֹהִים לְנֹחַ קֵץ כָּל־בָּשָׂר בָּא לְפָנַי כִּי־מָלְאָה הָאָרֶץ חָמָס מִפְּנֵיהֶם וְהִנְנִי מַשְׁחִיתָם אֶת־הָאָרֶץ :

---

cular habitation whatever, a sphere. If one relates the first of these ideas to a temporal duration, then the word רוּר signifies a cyclic period, an age, a century, a generation. If, by the second, one understands an inhabited space, then the same word designates a city, a world, a universe; for I must say, *en passant*, that in ancient times, every duration, like every habitation, was conceived under the picture of a circle. The Arabic words دار and کوره , the Greek words πόλις or πολεῖν, the Latin words *orbis* and *urbs*, are unimpeachable proofs.

v. 10. See v. 32 ch. V.

v. 11. וַתִּשָּׁחֵת, *And-it-was-debased*.... The root חת expresses an idea of terror, consternation, sinking, downfall; literally as well as figuratively. In this verb the root being governed by the sign of relative movement שׁ, characterizes a continual state of downfall and debasement, a progressive degradation.

חמס, *a violent-heat*.... This is the same root חם which I have

11. A n d-i t-was-debased (depressed, vilified) t h e-earth, in the-face of-HIM-the-Gods; and-it-was-filled, the earth, with-a-violent-de-praving-heat.

12. And-he-did-ken, HE t h e-Gods, the-selfsameness of-the-earth, and-lo : being-depraved, because-hastened-to-deprave, e v e r y-bodily-shape, the-way-its-own up-on-the-earth.

13. And-he-said, HE-the-Being-of-beings, t o - *N o a h* (nature's rest) the-end of-e v e r y corporeal-shape is-coming to-the-face-mine : for-it-is heaped, the-earth, with-a-violent-v i l i f y i n g-h e a t through-the-whole-face : and -h e r e-a m-I causing-to-de-press-quite-o v e r t h e-self-sameness-of-the-earth.

11. E t-elle-s e-déprimait (se ravalait, se dégradait) la-terre-à-la-face de-LUI-les-Dieux et-elle-se-remplissait, la-t e r r e, d'une-ardeur-de-plus-en-plus-dégradante.

12. Et-il-considéra, LUI-l'Être-des-êtres, l'ipséité-de-la-terre, et-voici : étant-dé-gradée parceque laissait-dé-grader, toute-forme-corpor-elle, la-voie - propre - sienne, sur-la-terre.

13. Et-il-dit,LUI-l'Ê t r e-des-êtres, à-*Noah*, (le repos de la nature) : la-terme de-toute forme-corporelle est-venant à-la-face-m i e n n e : car-elle-s'est-comblée, la-ter-re, d'une-ardeur dépravante, par-la-face-entière : et-voici-moi laissant-dégrader (avi-lir, détruire) entièrement l'ipséité-terrestre.

---

explained in v. 32 ch. V. Its action taken in the bad sense, is further increased by the addition of the circular movement ס•

v. 12. אֶת־דַּרְכֹּו, *the-way-its-own*.... I have spoken of the root דּוּר, in v. 9 of this chapter. The root אֶק, which is now joined to it by contraction,דַּר־אֶק, fixes the idea and determines it. Thus the word דֶּרֶךְ, expresses every circumscribed law, every orbit, every way, every line whether speaking of time or life, or speaking of intel-lectual or physical things.

v. 13. מִפְּנֵיהֶם, *through-the-whole-face*.... Neither the Hellenists nor the author of the Latin Vulgate, have perceived that the nominal affix הֶם, was used in this case, as collective final and they have

14. Hôsheh le-c̀ha thebath hotzeî-gopher, kinnîm tha-hosheh æth-ha-t h e b a h, w' c̀hapharetha â o t h-ha mi-baîth w'mi-houtz b'c̀hopher.

עֲשֵׂה לְךָ תֵּבַת עֲצֵי־גֹפֶר קִנִּים תַּעֲשֶׂה אֶת־הַתֵּבָה וְכָפַרְתָּ אֹתָהּ מִבַּיִת וּמִחוּץ בַּכֹּפֶר׃

---

connected it with the preceding word נשר; associating thus, without regard for the simplest rules of grammar, a plural with a singular. That Saint Jerome should have made this mistake, can be conceived; but that the Jews, the Essenes, interpreting the tongue of their an-cesters, should not have better understood the Sepher of Moses, is inconceivable. For how could they have ignored the fact that the characters ם or הם, added to the end of words, generalized the mean-ing in the same manner and by the same grammatical rule, that the characters ן or וֹן increased it?

Did they not see written יוֹמָם, *all the day*, שׁמָם, *a generic name*, אָמְנָם *the whole truth*, and שְׁנֵיהֶם, *both of them?* Why have they been deceived in the meaning of the verb נוּחַם, of which I spoke in v. 6. of this chapter? Why have they not recognized the collective sign ם , in the word which is the subject of this note and in the word following? I have already explained this in my Introductory Dis-sertation. They did not wish to give the knowledge of their tongue nor of their sacred books.

מַשְׁחִיתָם, *causing-to-depress-quite....* This is the same verb שָׁחֹר , *to disparage, to abase, to lower,* which Moses used according to the positive form, passive movement, in speaking of the earth, in v. II of this chapter, and which he uses now, according to the excitative form, continued facultative, in speaking of the Being of beings. This observation, that no translator had been in a position to make, was very important. It leads to the real thought of Moses, which is, that the Being of beings destroys the earth only by abandoning it to the degradation, to the corruption which is its own work: this thought is contained in the renunciation referred to in v. 6. It is needless to repeat here, how the ignorant or de-ceiving translators have seen *a repentance* in this divine renuncia-tion. It is because they have not comprehended the force of the collective sign ם , added again to the facultative מַשְׁחִית, in order to generalize its action.

14. Make to-thee a-*thebah* (sheltering abode) of-an-elementary-growth preserving-and-corporeal: hollowed-and-r o o m e d thou-s h a l t-m a k e the-whole-of-that-m u t u a l-abode: and-thou-shalt-smear the-whole-of-it within and-without-the -circumference, w i t h-a-viscous body-like-substance.

14. Fais à-toi une-*thebah* (une retraite, un refuge, un a s i l e mutuel) d'une-substance-élémentaire-conservatrice: de-canaux (lieux propres à contenir) tu-feras l' ensemble de-cette-retraite; et-tu-lieras (englueras) l' ensemble-d'elle, par-l'intérieur e t-p a r-l'extérieur-cir-conférenciel avec-une-mati-ère-corporisante.

---

v. 14. תבה, *a-thebah*.... It appears to be the Samaritan translator who, rendering this word by 𐤟𐤟𐤟𐤟 , *a vessel*, was the first to give rise to all the absurd ideas that this error has brought forth. Never has the Hebrew word תבה signified *a vessel*, in the sense of *a ship*, as it has since been understood; but *a vessel* in the sense of a thing destined to contain and to preserve another. This word, which is found in all the ancient mythologies, merits particular attention. It has so many significations that it is difficult to assign a definite one. It is, on the one hand, the symbolic name given by the Egyptians to their sacred city, *Theba*, considered as the shelter, the refuge, the abode of the gods; that famous city whose name transported into Greece to a straggling village of Beotia, has sufficed to immortalize it. On the other hand, it is a circuit, an orbit, a globe, a land, a coffer, an ark, a world, the solar system, *the Universe*, in fact, that one imagined contained in a sort of vessel called אוב : for I must recall here the fact that the Egyptians did not give chariots to the Sun and Moon as did the Greeks, but a sort of round vessel. The vessel of Isis was no other than that *theba*, that famous ark which we are considering; and it must be stated, the very name of Paris, of this city where are concentrated the rays of glory escaped from a hundred celebrated cities, where again flourish after long darkness, the sciences of the Egyptians, the Assyrians and the Greeks; the name of Paris, I say, is only the name of the Thebes of Egypt and of Greece, that of ancient Syparis, of the Babel of As-

15.   W'zeh âsher thahos-
heh âoth-ha shilosh mâôth
âmmah ârèch ha-thebah ha-
moshîm âmmah raheb-ha w-
shiloshîm âmmah kômath-
ha.

וְזֶה אֲשֶׁר תַּעֲשֶׂה אֹתָהּ שְׁלֹשׁ
מֵאוֹת אַמָּה אֹרֶךְ הַתֵּבָה חֲמִשִּׁים
אַמָּה רָחְבָּהּ וּשְׁלֹשִׁים אַמָּה
קוֹמָתָהּ :

---

syria, translated into the tongue of the Celts.   It is the vessel of
Isis, (Bar-Isis) that mysterious ark, which, in one way or another,
carries ever the destinies of the world, of which it is the symbol.

Besides, this word אוּב, whose vast meaning could not be exactly rendered by any of those that I know, and which the wisest
Egyptians alone were in position to comprehend, given over to
vulgar Hebrews and following the proneness of their gross ideas, was
finally restricted and corrupted to the point of signifying literally
the belly, a leather bottle; and figuratively, *a magic spirit,* a sort of
demon to which the Jews attributed the oracles of their sibyls.   But
there exists in the Hebraic idiom as well as in the neighbouring
idioms from the same source, a mass of expressions, which starting
from the same radical principle, show all its importance.

It is first its analogue אב, developing the general idea of fructification, of generation, of paternity; then, it is that of the will, in
אבה; that of love, in אהב: it is all blossoming, in the Syriac
ܘܚܒܐ: it is every awakening, in the Arabic هب ; all immensity,
every unknown place, in هوب ; every inner and profound sentiment, in واب: finally, without seeking to link with this root any
other signs than the one which enters into the composition of the
word תבה, it is the action of being moved in oneself, of returning,
of retiring into, of withdrawing to oneself through desire, in the
three verbs הוב, תוֹבב, and תאוב: it is even the name of the Universe, in the compound תבל.   One cannot see in all this, either
the coffer of the Hellenists, $κιβωτός$, or *the chest* of the Latin
translator, "arca".

עצי-גפר, *of-an-elementary-growth-preserving....*   The Hellenists
have said $ἐκ ξύλων τετραγώνων$ of *quadrangular wood;* Saint Jerome
has said "de lignis levigatis" *of polished wood;* the Chaldaic
paraphrast ראעין דקדרוֹם *of planks of cedar;* the Samaritan translator
ᛉᛦᛘᛁᛉ . ᛒᛉᛐ, *of an ebony substance, or of papyrus.*   None

15. And-thus this shalt-thou-make three hundred-fold of-mother-measuring the-length of-t h e-*t h e b a h* (t h a t sheltering abode): five-tens of-measuring, the-breath-of-it, and-three-tens of-measuring the-bulk (the whole heap, the substantiality)-of-it.

15. Et-c'est-ainsi que tu-feras la-séité-d'elle: trois centuples de-measure-mère (régulatrice) l a-longitude de-la-*thebah* (cette retraite sacrée) c i n q-décuples de-mesure, la-latitude-sienne; et-trois-décuples de-mesure, la-solidité (la substantialité) sienne.

---

of them having understood, or having wished to understand, what the *thebah* was; and being represented for the most part under the figure of a rude bark, it was impossible that they should not fall into the grossest errors. I have already proved that the word עץ does not signify *wood*. It should be known that it is not any kind of *tree* whose use had been forbidden to universal man, *Adam*. Here is the hieroglyphic composition of the word גפר. The root גף which developing, in general, all ideas of conservation, of protection, of means, of exterior guarantee, and which, signifying in a more restricted sense, *a body*, is found united to the elementary root אר. The Chaldaic verb גוף, which comes from the root גף, expresses the action of closing outwardly, of embodying, of furnishing with conservatory means, etc.

קנים, *hollowed-and-roomed*.... This is the root קן, used here for the root גן, so as to give more force to the expression. I call attention to this so that one may see nothing in it similar to קין.

בכפר, *with-a-viscous body-like-substance*.... כפר is the same word as גפר, used above, but whose force is now augmented by the hieroglyphic substitution which Moses has made of the assimilative sign כ, for the organic sign ג.

v. 15. אמה, *of-mother-measuring*.... The translator who has in this case rendered the word אמה, *a cubit*, has made the same mistake in rendering the word שנה *a year;* he has restricted in determined limits that which had only relative limits. Thus, as by שנה should be understood any duration relative to the being of which it is the object, so in אמה should be seen a measure peculiar

16.   Tzohr thahosheh la-thebah w'æl-âmmah thebale-uah mi-lemahel-ha w'phat-hah ha-thebah b'tzid-ha tha-shîm thahethiîm sheniîm w-shelishîm thahoshe-ha.

צֹהַר תַּעֲשֶׂה לַתֵּבָה וְאֶל־אַמָּה תְּכַלֶּנָּה מִלְמַעְלָה וּפֶתַח הַתֵּבָה בְּצִדָּהּ תָּשִׂים תַּחְתִּים שְׁנִיִם וּשְׁלִשִׁים תַּעֲשֶׂהָ׃

17.   Wa-ânî hin-nî mebîâ æth-ha-mabboul maîm hal-ha-âretz l'shaheth-čhol-bas-har âsher-b'ô rouah haîîm: m i-t h a h a t h ha-shamaîm čhol-âsher b'âretz îgwah.

וַאֲנִי הִנְנִי מֵבִיא אֶת־הַמַּבּוּל מַיִם עַל־הָאָרֶץ לְשַׁחֵת כָּל־בָּשָׂר אֲשֶׁר־בּוֹ רוּחַ חַיִּים מִתַּחַת הַשָּׁמָיִם כֹּל אֲשֶׁר בָּאָרֶץ יִגְוָע׃

---

to the thing in question.   This word signifies literally, *a metropolis*, an original maternal nation, relative to another; a thing upon which others depend, and by which they must be ruled; *a measure*, *a rule*.   Its root is אם, which develops all ideas of maternity.   I believe it unnecessary to dwell upon the other terms which compose this verse, inasmuch as the most important, the names of the numbers have been explained.

v. 16.   צֹהַר, *Gathering-light......*   The interpretation of this facultative by the Hellenists and the Latin translator differs widely. The former have seen ἐπισυνάγων, *gathering*, and the latter "fenestram" *a window*.   They might have easily perceived their error, if they had observed that its derivative יִצְהָר, designated *oil;* that is to say, that kind of liquid which seems to gather to itself the luminous principle to shed it without.   The facultative here referred to, rests upon two contracted roots צֹור־אֹר.   The first צֹור, contains the idea of an impressed movement, of direction given to a thing: the second אֹר or אֹור is the symbol of elementary principle, or light.

16. G a t h e r i n g-light, shalt-thou-make unto-t h e-*t h e b a h,* a n d-a f t e r-the-mother-measuring, the-orbicular-extent-its-own, as-to-the-uppermost-part-its-own; and-the-opening of-that-mutual-asylum, in-the-opposite-p a r t-i t s-o w n, shalt-thou-place: t h e-lowermost-parts two and-three-fold s h a l t-thou-make-to-it.

16. Dirigeant-la-lumière, tu-feras à-la-*thebah,* et-selon -l a-mesure-régulatrice, l'orbe (l'étendue orbiculaire)-sienne, e n-c e-qui-concerne-l a-partie-supérieure-sienne; e t-l a dilatation (la solution, l'ouverture), de-cette-r e t r a i t e en-la-partie-opposée-sienne tu-mettras: les-parties-basses, doubles et-triples, tu-feras-à-elle.

17. And-even-I, t h e r e-am-I bringing the selfsameness-o f-the-g r e a t-swelling (the flood) of-waters upon-the-earth, to depress (annihilate) e v e r y-bodily-shape that-has i n t o-it s e l f the-breath of-lives: from-below t h e-heavens all-that-is in-the-earth, shall-expire.

17. Et-moi-m ê m e, me-voici faisant-venir c e-q u i-constitue-la-grande-intumescence des-eaux (le déluge) sur-la-terre, pour-déprimer (détruire) toute-forme-corporelle qui-a dans-soi le-souffle des-vies: par-en-bas des-cieux, tout ce-qui-est en-la-terre expirera.

תבלנה, *the-orbicular-extent-its-own* .... The word תבל by which is generally understood, an orbicular extent, *the universe,* signifies in the most restricted sense, the globe of the earth, the earth, the terrestrial superficies. It is attached to the same root as the word תבה, as I have said, and differs from it only by the expansive sign ל, which communicates to it its particular movement.

v. 17. את־המבול, *the-selfsameness-of-the-great-swelling* .... This is that universal deluge related by Moses, that terrible event, the memory of which remains among all peoples, like tracks upon the face of the whole earth. If I should consult the annals of the world, I could easily prove that, from the Chinese to the Scandinavians, from the Syrians to the Iroquois, there does not exist a single people that has not had knowledge of this catastrophe; if I should call, in its turn, natural history to give evidence, I could not

18.   Wa-hakimothî æt h-
berith-î   âitha-ĉha-w-bâtha
æl-ha-thebah âthah! w-
banei-ĉha, w-âisheth-ĉha w-
neshei-baneî-ĉha âitha-ĉha.

וַהֲקִמֹתִי אֶת־בְּרִיתִי אִתָּךְ וּבָאתָ
אֶל־הַתֵּבָה אַתָּה וּבָנֶיךָ וְאִשְׁתְּךָ
וּנְשֵׁי־בָנֶיךָ אִתָּךְ

---

take a single step without encountering unimpeachable proofs of this truth of natural philosophy.

The root כול , composed of the two signs כ and ל , indicates a force eminently dilating, which, acting from the centre to the circumference, increases the volume of things, causing a boiling up, a flux, an extraordinary swelling.   All the words which come from this root are connected with this idea.   Sometimes it is a crowd, a tumultuous gathering; sometimes, an unusual abundance, an inundation, etc.   The character מ which governs it, ought to be considered on this occasion, not alone as sign of exterior and plastic action; but as representing the word *mah*, which, as we have already seen in explaining the word מאה *one hundred*, is applied to that which is great, to that which attains its utmost dimensions.

מים , *the waters....*   The deluge is not expressed by one single word in Hebrew, as might be believed, following the vulgar translations, but by two, מבול־מים , *the great intumescence, the great swelling of the waters.*   The hierographic writer clearly indicates here, that the divine will influencing the waters, they extend and increase in volume and cause the universal inundation.   Thus the calculations of the savants to determine whether the actual mass of the waters can be sufficient for this effect, are ridiculous and prove their ignorance.   It is not a question of computing whether the waters with which the seas are filled, can, in their state of

18. And-I will-cause-to-stand, t h e-creating-might-mine together-t h e e, a n d-thou-wilt-repair toward-the *thebah,* thou! and the-sons-of-thee (thy spiritual off-spring) a n d-t h e-intellect-ual-mate-thy-own (thy voli-tive faculty) a n d-the-cor-poreal-mates of-the-sons-of-thee (their natural facul-ties) together-thee.

18. E t-j e-ferai-subsister la-force-créatrice-mienne en-semble-t o i e t-t u-viendras vers-la-*t h e b a h,* toi! et-les-fils-à-toi (tes productions) et-l a-femme-intellectuelle-à-toi (ta faculté efficiente) et-les-épouses-corporelles-des-fils-à-toi (leurs facultés physi-ques) ensemble-toi.

---

depression, cover the whole earth and rise above the highest moun-tains; this is obviously impossible: but it is a question of knowing whether, in a state of extreme dilation and swelling caused by the effect of a certain force chained to the centre of the waters, they would suffice for this.

v. 18. בריתי, *the-creating-might-mine....* It is very difficult to divine how the Hellenists and Saint Jerome, can see a pact, a treaty of alliance, in a word so plainly derived from the verb ברא, *to create.* The reader must feel that it is more simple to believe that the Being of beings, ready to abandon the earth to the destruc-tion toward which it tends, leaves his creative force to subsist with *Noah,* the repose of nature, than to believe that he establishes some sort of contract or pact between them.

ונשי, *and-the-corporeal-mates....* I would call attention to the fact that Moses does not use, to designate the *mates* of the sons of Noah, the same word אשה, as he does in characterizing the *in-tellectual mate* of the latter, his *volitive faculty.*

19. W-mi-chol h-haî mi-chol bashar shenaîm mi-chol-thabîâ æl-ha-thebah l' hahoîoth âitha-cha: zachar w-nekebah îhîou.

וּמִכָּל־הָחַי מִכָּל־בָּשָׂר שְׁנַיִם מִכָּל
תָּבִיא אֶל־הַתֵּבָה לְהַחֲיֹת אִתָּךְ
זָכָר וּנְקֵבָה יִהְיוּ׃

20. Me-ha-hôph l'mîn-hou, w-min ha-behemah l' mîn-ha, mi-chol remesh ha-âdamah l'mîn-hou shenaîm mi-chol îaboâou æleî-cha l' hahoîôth.

מֵהָעוֹף לְמִינֵהוּ וּמִן־הַבְּהֵמָה
לְמִינָה מִכָּל רֶמֶשׂ הָאֲדָמָה
לְמִינֵהוּ שְׁנַיִם מִכֹּל יָבֹאוּ אֵלֶיךָ
לְהַחֲיוֹת׃

21. W'âthah kah-le-cha mi-chol maâ-chol âsher îeâ-chel w'assaphetha æleî-cha w'haîah l'cha w-la-hem l' âchelah.

וְאַתָּה קַח־לְךָ מִכָּל־מַאֲכָל אֲשֶׁר
יֵאָכֵל וְאָסַפְתָּ אֵלֶיךָ וְהָיָה לְךָ
וְלָהֶם לְאָכְלָה׃

22. Wa-îahash Noah ch' chol âsher tziwah âoth-ô Ælohîm; chen hashah.

וַיַּעַשׂ נֹחַ כְּכֹל אֲשֶׁר צִוָּה אֹתוֹ
אֱלֹהִים כֵּן עָשָׂה׃

---

v. 19. and 20.   All these terms have been explained.

v. 21. וְאָסַפְרֵּ, *that-thou-shalt-lay up*.... The conjunctive article וְ holds here the place of the relative אֲשֶׁר as we have seen it in other cases. The words used in this verse offer no difficulty as to their literal and grammatical signification; as to their figurative and hieroglyphic meaning, that is different; a long note would be necessary for me to make them understood and besides, I should not attain this point if the reader did not first recognize *Noah*, for upon

19. A n d-from-all-living-kind, from-all-bodily-shape, two-twains from-all t h o u-s h a l t-c a u s e-to-repair toward-the-*thebah*, for-being-kept-existing together-thee: male and-female they-shall-be.

20. From-t h e-f l y i n g-fowl after-the-kind-its-own, from the quadrupedly-walk-ing-a n i m a l i t y, after-the-kind-its-own, from-all-creep-ing-life elementary-e a r t h-born after-the-kind-its-own, two-and-two, they-shall-re-pair toward-thee for-being caused-to-exist.

21. A n d-t h o u ! t a k e (draw) unto-thee, from-all food which-c a n-feed, that-t h o u-shalt-lay up-toward-thee: and-it-shall-be unto-t h e e, a n d-unto-them for-food.

22. And-he-did, *N o a h*, t h e-s a m e-all which had-w i s e l y-prescribed HE-the-Gods; thus-doing.

19. Et-de-toute-existence, d e-t o u t e-forme-corporelle, deux-à-deux de-tout tu-fe-ras-venir vers-la-*t h e b a h*, afin-d'exister ensemble-toi: mâle et-femelle ils-seront.

20. Du-genre-volatile se-lon-l'espèce-s i e n n e, et-du-genre-quadrupède selon-l'es-pèce-sienne, de-tout-animal-reptiforme issu-de-l'élément-adamique, selon-l'espèce-à-lui, les-deux-doubles de-tout, ils-viendront p r è s-d e-t o i afin-d'y-c o n s e r v e r-l'exis-tence.

21. Et-toi ! prends (sais-is, tire) à-toi de-tout-ali-ment q u i-p e u t-alimenter que-tu-ramasseras d e v e r s-toi: et-il-sera-à-toi, et-à-eux pour aliment.

22. Et-il-fit, *Noah*, le-semblable-tout lequel avait-sagement-prescrit L U I-les Dieux: ainsi-faisant.

---

this knowledge depends that of the children of *Adam*. In regard to them, I have said all that I can say.

v. 22. ככל, *the-same-all*.... I quote this word only to point out the use of the assimilative article כ: an article which the trans-lators of the Sepher have not recognized, whether through ignorance or deliberate intent, in very essential instances where it **was quite as** obvious as it is here.

SEPHER BERÆSHITH.
Z.

ספר בראשית ז׃

1. Wa-îâomer Ihôah l'
Noah boâ âthah w'chol beîth
-cha æl-ha-thebah chi âoth-
cha râîthi tzaddîk l'phana-î
ba-dôr ha-zeh.

וַיֹּאמֶר יְהֹוָה לְנֹחַ בֹּא־אַתָּה
וְכָל־בֵּיתְךָ אֶל־הַתֵּבָה כִּי־אֹתְךָ
רָאִיתִי צַדִּיק לְפָנַי בַּדּוֹר הַזֶּה ׃

2. Mi-chol ha-behemah
ha-tehôrah thikkah - le - cha
shibehah shibehah! âîsh w'
âisheth-ô w-min-ha-behemah
âsher loâ theorah hiwâ shenaîm âîsh w'âisheth-ô.

מִכֹּל הַבְּהֵמָה הַטְּהוֹרָה תִּקַּח־
לְךָ שִׁבְעָה שִׁבְעָה אִישׁ וְאִשְׁתּוֹ
וּמִן־הַבְּהֵמָה אֲשֶׁר לֹא טְהֹרָה
הִוא שְׁנַיִם אִישׁ וְאִשְׁתּוֹ ׃

---

v. 1.   There is nothing perplexing in these terms.

v. 2.   איש ואשתו, *the-very-principle* and-the-volitive-intellectual
faculty-its own....   Here is a decisive passage which makes one
of the most astounding incoherences, one of the strongest physical
contradictions, disappear from the narrative of Moses. For if the
thebah was really a boat, as the translators leave it to be understood, of only three hundred cubits in length, fifty in breadth, and
thirty in height, I ask how the terrestrial and aerial animals, by
sevens of the pure and by twos of the impure, could lodge there?
How could the provisions necessary for this innumerable multitude
of famished beasts be placed therein, both during all the time of
their sojourn in the boat, and during that time when, even after
their going out, the earth, ravaged by the deluge, could offer them
none?   Has one ever considered how much so many carnivorous
animals would consume; the tremendous quantity of animals that

GENESIS VII.

COSMOGONIE VII.

1. And-he-said, I H O A H, unto *Noah* come-thou! and-the-whole-interior-thine toward-the-*thebah* (sheltering a b o d e): for-the-selfsameness-t h i n e I-d i d-view-as righteous in-t h e-face-mine, by-the-age this.

2. From-all the-quadrupedly-w a l k i n g-kind, the-pure! thou-shalt-draw unto-thee, by-seven seven! the-very-principle and-the-volitive-intellectual-faculty-i t s-o w n a n d-f r o m-the-quadruped, which-is not-pure initself, by-twains, the-principle and-the-v o l i t i v e-faculty-its-own.

1. Et-il-dit, IHOAH, à-*Noah*, vient-toi! et-tout-l'intérieur-à-toi, devers-la-*thebah* (la place de refuge) car l'i p s é i t é-tienne j'ai-considerée j u s t e à-m a-f a c e, dans-l'âge celui-ci.

2. De-tout le-genre-quadrupède, le-pur! tu-prendras (tu retireras) à-toi, sept à-s e p t! le-principe et-la-fa-c u l t é-volitive-efficiente-à-lui; et-du-genre-quadrupède qui-est non-pur en-lui-même, deux-à-deux, le-principe et-la-faculté-efficiente-à-lui.

---

would be required for their nourishment, and the amount of herbs, or of grain necessary for those even which must be devoured to sustain the others? Obviously a physical impossibility.

But Moses was not unlearned. The instructions that he had received in the sanctuaries of Egypt were not nonsense, and the particular inspiration which animated him did not lead him to absurdities. I believe I have had the pleasure of giving several times evident proof of it. I repeat that it is always as translator and not as commentator, that I have done so. These are not my ideas that I am giving; these are his own that I am restoring.

Whatever may be the *thebah*, sacred storehouse of Nature given over to the repose of existence, whose mystery can never be wholly divulged, it is at least certain that it is not a boat, properly so-called. It is a place of refuge, an inaccessible retreat, where elementary life

3. Gam me-hôph ha-shamaim shibehah shibehah! zachar w-nekebah l'haiôth zerah hal-pheneî chol-ha-âretz.

נֻם מֵעוֹף הַשָּׁמַיִם שִׁבְעָה שִׁבְעָה
זָכָר וּנְקֵבָה לְחַיּוֹת זֶרַע עַל־פְּנֵי
כָל־הָאָרֶץ :

---

itself, is concentrated during great catastrophes, cataclysms and conflagrations which the universe undergoes. When the fountains of the deep rise in tempestuous violence covering and ravaging the earth, the principle and the efficient volitive faculty of all the beings of the animal, aerial or terrestrial kingdom, must be united there in that holy *thebah*.

Now, what is a principle? What is an efficient volitive faculty? A principle is that which constitutes the being such as it is in general; for example, that which makes the lamb not a wolf: the hind, not a panther; the bull, not a hippopotamus. A principle produces its efficient faculty in the same manner that fire produces heat. It is by the action of its faculty that every principle is in-dividualized: for every faculty reproducing in its turn its principle, in the same manner that heat produces fire, multiplies the being by a sort of division. It is the efficient faculty which manifesting the principle, causes, for example, the bear not to be inclined in the same fashion as a rabbit; a sparrow hawk as a dove; a rhinocerous as a gazelle. It is by its efficient volitive faculty emanated from its principle that every being conforms exteriorly. The naturalists who have assumed that the tiger was tiger because he had teeth, claws, stomach and intestines, fashioned in a particular way, have spoken thoughtlessly and without understanding. They might have done better by saying, that the tiger had those teeth, claws, stomach and intestines because he was tiger, that is to say, because his efficient volitive faculty constituted him such. It is not the instrument which gives the will, but the will the instrument. The compass no more makes geometry, than the dagger makes the assassin, or the violin the virtuoso. These men can use these things to help them-selves but their will must always have precedence over the usage.

Moses expresses as usual, the principle of being and its ef-ficient volitive faculty by the words אִישׁ and אִשָּׁה. I have given

3. And-also from the-fly-ing-fowl of-heavens, by-se-vens; male and-female for-being-kept-existing in-germ upon-t h e-face of-the-whole-earth.

3. Aussi du-genre-vola-tile des-cieux sept à-sept; mâle et-femelle afin-d'être-fait-exister sementiellement •sur-la-face de-toute-la-terre.

---

the etymology and the hieroglyphic meaning of both. It is un-necessary for me to repeat. To ask why his translators have not rendered these important expressions, is vain repetition: it is ask-ing on the one hand, why they have not wished to betray the mys-teries of the Sepher, knowing them; or, on the other, why not know-ing them they have not betrayed them.

The Hellenists have distorted the Mosaic phrase in saying here ἄρσεν καὶ θῆλυ , *male and female*, because they knew or ought to have known that אִישׁ and אִשָּׁה never had that signification: but could they do otherwise? Could they expose for destruction all that they had done? Rather than to disclose the true meaning of this expression, or to become ridiculous by continuing to see there *man and woman*, they preferred to copy the Samaritan which had solved the difficulty in reading צֶ֗כָּר . צֶ֗קֵבָ֗ה *male and female*, without concerning themselves whether these words, analogous to the Hebraic words זכר ונקבה , were not announced further on as a warning not to confuse them. I have already said that these interpreters preferred to be accused of incoherences and contradictions, than to violate the mysteries of Moses. As to Saint Jerome, he could not diviate on this occasion from the meaning of the Hellenists, without disturbing their version entirely and without inopportunely shedding light on this conscious reticence.

v. 3. לְחַיּוֹת זֶרַע , *for-being-kept-existing-in-germ*.... This is per-fectly obvious and corroborates in an irresistible manner, what I have said. The quadrupeds are placed in the *thebah*, in principle and in faculty, and the flying fowl, male and female, in germ only. This distinction sustains the system of Moses, which gives to birds the same origin as to fishes, in making them both multiply by the aqueous element, whereas he correlates the quadruped kind with the adamic element. It suffices therefore to conserve the germ ex-

4. Chi l'îamîm hôd shib-
ehah, anochî mametîr hal-
ha-âretz ârbahîm îôm w'ârbahîm laîlah: w-m a h î t h î
æth-chol ha-îekoum â s h e r
hashîthî me-hal pheneî ha-
âdamah.

כִּי לְיָמִים עוֹד שִׁבְעָה אָנֹכִי
מַמְטִיר עַל־הָאָרֶץ אַרְבָּעִים יוֹם
וְאַרְבָּעִים לַיְלָה וּמָחִיתִי אֶת־כָּל
הַיְקוּם אֲשֶׁר עָשִׂיתִי מֵעַל פְּנֵי
הָאֲדָמָה :

5. Wa-îahash Noah che-
chol âsher tziwa-hou IHÔAH.

וַיַּעַשׂ נֹחַ כְּכֹל אֲשֶׁר צִוָּהוּ יְהֹוָה :

---

istence of birds upon the breast of the waters; whereas terrestrial
animals which emanate from another principle, require that this
principle be conserved.

The Hellenists not knowing how to express this phrase, have
resolved to distort it like the preceding one, by saying διατρέψαι
σπέρμα, *that the germ be nourished;* which has no sense.   The
author of the Latin Vulgate, to repair this absurdity, translates "ut
salvetur semen," *that the germ be saved;* which has more truth but
which absolutely contradicts the Hebrew; for the verb חיות does not
signify *to save*, but *to exist, to live;* so that the words לחיות זרע
signify literally, *for the action of existing*, or *of living*, germ, that is
to say, *in germ.*

v. 4. אַרְבָּעִים, *four-tens....*   What I have said upon the composition of this word and upon the signification of its root, can
be reviewed in v. 10, ch. II.   One can also consult the Rad. Vocab.
concerning the roots יו, ים and עוֹד.

וּמָחִיתִי, *and-I-shall-wash-off....* It is the root מרה changed to
מח to increase its force, which develops in the verb מהוֹר, all ideas
attached to the action of water.

4. For-in-the-days (manifested lights) of-the-present-cyclic-period, t h e-seventh, myself-I-am causing-to-rain upon-the-earth four-tens of-day (a great quaternion of light) a n d-f o u r-t e n s of-night (a great quaternion of d a r k n e s s) : a n d-I-shall-wash-o f f that-whole-standing-plastic-nature, which-I-have-framed from-over the-face of-the-adamic (elementary ground).

4. Car aux-j o u r s (aux manifestations phénoméniques) de-la-période-actuelle, septième, moi-même-je-suis faisant-pleuvoir sur-la-terre quatre-décuples de-jour (un grand quaternaire de lumière) et-quatre-décuples de-nuit (un grand quaternaire d' obscurité) : et-j'effacerai cette-toute la- nature-plastic-substantielle q u e-j' a i-faite, de-dessus la-face de-l' élément adamique.

5. And-he-did, *Noah,* the same-all w h i c h had-carefully-p r e s c r i b e d to-him, IHOAH.

5. Et-il-fit, *Noah* le-semblable tout lequel avait-prescrit-à-lui-avec-soin, IHOAH.

היקום *standing-plastic-nature....* The root קו characterizes in general, indefinite material extent, a thing indeterminate, obtuse, vague. The verb which is formed of it קוה, expresses the action of stretching, of extending, of being carried toward an object; the action of forming a desire, emitting a sound, etc. The same root קו, having asssumed the sign of exterior and plastic action, in קום, signifies as noun, *a substance,* in general, *an extensive thing, a material object;* as verb, it presents the action of existing materially, of subsisting, of being clothed with form and substance, of being formed, of coagulating, of rising with force, of opposing, etc. These various significations which, as one can see, have their source in the extent or in the indefinite material substance, of which the root קו is the symbol, are united in the word יקום by the sign of potential manifestation ׳, which here adds the sense that I give it of *substance* or of *plastic, substantial nature.*

This word, however, not being expressible by any analogue, must be considered carefully. The Chaldean paraphrast has preserved it in its integrity; but the Samaritan has deemed proper to change it, and has substituted ꜟꞨꞩꞨꞩ, which, coming evidently from the root

6. W-Noah b e n-s h e s h maôth s h a n a h w'ha-mab-boul haîah maîm hal-ha-âretz.

וְנֹחַ בֶּן־שֵׁשׁ מֵאוֹת שָׁנָה וְהַמַּבּוּל הָיָה מַיִם עַל־הָאָרֶץ:

7. Wa-îaboâ N o a h w-banaî-ô w'âisheth-ô w-nes-heî-banaî-ô âith-ô æl-ha-the-bah mi-pheneî meî ha-mab-boul.

וַיָּבֹא נֹחַ וּבָנָיו וְאִשְׁתּוֹ וּנְשֵׁי־בָנָיו אִתּוֹ אֶל־הַתֵּבָה מִפְּנֵי מֵי הַמַּבּוּל

8. Min-ha-behemah ha-te-hôrah w-min-ha-behemah âsher âîne-nah tehôrah w-min-ha-hôph w-čhol âsher ꞏomesh hal-ha-âdamah:

מִן־הַבְּהֵמָה הַטְּהוֹרָה וּמִן־הַבְּהֵמָה אֲשֶׁר אֵינֶנָּה טְהוֹרָה וּמִן־הָעוֹף וְכֹל אֲשֶׁר רֹמֵשׂ עַל־הָאֲדָמָה:

מוּן or מִין signifies *that which constitutes the form, the mien of things*. The Hellenists in rendering this word by ἐξανάστασιν, *re-surrection*, have had a very singular idea. Saint Jerome has not followed them in this instance; he has translated it simply "sub-stantiam" *the substance*.

v. 5. All these terms are understood.

v. 6. בֶּן־שֵׁשׁ *the-son-of-six*.... I beg the reader to observe that Moses speaking of *Noah* names him here again, son of an on-tological duration. This hierographic writer had said, v. 32, ch. v. that *Noah* was son of *five* hundreds of temporal mutation, when he begat *Shem, Ham* and *Japheth;* now he announces that he was son of *six* hundreds of like mutation when the deluge inundated the earth.   If the reader would penetrate the profound thought which Moses encloses in these hieroglyphic expressions, he should remember

6. And-*Noah*-was-the-son (consequent offspring) of-six hundreds of-beings-revolving-c h a n g e, that-the-great-swelling was of-waters upon-the-earth.

7. And-he-went, *N o a h*, and-the sons-of-him (his issued offspring) and-the-intellectual-mate-his-own (his volitive faculty), a n d-t h e-corporeal-mates of-the-sons-of-him (their natural faculties) toward-t h e-*t h e b a h* (sheltering abode), f r o m-the-face of-the water's great-swelling.

8. From-t h e-quadrupedly-walking-kind of-the-pureness, a n d-from-the-quadrupedly-walking-k i n d which not-being-itself of-the-pureness, a n d-f r o m-the-flying-fowl, a n d-from-every-creeping-life upon-the-adamic.

6. Et-*Noah*-était l e-f i l s (le r é s u l t a t) de-six-centaines de-mutation-temporelle-ontologique, que-la-grande-intumescence é t a i t des-eaux sur-la-terre.

7. Et-il-alla, *Noah*, et-les-fils-à-lui (ses productions) et-la-femme- intellectuelle-à-lui (sa faculté volitive efficiente), e t-l e s-épouses-corporelles des-fils-siens (leurs facultés physiques), vers-la-*thebah* (l'asyle sacré), de-la-face des-eaux de-la-grande-intumescence.

8. D u-genre-quadrupède de-l a-p u r e t é, et-du-genre-quadrupède lequel non-être-lui de-la-pureté, et-du-genre-volatile, et-d e-t o u t-ce-qui-e s t-animé-d'un-mouvement-reptiforme s u r - l' élément-adamique.

---

that in the Hebraic decade whose etymology I have carefully sought, I have found that the number *five* חמש, was that of physical compression; that number *six*, שש, contained the ideas of a proportional and relative measure; and that, by the number *one hundred*, משרה, should be understood the extension of a thing which fills its natural limits.

v. 7. ונשי־בניו, *and-the-corporeal-mates of-the-sons-of-him....* I make here the same observation that I have made in v. 18, ch. VI. Moses who uses the word אשת, to characterize the volitive faculty of *Noah*, makes use of the word נשי to designate the physical faculties of the beings emanated from it. This recidivism ought to

9. Shenaîm shenaîm bâou æl-Noah æl-ha-thebah zaĉhar w-nekebah ĉh' âsher tziwah Ælohîm æth-Noah.

שְׁנַיִם שְׁנַיִם בָּאוּ אֶל־נֹחַ אֶל־הַתֵּבָה זָכָר וּנְקֵבָה כַּאֲשֶׁר צִוָּה אֱלֹהִים אֶת־נֹחַ׃

10.   W a-î h î l'shibehath ha-iamîm w-meî ha-mabboul haîou hal-ha-âretz.

וַיְהִי לְשִׁבְעַת הַיָּמִים וּמֵי הַמַּבּוּל הָיוּ עַל־הָאָרֶץ׃

---

prove to those who might think hazard alone had decided this arrangement of words, that Moses had had a real intention in disposing of them in this manner.

v. 8. הַטְּהוֹרָה, *of-the-pureness*.... I note this word to call attention to the fact that the root from which it comes, הוּר, *fire*, is precisely the same as that from which the word *purity* is derived: for our qualificative *pure*, evidently comes from the Greek πῦρ, *fire*, which finds its principle in the elementary root אוּר, the history of which can be seen in v. 3 and 10, ch. I.   The Hebrew word טהוֹר and the English word *pure*, differ from each other only by the initial sign.   It is always fire which constitutes its radical principle, and from which the genius of the two tongues draws the idea of purification.   The Hellenists who, in this instance, have employed the word καθαρός are not far from the primitive root אוּר, since this facultative is derived from the verb καθαίρειν, which means *to pass through fire, to make like fire*: but they have not been followed by the Latin translator, who, having before him the qualificative "purus", has taken "mundus", whose root *und*, denatures entirely the thought of the hierographic writer.   For this latter word, being related, as can be seen, to the action of the waters, depicts only a sort of exterior cleanness, whereas the word "purus", being attached to the root אוּר, *fire*, would express an interior purification resulting from its action.   This distinction, trifling as it may appear to certain minds, is of the greatest importance for the mystagogues.   Air, fire and water were considered in the mysteries as three purifying elements; but one was careful not to confuse their action.

I ought, moreover, to say that the Samaritan in making use of

9. Twains-by-twains they-went t o w a r d-*Noah* (nature's rest) toward-the-*thebah*, male and-female, so-as w i s e l y-prescribed HE-the-Gods, together-*Noah*.

10. And-i t-w a s on-the-seventh of-the-days (mani-,fested lights) that-the-waters of-the-g r e a t-swelling were upon-the earth.

9. De-deux en-deux, ils-allèrent vers-*Noah* (le repos de l'existence) vers-la *thebah*, mâle et-femelle, se-lon-que prescrivit-sagement LUI-les-D i e u x, a u-m ê m e-*Noah*.

10. Et-c e-f u t a u-sept-ième des-jours (manifestations phénoméniques) que-l e s-eaux de-la-grande-intumescence furent sur-la-terre.

---

the word 𝔸𝔸𝔸𝔸𝔸, had much earlier, committed the same error as that with which I reproach the Latin translator, corrupting in this instance, as in many others, the hieroglyphic meaning of Moses.

v. 9. All these terms are understood.

v. 10. לשבעת, *on-the-seventh*.... We have seen in searching for the etymology of the Hebraic decade, that number *seven* שבע, was that of the consummation of things and times.

v. 11. בחורש, *in-the-moon-renewing*.... The root חר from which this word comes, and which expresses unity, is only the root ער which develops all ideas attached to time, and in which the elementary sign ה has been replaced by that of physical sense ע. These two roots, closely allied to each other, are often confused in pronunciation, thus confusing the diverse expressions of elementary and of temporal existence. This is the case here. The sign of relative movement ש added to this root, carries the idea of a beginning of existence, either in the order of things or in the order of time. Thus the word חרש characterizes that which is new, that which is renewed; that which reappears. With the luminous sign, this same word חורש, becomes the expression of a *neomenia, a festival of the new moon*: and in a restricted sense, it indicates a month measured by the course of the moon.

נבקעו, *were-unlocked*.... This is the verb בקע employed according to the positive form, passive movement. One can see in

11. B i-s h e n a t h shesh mæôth shanah l'haîî-Noah ba-hodesh ha-shenî, b'shibe-hah-hashar îôm la-hodesh ba-îôm ha-zeh nibekehou èhol-maheinoth thehôm rabbah w'ârubboth ha-shamaîm ni-phethahou.

בִּשְׁנַת שֵׁשׁ־מֵאוֹת שָׁנָה לְחַיֵּי־נֹחַ בַּחֹדֶשׁ הַשֵּׁנִי בְּשִׁבְעָה־עָשָׂר יוֹם לַחֹדֶשׁ בַּיּוֹם הַזֶּה נִבְקְעוּ כָּל־ מַעְיְנֹת תְּהוֹם רַבָּה וַאֲרֻבֹּת הַשָּׁמַיִם נִפְתָּחוּ :

12.   Wa-î, h î ha-gheshem hal-ha--âretz arbahîm îôm w'ârbahîm laîlah.

וַיְהִי הַגֶּשֶׁם עַל־הָאָרֶץ אַרְבָּעִים יוֹם וְאַרְבָּעִים לָיְלָה :

---

the Rad. Vocab. and in v. 4 of this chapter, what I have said of the root קוֹ from which it comes.   This root, governed by the sign of generative action בּ and terminated by that of physical sense עָ, ex-presses the action of giving unlimited extension to a thing; of un-locking, of breaking the bonds which restrict it; of disuniting it, etc.

מֵעְיְנֹת, *springs-of-the-deep*....   The root עוּ characterizes in the literal sense, *an inflection, a curvature, a thing concave* or *convex*.   Terminated by the final character וֹ, it is the symbol of a curvature, of an entire inflection; it depicts a circle, which, con-sidered relative to its circumference, presents a globe; and relative to its centre, a recess, a hole.   This root thus formed, עוּי, enlightened by the sign of potential manifestation, becomes the word עְיִן, which, according as it is examined exteriorly or interiorly, designates some-times the eye and sometimes the depth of a spring.   It is in this latter sense that it is employed on this occasion, having for initial character the plastic sign of exterior action, מ.

תְהֹם רַבָּה, *indefinite-potential-might*....   I have . explained the

11. By-the-revolving six-hundreds of-revolving-change, regarding-t h e-lives of-*Noah*, in-the-moon-renewing the-second, in-the-seventeenth manifested-light of-that-renewing, at-the-day it-self, were-unlocked all-the-springs o f-t h e-deep's inde-finite potential-might; and-the-multiplying-quaternions of-h e a v e n s were-loosened (unfastened, g i v e n u p t o their own dilating motion).

11. Dans-la-mutation-ontologique des-six-centaines d e - mutation, touchant - les-vies de-*Noah* dans-le-renouvellement-lunaire le-second; dans-la-d i x-septième manifestation-lumineuse de -c e-renouvellement, au-jour ce-lui-là, furent-lâchées toutes-les-sources de-la-puissance-d' ê t r e-universelle, indéfinie: et-les-f o r c e s quaternaires-multiplicatrices des-c i e u x furent déliées (abandonnées à leur propre extension).

12. And-there-was t h e-massy-shower (waterish atmosphere falling down in-cessantly) upon-t h e-earth, four-tens o f-d a y and-four-tens of-night (an entire qua-ternion of light and dark-ness).

12. Et-fut la-chute-d'eau (l'atmosphère aqueuse tom-bant en masse) sur-la-terre, quatre-décuples de-jour et-quatre-décuples de-nuit (un quaternaire entier de lum-ière et d'obscurité).

---

word תהום in v. 2., ch. I; and the root of the word רבה is found suf-ficiently developed in v. 10, ch. II.

נפתחו, *were-loosened*.... This is the verb פתׂח, employed after the positive form, passive movement. The root פׂת, from which it comes, has been explained under the proper name of *Japheth*, v. 3. ch. V.

v. 12. הגשם, *the-massy-shower*.... The Hebrew word has an almost incredible forcefulness which can scarcely be understood by the word-for-word French or English, for the reader who has not some idea of those masses of water which, lowering suddenly like a sheet of water falling from the atmosphere, inundate at times cer-tain countries of Asia. These cataclysms are of short duration, for if they were continued as that one which Moses characterizes by the word גשם, to which he attributes an immense duration, they would

13. B'hetzem ha-îôm ha-
zeh bâ Noah w-S h e m-w-
Ham-wa-Jepheth benei Noah
w'æsheth N o a h w-shelos-
heth nesheî-banaî-ô-âitham
æl-ha-thebah:

בְּעֶצֶם הַיּוֹם הַזֶּה בָּא נֹחַ וְשֵׁם־
וְחָם־וָיֶפֶת בְּנֵי־נֹחַ וְאֵשֶׁת נֹחַ
וּשְׁלֹשֶׁת נְשֵׁי־בָנָיו אִתָּם אֶל־
הַתֵּבָה׃

14. Hemmah! w'òhol-ha-
haîah l'min-ha w'òhol-ha-be-
h e m a h l'min-ha w'òhol-ha-
remesh ha - romesh hal - ha-
â r e t z l'min-hou w'òhol-ha-
hôph l'min-hou òhol tziphôr
òhool òhanaph:

הֵמָּה וְכָל־הַחַיָּה לְמִינָהּ וְכָל־
הַבְּהֵמָה לְמִינָהּ וְכָל־הָרֶמֶשׂ
הָרֹמֵשׂ עַל־הָאָרֶץ לְמִינֵהוּ וְכָל־
הָעוֹף לְמִינֵהוּ כֹּל צִפּוֹר כָּל־כָּנָף׃

---

cause frightful catastrophes. The words ύετός, "pluvia", *rain*, as it
has been rendered by the translators, depicting water falling by
drops or by slender streams, does not make the force of the Hebraic
expression felt.

The root from which this word comes is גשׁ, by which should
be understood a thing continued, palpable and without solution of
continuity. Thence, the Hebrew verb גוּשׁ *to feel, to recognize with
the hand;* and the Chaldaic words גשתא *substance continued and palpable;* גושמא *a body,* גשמי *corporeal,* גשמות *corporeity,* etc. Thence,
the Syriac ﻟﻤﺴﻮ *sense and sensation;* and the Arabic جش,
a thick thing, a profound obscurity.

It is easy to see, after this explanation, that the root גשׁ, universalized in the word גשׁם, by the collective sign ם, characterizes an
aqueous atmosphere, forming a kind of dark and palpable body. I
invite the physicists who have sought the origin of the waters of the
deluge, to meditate a little upon this illuminating etymology. The
Samaritan translator has allowed the terrible picture offered here by
Moses to escape by substituting for the original word, the word
ᔖᘉᔖᗅ *a heavy rain.* The Chaldaic paraphrast seems to have
been more fortunate in giving at least מטרא גחית *a contiguous, palpable rain.*

13. F r o m-the-very-sub-stantial-principle of-this-day itself, went *Noah*, and-*Shem*-and-*Ham*-a n d-*Japheth*, issued-offspring-of-*Noah*, and-t h e - volitive-faculty-*Noah's* and-the-three natural-faculties o f-t h e-offspring-h i s-own, together-them toward-the-*thebah* (m u t u a l asylum) :

14. Themselves! and-the-whole-animality, after-t h e-kind-its-own; all-quadruped after-the-kind-its-own; and-a l l-creeping-l i f e trailing-along upon-the-earth, after-the-kind-its-own; a n d-all-fowl after-the-kind-its-own, every-thing-running, every-thing-flying:

13. Dès-le-principle-sub-s t a n t i e l du-jour celui-là, alla *Noah*, et-*Shem* et-*Ham*-et-*Japhcth*, productions-de-*Noah*, e t-l a-faculté-volitive de-*Noah*, et-l e s-trois-facul-tés-physiques des-product-ions-à-l u i, ensemblement, devers-la-*t h e b a h* (l'asile mutuel) :

14. E u x-m ê m e s ! et-toute-l'animalité selon-l'es-pèce-sienne; t o u t-quadru-pède s e l o n-l'espèce-sienne, et-tout-reptile rampant sur-la-terre, selon-l'espèce-sien-ne, et-tout-volatile selon-l' espèce-sienne: toute-chose-courant, toute-chose-volant:

---

v. 13. בעצם, *From-the-very-substantial-principle....* This word is presented here in a very singular manner. It affords matter for reflection. In whatever way one wishes to understand it, I defy anyone to see either *wood*, or *bones*, or *tree*, following the interpretation that the Hellenists have given it in other instances. See v. 9. and 23, ch. II.

ושלשת נשי, *and-the-three-natural-factulties....* It can be seen again with what constancy Moses distinguishes the word אשה belonging to the intellectual mate of *Noah*, from the word נשים appropriate for the mates of his sons.

אתם, *together-them....* This word depicts very well the effect of the collective sign ם, added to the designative preposition את.

v. 14 and 15. All these terms have been explained, or offer no difficulty.

15. Wa-îaboâou æl-Noah æl-ha-thebah shenaîm shenaîm mi-ċhol ha-bashar âs her b'o rouah haîîm.

וַיָּבֹאוּ אֶל־נֹחַ אֶל־הַתֵּבָה שְׁנַיִם שְׁנַיִם מִכָּל־הַבָּשָׂר אֲשֶׁר בּוֹ רוּחַ חַיִּים :

16. W'ha-baîm zaċhar w-n e k e b a h mi-ċhol-bashar bâou ċh'âsher tziwa âoth-â Ælohîm : wa-issegor IHOAH ba-had-ô.

וְהַבָּאִים זָכָר וּנְקֵבָה מִכָּל־בָּשָׂר בָּאוּ כַּאֲשֶׁר צִוָּה אֹתוֹ אֱלֹהִים וַיִּסְגֹּר יְהֹוָה בַּעֲדוֹ :

17. W a-î h î ha-mabboul ârbahîm îôm hal-ha-âretz : wa-îrebou ha-maîm, wa-ish-æou æth-ha-thebah, wa-tha-ram me-hal-ha-âretz.

וַיְהִי הַמַּבּוּל אַרְבָּעִים יוֹם עַל־הָאָרֶץ וַיִּרְבּוּ הַמַּיִם וַיִּשְׂאוּ אֶת־הַתֵּבָה וַתָּרָם מֵעַל־הָאָרֶץ :

---

v. 16. בַּעֲדוֹ, *by-the-removing-himself*.... The Hellenists who had no doubt their reasons for hiding from the vulgar the theo-sophical ideas of the Sepher, chose the part here of making IHOAH, a kind of door-keeper who shuts the door upon *Noah:* καὶ ἔκλεισε κύριος ὁ Θεὸς ἔξωθεν ; an idea quite ridiculous, which the Latin trans-lator has not failed to copy "et includit eum Dominus deforis"; but the Hebraic verb עָרֹה as well as the Chaldaic, Ethiopic and Arabic analogues, all signify *to be removed, to go away, to disap-pear:* which proves that the root עַר, which develops, in general, all ideas relative to time, and to things temporal and transitory, ex-presses *a separation, a departure, an eclipse, a disappearance.* In the present case, this root, taken in the latter sense, is inflected by the mediative article בַ, and followed by the nominal affix וֹ.

v. 17. וַיִּרְבּוּ, *and-they-did-quaternify*.... I have believed it neces-sary to coin this word taken from the language of numbers, in order to make felt the force of the root בַּר, from which are equally derived, both the name of the number אַרְבָּעִים which ex-presses the duration of the great swelling of the waters, and the verb רְבֹה which characterizes its action.

15. And-t h e y-went to-ward-*Noah* (nature's rest) toward-the-sheltering-abode, t w a i n s b y-twains, from-e v e r y-c o r p o r e a l-shape which-h a s in-itself breath of-lives.

15. E t-i l s allèrent de-vers-*Noah* (le repos de la nature) vers-la-retraite-in-accessible deux à-deux, de-toute-forme-corporelle, qui-a dans-soi souffle-des-vies.

16. And-thus-going, male and-female from-every-bod-ily-shape, they-went accord-ing-to-what had-prescribed to-himself, HE-the-Gods: and -he-shut-up, IHOAH, by-the-removing-himself.

16. Et-les-allants, m â l e et-female, de-t o u t e-forme-corporelle, allèrent suivant-c e-q u'a v a i t-prescrit cela-même-à-soi LUI-les-Dieux, et-il-conclut, IHOAH, au-moyen-de-l'éloignement-sien.

17. And-itwas, the-great-swelling four-tens o f-d a y u p o n-the-earth; and-they-d i d-quaternify (multiply-themselves) the-w a t e r s; and-they-bare the-*t h e b a h* which was-raised from-over-the-earth.

17. Et-elle-fut, l a-gran-de intumescence, quatre-dé-cuples de-jour sur-la-terre; e t-e l l e s-s e-quaternisèrent (se multiplièrent) les-eaux, et-elles-portèrent l a-*thebah* qui fut-enlevée-de-dessus la-terre.

וישׂא, *and-they-bare....* This is the verb נשׂא, employed according to the positive form, active movement, in the future made past by the convertible sign ו. This verb is attached to the root שׂ, of which I have spoken in giving the etymology of number *six* שׂש, v. 3 ch. V. It depicts a sort of *libration*, of support in equilibrium.

ותרם, *which-was-raised....* The verb רום designates literal-ly that sort of action or movement by means of which a thing runs through or fills an extent or a place which it did not occupy former-ly. It is composed of the sign of movement proper ר, united to that of exterior and plastic action מ.

v. 18. ויגברו, *and-they-prevailed-intensely....* Review in v. 14, ch. VI, what I have said concerning the famous word גבור. This word signifying, according to its exact etymology, *a superior*

18.   W a-îghebbrou h a-
maîm wa-îrebbou mæôd hal-
ha-âretz: wa-thelech ha-thebah hal-pheneî ha-maîm.

וַיִּגְבְּרוּ הַמַּיִם וַיִּרְבּוּ מְאֹד עַל־
הָאָרֶץ וַתֵּלֶךְ הַתֵּבָה עַל־פְּנֵי
הַמָּיִם :

19.   W'ha-maîm gabrou
mæôd mæôd hal-ha-âretz:
wa-iechussou chol he-harîm
ha-ghebohîm âsher thahath
chol-ha-sha-maîm.

וְהַמַּיִם גָּבְרוּ מְאֹד מְאֹד עַל־
הָאָרֶץ וַיְכֻסּוּ כָּל־הֶהָרִים
הַגְּבֹהִים אֲשֶׁר־תַּחַת כָּל־
הַשָּׁמָיִם :

20.   H a m e s h heshereh
âmmah milmahelah gabrou
ha-maîm wa-iechussou he-
harîm.

חֲמֵשׁ עֶשְׂרֵה אַמָּה מִלְמַעְלָה
גָּבְרוּ הַמָּיִם וַיְכֻסּוּ הֶהָרִים :

21.   Wa - ighewah c h o l-
bashar ha-romesh h a l-h a-
âretz ba-hôph ba-behemah w'
ba-h a î a h w-b' chol-ha-sher-
etz ha-shoretz hal-ha-âretz
w'chol-ha-Adam.

וַיִּגְוַע כָּל־בָּשָׂר הָרֹמֵשׂ עַל־
הָאָרֶץ בָּעוֹף וּבַבְּהֵמָה וּבַחַיָּה
וּבְכָל־הַשֶּׁרֶץ הַשֹּׁרֵץ עַל־הָאָרֶץ
וְכֹל הָאָדָם :

---

man, a high-baron, a master, the verb which is formed from it should
express the action of prevailing, dominating, acting, commanding as
master, etc.   This verb is used here according to the intensive form,
which increases its force.

v. 19 and 20. The terms offer no difficulty in the literal sense.
The figurative sense springs from that which has been previously
cited.

v. 21. וַיִּגְוַע, thus-expired....   The radical verb גּוע, such as
is used here, indicates a total dissolution of the organic system, of
which the root גּו is the symbol.   The sign ו materialized by the
addition of the sign ע, thus makes this root pass from the state of
crganic life to that of inorganic life or material death.   Our attention has already been called to this same verb in v. 3, ch III.

18. A n d-they-prevailed-intensely, the-waters; and-t h e y-d i d-quaternify (increase themselves) at-their-h i g h e s t-r a t e, upon-the-earth: and-it-moved-to-and-fro,the-*thebah,* on-the-f a c e of-the-waters.

19. And-the-waters per-vailed a t-their-highest-rate s o-m u c h u p o n-the-earth that-were-covered a l l-t h e-hills u p p e r-m o s t which-were-below t h e-whole-hea-vens.

20. Fifteen o f-mother-measuring from-over-above, prevailed the-waters: a n d-were-quite-covered the-hills.

21. Thus-expired (w a s dissolved) every-corporeal-shape moving on-the-earth, i n-t h e-f o w l, a n d-in-the-quadruped, and-in-the-life-e a r t h-b o r n, a n d-in-the-whole-worm-l i f e creeping-along on-the-earth; and-the-whole-collective-man (man-kind).

18. Et-elles-prévalurent-avec-force, l e s-eaux, et-se-quaternisèrent (augmentèr-ent) autant-que-possible sur-la-terre: et-elle-se-mouvait-en-tous-sens la-*thebah,* sur-la-face des-eaux.

19. Et-les-eaux prévalu-rent autant-que-possible tel-lement-que, sur-la-terre, fu-rent-couvertes toutes-l e s-montagnes supérieures les-quel-les-étaient e n-b a s de-tous-les-cieux.

20. Quinze de-measure-m è r e p a r-dessus-le-haut, prévalurent les-eaux: et-fu-rent - couvertes-entièrement les-montagnes.

21. Ainsi-e x p i r a (dis-parut) toute-forme-corpor-elle se-mouvant sur-la-terre, dans-le-volatile, e t-dans-le-quadrupède et-d a n s-l'exis-tence-animale et-dans-toute-l'originante-vie vermiforme, sur-la-terre; a i n s i- q u e-tout-l'homme-universel (l e règne hominal).

וכל - האדם, *and-the-whole-collective-man....* The reader who follows with impartial mind the development of these notes, will see that it is impossible for the word אדם to have other signification than that which I have given to it, of *universal man* or *mankind.* If this word indicated simply *a man,* as the Hellenists and the other interpreters have made it understood in this passage, what is it then

22. C h o l â s h e r nishe-
math-rouah haîim b'aphaî-ô,
mi-ċhol âsher b'harabah me-
thou.

כֹּל אֲשֶׁר נִשְׁמַת־רוּחַ חַיִּים בְּאַפָּיו
מִכֹּל אֲשֶׁר בֶּחָרָבָה מֵתוּ :

23.   Wa-îmmah æth-ċhol-
ha-îekoum âsher hal-pheneî
ha-âdamah, me-Adam had-
behemah had-remesh w-had-
hôph ha-shamaîm: wa-îm-
mahou m i n - h a - â r e t z : wa-
îsh-aær aċh-N o a h w'âsher
âith-ô ba-thebah.

וַיִּמַח אֶת־כָּל־הַיְקוּם אֲשֶׁר עַל־
פְּנֵי הָאֲדָמָה מֵאָדָם עַד־בְּהֵמָה
עַד־רֶמֶשׂ וְעַד־עוֹף הַשָּׁמַיִם
וַיִּמָּחוּ מִן־הָאָרֶץ וַיִּשָּׁאֶר אַךְ־נֹחַ
וַאֲשֶׁר אִתּוֹ בַּתֵּבָה :

---

that Moses intended by the word כל *all*, which he unites to it by
means of the determinative article ה ?   Is it that, when it is a
question of dying, of expiring, by the effect of a frightful catastrophe,
a man can be divided?   Is it not more natural to understand here,
even literally, that all mankind expired, than to rack one's brains to
find an hebraism where the phrase is perfectly simple; or, to change
the word as the Latin translator who says "universi homines" *all
men*, not being able to rise to the point of seeing "omnis universus
homo" *all universal man*, which would exactly render the Hebrew?

v. 22. נשמת, *a-being-exalted*.... Refer to v. 7, ch. II.

בחרבה, *in-the-wasting-havock*....   I cannot conceive how it is
possible that all the translators, without exception, have missed the
meaning of this word, it is so simple. Its root חר is evident; it is
united to the sign of interior action ב, to express *ravage*, *extermina-
tion*, *desolation*, *scourge*. In giving it the sense of a *desert*, of a
dry land and even simply of *the earth*, as the Latin translator, they
have made Moses say a futile and ridiculous thing.   It was not the
inhabitants alone of the desert or the dry lands who perished, but all
beings whatsoever, who were struck at the same time by this disaster,
this devastating flood.

22. All that-had a-being-exalted (an essence)of-the-breath of-lives in-the-spiritual-faculty his-own among-the-w h o l e that-underwent the-w a s t i n g-havock (t h e flood) they-died.

22. T o u s-les-êtres qui-avaient un-étant-élevé (une essentialité) de l'esprit-des-v i e s dans-la-faculté-spirituelle-à-e u x, parmi-tous-ceux qui étaient dans-le-désastre (atteints par le fléau) ils moururent.

23. A n d-h e-washed-o f f (IHOAH) even-the-selfsameness-of-t h e-whole-standing-plastic-nature w h i c h-w a s on-the-f a c e of-the-adamic, from-mankind, to-the-quadrupedly-walking, the-creeping-one, t h e-f o w l of-heavens; and-they-were-washed-off from-the-e a r t h: and-there-remained only-N o a h (nature's r e s t) and-what-was together-h i m i n-t h e-sheltering-abode.

23. Et-il-effaça (IHOAH) l'ipséité-même-de-t o u t e-nature-plastique-substantielle, qui-était sur-la-f a c e de-l' élément-adamique, depuis-le-genre-humain, jusqu'au-genre-quadrupède, au-reptiforme, au-volatile-des-cieux : e t-i l s-furent-effacés-d e-l a-terre; et-il-resta seulement-*Noah* (le repos del'existence élémentaire) et-ce-qui-était ensemble-lui dans la *thebah.*

---

v. 23. האדמה, *of-the-adamic.* . . . An attentive reader should have perceived that, in the narration of the deluge, Moses did not use indifferently the name of *adamah* אדמה, primitive, homogeneous land, adamic element, and that of *artz,* ארץ, the earth properly so-called. The action of the Divinity is exercized particularly upon *adamah;* the action of the flood, always upon *artz.* There is in this verse a singular difference between these two words. The Divinity, says Moses, effaces the selfsameness, the ipseity, the objectivity of corporeal beings upon the face of *adamah,* adamic element, and all corporeal beings are effaced upon *artz,* elementary earth. There are many things to be said here, but I could not undertake the explanation without involving myself in a long commentary and going beyond my position of simple translator. Perhaps I shall one day make amends for my silence in this regard. It was necessary first, to reëstablish the meaning of the words and make the Hebraic text understood in its purity; but this text once understood, it will no doubt be im-

24.   W a-îghebbrou h a - וַיִּגְבְּרוּ הַמַּיִם עַל־הָאָרֶץ חֲמִשִּׁים
maîm hal-ha-â r e t z hamis-
hîm w'màth îôm.   וּמְאַת יוֹם :

---

portant to examine the doctrine that it contains so as to fathom all
its thoughts.   This is what I intend doing, if my labour, welcomed
by the true savants appears to them useful for the advancement of
knowledge and the welfare of humanity.

וַיִּשָּׁאֶר, *and-there-remained*....   The word שָׁאַר is applied
literally to that sort of residue which falls to the bottom of a
receptacle, after its fluid being agitated comes to equilibrium.   It is
composed of the root שָׁא or שׁוּ, which develops all ideas of measure
and of equilibrium, joined to the sign of movement proper ר.   The
verb which is derived from it, applied here to *Noah*, the repose of
natural existence, is very worthy of attention.

אַךְ, *only*....   This is the same root אַךְ, which contains all
ideas of restriction, of compression, of closing upon oneself, which
Moses uses as adverbial relation, uniting it by hyphen to the name
of *Noah*.   This hierographic writer neglects no means to enlighten
the mind of the reader and initiate him into mysteries that he cannot entirely divulge.   This simple hyphen forms an hieroglyphic

24. And-t h e y-prevailed, t h e-waters, upon-the-earth, f i v e-tens and-one-hundred of-day (periodical light).

24. E t-elles-dominèrent, les-eaux, sur-la-terre, cinq-décuples et-une-centaine de-jour (manifestation lumin-euse).

---

figure, the translation of which is impossible. The use of this fig-ure is quite frequent in the tongue of Moses and demands medita-tion. A striking example can be seen in v. 13 of this chapter; when the hierographic writer, wishing to make understood that the three productions of Noah, Shem, Ham and Japheth, who are contained with him in the *thebah*, are not three distinct beings, but one unique triad, links them together; and their three names united, form only one single name: בא נח ושם־וחם־ויפת, "he went, Noah, (in the thebah) and-Shem-and-Ham-and-Japeth," Now, this triad, thus rep-resented hieroglyphically, is precisely to the cosmogonic being called *Noah*, what the three geometrical dimensions are to all natural bodies.

v. 24. All these terms are understood.

SEPHER BERÆSHITH
H.

ספר בראשית ח.

1. Wa - îzeċhar Ælohîm
æth-N o a h w'æth-ċhol-h a-
h a î a h w'æth-ċhol-ha-behe-
mah âsher âith-ô ba-thebah:
wa-îahober Ælohîm r o u a h
hal-ha-â r e t z wa-îashoċhou
ha-maîm.

וַיִּזְכֹּר אֱלֹהִים אֶת־נֹחַ וְאֶת־כָּל־
הַחַיָּה וְאֶת ־ כָּל ־ הַבְּהֵמָה אֲשֶׁר
אִתּוֹ בַּתֵּבָה וַיַּעֲבֵר אֱלֹהִים רוּחַ
עַל־הָאָרֶץ וַיָּשֹׁכּוּ הַמָּיִם :

2. Wa-issaċhron maheîn-
oth thehoûm w a-arubboth
ha-shamaîm wa-iċċhallâ ha-
gheshem min-ha-shamaîm.

וַיִּסָּכְרוּ מַעְיְנֹת תְּהוֹם וַאֲרֻבֹּת
הַשָּׁמָיִם וַיִּכָּלֵא הַגֶּשֶׁם מִן
הַשָּׁמָיִם :

---

v. 1. ויזכר, *and-he-remembered*....   In giving the etymology
of the word זכר *male*, in v. 27, ch. I, I have spoken of the root
כר which forms its basis, and which, as I have said, characterizes
that which is apparent, eminent; that which is engraved or
serves to engrave; that which is of a nature to conserve the memory
of things.   It is remarkable that this root, governed by the demonstrative sign ז, develops on the one side, the idea of masculinity,
and on the other that of memory; for the word זכר, which signifies
literally *male*, designates figuratively, that faculty of the human understanding which preserves the impression of sensations, images
and evidences of ideas: but what is no less remarkable is, that in a
tongue far removed from the Hebrew in appearance, the Celtic
tongue, from which the French is derived through the Teutonic and
the Latin, a same root has of yore likewise developed these two ideas
of masculinity and memory, which appear today so dissimilar.   This
root is AL, representing that which is raised, not only in Celtic but
in Hebrew and in all the ancient tongues.   Now, this root governed

GENESIS VIII.

1. A n d-h e-remembered, HE-t h e-Gods, the-selfsame ness-o f-*N o a h*, and-that-of-t h e-whole-earth-born-e x i s-tence, a n d-t h a t-of-all-the-quadruped-kind, which-were together-him i n-the-*thebah* (sheltering abode) : and-he-c a u s e d-to-move-over, HE-the-G o d s, a-breath on-the-e a r t h : and-t h e y-were-checked, the-waters.

2. And-t h e y-were-shut-up the-springs of-the-deep's infinite - potential - p o w e r, and-the-multiplying-quatern-ions of-heavens: a n d-w a s-wholly-exhausted t h e-mas-sy-shower (waterish atmos-phere falling down) from-the-heavens.

COSMOGONIE VIII.

1. Et-il-se-rappela, LUI-l e s-Dieux, la-séité-de-*Noah*, et-celle-de-toute - l'existence-terrestre, e t-celle-de-toute-l e-genre-quadrupède, q u i-étaient ensemble-lui d a n s la-*thebah* (la place de re-fuge) : et-il-fit passer-d'une-extrémité-à-l'autre, L U I-les-Dieux un-souffle sur-la-ter-re: e t-furent-resserrées-en-elles-mêmes les-eaux.

2. Et-furent-fermées les-sources d e-l a-puissance-d'être-indéfinie, et-les-forces-quaternisantes - multiplicat-rices d e s-cieux: et-fut-en-tièrement-consommée la-chute-d'e a u (l'atmosphere épaissie tombant) des-cieux.

---

by the emphatic sign P or PH, has produced *pal* or *phal*, whence is derived in French, the ancient word *pal*, changed to *pieu*, and in Latin, the word "phallus" copied from the Greek φαλλός which, as one knows, characterizes the sign of masculinity. But among the Celts, a *pal*, was a sort of monumental post raised in any place what-ever to serve for rallying; from there the word *appeal*, and the French words *appeler* and *rappeler*.

ויעבר, *and-he-caused-to-move-over*.... The verb עבר means, liter-ally speaking, *to pass beyond, to go to the other side.* I have been obliged to change its form which is positive in Hebrew, to show the force of the superactive movement rendered active in this in-stance.

3. Wa-Ïashubou ha-
maîm ma-hal ha-âretz hal-
ôch wa-shôb wa-ahesserou
ha-maîm mi-ketzeh ha-mis-
hîm w-mâth îôm.

וַיָּשֻׁבוּ הַמַּיִם מֵעַל הָאָרֶץ הָלוֹךְ
וָשׁוֹב וַיַּחְסְרוּ הַמַּיִם מִקְצֵה
חֲמִשִּׁים וּמְאַת יוֹם:

וַיָּשֻׁבוּ, *and-they-were-checked*.... The root אָךְ which develops all
ideas of repression, of compression, of drawing into itself, ruled
by the sign of relative movement שׁ, forms the verb here referred to
שֹׁכְךָ or שׁוּךְ : this verb depicts in most decisive manner the action
of the Divine breath upon the watery swelling: for it must not be
forgotten that it is in consequence of the absence of this breath that
the waters had been dilated; that is to say, abandoned to their own
impulse.   It deals now with reëstablishing the broken equilibrium,
and it is this which Moses expresses admirably by the verb שׁוּךְ .   I
am, furthermore, only the translator of this great man. The verb
check which comes from the same source as the Hebraic, renders very
well this meaning.

v. 2.   All these terms have been explained.   Refer to v. 11 and
12 of the preceding chapter.

v. 3.   וַיָּשֻׁבוּ, *and-they-restored-themselves-as-formerly*....   I have
often had occasion to speak of the root שב which brings with
it every idea of return and of reëstablishment.   The radical verb
שׁוּב, which is formed from it, is employed here according to the
positive form, active movement, future tense made past by the convertible sign וּ.   One finds a little later on, this same verb used in
the nominal and united to the verb הָלוֹךְ *to go before, to be carried
to and fro*, to indicate a contrary movement.   Now this singular
phrase הָלוֹךְ וָשׁוֹב is very remarkable in what it seems to indicate
in the seas, and in the waters which covered the earth, in general,
that alternating movement of going and coming, which the modern
physicists have begun to suspect.

Concerning the four original translators whose versions are ever
before my eyes, two have evaded the sense of this phrase and two
have felt it. The Samaritan, not understanding what this alternating movement impressed upon the waves could be, has said, corrupt-

3. And-t h e y-restored-themselves-as-formerly, the-waters, from-over-the-earth, by-the-g o i n g-off and-the-c o m i n g back: and - they-withdrew (they shrunk) the-waters, a t-t h e-end of-five - tens a n d-one-hundred of-day (manifested universal light).

3. Et-revinrent-à-l e u r-premier-état les-eaux de-des-sus-la-terre du movement d' a l l e r-e n-avant et-de-reve-nir-s u r-s o i : e t-elles-se-re-tirèrent-en-elles-mêmes, l e s e a u x, a u-bout-de-cinq-dé-cuples e t-u n e-centaine de-jour (de manifestation lu-mineuse, universelle).

---

ing the text ....תַּשָׁבַ מַעַל הָאָרֶץ הַלּוֹך, they-went, and-returned, and-were-abated, the-waters....which the Hellenists, faithful in following the most vulgar meaning, have imitated. But the Chaldean, adhering closer to the text, has translated this passage very clearly...... אוּלִין וּתִיבִין .... וְתָבוּ מִיָּא : and-they-were-restored-in-their-primitive-state, the-waters...... going-and-returning-alternate-ly...... In which it has been followed by the author of the Vulgate.

וַיַּחְסְרוּ, and-they-withdrew.... The root הוּם from which this verb comes, merits the attention of the reader; through it, he can gradually penetrate the thought of Moses pertaining to the physical causes of the deluge. This root is composed of the sign of elementary existence ה, image of the travail of Nature, united to the sign of circular movement, and of all circumscription ם. It develops in its verbal state the action of conquering one's self; of experiencing a sentiment of sorrow and contrition; of shrinking. The sign of movement proper ר, being joined to this root to form the derivative verb חסוֹר, only adds to the force of this expression which is quite accurately rendered by the word shrink. I observe that the hierographic writer, after having displayed all the resources of the Hebraic tongue, to depict the dilatation and swelling of the waters, neglects none of the means afforded in the literal sense, as well as in the figurative or hieroglyphic, to express with the same energy their shrinking and their contraction.

v. 4. וַתָּנַח, and-it-rested.... It is not without purpose that Moses employs the verb נוּח, which comes from the same root as the name of Noah, to express the repose of the thebah which bears this cosmogonic personage.

4. Wa-thanah ha-thebah
b'ha-hodesh h a-shebîhî bi-
shibehah-hashar îôm la-hodesh hal-hareî **Ararat.**

וַתָּנַח הַתֵּבָה בַּחֹדֶשׁ הַשְּׁבִיעִי
בְּשִׁבְעָה־עָשָׂר יוֹם לַחֹדֶשׁ עַל־
הָרֵי אֲרָרָט :

הַשְּׁבִיעִי, *the-seventh*.... It should not be forgotten that, in
a work of this nature, issued from the Egyptian sanctuaries, all the
words are chosen with calculation and forethought. I have taken
care to explain, as much as possible, the meaning of the Hebraic
decade.   The names of numbers here contain great mysteries; they
are far from being limited to cold dates, as the vulgar translators
have thought.   They must be examined.   It is necessary to remember for example, that number *seven* שֶׁבַע, is always that of the consummation of things and times.   The *thebah*, which was put in
movement in the *second* lunar renewal, is stopped in the *seventh*.
Now, we ought to know also, that number *two* שְׁנַ, is the emblem of
every mutation, of every transition, and of every passing from one
state to another.

אֲרָרַט, *of-Ararat*.... Here is a word which would afford a
vast subject for commentary, but I have resolved to limit myself to
translating.   All peoples who have preserved the memory of the
deluge, and nearly all have preserved it, have not failed to relate
the name of the alleged mountain upon which rested the mysterious
thebah, which bore within it the hope of nature and the seed of a
new existence.   Nicholas of Damas, cited by Josephus, called it
Mount *Barris*, a name which is not very unlike that of *Syparis* or
Sypara, which Berosus gave to that city of the sun, in which an
Assyrian monarch deposited the archives of the world when he knew
that the catastrophe of the flood was imminent.   It is well known
that the Greeks called λυκορεός, *the luminous mountain*, the place
on Parnassus where Deucalion rested; but perhaps it is not generally
known that the Americans had also a celebrated mountain, upon
which they declared that the remnants of mankind had taken refuge,
and whose name they consecrated by the erection of a temple dedicated to the sun. This name was *Olagmi*.   It would certainly
be very easy for me to prove that these names, more or less direct.
all have a connection with the course of light; but without citing.
at this moment, other tongues than the Hebraic, let us content our-
selves with examining the word which is the subject of this note.

4. And-it-rested, the-*the-bah*, in-t h e-moon-renewing the-s e v e n t h, by-the-seventeenth manifested-light of-t h a t-r e n e w i n g, on-the-heights of-Ararat (reflected light's stream).

4. Et-elle-se-reposa, l a *thebah*, dans-le-renouvelle-ment-l u n a i r e le-septième, au-dix-septième jour de-ce-r e n o u v e l l e m e n t, sur-les-sommets de-l'Ararat (le cours réfléchi de la lumi-ère).

---

and in which the thoughtless savants have been so unfortunate as to see an object of terror or of malediction.

This word is composed of the two roots אוֹר־רט : the first אוֹר, is understood: it is *light* and all ideas which are related to it. The second, רט, formed of the signs of movement proper and of resistance, characterizes a course accompanied, inflected or directed by anything whatsoever. Thence, the Chaldaic verb רהט, *to concur with a thing, to follow it in its course, to direct it;* as light or water, for example; thence, the Hebraic word רהיט, *a channel, a conduit, a promenade;* thence, the Syriac derivative ܡܐܠܒܘܣ *an inflection, a reflection,* etc.

After this explanation one can feel that the word ארט, does not signify the *mount of malediction* or *of terror,* as has been believed without examination; but indeed that of *the reflected course of light;* which is very different. Besides, it is well to know that the Samaritan translator, the most ancient interpreter of Moses, has not rendered the word אֲרֹט, by a simple transcription of the characters, as it seems that he might have done, had he thought that this was simply a proper name of the Mount, but he has translated it by the word ᛒᛘᚦᛒᛘᛉ, which differs entirely. The resemblance of this word with the ancient name of the island of Ceylon, *Serandip,* in the *Sanskrit* tongue, *Sinhala-dwip,* has caused some savants to think that Moses had perhaps designated a famous rock which commands that isle, and where the Brahmans declare that Buddha or Rama has left the imprint of his foot: but, without combatting this opinion wholly, I shall state that this word appears to be composed of the Chaldaic and Samaritan words, סרנא, *axis, wheel, orbit;* and רוב or ריב *effluence, emanation:* so that it offers a translation quite exact of the sense that I have given to the word ארט : that is to say, instead of signifying simply *the reflected course of light,* it signifies *the orbit of luminous effluence.*

5. W'ha-maîm haîou ha-lôċh w'hassôr had ha-ho-desh ha-hashîrî: ba-hashîrî b'æhad l'hodesh niRâou Râ-sheî he-haRîm.

וְהַמַּיִם הָיוּ הָלוֹךְ וְחָסוֹר עַד הַחֹדֶשׁ הָעֲשִׂירִי בָּעֲשִׂירִי בְּאֶחָד לַחֹדֶשׁ נִרְאוּ רָאשֵׁי הֶהָרִים:

6. Wa-îhî mi-ketz âRba-hîm îôm: wa-îphethah Noah æth-hallôn ha-thebah âsher hashah.

וַיְהִי מִקֵּץ אַרְבָּעִים יוֹם וַיִּפְתַּח נֹחַ אֶת־חַלּוֹן הַתֵּבָה אֲשֶׁר עָשָׂה:

---

v. 5. הָעֲשִׂירִי, the-tenth.... We know that number ten, עֶשֶׂר is that of aggregate power, of efficient elementary force. The words which compose this verse and in general all those of this chapter, are chosen with such art, and the literal meaning connected and blended so closely with the figurative and hieroglyphic meaning, that it is impossible to separate them without weakening or destroy-ing them. No translation can give the force of the original; for to attain this, it would be necessary to find words which might always contain three distinct ideas; which cannot be in our modern tongues, where the separation in the three significations, has long since been made by derivatives whose analogy is no longer perceived. Thus, for example, how can one understand all that Moses intended by these words רָאשֵׁי הֶהָרִים? The literal sense is, *the heads, the summits of the mountains;* the figurative sense, *the principles, the beginnings of pregnancies;* the hieroglyphic sense, *the principiations of elementary conceptions.* All that I can do when it presents these difficulties is to manœuvre, as it were, among the three meanings, furnishing the reader with all means possible to penetrate them, if he will take the pains to do so.

v. 6. חַלּוֹן, *the-opening....* As this word is written with the character ח as initial, it does not appear to have any other

5.   And-the-waters were by-the-going-off and-by-the-withdrawing, till-the-moon-renewing the-tenth: and-in-that-tenth, by-the-first of-the-renewing were-seen the-h e a d s of-the-hills (principles of nature's pregnancies, foremost elementarities).

5.   Et-les-eaux furent du-mouvement-d'aller-en-avant et-d e-celui-de-se-retirer-en-elles-m ê m e s, jusqu'au renouvellement-lunaire le-dixième; et-dans-ce-dixième, a u-premier d u-renouvellement furent-vues les-t ê t e s des-montagnes (les principes d e s-enfantemens naturels, les prémices des elemens).

6.   And-it-was, at-the-determined-end o f-t h e-great-quaternion of-day that-he-unfastened, *Noah*, the-opening of-the-*thebah*, which he-had-made.

6.   Et-ce-f u t à-la-fin-déterminée d u-grand-quaternaire de-jour, qu'il-dégagea, *Noah*, l'ouverture de-la-*thebah*, qu'il-avait-faite.

---

meaning than that of *opening*, being derived from the root חל which develops the idea of a distention, a solution, a separation operated with force; but if, as it might very well be, this initial character had been in the original only the determinative article ה, which the negligence of certain copyists might have caused to be confused with its analogue ח, then the word חלון, instead of signifying *an opening*, would signify *a nocturnal light, a night-light;* that is to say, a lamp destined to lighten the night, and which *Noah* might at first have released from the thebah to lighten the darkness.

I take this opportunity, which has perhaps more importance than one imagines, to call attention to the fact that the French word *lune*, formed from the Latin "luna", is derived from the word לון, referred to in this note, and that it means as I have indicated, *a nocturnal light, a night-light.*   The Arabic analogue employed as verb, expresses the action of colouring, adorning, distinguishing, etc.

v. 7. הערב, *Ereb*. . . .   I am well aware that the Hellenists, and after them, the author of the Latin Vulgate, have seen in *Ereb*, that famed *Ereb* of ancient cosmogonies, only a simple raven: transforming thus a vast and mysterious idea into an idea petty and

7. Wa-îshallah æth-ha-
horeb, wa-ietzâ iotzôâ wa-
shôb had îbosheth ha-maîm
me-hal ha-âretz.

וַיְשַׁלַּח אֶת־הָעֹרֵב וַיֵּצֵא יָצוֹא
וָשׁוֹב עַד־יְבֹשֶׁת הַמַּיִם מֵעַל
הָאָרֶץ :

8. Wa-îshallah æth-ha-
ionah me-âith-ô li-raôth ho-
k a l l o u h a-maîm me-hal
pheneî ha-âdamah.

וַיְשַׁלַּח אֶת־הַיּוֹנָה מֵאִתּוֹ לִרְאוֹת
הֲקַלּוּ הַמַּיִם מֵעַל פְּנֵי הָאֲדָמָה :

---

ridiculous: but I am also aware that these same Hellenists who
worked upon the version which bears the name of Septuagint, Essenes, and consequently initiates in the oral law, penetrated the
hieroglyphic meaning of the Sepher deeply enough not to be the
dupes of such a metamorphosis. One cannot read them with any
kind of attention without discovering their perplexity. Not knowing how to disguise the periodic returns of this alleged bird, and
fearing that the truth might shine forth in spite of them, they decided to change completely the original text and be delivered of this
Ereb which perturbed them, by saying that the raven being sent
forth returned no more, οὐκ ἀνέστρεψεν .   But in this instance,
everything betrays their pious fraud.   The Samaritan text agrees
with the Hebraic text and makes it unassailable; the Samaritan
Version and the Chaldaic Targum say alike that *Ereb*, given liberty,
takes an alternating movement of going forth and coming back;
finally Saint Jerome, forced to recognize this truth, can only weaken
the force of the phrase by saying, without doubling the first verb
and changing their temporal modification of it, "qui egrediebatur et
revertebatur."

It must be remembered that to reveal the depth of this hieroglyphic expression, this *Ereb* was not set at liberty, and did not take
this periodic movement until after the release of the nocturnal light
referred to in the preceding verse.

v. 8.   הַיּוֹנָה, *Ionah*.... Here again is an emblem famous
in ancient cosmogonies; emblem, that the Greek and Latin interpreters have again presented under the least of its characteristics;

7. And-he-let-out what-constitutes *Ereb* (westerly darkness) that-issued-forth by-the-issuing a n d-periodi-cally-repairing, till-the-dry-ing-up of-the-waters from-off-the-earth.

8. A n d-n e x t-he-let-out the-selfsameness of-*I o n a h* (the brooding dove, nature's p l a s t i c power) from-his-own-self; to-see if-they-be-came-light, the-waters, from-over the-face of-the-adamic.

7. Et-il-laissa-a l l e r (il l â c h a) c e-qui-constitue-l' *Erebe* (l'obscurité occiden-tale) qui-sortit du-mouve-ment-de-sortir et-de-revenir-périodiquement jusqu'au des-séchement des-eaux de-des-sus-la-terre.

8. Et-ensuite-il-laissa-al-ler ce-q u i-constitue-l'*Ionah* (la colombe génératrice, la f o r c e plastique de la na-ture) d e h o r s-d'avec-lui; pour-voir-si-e l l e s se-faisa-ient légères, les-e a u x, de-dessus la-face-de-l'élément-adamique.

---

under that of a dove. It is indeed true that the Hebrew word יֹונה , signifies *a dove*, but it is in the same manner that the word ערב, signifies *a raven;* that is to say, that the names of these two birds have been given them, in a restricted sense, in consequence of the physical or moral analogies which have been imagined between the primitive signification attached to the words ערב and יֹונה, and the apparent qualities of the raven and the dove. The blackness of *Ereb*, its sadness, the avidity with which it is believed that it de-vours the beings which fall into its pale, could they be better char-acterized than by a dark and voracious bird such as the raven? The whiteness of the dove on the contrary, its gentleness, its inclination to love, did not these qualities suggest it as emblem of the generative faculty, the plastic force of Nature? It is well known that the dove was the symbol of Semiramis, of Derceto, of Mylitta, of Aphrodite, and of all the allegorical personages to whom the ancients attributed the generative faculty, represented by this bird. This emblem ap-pears to have been known from most ancient times, by the Brahmans, by the Chaldeans, and even by the Sabæan priests of Arabia. It is known that at the time when Mohammed entered victorious into Mecca, he caused an image of the dove, sculptured in the temple of that celebrated city, to be broken by the hands of Ali. In short,

9.   W-loâ   m a t z â h   ha-îônah manôah l'ĉhaph-rag-h e l-h a-, wa-thashab ælaî-ô æl-ha-thebah ĉhi-maîm hal-pheneî ĉhol-ha-âretz wa-îs-h e l a h îad-ô, wa-ikkah-ha wa-îabâ âoth-ha ælaî-ô æl-ha-thebah.

וְלֹא מָצְאָה הַיּוֹנָה מָנוֹחַ לְכַף־רַגְלָהּ וַתָּשָׁב אֵלָיו אֶל־הַתֵּבָה כִּי מַיִם עַל־פְּנֵי כָל־הָאָרֶץ וַיִּשְׁלַח יָדוֹ וַיִּקָּחֶהָ וַיָּבֵא אֹתָהּ אֵלָיו אֶל־הַתֵּבָה :

If one open any ancient book treating of religious mysteries, he will find therein traces of the veneration of the peoples for the dove. Assyria was particularly characterized by this bird and it can be inferred from a passage in Isaiah (v. 6. ch. XX) that it was an ensign for the Assyrians.   But let us return to its Hebraic name the etymology of which is a matter of importance.

It is evident that the name of Ionia, that famous country claimed equally by Europe and Asia, comes from the same source as this word יוֹנח.   The Chaldaic and Hebrew יוֹן, יוֹנִי, or יוֹנָאִ, always designate Greece, or that which belongs to her: these are the Greek analogues, 'Ιωνία, 'Ιωνικός.   For, if we examine Greece, concerning the inner meaning of the name which she gives herself, we shall find that she attaches to the word 'Ιωνικός, all ideas of softness, sweet-ness and amorous langour, which we attach to that of the *dove;* if we go further and explore in Greek itself the root of this word, we shall see that this root, 'Ιον or 'Ιων, contains in that tongue, the ideas of cultivated, fertile land; of productive soil; of existing being, in general; of the violet, flower consecrated to Juno, etc.

Now what do we find in the Hebraic root יוֹן ?   We find, in gen-eral, the idea of a thing indeterminate, soft, sweet, easy to receive all forms, and in particular, a clayey, ductile land.   If, following our method, we proceed to the hieroglyphic sense, and if we examine the signs of which this root is composed, we shall easily find in יוֹן, the mysterious root   אוִי, where the sign of manifestation י, has replaced the sign of power א : so that, if the root אוֹן designates indefinite being, the root יוֹן will designate this same being passing from power into action.

9. And-not it-found, *Ionah* (nature's plastic power), a place-of-rest to-bend (to impart) the-breeding-motion-its own: and-it-returned unto-him, toward-the-*thebah*, because-of-the-waters-being on-the-face of-the-whole-earth: and-he-put-forth the-hand (the power)-his-own; and-he-took-it-up; and-he-caused-it-to-come unto-him toward-the-*thebah*.

9. Et-non-pas elle-trouva, l'*Ionah* (la colombe génératrice), un-lieu-de-repos pour-infléchir (communiquer) le-mouvement-sien: et-elle-retourna devers-lui, vers-la-*thebah*; à-cause-que les-eaux étaient sur-la-face de-toute-la-terre: et-il-étendit la-main-sienne (sa puissance) et-il-retira-elle; et-il-fit-aller elle-même devers-lui, vers la-*thebah*.

Have we still need of other proofs to know that the word יונה expresses the generative faculty of Nature? We shall see that in Hebrew, the compound word אביונה, signifies *desire of amorous pleasures;* and that one understands by the words יונח עלם, *a song, tender, melodious and capable of inspiring love.*

If I have entered into so great details concerning the word יונה it is because it holds very closely to the history of Nature, and because the reader will perhaps be interested to learn that the name of this soft Ionia, from which we have imbibed all that we have which is delightful in art and brilliant in knowledge, is attached, on the one side to the mysterious dove of Moses, to that of Semiramis; and loses itself on the other, in that sacred emblem called *Yoni* by the Brahmans; *Yng*, by the Chinese *Tao-teh*, over which it is necessary that I draw an impenetrable veil.

v. 9. מנוח, *a-place-of-rest....* This word is remarkable because it is attached to the name itself of *Noah.*

לכך־רגלה, *to-bend-the-breeding-motion-its-own....* This is an expression with double and even triple meaning, according to the literal, figurative or hieroglyphic relation under which it is considered. The root כף, which composes the first word, contains the idea of bending, of inflection, of cavity: it is, in a restricted sense, the palm of the hand, or the sole of the foot. The root רג, from which the second comes, develops every idea of organic movement. United to the directive sign ל, it expresses, figuratively, every con-

10. Wa-iahel hod shibe-hath îamîm âherîm, wa-îos-seph shallah æth-ha-Iônah min-ha-thebah.

וַיָּחֶל עוֹד שִׁבְעַת יָמִים אֲחֵרִים וַיֹּסֶף שַׁלַּח אֶת־הַיּוֹנָה מִן־ הַתֵּבָה :

11. Wa-thaboâ ælaî-ô ha Iônah l'heth hereb: w'hin-neh holeh zaîth taraph b' phi-ha wa-îedah Noah ĉhi-kallou ha-naîm me-hal ha-âretz.

וַתָּבֹא אֵלָיו הַיּוֹנָה לְעֵת עֶרֶב וְהִנֵּה עֲלֵה־זַיִת טָרָף בְּפִיהָ וַיֵּדַע נֹחַ כִּי־קַלּוּ הַמַּיִם מֵעַל הָאָרֶץ :

---

tinued action, every movement, every effort of the body or the soul toward a physical or moral object: literally, it is the foot, or the foot-print.   Now, if in the word יונה, one sees only a *dove*, one must see only the bending of its foot in the words לכף רגלה : but, if by the one is understood, as it should be, *a generative faculty*, by the others would be understood, the communication, the application of the generative movement to this same faculty.

ידו, *the-hand-his-own*....   Another similar expression. If Noah is a man of flesh and bones as the Hellenists feign to believe, nothing is more simple than making him stretch out his hand to seize a bird and shut it up in his boat: but, if this is a cosmogonic personage representing the repose of Nature, and the conservator of elementary existence, it is its protective power which it uses to draw unto itself a faculty that it has sent forth prematurely.   The root יד , which in a very restricted sense characterizes *the hand*, designates in a broader sense, every manifestation of power, of ex-ecutive force, of ministry, etc.

v. 10. These terms present no difficulties.

v. 11.   לעת ערב , *at-the-same-time-Ereb*....   The Hellenists seeing reappear here this same Ereb which they had travestied as a raven, and of which it was said positively that it returned no

10. And-he-waited yet-a-septenary o f-d a y s more; a n d - he-added the - letting-forth of-that-same-*I o n a h,* from-out-the-*thebah.*

11. And-it-came toward-him, *I o n a h* (the brooding dove) at-the-same-time *Ereb* (as a dove flying off from the raven) and-lo! a-bough of-olive-tree (elevated pro-duct of the fiery essence) plucked-off i n-t h e-mouth-its-own (seized by her be-getting faculty) : t h u s-he-knew, *Noah* (nature's rest) t h a t-t h e y-lightened, the-waters, from-off-the-earth.

10. Et-il-attendit encore un-septenaire de-jours aut-res; e t-i l-ajouta-l'émission de-cette-même-*Ionah,* hors-de-la-*thebah.*

11. Et-elle-v i n t devers-lui, l'*Ionah,* (la colombe gé-nératrice) a u-temps-même de-l'*Erebe* (au retour de l' obscurité occidentale) e t-v o i c i un-rameau d'olivier (une élévation de l'essence ignée) détaché dans-le-bec-à-elle (saisi par sa f o r c e conceptive) : ainsi-il-connut, *Noah* (le r e p o s de l'exis-tence) que-s'allégeaient les-eaux, de-dessus-la-terre.

---

more, have assumed the part of ignoring it completely. The author of the Latin Vulgate, being unable to do such great violence to the Hebrew text, is contented with changing it, seeing no longer a raven in the word ערב, but simply a part of the day and in saying that the dove came back *at-even-tide,* "ad vesperam".

עלה־זית, *a-bough of-olive-tree....* This again, is a symbolic expression, to which is given a meaning relative to the one which has been given to the word יונה. If in this one is seen a dove, pure and simple, in the other two will be seen an olive branch, a generative force of Nature, and one is led to understand, an eleva-tion of igneous essence. It is the same with the word פי, which in either case is taken for the beak of the bird, or for the conceptive force of the moral being. Such was the genius of the Egyptian language, whose most secret sources had been opened to Moses.

I have explained in another passage the various significations attached to the word עלה, whose root על designates, in general, that which is superior, sublime; that which is raised above another

12. Wa-îîahel hôd shibe-hath îamîm aherîm wa-îs-hallah æth-ha-Iônah, w'loâ îassephah shoub-ælaî-ô hôd.

וַיָּ֫חֶל ע֖וֹד שִׁבְעַ֣ת יָמִ֣ים אֲחֵרִ֑ים וַיֹּ֛סֶף שַׁלַּ֥ח אֶת־הַיּוֹנָ֖ה וְלֹֽא־יָסְפָ֥ה שׁוּב־אֵלָ֖יו עֽוֹד׃

13. Wa-î h î b'ahath w' shesh-mâôth shanah ba-riâ-shon b'æhad la-hodesh har-bou h a-m a î m me-hal ha-âretz, wa-îassar Noah æth-michesseh ha-t h e b a h wa-îarâ w'hinneh harbou phe-neî ha-âdamah.

וַיְהִ֡י בְּאַחַת֩ וְשֵׁשׁ־מֵא֨וֹת שָׁנָ֜ה בָּרִאשׁ֗וֹן בְּאֶחָ֤ד לַחֹ֨דֶשׁ֙ חָֽרְב֣וּ הַמַּ֔יִם מֵעַ֖ל הָאָ֑רֶץ וַיָּ֤סַר נֹ֨חַ֙ אֶת־מִכְסֵ֣ה הַתֵּבָ֔ה וַיַּ֕רְא וְהִנֵּ֥ה חָֽרְב֖וּ פְּנֵ֥י הָאֲדָמָֽה׃

---

thing. The word זית signifies clearly in its literal sense, *an olive, an olive-tree;* but it signifies in its figurative, not only *oil,* but according to its hieroglyphic sense, *the luminous essence of a thing.* It comes from the root אור, which characterizes the *essence* in general, contracted with the root זי, whose object is to depict that which shines and is reflected as the light.

v. 12.   All these terms are understood or easy to understand.

v. 13.   באחד, *in-the-unity....*   This number is the symbol of the stability of things.   Moses uses it twice in this verse, where he indicates the beginning of a new existence and, as it were, the awakening of nature.   Attention should be given to the fact that number seven, which characterizes the consummation of things and end of temporal periods, is employed in the preceding verse.

בראשון, *in-the-very-principle....*   This is the word ראש, to which Moses adds designedly the extensive syllable ון.   What I have said concerning this root can be seen in v. 1, ch. I.

חרבו, *that-they-wasted....*   The verb חרוב which appears twice in this verse in speaking of the waters, is worthy of notice. It does not signify *to be dried up,* as the Latin translator has appeared to believe, but *to be destroyed, to leave off, to waste,* as the Hellenists have better interpreted ἐξέλιπε τὸ ὕδωρ .   The Hebraic verb חרוב belonging to the root חר, which characterizes elementary, devouring heat, an igneous focus, contains the idea of devastation.

12. And-he-waited yet a-
septenary of-d a y s m o r e;
a n d-h e-s e n t-forth   that-
same-*Ionah*, and-not-did-it-
add t h e-repairing toward-
him again.

12. Et-il-attendit encore
un-septenaire de-jours aut-
res; et-il-laissa-aller cette-
même *Ionah*, et-non-pas el-
la-ajouta le-retour vers-lui
encore.

13. A n d-i t-was in-the-
unity and-six-hundreds of-
revolving-c h a n g e, in-the-
very-principle, by-t h e-first
of-the-moon-renewing, t h a t
t h e y-w a s t e d, the-waters,
from-off-the-earth: and-he-
reared-up, *N o a h*, the-shel-
tering-o f-t h e-*thebah*, and-
h e-d i d-k e n, and lo! that-
wasted (the waters) from-
off-the-faces of-the-adamic.

13. Et-ce-fut dans-l'unité
e t-s i x centaines de-mutation-temporelle, d a n s - l e-
principe au-premier du-re-
nouvellement - lunaire-que-s'
usèrent (se défirent) les-
eaux de-dessus-la-terre: et-
il-éleva, *Noah*, le-comble de-
la-*thebah*, et-il-considéra et-
voici! qu'elles-s'usaient (les
eaux) d e s-f a c e s de l'élément-adamique.

---

of ravage, of total exhaustion.   The word *waste* renders the Hebrew
with exactitude.

ויסר, *and-he-reared-up*.... This expression is very remarkable.   Whether one takes the radical verb סור, or one of the compound radical verbs יסר or נסר, it will always signify *to rear up*,
in the sense of *instructing, educating, training in knowledge*. Moses,
in making use of this amphibological expression, with regard to *a
sheltering* has no doubt had the intention of making it understood,
that the word מכסה, ought not to be taken in the literal and material
sense which it presents at first glance.   All that I can do as its
interpreter, is to acquaint one with its purpose.   I have said that
the *thebah*, to which belongs this shelter or this vaulted superficies,
was neither a boat nor an ark, nor a coffer, but a mysterious refuge.

v. 14. יבשה, *was-dried-up*....   I only cite this word to show
that Moses puts it in its place, and that his translators have been
wrong in confusing it, as they have done, with the verb חרוב, of
which I spoke in the preceding verse.   It was essential before announcing the drying up of the land, to say that the waters, having

14. W-ba-h o d e s h h a-
s h e n î b'shibehah w-heshe-
rîm îôm la-hodesh îbeshah
ha-âretz.

וּבַחֹדֶשׁ הַשֵּׁנִי בְּשִׁבְעָה וְעֶשְׂרִים
יוֹם לַחֹדֶשׁ יָבְשָׁה הָאָרֶץ :

15. Wa-idabber Ælohîm
æl-Noah l'æmor:

וַיְדַבֵּר אֱלֹהִים אֶל־נֹחַ לֵאמֹר :

16. Tzeâ min-ha-thebah,
a t h a h ! w'âisheth-ċha w-
b a n e î-ċha w-nesheî-baneî-
ċha âitha-ċha.

צֵא מִן־הַתֵּבָה אַתָּה וְאִשְׁתְּךָ
וּבָנֶיךָ וּנְשֵׁי־בָנֶיךָ אִתָּךְ :

---

grown less and less, or destroyed, had disappeared from its surface.
If one will give attention to the gradation which the hierographic
writer observes, from the great swelling which causes the deluge to
the entire disappearance of the waters, it will be found wonderful.

He first says in v. I, that the waters were checked ישׂכו; and
soon in v. 3, that they restored themselves as formerly, ישׁבו; these
two Hebrew words are constructed and employed with such an art
that they have been judged the same; they differ only by the sign of
interior action ב, which in this one has replaced the assimilative
and centralizing sign כ, which is found in the other.   Next, in v.
4 and 5, the waters experience a sort of libration, of periodic movement of going and coming, and as it were, of flux and reflux, הלוֹך
ושׁוב   and   הלוֹך וחסוֹר, which seems to depict, in particular, the
effect of the seas, and in general, that of a colossal tidal wave.   Then
the waters become more and more abated, הקלו and קלו, even as it
is said in v. 8 and 11; and when at last they are wasted by this
sort of friction, done away with, entirely exhausted, חרבו, the land
is dried up, יבשה הארץ.   Let the reader who recalls with what
obstinacy Moses has been reproached for his bad natural philosophy,
examine this gradation and see if these reproaches would not apply
better to his slanderers.

v. 15. וידבר, and-he-informed-by-the-speech....   The two con-

14. And-i n-the-moon-re-
newing the-second, in-the-
seven and-twentieth day of-
that-renewing, was-dried-up
the-earth.

14. E t-dans-le-renouvel-
lement-lunaire le-s e c o n d,
dans-le-vingt-septième jour-
d e-c e-renouvellement f u t-
séchée la-terre.

15. And-he-informed-by-
the-speech, HE-the-Gods, to-
ward-*N o a h*,   pursuing-t o-
say :

15. Et-il-informa-par-la-
parole, L U I-les-Dieux, en-
vers-*Noah*, selon-ce-dire :

16. Issue from-t h e-*thebah* (sheltering p l a c e),
t h o u, and-the-intellectual-
wife-of-theee (thy volitive
faculty) and-the-issued-off-
spring-of-thee   a n d-the-cor-
poreal-m a t e s of-those-off-
spring-of-t h e e (t h e i r natural faculties), together-
thee.)

16. Sors (produis-toi en
dehors) de la-*thebah*, toi, et-
la-femme-intellectuelle-à-toi
(ta faculté volitive), et-les-
fils-à-toi (t e s productions
manifestées), et-les-épouses-
corporelles   des - fils - à - toi
(leurs facultés physiques),
ensemble-toi.

---

tracted roots רכ־בר, one of which designates *a course* and the
other *a production*, form the compound רבר, which signifies literally
an effusion, that is to say, an exterior thing by means of which an
interior thing is made manifest. In a restricted and physical sense,
it is *a thing, an affair, an object, a word*: in a broad and moral
sense, it is *an idea, a speech, a discourse, a precept*, etc.

v. 16. צא, *issue....*   The word *issue* renders well the Hebrew.
I have explained in v. 12 ch. I, the origin and force of this verb,
the application of which is here of the highest importance.

v. 17 and 18. All these terms have been explained: if I give
them an acceptation a little different from what they seem to present,
it is so that the reader may be able to grasp better the inner meaning, and that he may become familiar with the genius of the Hebraic
tongue in particular, and in general, with that of the primitive
tongues.   For the writers of these remote times, restricted to the
narrow limits of an original tongue, having only a small number of
words at their disposal, and not being able to draw elsewhere the

17. Čhol-ha-haîah asher-âith-čha miċhol-bashar ba-hôph ba-behemah w-b'ċhol-ha-remesh ha-romesh h a l-ha-âretz, hawtzeâ âith-čha w-shartzou ba-âretz w-pha-rou w-rabou hal-ha-âretz.

כָּל־הַחַיָּה אֲשֶׁר־אִתְּךָ מִכָּל־בָּשָׂר בָּעוֹף וּבַבְּהֵמָה וּבְכָל־הָרֶמֶשׂ הָרֹמֵשׂ עַל־הָאָרֶץ הַוְצֵא אִתָּךְ וְשָׁרְצוּ בָאָרֶץ וּפָרוּ וְרָבוּ עַל־הָאָרֶץ:

18. Wa-ietzeâ-N o a h w' banaî-ô w'âisheth-ô w-nes-heî banaî-ô âith-ô.

וַיֵּצֵא־נֹחַ וּבָנָיו וְאִשְׁתּוֹ וּנְשֵׁי־בָנָיו אִתּוֹ:

19. Čhol-ha-haîah čhol-ha-remesh w-č h o l-ha-hôph čhol rômesh hal-ha-âretz le-wishephehotheî-hem îatzâou min-ha-thebah.

כָּל־הַחַיָּה כָּל־הָרֶמֶשׂ וְכָל־הָעוֹף כֹּל רוֹמֵשׂ עַל־הָאָרֶץ לְמִשְׁפְּחֹתֵיהֶם יָצְאוּ מִן־הַתֵּבָה:

---

expressions which they needed, were obliged to attach to each of these words, a considerable number of analogous ideas, literally as well as figuratively: therefore, they were careful to examine the root, following the etymological science which for them held the place of erudition. It cannot be doubted, in reading the Sepher of Moses, that this extraordinary man, initiated into this science by the Egyptian priests, possessed it in the highest degree.

v. 19. למשפחתיהם, *after-the-tribes-their-own*.... Two distinct roots enter into the composition of this word. The first מש, characterizes every thing united and forming, so to speak, *a mass*: the second, פח, on the contrary, designates everything which opens to embrace a greater extent, to envelop and to include as *a net*, for

17. All-living-life which-together-thee, f r o m-every-bodily-shape, b o t h-in-fowl and-in-quadruped, a n d-i n-t h e-w h o l e-creeping-kind, t r a i l i n g-along upon-the-earth, let-i s s u e together-thee: and-let-them-pullulate in-the-earth, and-teem and-breed-multiplying upon-the-earth.

18. A n d-he-issued-forth (he waked out) he-*N o a h,* a n d-t h e-offspring-of-h i m , a n d-t h e-volitive - efficient - might-his-own, and-the-corporeal-faculties o f-t h e-off-spring-of-him, together-him.

19. T h e-w h o l e-earth-born-life, the-whole - creep-ing-kind, a n d-the-w h o l e-fowl, everything - crawling-along upon-the-earth, after-the-tribes-their-own issued forth from-the-*thebah.*

17. Toute-vie-animale la-quelle-est ensemble - toi, de-toute-forme-corporelle, e n-genre-volatile, e t-e n-quad-rupède, et-en-tout-genre-rep-tiforme serpentant sur-la-terre, fais-sortir (produire dehors) ensemble-toi ; et-qu' ils-pullulent en-la-terre, et-fructifient, e t - multiplient sur-la-terre.

18. Et-il-sortit (il se re-produisit au d e h o r s) lui-*Noah,* et-les-productions-à-lui, et-la-faculté-volitive ef-ficiente-à-lui, et-les-facultés-corporelles-des-productions-à-lui, ensemble-lui.

19. T o u t e-l'animalité-terrestre, toute-l'espèce-rep-tiforme, et-toute-l'espèce-vo-latile, t o u t-ce-qui-se-meut-d' un-mouvement-contractile sur-la-terre, selon-les-famil-les-à-eux, sortirent (se pro-duisirent h o r s) de-la-*the-bah.*

---

example. United to form the word מִשְׁפָּחָה, they depict, in the most energetic manner, the formation of the family, the tribe, the nation, which, departing from a central point embraces a greater extent. This word, inflected by the directive article לְ, is here used in the constructive plural, and united to the nominal affix הֶם .

v. 20. מִזְבֵּחַ, *an-offering-place....* The word זֶבַח, which des-ignates in Hebrew, *a sacrifice,* being governed by the sign of ex-terior and plastic action מְ, characterizes a place destined for sacri-

20. Wa-îben Noah mizeb-beha la-I H Ô A H wa-ikkah mi-ċhol ha-bemah ha-teho-rah w-mi-ċhol ha-hôph ha-tahôr: wa-îahal holoth ba-mizzebbeha.

וַיִּבֶן נֹחַ מִזְבֵּחַ לַיְהוָֹה וַיִּקַּח מִכֹּל הַבְּהֵמָה הַטְּהֹרָה וּמִכֹּל הָעוֹף הַטָּהוֹר וַיַּעַל עֹלֹת בַּמִּזְבֵּחַ :

21. W a-i a r a h IHÔAH æth-r e î a h ha-nîhoha, wa-îîomer IHÔAH ællibb-ô loâ-âossiph l'kallel hôd æth-ha-âdamah ba-hobour ha-Adam ċhi-îetzer leb ha-Adam rah mi-nehuraî-ô: w-loâ âossiph hôd l'haċhôth æth-ċhol-haî ċha-âsher hashîthî.

וַיָּרַח יְהוָֹה אֶת־רֵיחַ הַנִּיחֹחַ וַיֹּאמֶר יְהוָֹה אֶל־לִבּוֹ לֹא־אֹסִף לְקַלֵּל עוֹד אֶת־הָאֲדָמָה בַּעֲבוּר הָאָדָם כִּי יֵצֶר לֵב. הָאָדָם רַע מִנְּעֻרָיו וְלֹא־אֹסִף עוֹד לְהַכּוֹת אֶת כָּל־חַי כַּאֲשֶׁר עָשִׂיתִי :

fice, an altar. I should not have noticed this word, which otherwise offers nothing difficult, if I had not believed to give pleasure to the reader, in showing him that its root זב, is not used in this sense in Hebrew, that it does not appear even of Egyptian origin, and that it is necessary to penetrate as far as the Ethiopians to find it. The verb **ዘብሐ** (zabh), signifies among this ancient people, to sacrifice; and I quite believe that its origin goes back to a very remote time when Sabæanism flourished in that country. At the epoch when Moses employed the word זבח, it was already ancient enough to be naturalized in the Egyptian tongue without preserving the idea of its origin, which no doubt would have appeared profane to this theocratic legislator.

ויעל עלת, and-he-raised-up a-rising-sublimation.... Both the noun and the verb which the hierographic writer uses to express the action of Noah sacrificing to the Divinity, issue alike from the root על־, which characterizes every thing which is raised with energy, which mounts from a low place toward a higher, which is exhaled, which is sublimated chemically, evaporates, is spiritualized, etc. This expression merits close attention in its hieroglyphic sense.

20. And-he-erected *Noah,* an-o f f e r i n g - place unto- I H O A H ; a n d-he-t o o k-up f r o m-every-quadruped of-the-purity, and-from-every-fowl of-the-purity, a n d-he-raised-up a-rising - sublima-tion f r o m-t h a t-offering-place.

21. And-he-b r e a t h e d, IHOAH, that-fragrant-breath of-sweetness; a n d-he-said, I H O A H, inward-the-heart-his-own, n o t-will-I-certain-ly-add the-cursing-yet-again t h e - a d a m i c-for-the-sake-*Adam's* because-it-framed, the-heart of-that-collective-man, evil, f r om-the-first-ling-impulses-his-own : and-not-will-I-certainly add yet-a g a i n the-smiting-so-l o w a l l-earth-born-life such-as-that I-have-done.

20. Et-il-édifia, *N o a h,* un-lieu-d e-s a c r i f i c e à- I H O A H ; et-il-prit de-tout-quadrupède de-la-p u r e t é, et-de-tout-v o l a t i l e de-la-pureté ; et-il-éleva une-élé-vation (il fit exhaler une exhalaison) d e-c e-lieu-de-sacrifice.

21. Et-il-respira, IHOAH, c e t-esprit-odorant de - dou-ceur ; et-il-dit, IHOAH, de-vers-l a-cœur-sien, non-pas-j'ajouterai - certainement l' action-de-maudire e n c o r e la-terre-adamique d a n s-le-rapport-d'*A dam*, car-il-for-ma, le-cœur de-cet-homme-universel, l e-m a l, dès-les-premières - impulsions-sien-nes : et-non-pas-j'ajouterai-certainement encore l'act-ion de - frapper - si - violem-m e n t toute-l'existence-élé-mentaire de-même-que j'ai-fait.

---

v. 21. אֶת־רִיחַ, *that-fragrant-breath....* This noun as well as the verb which precedes it, are both attached to the root רוּחַ, of which I spoke in v. 2, ch. I. But it must be noticed that in the word רִיחַ, the sign of potential manifestation has replaced the sign of the convertible link.

לֹא־אֹסֵף, *not-will-I-certainly-add....* The root סָף, indicates any capacity whatever; employed as verb it signifies that an action already done is continued, or that it takes place again. The iterative syllable *re*, which we take from the Latins, put at the head of a verb, renders quite well this Hebraic idiomatism. Thus, for example, when in v. 12 of this chapter Moses says, in speaking of *Ionah,*

22. Hôd ĉhol-îemeî ha-
âretz zerah w-katzîr w-kor
wa-hom w-kaîtz wa-horeph
w'îôm wa-laîlah loâ îsheb-
bothou.

עֹד כָּל־יְמֵי הָאָרֶץ זֶרַע וְקָצִיר
וְקֹר וָחֹם וְקַיִץ וָחֹרֶף וְיוֹם וָלַיְלָה
לֹא יִשְׁבֹּתוּ :

ולֹא־יִסְפָה שׁוּב *and not-did-it-add-the-returning;* we would say, *and it did not return.*

יָצַר, *it-framed....* I have explained as much as possible for me, this difficult word of the Hebraic tongue in v. 7. ch. II.

רַע, *evil....* As this word offers no difficulty either in the literal or in the figurative sense, I have not dwelt upon it until now. Its etymology is so very simple. The hieroglyphic meaning only, is very profound. Its etymological composition results from the sign of movement proper ר, united to the root וע, not used in Hebrew, and changed in its analogue עו to signify literally, every bending, obliquity, inclination, declination of things; and figuratively, every perversity, iniquity, moral depravation. The hieroglyphic meaning is drawn from the symbolic union of the signs of movement proper and material sense. The Arabic analogue روِاغ, characterizes that which leaves its path, its sphere, by a disordered movement; that which bends, twists or is perverted. The Chaldaic expresses this word by בִּישׁ, which is the analogue of the Samaritan ᵐᵐᴥ‌ᴥᴥ, of which I have spoken. The Teutonic *bös* is the exact copy of the Chaldaic, of which the Latin *vitium* is a derivative.

מִנְעֻרָיו, *from-the-firstling-impulses-his-own....* The root נוּע develops every idea of impulse given to a thing to agitate, to stir it, to draw it from its torpor. This root, united by contraction to the elementary root אֹר, forms the word נַעַר, which is taken in a broader sense for elementary impulse, and in a more restricted sense, for youth and childhood.

v. 22. The terms of this verse are not difficult. I shall limit myself to giving briefly the etymology, as much to satisfy the curiosity of the reader, as to show him how the hieroglyphic meaning can pass to the figurative and to the literal, for nearly all these terms have been hieroglyphic in their origin.

---

22. While-shall-revolve-all-the-lights o f-t h e-earth (phenomenal u n i v e r s a l light's manifestation), seed-time and-harvest, and-cold and-heat, and-summer and-winter, and - day and-night shall-not sabbathize (shall not cease).

22. Pendant-t o u s-l e s-jours de-la-terre (les mani-festations lumineuses, phé-noméniques), le-germe et-la-récolte, et-le-froid et-le-chaud, et-l'été et-l'hiver, et-le-jour et-la-nuit non-pas-septeniseront (ne cesseront pas).

זרע , *seed-time*: that is to say, the dispersion, the division, the attenuation of evil; as is proved by the two contracted roots זר-רע.

קציר , *harvest*: that is to say, the term, the end of pain, of agony; as can be seen in the two contracted roots קץ-צר.

קר , *cold*. This root contains in itself the idea of that which is incisive, penetrating, stiff, strong, etc.

חם , *heat*. I have frequently had occasion to speak of this root which is attached to that which is inclined, bent, restricted, scorched, etc.

קיץ , *summer*. This is the root קץ , expressing the term, the summit, the end of all things; to which the sign of manifestation has been added.

חרף , *winter*. These words are composed of two contracted roots חר-רוף, one of which, חר, characterizes elementary heat; the other רוף, expresses the action of breaking, of interrupting, of striking, etc. *Winter* is therefore, in Hebrew, the solution, the rup-ture of elementary heat, as *summer* is the summit and the end manifested. *Cold* is therefore, a thing that is keen, penetrating, straight and clear; and *heat*, on the contrary, a thing obtuse, envelop-ing, bent and obscure. *Seed-time* can therefore be considered as a thing destined to divide, to attentuate evil more and more. One realizes how far the exploration of these hieroglyphics and others similar, might lead into the physical and metaphysical ideas of the ancient Egyptians.

I have firm reasons for thinking that this twenty-second verse and perhaps a part of the twenty-first, are foreign to Moses; I be-lieve them to be a fragment of an early commentary passed from the margin into the text.

SEPHER BERÆSHITH
T.

סֵפֶר בְּרֵאשִׁית ט ·

1. Wa - îbareĉh Ælohîm
æth-N o a h w'æth-b a n a î-ô
wa-îâomer l a-h e m, phrou
w-rebou, w-milaou æth-ha-
âretz.

וַיְבָרֶךְ אֱלֹהִים אֶת־נֹחַ וְאֶת־בָּנָיו
וַיֹּאמֶר לָהֶם פְּרוּ וּרְבוּ וּמִלְאוּ
אֶת־הָאָרֶץ :

2. W - môrâo - ĉhem w -
hith-ĉ h e m îhîeh hal-ĉhol-
haîath ha-âretz w-hal-ĉhol
hôph ha-shamaîm b'ĉhol âsher thiremoth ha-âdamah
w-b'ĉhol-degheî ha - îam b'
îed-ĉhem nithanou.

וּמוֹרַאֲכֶם וְחִתְּחֶם יִהְיֶה עַל־חַיַּת
הָאָרֶץ וְעַל־כָּל־עוֹף הַשָּׁמַיִם
בְּכֹל אֲשֶׁר תִּרְמֹשׂ הָאֲדָמָה
וּבְכָל־דְּגֵי הַיָּם בְּיֶדְכֶם נִתָּנוּ :

---

v. 1.   All the terms in this verse have been previously explained.

v. 2.   וּמוֹרַאֲכֶם *and-the-dazzling-brightness-yours....*   The Hellenists and their imitators who have seen in the word מוֹרָא an
expression of terror or fright, have therefore rendered *Noah* and
his productions, as objects of fear for terrestrial animality; but this
is not what Moses has intended.   The root of this word is אוֹר
light, whence מָאוֹר, *splendour, brightness, a torch.*   The verb מָרוֹא
which is formed from it signifies *to rule by its lights* and not to
terrify.   One finds in Chaldaic the word מָרָא, and the analogues in
Syriac and in Arabic to designate, *a master, guide, lord.*   From this
word is formed the Latin "maritus", from which comes the French
mari (husband), that is to say exactly, the torch, the enlightened
guide of the woman: name given at first out of respect or flattery
but which habit has finally distorted utterly.

I must admit that the Samaritan translator had already corrupted
the meaning of Moses before the Hellenists, since rendering the word
מוֹרָא by ⳥ⳡⳘⳘⳤ, which designates a gigantic formidable object, he

GENESIS IX.

1. A n d-h e-blessed, HE-t h e-Gods, the-selfsameness-of-*Noah,* and-that-of-the-off-spring-h i s-o w n; a n d-he-said unto-them : breed and-multiply, and-fill the-self-sameness-of-earth.

2. And-the-d a z z l i n g-brightness-yours, a n d-the-dreadful-awe-o f-y o u shall-be u p o n-the-whole-animal-ity e a r t h-born, and-upon-e v e r y-fowl of-heavens, in-all that can-breed from-the-adamic-pristine-e l e m e n t, and-in-every-fish of-the-sea : i n t o-t h e-hand-yours they-were-given-over.

COSMOGONIE IX.

1. Et-il-b é n i t , LUI-les-Dieux, l'ipséité-de-*Noah,* et-celle-des-émanations-à-l u i ; et-il-dit-à-eux : fructifiez et-multipliez et-remplissez-en-tièrement l'ipséité-terrestre.

2. E t - l a-splendeur-éb-louissante-v ô t r e, e t-le-re-spect-terrifiant-à-vous, sera s u r-toute-l'animalité-terres-tre et-sur-toute-l'espèce-vola-tile d e s-régions-é l e v é e s; dans-tout ce-qui recevra-le-mouvement-originel de-l'élé-ment-adamique, e t-d a n s-tous-les-poissons de-la-mer; sous-la-main-à-vous, ils-ont-été-mis.

---

had effaced this imposing light, whence the hierographic writer causes the respect of animals for the posterity of *Noah* to be derived.

v. 3. I have nothing more to say upon the meaning of these words; except that animal life is given as food to Noah and to his posterity, which had not been done with regard to that of Adam. This life is given to them the same as the green herb, כירק עשב. Here the assimilative article כ is used in the most picturesque, and in the least equivocal manner: the root אך, makes, in the following verse, an effect no less striking, as adverbial relation.

v. 4. אך־בשר, *but-the-bodily-shape....* I regret assuredly the

3. Čhol-r e m e s h asher houâ-haî la-čhem îhîeh l' ačhelah: čh'îerek h e s h e b nathathî la-čhem æth-čhol.

כָּל־רֶמֶשׂ אֲשֶׁר הוּא־חַי לָכֶם
יִהְיֶה לְאָכְלָה כְּיֶרֶק עֵשֶׂב נָתַתִּי
לָכֶם אֶת־כֹּל :

4. Ačh-b a s h a r b'nap-hesh-ô dam-ô loâ thâočhelou.

אַךְ־בָּשָׂר בְּנַפְשׁוֹ דָמוֹ לֹא־
תֹאכֵלוּ :

---

trouble that the Hellenists have taken to disguise the force of this verse and the ensuing ones; I would gladly imitate the discreet complaisance of the Latin translator, who has chosen to pass in silence the words which perplexed him; but at last it is necessary that Moses be translated. If this extraordinary man has said things which alarm the rabbis, or which shock their pride, he has also said things which ought to make them proud: thus is every-thing balanced. Long enough have these magnificent tableaux been degraded by the sorry caricatures which have been made of them. They must be known in their original conception. The disagreeable truths to be met with here are nothing in comparison to the false or ridiculous things which the copyists have introduced.

In fact, this is beyond doubt: Moses, by the mouth of the Divin-ity, forbids the posterity of *Noah* to feed upon corporeal substance, the similitude of that which his soul bears in himself, that is to say, the very flesh of man. Certainly one should regard this decree only as a general law which concerns the entire human race, since it is also addressed to the posterity of *Noah*, which here represents mankind; but in supposing that the Hebrews might be found at that time in circumstances lamentable enough to have required it, I must apprise the modern Jews, if anything can console them for this, that not only had Zoroaster already made this decree to the Parsees, a people today very pacific, and who even abstain from the flesh of animals; but that he had moreover, commanded them to confess hav-ing eaten human flesh, when this had happened; as can be seen in the *Jeschts sadés*, traduit par Anquetil-Duperron (p. 28, 29, 30 et suiv.).

3. Every-moving - thing, which-is itself-life, to-you shall-be for-food : even-as-the-green herb, I-have-given unto-you together-all.

4. B u t-the-bodily-shape-h a v i n g by-the-soul-itself, the-likeness-its-o w n, n o t-shall-you-feed-upon.

3. Tout-c h o s e-s e-mou-vant qui-a en-soi l'existence, à-vous s e r a pour-aliment: de-m ê m e-que-la-verdoyante herbe, j'ai-donné-à-vous en-semble-tout.

4. Mais-la-forme-corpor - elle-ayant dans-l'âme-sienne l'homogénéité (la similitu-de) à-elle, non-pas-vous-con-sommerez.

I shall not expatiate upon this subject as I shall doubtless have occasion to treat of it elsewhere. I pass on to the explanation of the verse under consideration.

Moses, after having likened all terrestrial animality to the green herb and having given it as food for the posterity of Noah, opposes to the assimilative article כ which he has just used, the adverbial relation אך, thus giving a contrary movement to the phrase, restricting with greatest force, and making exception of that corporeal form which receives its likeness from its soul by means of *blood*. For in whatever manner one may examine the words which compose this verse, here is their meaning; one cannot interpret them otherwise without mutilating them or making them utterly unrecognizable.

When the Hellenists have said, *ye shall not eat the flesh which is in the blood of the soul*: κρέα ἐν αἱματι ψυχῆς ; they have not only misunderstood the true signification of the word דם by limiting it to signifying only *blood*, but they have again overthrown all the terms of the phrase, by attributing to this word the mediative article ב which belongs to *the soul* in the Hebrew text, and by suppressing the two nominal affixes which make *the corporeal form* בשר, dependent upon sanguineous homogeneity דמו , residing *in its own soul*, בנפש׳ .

When the Latin translator has said, *ye shall not eat the flesh with the blood*, "carnem cum sanguine", he has, like the Hellenists, wrongly interpreted the word דם ; he has given it a relation that it has not, and finally, he has suppressed entirely the word נפש , *soul*, not knowing what to do with it. The great difficulties of this verse

5. W'âċh æth-dime-ċhem l'napheshothî-ċhem âedrosh mi-îad ċhol-haîah âedresh-nou w-mi-îad ha-Adam, mi-îad Aîsh æhî-ô âedrosh æth-nephesh ha-Adam.

וְאַךְ אֶת־דְּמְכֶם לְנַפְשֹׁתֵיכֶם אֶדְרֹשׁ מִיַּד כָּל־חַיָּה אֶדְרְשֶׁנּוּ וּמִיַּד הָאָדָם מִיַּד אִישׁ אָחִיו אֶדְרֹשׁ אֶת־נֶפֶשׁ הָאָדָם׃

---

and those following consist, first, in the meaning which Moses has attached to the word דם; secondly, in the manner in which he has made use of it.

The word does not signify literally *blood*, as the Hellenists have wished to make it believed and as Saint Jerome has believed; but, as I have already said elsewhere, every homogeneous thing, formed by assimilation of similar parts, and belonging to the universal organization. If this word, taken in a restricted sense, designates *blood*, it is because, following the Egyptian ideas of natural philosophy, the blood was regarded as formed of homogeneous molecules, united by an universal, assimilative force, serving as bond between the soul and body, and in consequence of the laws which preside at the organization of beings, of designing exteriorly the corporeal form, according to the impulse which it receives from the efficient volitive faculty, inherent in the soul.

Whatever opinion one may take of these ideas of natural philosophy it is not my purpose to discuss their advantages over those of our modern physicists; it is enough for me on this occasion, to bring them out and to state that they were all contained in the word רם , by virtue of its hieroglyphic composition. When this word designated *blood*, it was in its quality of assimilative link between the soul and body, of organizing instrument, as it were, destined to raise the edifice of the body according to the plan furnished by its soul.

Now, in this instance the hierographic writer has made use of its literal, figurative and hieroglyphic sense to its fullest extent, by means of a oratorical figure of speech peculiar to the genius of the Hebraic tongue, and which I have already explained several times. There is no translation in any modern European tongue which can wholly express his thought. All that I can do is to present it so that an intelligent reader can penetrate it readily.

Let us listen now to the Samaritan translator; he has not de-

5. For that-sanguineous-likeness-yours (which acts according) t o-t h e-s o u l s-yours I-will-prosecute from-the-hand of-every-living: I-will-prosecute-it (I will a v e n g e it) and-from-the-hand of-*A d a m* (collective man); a n d-from-the-hand of-*Aish* (intellectually indi-viduated man) brother-of-him, I-will-prosecute that-v e r y-s o u l, universal-like-ness.

5. Car cette-assimilation-sanguine-à-vous (q u i est) selon-les-âmes-vôtres, je-re-chercherai d e-l a-m a i n de-tout-vivant: je-rechercherai-elle (j'e n poursuivrai la vengeance) et-de-la-main d' *Adam* (l'homme universel); et-de-la-m a i n d'*A i s h* (l' homme individualisé par sa volonté) frère-à-lui, je - re-chercherai (j e vengerai) cette-même-âme-adamique.

---

viated greatly from his model: and he has been abandoned by the Hellenists who did not wish so much clarity.   Here is his entire phrase interpreted word-for-word.

פֶּל־בֶּף־בֶּם־ִי־אִישֶׁךְ
:וֹ2אֹמֶה־אֲכֶל

However the form-corporeal, by-the-soul-its-own a d a m i c, not-shall-you-consume.

That is to say, you shall not eat of the animal substance assimilated by the soul of universal man. This seems clear. The following verses will complete its evidence.

v. 5.   In this verse the Divinity announces that it will avenge this blood assimilation, analogous to the adamic soul, that is to say, plainly, that it will avenge the human blood shed, מִיַד כֹּל־חַיָּה, "at the hand of every living being"...... וּמִיַד הָאָדָם, "and at the hand of universal Adam"...... מִיַד אִישׁ אָחִיו "at the hand of in-tellectual Aish, his brother"...... I urge the reader to observe, be-sides the proofs which I have just advanced, the irresistible proof of the distinction which I have established according to Moses, between *Adam*, universal man, mankind, and *Aish*, intellectual man, in-dividualized by his volitive faculty.   This hierographic writer nam-ing them together in this verse, is careful not to confuse them, as his translators have done.   On the contrary, he designates the one as brother of the other.

6. Shopheċh d a m h a-
Adam b'Adam dam-ô îshap-
heċh : ċhi b'tzelem Ælohîm
hashah æth-ha-Adam.

שָׁפֵךְ דַּם הָאָדָם בָּאָדָם דָּמוֹ
יִשָּׁפֵךְ כִּי בְּצֶלֶם אֱלֹהִים עָשָׂה
אֶת־הָאָדָם :

7. W'âthem, phrou w-re-
bou, shirtzou ba-âretz, w-rebou b'ha.

וְאַתֶּם פְּרוּ וּרְבוּ שִׁרְצוּ בָאָרֶץ
וּרְבוּ בָהּ :

8. W a-îâomer Ælohîm
æl-Noah w'æl-banaî-ô, âith-
ô, l'æmor.

וַיֹּאמֶר אֱלֹהִים אֶל־נֹחַ וְאֶל־בָּנָיו
אִתּוֹ לֵאמֹר :

9. Wa-âni hin-nî mekîm
æth-berith-î, âith - ċhem w'
æth-zarehaċhem â h o r e î -
ċhem.

וַאֲנִי הִנְנִי מֵקִים אֶת־בְּרִיתִי
אִתְּכֶם וְאֶת־זַרְעֲכֶם אַחֲרֵיכֶם :

---

v. 6.   This verse contains a terrible mystery, which Plato has
very clearly understood and developed very well in his book of
Laws.   I refer the reader to it in order to avoid commentaries.
As to the terms themselves, they have either been already explained
or they offer no kind of grammatical difficulty.

v. 7.   וְאַתֶּם, and-ye-collective-self.... The designative relation אֵת, taken substantively and invested with the collective sign
ם, is applied here to Noah and to his productions; that which gives
to the apostrophe a force that no translator of Moses has made felt.

וּרְבוּ בָהּ, and-spread-yourselves on-it.... It must be observed
that the verb רָבֹה, is employed twice in this verse.   The first, in
the sense of growing in number; the second, in that of growing in
power; so that it is difficult to say whether the mediative article
ב, employed with the nominal affix ה, to designate the earth, in-

6. The-shedding-one the-s a g u i n e o u s-likeness of-*Adam* (mankind) through-*A d a m* t h e-blood-his-own s h a l l-be-shed: because-in-the-universal-s h a d o w of-HIM-the-Gods HE-made the-selfsameness-of-*Adam*.

7. And-ye-collective-self! f r u c t i f y and-increase-in-number; breed in-the-earth, and-spread-yourselves on-it.

8. And-he-declared, HE-the-Gods, unto-*Noah*, and-unto-t h e-offspring-of-h i m, together-hi m, pursuing-to-say:

9. And-I, lo-I-am causing-to-stand-substantially t h e-c r e a t i n g-might-mine to-gether-you, a n d together-the-seed-yours, after-you.

6. L'épandant (celui qui épandra) l'assimilation-san-guine d'*Adam* (le règne ho-minal) p a r-l e-m o y e n-d' *A d a m* le-sang-à-lui sera-épandu: c a r-dans-l'ombre-u n i v e r s e l l e de-LUI-les-D i e u x IL-fit l'ipséité-d' *Adam*.

7. Et-vous-existence-uni-verselle! fructifiez et-multi-pliez: propagez-vous en-la-terre, et-étendez-vous en-el-le.

8. Et-il déclara, LUI-les-Dieux, envers-*Noah*, et-en-vers-les-émanations-à-lui, en-semble-lui, selon-ce-dire:

9. Et-moi, voici-moi fai-sant-exister-en-substance la-f o r c e-créatrice-mienne en-semble-vous et-ensemble-la-generation-vôtre, après-vous.

---

dicates simply that the earth will be the place, or the means of this power.

v. 8. All these terms are understood.

v. 9. מקים, *causing-to-stand-substantially....* This is the verb קום, used according to the excitative form, active movement, continued facultative. For the meaning which I give it, refer to the history of this important root, v. 4, ch. II.

את־בריתי, *the-creating-might-mine....* See v. 18, ch. VII. If one glances at the vulgar translations, he will see the Divinity, (instead of the power or creative law which It gives to Noah and to

10.   W'æth-chol-nephesh
ha-haîah â s h e r âith-chem
ba-h ô p h ba-behemah w-b'
chol haîath ha-âretz âith-
chem mi-chol îotzeâî ha-thebah l'chol haîath ha-âretz.

וְאֶת־כָּל־נֶפֶשׁ הַחַיָּה אֲשֶׁר אִתְּכֶם
בָּעוֹף בַּבְּהֵמָה וּבְכָל־חַיַּת הָאָרֶץ
אִתְּכֶם מִכֹּל יֹצְאֵי הַתֵּבָה לְכֹל
חַיַּת הָאָרֶץ :

11.   W a-hokimothî. æth-
berith-î âith-ê h e m w-loâ-
îchareth chol-b a s h a r hôd
mi-meî ha-m a b b o u l w-loâ
îhîeh hôd m a b b o u l l'shaheth ha-âretz.

וַהֲקִמֹתִי אֶת־בְּרִיתִי אִתְּכֶם וְלֹא־
יִכָּרֵת כָּל־בָּשָׂר עוֹד מִמֵּי הַמַּבּוּל
וְלֹא־יִהְיֶה עוֹד מַבּוּל לְשַׁחֵת
הָאָרֶץ :

12.   Wa-îâomer Ælohîm
zoâth âôth ha-berith âsher
anî nothen bein-î. w-beineî-
ê h e m w'beîn chol-nephesh
haîah âsher âith-chem l'do-
roth hôlam.

וַיֹּאמֶר אֱלֹהִים זֹאת אוֹת־הַבְּרִית
אֲשֶׁר אֲנִי נֹתֵן בֵּינִי וּבֵינֵיכֶם וּבֵין
כָּל־נֶפֶשׁ חַיָּה אֲשֶׁר אִתְּכֶם
לְדֹרֹת עוֹלָם :

---

his productions according to the Hebrew text), consenting with them
and with all the animals coming out from the ark; and following
the Hellenists and Latin interpreters, he will see a sort of pact,
treaty or alliance, the articles of which it is none too easy to conceive.

v. 10. All these terms are understood.

v. 11. וְלֹא־יִכָּרֵת, *and-no-more-shall-be-cut-off*.... This is the
verb כָּרֹת, used according to the positive form, passive movement.
This verb, which signifies literally *to arrest the scope of a thing*, is

10. And-t o g e t h e r-all-soul of-life w h i c h-was to-gether-you, in-the-fowl, in-the-quadruped, a n d-in-the-whole animality earth-born, together-y o u, amongst-all the-issuing-b e i n g s of-the-*thebah*, including-the-whole animality of-the-earth.

11. A n d-I-will-cause-to-exist-i n-a-material - s h a p e that-creating-might-mine. to-gether-y o u; a n d-no-more-shall-be-cut-o f f every-cor-poreal-shape again, through-t h e-w a t e r s of-the-great-swelling; and-no-more-shall-be yet a-flood for-the-des-troying-quite-o v e r o f-the-earth.

12. And-he-said, HE-the-G o d s, t h i s-i s t h e-token (symbolical s i g n) of-the-creating-might which I-am l a y î n g-down betwixt-me and - betwixt - you a n d - be-twixt e v e r y-s o u l of-life, which-shall-be together-you unto-the-ages of-the-bound-less-time.

10. Et-ensemble-t o u t e-âme de-vie, laquelle-était ensemble-vous, en-genre-vo-latile, en-quadrupède, et-en-t o u t e animalité terrestre, ensemble-vous, parmi-tous-les-provenans d e-l a-*thebah*, comprenant-toute l'anima-lité terrestre.

11. Et-j e-f e r a i-exister-dans-l'ordre-matériel cette-loi-créatrice-mienne, ensem-ble-vous; et-non-pas sera-re-tranchée t o u t e-forme-cor-porelle encore, par-l'eau de-la-grande-intumescence : et-non-pas-sera e n c o r e une-grande-intumescence p o u r-la-dépression (la destruct-tion) de-la-terre.

12. E t-i l-d i t, LUI-les-Dieux, ceci-est le-signe de-la-loi-créatrice laquelle je-suis mettant entre-moi et-entre-vous, e t-entre-toute-âme de-vie, laquelle-sera en-semble-vous aux-âges de-l' immensité (des temps).

---

formed of the two contracted roots כר־רת of which the one, כר, contains the idea of that which grows, rises, unfolds; and the other, רת , expresses on the contrary, that which chains, arrests, coagu-lates, etc.

v. 12. אני נותן, *I-am laying-down*.... Here is the source of this facultative whose signification can here be of some import-

13.   Æth-kasheth-î   nathathî b'hanan w'haîthah l'
aóth berith beîn-î w'beîn ha-
âretz.

אֶת־קַשְׁתִּי נָתַתִּי בֶּעָנָן וְהָיְתָה
לְאוֹת בְּרִית בֵּינִי וּבֵין הָאָרֶץ :

14.   W'h aî a h b'hanan-î
hanan hal-ha-âretz w'nirâ-
thah ha-kesheth b' hanan.

וְהָיָה בְּעַנְנִי עָנָן עַל־הָאָרֶץ
וְנִרְאֲתָה הַקֶּשֶׁת בֶּעָנָן :

15.   W-zaċharethî æth-be-
rîth-î â s h e r beîn-î w-beî-
neî-ċhem w-beîn ċhol-nep-
hesh haîah b'ċhol-bashar w-
loâ î h î e h hôd ha-maîm l'
mabboul l'shaheth ċhol-bashar.

וְזָכַרְתִּי אֶת־בְּרִיתִי. אֲשֶׁר בֵּינִי
וּבֵינֵיכֶם וּבֵין כָּל־נֶפֶשׁ חַיָּה בְּכָל־
בָּשָׂר וְלֹא־יִהְיֶה עוֹד הַמַּיִם
לְמַבּוּל לְשַׁחֵת כָּל־בָּשָׂר :

---

ance. The root תן develops in a general sense, an extension of itself, an enlargement: in a particular sense, it is a gift, a largess.
Preceded by the verbal adjunction נ , it expresses the action of
putting in the possession of another, of delivering for his disposition, of giving.   It is to this latter meaning that the facultative
נותן is related.

v. 13. את־קשתי, *that-bow-mine....*   The root of the word
קשת, *a bow*, is not found in the Hebrew tongue; it must be
sought for in the Arabic قاس, in which it is a kind of idiomatic
onomatopoeia.   It is from the word قوس *a bow*, that the Hebrew is
formed as feminine derivative.

בענן , *in-the-cloudy-expanse....*   I beg the reader to recall
what I have said concerning the extraordinary root אן, which sometimes characterizes indefinite being, the world, and sometimes void,
nothingness.   If this root, conceived as characterizing void, loses
its radical vowel א to take ע which designates the material sense,
then it seems that void itself is corporified and becomes palpable.
It is a heavy air, an obscure vapour, a lugubrious veil, thrown over

13. That-bow-mine I-have-laid-down in-the-cloudy-expense; and-it-shall-be for-token of-the-creating-might betwixt-me and-betwixt the-earth.

14. And-it-shall-be by-the-clouding-mine the-cloudy-expanse, upon-the-earth, that-shall-be-seen the-bow in-the-cloudy-expanse.

15. And-I-will-remember that-creating-law which-is betwixt-me and-betwixt-you, and-betwixt all-soul of-life into-all-corporeal-shape; and-not-shall-be-there an-again (a coming back) of-the-water's great-swelling to-depress (to destroy, to un-do) every-corporeal-shape.

13. Cet-arc-mien j'ai-mis dans l'espace-nébuleux; et-il-sera pour signe de-la-loi-créatrice entre-moi et-entre la-terre.

14. Et-ce-sera-dans-l'action-mienne d'obscurcir l'espace-nébuleux sur-la-terre, qu'il-sera-vu l'arc dans l'espace-nébuleux.

15. Et-je-me-rappellerai cette-loi-créatrice laquelle-sera entre-moi et-entre-vous, et-entre-toute-âme de-vie, en-toute-forme-corporelle; et-non-sera un-encore (une révolution nouvelle) des-eaux de-la-grande-intumescence pour-déprimer (abîmer) toute-forme-corporelle.

---

the light. Now, this is what the root עֵן signifies properly. In its state of verb it develops the action of obscuring, covering, hiding, obstructing; *fascinans oculis*. In its state of noun and united to the syllable וֹן, it designates nebulous space and all clouds in particular.

v. 14. בְּעַנְנִי, *by-the-clouding-mine*.... Moses, true to this style, derives the verb from the same root as the noun and uses them together. The effect of his phrase is here very picturesque, but the thought that it contains is again most profound. This thought is of such a nature that it cannot be explained. All that I can say is, that in the same action of obscuring the earth, the Divinity, according to this hierographic writer, places the striking

16. W'haîthah ha-kes-heth b'hanan w-raîthî-ha li-zeĉhor berîth holam beîn Ælohîm w-beîn ĉhol-nephesh haîah b'ĉhol-bashar âsher hal-ha-âretz.

וְהָיְתָה הַקֶּשֶׁת בֶּעָנָן וּרְאִיתִיהָ לִזְכֹּר בְּרִית עוֹלָם בֵּין אֱלֹהִים וּבֵין כָּל־נֶפֶשׁ חַיָּה בְּכָל־בָּשָׂר אֲשֶׁר עַל־הָאָרֶץ :

17. Wa-îâomer Ælohîm æl-Noah zâoth âôth ha-ber-îth âsher hokimothî beîn-î w-beîn ĉhol bashar âsher hal-ha-âretz.

וַיֹּאמֶר אֱלֹהִים אֶל־נֹחַ זֹאת אוֹת־ הַבְּרִית אֲשֶׁר הֲקִמֹתִי בֵּינִי וּבֵין כָּל־בָּשָׂר אֲשֶׁר עַל־הָאָרֶץ :

18. Wa-îhîou benei-Noah ha-îotzeâîm min-ha-thêbah: Shem w-Ham wa-Japheth: w-Ham houâ âbî Ĉhenahan.

וַיִּהְיוּ בְנֵי־נֹחַ הַיֹּצְאִים מִן־הַתֵּבָה שֵׁם וְחָם וָיָפֶת וְחָם הוּא אֲבִי כְנָעַן :

token of might, or the creative law which he gives to *Noah* and to his posterity.

v. 15. עוֹד *an-again*.... The root עוֹד, expresses the idea of a return to the same action, as I have announced in v. 19, ch. IV. It is ordinarily employed as adverbial relation; but in the example here referred to, it appears with the force of a real substantive governing the words הַמַּיִם לַמַּבּוּל, *the-waters of-the-great-swelling*.... This is what has determined me to make a substantive of the word *again*, to express exactly the Hebraic phrase.

v. 16 and 17. All these terms are understood.

v. 18. כְנָעַן, *Chanahan*.... I have given in the greatest detail, the etymology of the proper names of *Noah's* three sons,

16. And-t h e r e-shall-b e t h e-b o w in-the-cloudy-expanse; a n d-I-will-look-upon-it, to-remember the-creating-law (laid down for) a-boundless-time, b e t w i x t HIM-the-Gods, and-betwixt-all-soul of-life, in-every-corporeal-shape, w h i c h-is on-the-earth.

17. And-he-said, HE-the-Gods, unto-*Noah,* this-is the-token of-the-creating-might which I-caused-to-exist-substantially between-me and-b e t w e e n every-corporeal-s h a p e, w h i c h-is on-the-earth.

18. A n d-they-were t h e-s o n s o f-*N o a h,* (his offspring) issuing f r o m-the-*thebah* (sheltering abode). *Shem* (all that is upright and bright), *Ham* (all that is dark, curved and heated) and-*Japheth* (all that is extended and wide): then-*Ham* was-himself, the-father of-*Chanahan* (reality, material existence.

16. Et-il-sera, l'arc, dans-l'espace-nébuleux; et-je-considérerai-lui pour-rappeler la-loi-créatrice de-l'immen-sité-d e s-temps (existante) entre-LUI-les Dieux, et-en-tre-toute âme-vivante, dans-toute-forme-corporelle q u i-est sur-la-terre.

17. E t-i l-d i t, L U I-l e s-Dieux, à *Noah,* ceci-est le-s i g n e de-la-force-créatrice laquelle j'ai-fait-exister-sub-stantiellement entre-moi et-e n t r e toute-forme-corpor-elle qui-est sur-la-terre.

18. Et-ils-furent les-fils de-*Noah* (ses émanations) les-sortans de-la-*thebah* (la place de refuge), *Shem* (ce qui est élevé et brillant). *Ham* (ce qui est incliné, ob-scur, et chaud) et-*Japheth* (ce qui est étendu) : or-*Ham* fut-lui-même, père de-*Cha-nahan* (la réalité matér-ielle, l'existence physique).

Shem, Ham and *Japheth:* here is a fourth, *Chanahan,* whose sig-nification merits all the attention of the reader.   Although Moses declared him son of *Ham* and that he ought, as to his extraction to be considered such, we shall see nevertheless a little further on, that this writer speaks of him as a real son of *Noah,* thus associating him in the most expressive manner with *Ham* from whom he issued. · It is because *Ham* and *Chanahan* are but one sole and same thing,

19.   Sheloshath ælleh be-
nef-Noah w-m'ælleh nephet-
zah chol-ha-âretz.

שְׁלֹשֶׁת אֵלֶּה בְּנֵי־נֹחַ וּמֵאֵלֶּה
נָפְצָה כָל־הָאָרֶץ :

20.   Wa-îahel Noah Aish
ha-âdamah wa-ittah charem.

וַיָּחֶל נֹחַ אִישׁ הָאֲדָמָה וַיִּטַּע
כָּרֶם :

---

one sole and same cosmogonic personage, considered under two different relations.   *Chanahan* once produced by *Ham*, becomes *Ham*
himself.   This name comes from two distinct roots: בֶּן and עֶן.
By the first, בֶּן, should be understood all that which enjoys a central force sufficiently energetic to become palpable, to form a body
extended in every sense, to acquire solidity.   This root has many
analogies with the one of which I have spoken in explaining the
name of *Kain*.   The only difference which exists between them is
that קַן, being especially animated by the sign of potential manifestation in קִין, has a force of usurpation and of transmutation in
its proper nature, that the other קַן, has not.   This one seems reduced to a force of inertia which leaves it only an existence purely
passive and material.

Employed as substantive, the root קַן develops the idea of that
which pertains to the reality of things and to their physical essence.
As verb, it expresses the action of fixing and affirming, of placing
and arranging, literally as well as figuratively.

The second root from which the name of *Chanahan* comes, is
עֶן , which, according to the analysis that I have made in v. 13 of
this same chapter, should be understood as a sort of nothingness, of
materialized void, depicted by a heavy air, an obscure vapour, a
dismal veil, etc.   So that by now uniting the roots in question, according to their different significations, we shall find in כְּנַעַן , the
expression of a realized nothingness, of a shadowy air made solid and
compact, in short, of a physical existence.

This physical existence sometimes taken in good or in bad sense,
has furnished a great number of figurative expressions for the
Hebraic tongue.   The one most used is that by which one has
designated, by the same name of כְּנַעַן, artisans and merchants; that is
to say, those who are trained in real or physical things, who traffic

19. Three-were those the-o f f s p r i n g of-*Noah*, and-through-t h o s e was-shared the-whole-earth.

20. And-he-released (set f r e e, redeemed forcibly), *Noah*, the-intellectual-m a n of-the-adamic-ground; and-thus-he-tilled what-is-lofty (spiritual heights).

19. Trois-furent ceux-là les-fils (les êtres émanés) de-Noah, et-par-ceux-là fut-partagée toute-la-terre.

20. Et-il-délivra (rendit à la liberté, dégagea avec effort) *Noah*, l'homme-intel-lectuel de l'élément-adami-que; et-il-cultiva (ainsi) ce-qui-est-élevé (les productions spirituelles).

---

in, and maintain their existence from them: it has been, in the course of time, the cause of unenlightened or prejudiced interpreters believing that the son of *Ham* had been the father of merchants and perhaps himself a merchant.

v. 19. No difficulties here.

v. 20. וַיִּחֶל, *And-he-released....* The Hellenists, ever engrossed in restricting to the most insignificant and most trivial sense, the magnificent thoughts of Moses, instead of seeing *Noah*, the preserver of elementary existence, giving liberty to the human intelligence, weakened and held captive not only through the degradation of the earth, but by the terrible catastrophe which had taken place, far from seeing him restore birth to that intellectual man whom the vices of humanity had brought near to death, as far as death can be approached by an immortal essence; the Hellenists, I say, see in their *Noah* only a man of the fields who plants the vine: καὶ ἤρξατο Νῶε ἄνθρωπος γεώργος γῆς καὶ ἐφύτευσεν ἀμπελῶνα. "And Noah began to be an husbandman, and he planted a vineyard."

The author of the Latin Vulgate has faithfully rendered this singular idea, and has even augmented it by a verb which is found neither in the Greek, nor even in the Hebrew: "cœpit que Noe, vir agricola, exercere terram: et plantavit vineam."

But there is not a word of all that in the text of Moses.

21. Wa-îesheth min-ha- וַיֵּשְׁתְּ מִן־הַיַּיִן וַיִּשְׁכָּר וַיִּתְגַּל בְּתוֹךְ
jîn : wa-ishecchar, wa-itheg-
gal bethôch âholoh. אָהֳלֹה :

First, it is necessary to distort grievously the verb וַיָּחֶל, to make
it say, *and he began.* This verb is derived from the root חֶל, which
as I have already stated on several occasions, develops the general
idea of an effort made upon a thing to extend it, to draw it out, to
lead it toward another, to be clasped there, etc. This root, verbalized by
the convertible sign ו, offers, in the radical verb הוּל, an idea of
suffering caused by the violent effort that one makes upon oneself,
or upon another; and thence, the accessory ideas of wringing, of
moving in a convulsive manner, of suffering; of taking courage, of
being hardened against pain, of waiting, of hoping, etc.   The different compounds of this radical, formed either by the initial adjunc-
tions י or נ, or by the redoubling of the final character ל, par-
ticipate more or less in its original signification.   They always
signify opening a thing, resolving, dissolving, extracting, bringing
to light, making public, taking possession of, etc.

It must be seen after this explanation, that the most exact meaning which can be given to the expression of Moses, is not *he began,*
which can only be applied to the accessory idea of opening; but
rather, *he released* which proceeds from the first idea.   The Samaritan translator and the Chaldaic paraphrast, agree with me upon
this point: the former, using the verb ﬞ, and the latter, its
analogue שְׁרִי, which expresses the action of emitting, permitting,
allowing, letting go; as is proved by the Syriac ﬞ, and the Arabic
شرﻩ, which are attached to the same root   שׁוּר, whose literal
meaning is to direct and regulate a thing.

But let us continue the analysis of this important verse.   Moses
said therefore, not that *Noah* began to be an husbandman, but that
he released intellectual man from the adamic element, and opened
for him a new career.   The word אִישׁ which he uses in this instance, has been sufficiently explained in v. 23, ch. IV.   It is after
the revivification of this principle, that he applies himself to cul-
tivate that which is lofty or sublime.   Now, it was quite simple,
after having made an agricultural man of Noah, to see in this

21. A n d-h e - saturated-himself with-what-is spirit-uous; a n d-h e-intoxicated-his-thought (gave a delir-ious movement to his fan-cy); a n d-h e-revealed-him-self-in-the-bottom (i n t h e most secret part) of-the-ta-bernacle-his-own.

21. Et-il-s'abreuva de-ce-qui-est spiritueux; et-il-ex-alta-sa-pensée (donna un es-sor violent à son imaginat-ion); et-il-se-révéla dans-le-centre (dans le lieu le plus secret) du-tabernacle-à-lui.

---

spiritual elevation, *a vineyard*, the name of which taken in the physical order, was synonymous: and instead of the spirit, produc-tion of this same elevation, *wine*, equally synonymous with spirit.

For what does the word כרם, that the Hellenists have rendered by ἀμπλῶνα, signify? It signifies not only a *vineyard*, but a thing pertaining to an elevation, to an exaltation literally as well as figuratively. It is formed from the root רם, which characterizes that which moves upward from below, in the manner of a flame, em-ployed as substantive, and inflected by the assimilative article כ. In the figurative sense, כרם, designates an exaltation, a sublime move-ment of the understanding; in the literal sense *a vine*, a spirituous plant which enjoys elevated places, and which one raises higher by means of trellises and poles. I must say, besides, for those of my readers who might imagine that the word כרם has never before been taken in the figurative sense that I give it, that this word, famous throughout all Asia, signified, in Chaldaic, *a splendid thing, an academy, an assemblage of savants*, that the Syriac ܟܪܡܘܬܐ, designates *strength;* the Arabic كرم , *generosity, greatness of soul;* that this word expresses the action of fire in Coptic, as it expresses it morally in Egyptian; that in the Sanskrit tongue, *Karma* or *Kirmo*, is taken for the *motive faculty*, the *movement*. It is from the word כרם, that the Greek tongue has drawn χαρμονή, *jubilation*, and ἁρμονία, *har-mony*. It is from the word כרם in fact, and this etymology is worthy of close attention, that the Latin word "carmen", *poetry*, is derived; the word *charm* is the same as "carmen" only altered by pronunciation.

22.　Wa-îarâ H a m âbî   וַיַּרְא חָם אֲבִי כְנַעַן אֵת עֶרְוַת
Chanahan æth-herwath âbî-
ô: wa-îaghed li-shenei âhî-ô   אָבִיו וַיַּגֵּד לִשְׁנֵי־אֶחָיו בַּחוּץ :
ba-houtz.

---

v. 21.　מִן־הַיַּיִן, *with-what-is-spirituous*....　The word יַיִן,
which, in the natural order signifies simply *wine*, designates in the
moral order, and according to the figurative and hieroglyphic sense,
a spiritual essence, the knowledge of which has passed in all times,
as belonging to the most profound mysteries of Nature.　All those
who have written of it, represent this mysterious essence as a thing
whose profoundness cannot be known without revelation.　The Kabbalists are accustomed to say, in speaking of this *wine*, that he who
drank of it would know all the secrets of the sages.　I can only offer
to the reader the grammatical analysis of the Hebrew word, leaving
the rest to his sagacity.

I have often spoken during the course of my notes of the root
אָן, which enjoys the unusual privilege of characterizing alternately,
being and nothingness, everything and nothing.　Refer v. 2, ch. IV;
v. 25, ch. V; v. 8, ch. VII, and v. 13 of the present chapter.

It is evident that this root, emerging from the deepest abysses
of Nature, rises toward being or falls toward nothingness, propor-
tionally, as the two mother vowels אוֹ, enlighten or obscure it.
From its very principle, it suffices to materialize or to spiritualize
the convertible sign ו, in order to fix its expression upon objects
genuine or false.　Thus one sees it in אוֹן, virtue, strength, valour;
and in אָוֶן, *vice, vanity, cowardice;* in יוֹן, *the generative faculty of
Nature;* in יָוֵן, *the clay of the earth.*

In the word here referred to, the two vowels are not only enlightened but replaced by the sign of potential manifestation י,
image of intellectual duration.　This sign being doubled constitutes,
among the Chaldeans, one of the proper names of the Divinity.
United to the final sign ן, it seems, if I can so express it, to offer
the very body of that which is incorporeal.　It is a spiritual
essence which many peoples and particularly the Egyptians, have
considered under the emblem of light.　Thus, for example, one finds
in the Coptic, Oϑωπι, *light* or *torch.*　It is in conceiving this essence
under the form of *spirit*, that these same peoples, choosing for it

22. And-he-did-discover, *Ham*, the-father-o f *Chana-han*, the-self-secret-parts of-the-father-his-own, a n d-he-blabbed-o u t t o-b o t h-bro-thers-h i s-o w n, in-the-out-ward-enclosure.

22. Et-il-considéra *Ham*, père de-*Chanahan*, les-pro-pres-mystères-s e c r e t s du-père-sien; e t-il-les-divulgua aux-deux-frères-à-lui dans l' enceinte-extérieure.

---

an emblem more within the reach of the vulgar, have taken for its physical envelope *wine*, that liquor so vaunted in all the ancient mysteries because of the *spirit* which it contains and of which it was the symbol. This is the origin of these words which, coming from the same root appear so different in signification: אוֹן *being*, and יין, *wine*, of which the Greek analogues offer the same phenom-enon: ὤν *being*, and οἶνος, *wine*.

It is useless to continue these comparisons. However I can-not refrain from saying that it is by an almost inevitable con-sequence of this double sense attached to the word יין, that the cosmogonic personage called Διονύσος, *Dionysus*, by the Greeks, has finally designated for the vulgar, only the god of wine, after having been the emblem of spiritual light; and that the same word which we use has become such, only as a result of the same degrada-tion of the sense which was attached to it, a degradation always coincident with the hardening of the mother vowel: for, from the word יין, is formed the Teutonic *wein*, the Latin "vinum", and the French *vin*.

The Samaritan translator makes use in this place of the word עבּצֹף, and the Chaldaic paraphrast has imitated him in employ-ing the analogue חמרא. These two terms springing from the two contracted roots חב־מר, designate that which dominates by its vigour, or simply that which heats and lights.

וישׁכֵּר, *and-he-intoxicated-his-thought*.... After the long and detailed explanations into which I have entered, the reader should have no more need, except for the grammatical proof of the meaning that I give to this word or that I shall give to those which follow. The word שׂכֵי signifies *thought, the comprehension of the soul*. It is attached to the Arabic كَ, *he reflected. he thought*. This word, united to the sign of movement proper ר, forms the verb שׂכֹר, *to exalt one's thought, to be intoxicated, to be carried away*, etc.

23. Wa-ikkah Shem wa-
J a p h e t h æth-ha-shimelah
wa-îashîmou hal-s h e ĉ h-em
s h e n e î-h e m : w'îele ĉhou
âhoranîth wa-îeĉhassou æth-
herwath âbî-hem : w-pheneî-
h e m ahoranîth w-herwath
âbî-hemloâ râou.

וַיִּקַּח שֵׁם וָיֶפֶת אֶת־הַשִּׂמְלָה
וַיָּשִׂימוּ עַל־שְׁכֶם שְׁנֵיהֶם וַיֵּלְכוּ
אֲחֹרַנִּית וַיְכַסּוּ אֵת עֶרְוַת
אֲבִיהֶם וּפְנֵיהֶם אֲחֹרַנִּית וְעֶרְוַת
אֲבִיהֶם לֹא רָאוּ :

וַיִּתְגַּל, *and-he-revealed-himself-wholly* .... Here it is the verb
גָּלֹה *to reveal*, employed according to the reciprocal form, in
the future made past by the convertible sign ו. The Hellenists,
always adhering to the trivial and gross meaning, and seeing in *Noah*,
an husbandman overcome with wine, could not acknowledge the
meaning of this verb. Also, instead of saying that Noah revealed
himself, they have said that he stripped himself of his garments:
καὶ ἐγυμνώθη : "et nudatus est".

v. 22. אֶת־עֶרְוֹת, *the-secret-mysteries-his-own*.... This was a
consequence of the exaltation of *Noah*, that he revealed and disclosed the mysteries which ought to have remained hidden. The
Hellenists, faithful to their custom of looking at things, might have
translated by the word αἰδοῖα, that which they supposed *Ham* had
looked upon in his father; but it appears that they did not dare.
Saint Jerome, less scrupulous, has ingenuously said "verenda nu-
data". It is certain that the Hebrew word עֶרְוֹת, might have this
sense, in every other circumstance, if the rest of the discourse had
been relative to it; but it is quite easy to see here, that this word
taken in a figurative acceptation, expresses what the Chaldeans have
always made it signify; that is to say, *the mysteries of nature, the
secrets, a hidden doctrine*, etc. Also the Samaritan word is worthy
of comment: ᴧᕁᕳᛨ2ᕽ expresses, according to the Chaldaic roots
from which it springs, *that which must remain hidden*.

v. 23. אֶת־הַשִּׂמְלָה, *the-very-left-garment* .... All the hieroglyphic force of this verse is contained in this word. Moses has
chosen it with an art of which he, and his instructors, the Priests
of Egyptian Thebes, were alone capable. To explain it entirely is
for the moment, an impossible thing. It would demand, in order

23. And-he-took, *Shem* with *Japheth*, the-very-left-garment; and-they-uplifted-it upon-the-b a c k of-them-both; and-they-went backward; and-they-covered the-mysterious-parts o f-the-fa-ther-their's; and-their-faces-were backward; so-the-mys-terious-parts of-the-father-their's not-did-they-see.

23. Et-il-prit, *Shem* avec *J a p h e t h,* le-propre-vête-m e n t-de-la-gauche, et-ils-l' élevèrent sur-le-dos de-tous-deux; et-ils allèrent en ar-rière e t-i l s-couvrirent les-mystères cachés du-père-à-eux; et-les faces-à-eux-étai-ent en-arrière : ainsi-les-mys-tères - cachés du-père-à - eux non-pas_ils-virent.

---

to be understood and proved, a commentary more exhaustive than this volume. Perhaps I may one day have the good fortune to demonstrate to what point this mighty cosmologist has understood the history of the universe.

The root of this important word, is the same name as one of the beings emanated from *Noah,* שׁם *Shem,* which as we have seen, characterizes that which is raised, brilliant, remarkable. By means of the directive sign ל, which is here joined, this root is applied, in the figurative sense, to the Septentrion, to the Boreal pole, to that pole of the earth which dominates the other. I beg the reader to notice this point. In a more restricted sense it designates the left side. It is known that among the most ancient peoples, this side was the noblest and most honoured. When, in those remote times, a Sabæan priest turned his face toward the orient to worship the Sun, dazzling emblem of the Being of beings, he had on his left, the Boreal pole, and on his right the Austral pole; and as he was more initiated in the astronomic science than our modern savants ordinarily imagine, he knew that one of these poles was raised, whilst the other was inclined toward the equinoctial line.

But without dwelling now upon these comparisons which will find their place elsewhere, I shall content myself with saying that in the most ancient customs, the left side of a man was always the first enveloped and the most covered. Still in this day certain peoples, attached to the ceremonies of their ancestors, envelop the left arm before making their prayers. The modern Jews call טללים the cords which serve them for this usage. From this habit spring many analogous expressions. The Hebrews called the kind of gar-ment which enveloped this side שׂמלה, from the word שׂמל, *the*

24. Wa-îîketz Noah mi-jeîn-ô: wa-îedah æth âsher hashah l'ô ben-ô ha-katan.

וַיִּקֶץ נֹחַ מִיֵּינוֹ וַיֵּדַע אֵת אֲשֶׁר־עָשָׂה לוֹ בְּנוֹ הַקָּטָן :

25. Wa-îâomer: a r o u r Chenahan, h e b e d hobadîm îhieh l'æhî-ô.

וַיֹּאמֶר אָרוּר כְּנָעַן עֶבֶד עֲבָדִים יִהְיֶה לְאֶחָיו :

26. Wa-îâomer: barouch, IHÔAH Æloheî-Shem: w'îhî Chenahan hebed lam-ô.

וַיֹּאמֶר בָּרוּךְ יְהֹוָה אֱלֹהֵי־שֵׁם וִיהִי כְנַעַן עֶבֶד לָמוֹ :

27. Japheth Ælohîm l' Jepheth, w'ishechon b'aho-leî-Shem: w'îhî Chenahan hebed lam-ô.

יַפְתְּ אֱלֹהִים לְיֶפֶת וְיִשְׁכֹּן בְּאָהֳלֵי־שֵׁם וִיהִי כְנַעַן עֶבֶד לָמוֹ :

---

left side. The Arabs had the verb شمل which expressed the action of enveloping, of girding, of folding the left side, of turning toward the north; the Syrians, attaching more to the respect that this action inspired in them, than to the action itself, designated it by the word ܡܫܠܡܘ, *perfection*, the aim toward which one tends, the accomplishment of things, holy ordination, etc.

The reader should feel now that the Hellenists, having seen in the word שמלה only a simple mantle *ἱμάτιον*, have perceived only the gross exterior of a profound meaning, that Moses, besides, has not wished to explain otherwise than to attach it to the root שם, which designates one of the sons of *Noah*, and the name of the garment with which he covered his father, שמלה, as well as the verb itself which serves to express this action, ישם.

v. 24. הקטן, *the-little-one*....   This word offers no difficulty; but it indicates that Moses places no difference between *Chanahan*

24. A n d - h e-recovered, *Noah* f r o m-the-spirituous-delirium-his-o w n : and-h e-knew what had-done to-him the-little-one (the younger son).

24. Et-il-revint, *Noah* de l'exaltation-spiritueuse-sienne, et-il-connut ce qu'avait-fait à lui le petit (la moindre la dernière production).

25. And-he-said : cursed-be *Chanahan;* servant o f-servants he-s h a l l-be unto-the-brothers-his-own.

25. Et-il-dit : m a u d i t-soit *Chanahan;* serviteur des-serviteurs, il-s e r a aux-frères-siens.

26. And-he-said : blessed-be IHOAH, HE-the-Gods of-*Shem;* and-let-be-*Chanahan* servant toward-t h e-collect-ion-of-him.

26. E t-i l-d i t : soit-béni-IHOAH, LUI-les-D i e u x de *S h e m;* et-qu'il-soit, *Chanahan*, serviteur envers-la-collection-sienne.

27. He-will-give exten-sion, HE-the-Gods to Japheth, (w h a t is extended) who-shall-direct his-a b o d e in-the-tabernacles of-*Shem:* a n d-he-shall-be, *Chanahan*, a-servant to-t h e-collection-of-him.

27. Il-donnera-de-l'éten-due, LUI-les-Dieux à-*Japheth* (ce qui est étendu); qui-dirigera sa-d e m e u r e d a n s-l e s-tabernacles d e-*Shem:* et-il-sera, *Chanahan*, serviteur d e - l a-collection-sienne.

---

and his father *Ham;* as this appears plainly, moreover, in the verses following, where *Noah* curses *Chanahan*, for a fault of which *Ham* alone is culpable toward him.

v. 25. These terms are clear.

v. 26. למו, *toward-the-collection-of-him....* If Moses had written simply לו *his*, it would have indicated only that *Chanahan* would be subject to *Shem;* but in adding, by an ellipsis which has not been felt by his translators, the collective sign ם to the directive article ל, he has made understood, that it would be equally so to that which would emanate from *Shem*, to that which would be of the same nature, to that which would form the whole of his being.

28.   Wa-îhî N o a h âhar ha-mabboul shelosh mâôth shanah w a-hamishîm sha-nah.

וַיְחִי נֹחַ אַחַר הַמַּבּוּל שְׁלֹשׁ מֵאוֹת שָׁנָה וַחֲמִשִּׁים שָׁנָה :

29.   Wa-îhîou ċhol-îemeî-N o a h theshah mâôth sha-nah, wa-hamishîm shanah: wa-îamoth.

וַיִּהְיוּ כָּל־יְמֵי־נֹחַ תְּשַׁע מֵאוֹת שָׁנָה וַחֲמִשִּׁים שָׁנָה וַיָּמֹת :

---

v. 27.   יְפְתְּ, *he-will-give-extension*. . . .   This verb taken from the same root as the name of *Japheth*, is very remarkable.

וישכן , *who-shall-direct-his-abode*. . . . . .   It must be remembered that the abode of the ancient peoples to whom Moses makes allusion here, was transported from one country to another with the people itself, and was not so fixed as it became in time.   The verb שכן expresses besides, a movement of usurpation, of taking possession; being formed from the root כון, governed by the sign of relative movement ש.

v. 28 and 29.   These terms have been sufficiently explained in ch. V.   That is to say, that the signification I give them here has been grammatically proved.   The reader should not forget in run-ning through these Notes, that grammatical proof has been my only pledge, and the only one I could possibly fulfill without entering into lengthy commentaries.   In translating the Cosmogony of Moses, my purpose has been first, to make the sense of the words employed by this hierographic writer understood by following step by step the grammatical principles which I had set down in advance in restor-ing his tongue.   As to what concerns his ideas and the *ensemble* of his doctrine, that is a different point.   Moses, in enveloping it designedly with veils, has followed the method of the Egyptian priests among whom he had been brought up.   This method has

28. And-he-lived *Noah*, after t h e-great-swelling, t h r e e-hundreds of-being's-revolving-change, a n d-five-tens of-revolution.

29. And-t h e y-were all-the-days (manifested lights) of-*Noah*, nine-hundreds-of-revolving-change, and-f i v e tens of-revolution; and-he-deceased.

28. Et-il-vécut, *N o a h*, après la-g r a n d e-intumes-cence, trois-centaines-de-mu-tation - ontologique-tempor - elle, et-cinq-décuples de-mu-tation.

29. E t-furent, tous-les-jours (les manifestations lu-mineuses) de-*N o a h*, neuf-centaines - de-mutation-tem-porelle et-cinq-décuples de-mutation; et-il-passa.

---

been from all time that of the theosophists. A work of this nature wherein the most vast and most complicated ideas are enclosed in a very small quantity of words, and being crowded, as it were, into the smallest space possible, has need of certain developments to be entirely comprehended. I have already promised to give these developments later on, doing for his doctrine what has been done for that of Pythagoras; and I shall give them if my labour is judged useful for the welfare of humanity. I shall not be able to enter at present into the discussions which they will necessarily involve, without injuring the clarity of my grammatical explanations already difficult enough in themselves. The reader no doubt will have remarked certain reticences in this respect, and perhaps he will have been shocked; but they were indispensable. I only beg him to believe that these reticences, in whatever manner they may be pre-sented, have not been for the purpose of concealing any evil meaning, any meaning injurious to the doctrine of Moses, neither any which could call in question his dogmas upon the unity of God, the spiritual-ity and immortality of the soul, nor shake in the slighest the pro-found veneration of this sacred writer for the Divinity.

SEPHER BERÆSHITH
I.

ספר בראשית י•

1. W'ælleh thô-l e d o t h
benei-Noah Shem Ham wa-
Japheth wa-îwaledou la-hem
banîm ahar ha-mabboul.

וְאֵלֶּה תּוֹלְדֹת בְּנֵי־נֹחַ שֵׁם חָם
וָיֶפֶת וַיִּוָּלְדוּ לָהֶם בָּנִים אַחַר
הַמַּבּוּל :

This tenth chapter, belonging to a new order of things and
presenting a geologic tableau quite different from that which precedes, I would refrain from translating, if I had not been forced,
in order to terminate the Cosmogony, properly so-called, of which it
is the complement. But not wishing to increase indefinitely these
notes already very long, I refrain from all development and all comparison.   The reader will feel very well, in examining the version
of the Hellenists and that of Saint Jerome, into what interminable
discussion, I would have been drawn; there is not a single word of
this chapter which could not give rise to several volumes of commentaries; I am limited to presenting briefly the etymological proof
of the meaning which I assign to the physical and metaphysical
terms, of which the Hellenists, true to their method of materializing
and restricting everything, have made so many proper names of
individuals.   I have said, and I think proved sufficiently, that *Noah*
and the productions emanated from him, *Shem*, *Ham* and *Japheth*,
ought not to be taken for men of blood, of flesh and bone: therefore
I shall dispense with repeating and proving it again: assuming that
an impartial reader will not hesitate to admit with me that these
cosmogonic principles becoming developed, could not bring forth
human individuals, but other geologic principles, such as I represent
them.   The concatenation of this doctrine would alone be sufficient
proof, even if a mass of other proofs were not piled up beforehand,
to give it the force of a mathematical demonstration.

I ought, however, to warn the reader, that in the exposition of
a system of geology so extraordinary, placed in the midst of a mass
of new ideas, the analogous words have often failed me in French
as well as in English; and that instead of exaggerating the sense

GENESIS X.

1. N o w-these-are t h e-symbolical-progenies of-the-issued-beings of-*Noah*: *Shem* (w h a t i s upright and bright), *Ham* (what is curved and heated) and *Japheth* (what is extended and wide): which-were-begotten through-t h e m, issued-offspring after the-great-swelling (of waters).

COSMOGONIE X.

1. Or-celles-ci-sont l e s-caractéristiques-générations des-êtres-émanés-de-*N o a h*: *Shem* (ce qui est direct et incliné et chaud), *Ham* (ce qui est incliné et chaud), et-*Japheth* (ce qui est étendu): lesquelles-furent-p r o d u i t e s envers-e u x, émanations d' après la-grande-intumescence (des eaux).

---

of the Hebraic expressions, as one will be tempted to believe I have done, I have, on the contrary, been obliged more than once to weaken them. However extraordinary my assertion may appear to modern savants, it is none the less true to say that the geologic sciences among the ancient Egyptians were more advanced in every way than among us. So that many of their ideas coming from certain principles which we lack, had enriched their tongue with metaphorical terms, whose analogues have not yet appeared in our European idioms. It is a thing that time and experience will demonstrate to those who might doubt, in proportion as their understanding develops; let them be occupied more with things than with words, and let them penetrate more and more into the depths which I have opened for them.

v. 1. These terms have been previously explained.

v. 2. גמר, *Gomer....* This word is composed of the contracted roots גם־אר, one of which גם, contains every idea of accumulation, augmentation, complement; and the other, אר, is applied to elementary principle.

ומגוג, *and Magog....* The root גוה, which expresses a movement being opposed to itself, indicates in the word גוג, an extension continued, elastic, pushed to its utmost limits. This word

2. Beneî-Japheth Gomer w-Magôg w-Madaî w'Jawan w-Thubal w-Mesheĉh w-Thî-rass.

בְּנֵי־יֶפֶת גֹּמֶר וּמָגוֹג וּמָדַי וְיָוָן וְתֻבָל וּמֶשֶׁךְ וְתִירָם :

3. W-beneî Gomer Asheĉ-henaz w- Rîphath w-Thogar-mah.

וּבְנֵי גֹמֶר אַשְׁכְּנַז וְרִיפַת וְתֹגַרְמָה :

---

governed by the sign of exterior action מ, characterizes that faculty of matter, by which it is extended and lengthened, without there being any solution of continuity.

וּמָדַי, *and-Madai*....   These are the two contracted roots מד־די , the one, expressing that which fills its measure, that which is commensurable; the other, that which abounds, which suffices.

וְיָוָן, *and-Jawan*....   I have given the history of this word, which I read *Ion*, in v. 18, ch. VIII.

וְתֻבָל , *and-Thubal*....   This word is composed of the well known root בל, governed by the sign of reciprocity ת.

וּמֶשֶׁךְ, *and-Mesheĉh*....   This word is composed of the root שך, developing every idea of perception, conception, speculation, governed by the sign of exterior and plastic action מ.

וְתִירָם, *and-Thirass*....   The root תר contains every idea of determination given to element. It is a definition, a stable form in ראת; it is a disposition, a condition, a mode of being, in תור, or תיר; it is, in the word תרם, an impenetrable thing, a resistance, a persistence, an opposition.

2. T h e-issued-offspring of *Japheth* (that which is extended) (were) : *Gomer* (elemental heap), and-*Magog* (elastic stretching power), and-*M a d a i* (mensurability, mensural indefinite capacity), and-*Ion* (generative ductileness), and-*Thubal* (diffusive motion), and-*Meshech* (p e r c e p t i b l e cause), and-*Thirass* (modality, modal accident).

2. L e s-productions-émanées d e *Japheth* (l'étendu) (furent) : *G o m e r* (la cumulation élémentaire),et-*M a g o g* (la faculté extensive, élastique), et-*M a d a i* (la faculté commensurable, celle de suffire toujours et de se diviser à l'infini), et-*I o n* (l a ductilité generative), et-*Thubal* (la diffussion, le mélange), et-*Meshech* (la perceptibilité), et-*Thirass* (la modalité, la faculté de paraître sous une forme impassible).

3. A n d-t h e-issued-offspring of-*Gomer* (elemental heap) (were) : *Aschechenaz* (latent fire), and-*Riphath* (rarity, centrifugal force), a n d-*Thogormah* (density, universal centripetal force).

3. E t - l e s-productions-émanées de *Gomer* (la cummulation élémentaire) (furent) : *Aschechenaz* (le feu latent, le calorique), et *Riphath* (la rareté, cause de l' expansion), e t-*Thogormah* (la densité, cause de la centralisation universelle).

---

v. 3. אשכנז, *Aschechenaz*.... This extraordinary word comes from three roots. The first, אש, quite well known, designates the igneous principle; the second כן, characterizes that which serves as basis, as foundation; that which is gathered together, heaped up; and finally the third נז, expresses that which makes its influence felt in its vicinity. It was impossible to characterize better that which the modern physicists have named *caloric*.

ריפת, *Ripath*.... This is the same name as *Japheth* יפת governed by the sign of movement proper ר.

תגרמה, *Thogormah*.... This is the root תור, designating all giratory movement, all action which brings the being back upon

4. W-beneî Jawan Æli-
shah w-Tharshîsh Chithim
w-Dodanîm.

וּבְנֵי יָוָן אֱלִישָׁה וְתַרְשִׁישׁ כִּתִּים
וְדֹדָנִים׃

5. Me-ælleh nipheredou
âîeî ha-gôîm b'aretzoth'am:
âîsh li-leshon-ô le-mishep-
hehoth'am b'gôeîhem.

מֵאֵלֶּה נִפְרְדוּ אִיֵּי הַגּוֹיִם
בְּאַרְצֹתָם אִישׁ לִלְשֹׁנוֹ
לְמִשְׁפְּחֹתָם בְּגוֹיֵהֶם׃

---

itself and fixes it. This root is universalized by the collective sign
ם, and governed by that of reciprocity ה. The compound גרם
characterizes in general, that which is solid and hard, and in particular, the bones, the boney structure of the body.

v. 4. אלישה, *Ælishah*.... In this word, two contracted roots
should be distinguished, אל־לוש: the first אל, designates a superior
force: the second, לוש, an action which dilutes, kneads, and makes
a compact thing ductile. The Chaldaic word אלושא, signifies *a multitude, a crowd.*

ותרשיש, *and Tharshish*... The root ראש is known to us as
expressing *motive principle*. This root, of which the last character
is doubled, marks an intense and mutual principiation, a separation
among things of a divers nature.

כתים, *of-the-Chuthites*.... The root כות, develops every action of cutting off, of intrenching, of striking. The Chaldaic כת designates schism, schismatic, reprobate, damned, etc.

ודדנים, *and-the-Dodanites*.... Here it is the root דוד, expressing that which attracts, pleases and mutually suffices, whose expression is again increased by the addition of the extensive sign ן.

v. 5. איי הגוים, *the-propending-centres-of-reunion of-the-social-
bodies*...... The Hellenists have seen here νῆσοι τῶν ἐθνῶν, *isles
of the nations.* It can be clearly seen that this separation of the

4. And-the-i s s u e d-off-spring of-*I o n* (generative ductileness) (were) : *Æli-shah* (diluent and kneading force), and-*Tharshish* (prin-cipiating principle) of-the-*Chuthites* (the cut off, the barbarous, the schismatic) and-of-the-*Dodanites* (t h e selected, the covenanters).

4. E t - l e s-productions-émanées de-*Ion* (la ductilité générative) (furent) : *Æli-shah* (la force délayante et pétrissante), e t - *Tharshish* (le p r i n c i p e mutuel, in-tense) des-*Chuthéens* (l e s réprouvés, les barbares, les Scythes), et-des-*Dodanéens* (les élus, les civilisés, les confédérés).

5. Through-those were-moved-at-variance t h e-pro-pending-centres-o f - reunion of-the-social-bodies, in-the-earths-their-o w n ; e v e r y-principle-acting a f t e r-the-particular-speech-h i s-o w n, toward - t h e-general-tribes, b y-the-social-bodies-t h e i r-own.

5. Par-ceux-là f u r e n t-différenciés l e s-centres-de-volonté des-organisations-social, dans-les-terres-à-eux ; chaque-principe-agissant se-lon- l a - langue-particulière-sienne, envers-les-tribes-en-général, dans-les-organisa-tions-sociales-à-eux.

---

isles, understood literally, signifies nothing. These are not in fact isles which were divided; but the interests, the desires, the opinions, the inclinations, and ideas of the peoples who formed so many par-ticular *régimes*. All this is contained in the word אי, used here in the constructive plural. I cannot dwell at this time upon one of the profoundest mysteries of the history of the earth: it may be that I shall have the occasion of coming back to it in another work.

איש , *every-principle-acting*.... I have said enough concern-ing this word so that I can dispense with a long digression. The Hellenists have avoided it and have been careful not to show the dif-ference of the nominal affix ו which is connected here, with the other nominal affixes ם and הם, which concern the *Chuthites* and the *Dodanites* that is to say, the cut off and the elect, the rejected and the chosen, referred to in the preceding verse.

v. 6. כוש, *Choush*.... This word can be understood as formed

6. W-benei Ham Choush w-Mitzeraîm w-P h o u t w-Chenahan. · וּבְנֵי חָם כּוּשׁ וּמִצְרַיִם וּפוּט וּכְנָעַן :

7. W-benei Choush Sçebâ wa-H'a w î l a h w-Sçabethah w-Rahemmah w-Sçabethechâ : w-benei Rahemmah Shebâ w-Dedan. וּבְנֵי כוּשׁ סְבָא וַחֲוִילָה וְסַבְתָּה וְרַעְמָה וְסַבְתְּכָא וּבְנֵי רַעְמָה שְׁבָא וּדְדָן :

---

of two contracted roots כוה־אש, *the elementary force of the igneous principle;* or as being derived from the single root אוש *fire,* governed by the assimilative sign כ . In either case its signification differs but little.

ומצרים, *and-Mitzeraim....* In this word one finds the root אר , which develops in general, all ideas of compression and oppression, particularized and made more intense by the sign of exterior action מ.

ופוט, *and-Phut....* This is a consequence of the action of *Ham,* which produces elementary combustion; producing also suffocation, that is to say, the smoke which suffocates, after having brought forth victorious forces which centralize. The word פוט, formed of two contracted roots פוה־טו, signifies literally, *the cessation of breath.* It is understood in this sense by the Arabic فاط .

וכנען, *and-Chanahan....* I have explained as much as possible, the hieroglyphic force of this word in v. 18, ch. IX.

v. 7. סבא, *Seba....* The root אב, which develops in general, all ideas of cause, inclination, determining movement and fructification, has served in a great many dialects to designate particularly, aqueous element, regarded as principle or vehicle of all natural production. In the above word this root is ruled by the sign of circular movement ס.

6. A n d - t h e-issued-offspring of-*Ham* (w h a t is c u r v e d and hot) (were) : *Chush* (igneous power, combustion), a n d - *Mitzeraim* (subduing, overcoming power, compressing bodies to their narrowest b o u n d s), and-*Phut* (stifledness) and-*Chanahan* (material e x i s tence).

7. A n d-t h e-issued-offspring of-*C h u.s h* (igneous power) (were) : *Seba* (radical moisture, sap), a n d - *Hawilah* (striving energy), a n d-*Sabethah* (determinative motion), and-*Rahamah* (thunder) a n d-*Sabethecha* (determined motion) : and-t h e-issued-offspring of-*Rahamah* (thunder) (were) : *Sheba* (restoring rest), and -*Dedan* (selective affinity).

6. E t-l e s - productions émanées de-*Ham* (ce qui est incliné et chaud) (furent) : *Choush* (la force ignée la combustion), et - *Mitzeraim* (les f o r c e s subjuguantes, victorieuses opprimantes), et-*Phout* (la suffocation, ce qui asphyxie) et-*Chanahan* (l'existence physique).

7. E t-l e s - productions-é m a n é e s d e *Choush* (la force ignée) (furent) : *Seba* (l'humide radical, la sève, c a u s e de la sapidité), et-*Hawilah* (la travail énergique), et-*Sabethah* (la cause déterminante), et - *Rahammah* (le tonnerre), et-*Sabethecha* (la cause determinée, l'effect) : et-les-productions-émanées de-*Rahammah* (le tonnerre) (furent) : *Sheba* (le retour au repos), et-*Dedan* (l'affinité élective).

חוילה, *and-Hawilah*.... I have already had occasion to speak of this word in v. 11, ch. II. Only it must be considered that the energetic effort which it expresses as derivative of the root חול or חיל, being influenced by the generation of *Ham*. bears a character of violence, of suffering, that it did not have then.

וסבתה, *and-Sabethah* .... This word comes from the two roots סב-תה: in the one, resides the occasional, determining force, *cause;* in the other, the sympathetic reason, the determined force, *effect.*

ורעמה, *and-Rahamah*.... The root רעו, which indicates literally every rupture of order, every fraction, being generalized by

8. W-Choush îaled æth-
Nimerod houâ hehel li-heî-
ôth ghibor ba-âretz.

וְכוּשׁ יָלַד אֶת־נִמְרֹד הוּא הֵחֵל
לִהְיוֹת גִּבֹּר בָּאָרֶץ :

9. Houâ- haîah ghibor-
tzaîr li-pheneî Ihôah : hal-
ċhen îeamar ċhe-Nimerod
ghibor tzaîr li-pheneî
Ihôah.

הוּא־הָיָה גִבֹּר־צַיִד לִפְנֵי יְהֹוָה
עַל־כֵּן יֵאָמַר כְּנִמְרֹד גִּבֹּר צַיִד
לִפְנֵי יְהֹוָה :

---

the final sign ם, expresses in a manner as energetic as picturesque
and wise, the cause and effect of the lightning.

וסבתכא, *and-Sabetheċha*.... The root סב, which as we have
seen, indicates always, an occasional movement, is linked by means
of the constructive, sympathetic sign ת, with the root תך, which
characterizes, the effect which follows every cause. The effect here
is an enchaining, an extreme oppression, an infernal pain, a damna-
tion. I pray the reader to reflect a moment upon this signification.

שבא, *Sheba*.... Now as we know, the root שב is always the
emblem of restitution, and of return to an original state. This root,
being united on this occasion to the root בא, which contains every
idea of passing from one place to another, and being presented as
an effect of thunder, can here lead to the idea of electric repulsion.

ודרן, *and-Dedan*.... One can in the same manner, consider
this word as an emblem of electric attraction since it is found in the
root רור, which characterizes that which pleases, attracts and mutually suffices, united by contraction to the root דן, which expresses
every chemical *parting*, every judgment brought to bear upon conten-
tious things.

v. 8. נמרד, *Nimerod*.... The verb מרוד, of which this is
here the continued facultative, passive movement, signifies literally
to give over to one's own impulse, to shake off every kind of yoke, to

8. A n d-*Chush* (igneous power) begat *Nimerod* (self ruling will, arbitrary sway, a pregnant cause of revolt, anarchy, despotism, and of any power prone to follow its own v i o l e n t self impulse), h e-w h o strove for-being-the-high-lord i n-t h e-earth.

9. H e-w h o-was a-most-lordly-oppugner before-the-face of-IHOAH : wherefore it-was-said : e v e n-as-*Nimerod* (self ruling will), a-most lordly-oppugner before-the-face of-IHOAH.

8. Et-*Choush* (la force ignée) enfanta *Nimerod* (le principe de la volonté desordonée, principe de rébellion, d'anarchie, de despotisme, de t o u t e puissance n' obéissant qu'à sa propre impulsion) : lui-qui fit-des-efforts-violens p o u r-être le-dominateur (le héros, l'hyperboréen) sur-la-terre.

9. Lui-qui-fut le superbe-principe-de-tout-ce-qui-e s t - adverse (opposé à l'ordre) à-la-face de-I H O A H : sur-quoi ce-proverbe : sembla-ble-à-*Nimerod* (le principe d e l a volonté arbitraire), ce-superbe adversaire à-la-face de-IHOAH.

---

behave arbitrarily. It is formed from the root רר, which develops every idea of movement, proper and persevering, good or evil, ruled by the sign of exterior action מ.

I am not considering the version of the Hellenists, wherein this anarchical principle is transformed into a *mighty hunter*: γίγας κυνηγός, because I should have too much to do, as I have said, if obliged to mention all of the errors which are woven into this chapter.

v. 9. The kind of proverb inserted in this verse could very well be a marginal note passed into the text.

v. 10. בבל *Babel....* The root בל which expresses an extraordinary dilation, a swelling, is taken here in the bad sense, and depicts the effect of vanity. The resemblance of this name to that of Babylon, appears to excuse here, the version of the Hellenists who have placed in this city the origin of the empire of their pretended giant: but it would be sufficient to read attentively this verse alone, to see that the word בבל is not applicable to a city, even if the whole development of the chapter did not compel giving it another sense.

10. Wa-thehî, reâshith mamelacheth-ô Babel w' Arech w'Achad, w'Chalneh b'âretz Shinhar,

וַתְּהִי רֵאשִׁית מַמְלַכְתּוֹ בָּבֶל וְאֶרֶךְ וְאַכַּד וְכַלְנֶה בְּאֶרֶץ שִׁנְעָר :

11. Min-ha-âretz ha-hiwa iatzâ Asshour wa-îben æth-Ninweh w'æth-rehoboth hir wæth-Chalah.

מִן־הָאָרֶץ הַהוּא יָצָא אַשּׁוּר וַיִּבֶן אֶת־נִינְוֵה וְאֶת־רְחֹבֹת עִיר וְאֶת־ כָּלַח :

וְאֶרֶךְ, and-Arech.... I have spoken more than once of the root רך or רק, whose effect is to depict the relaxation, the dissolution of things, literally as well as figuratively.

וְאַכַּד, and-Achad...... Two contracted roots compose this word: אך־כר. They depict energetically that sort of sentiment the result of which is, that each is excepted from the general law, flees from it, acts for his own part. The word אכר, signifies properly *a particle, a spark.*

וְכַלְנֶה, and-Chalneh.... That is to say, according to the hieroglyphic sense: the concentration of the whole in the individual self. This is the root כל *all*, to which is joined the emphatic, nominal affix נה.

שִׁנְעָר, Shinar.... We already know that the root שן contains every idea of mutation, variation and change; now, the root ער, which is joined to it, indicates at the same time, both the vehemence which excites, and the city in which this change takes place. It was impossible to create a happier word for depicting a civil revolution.

v. 11. אַשּׁוּר, Asshour.... Causing order to come out from the heart of disorder, and the principle of legitimate government from the midst of revolutionary anarchy, is a trait of genius which astonishes, even after all that has been seen. I dispense with inviting the reader to reflect; he will be inclined enough to reflection both by the memory of the past and by the image of the present. Still if glancing in turn upon my version and upon that of the Hel-

10. A n d-such-was the-r i s e o f-the-kingly-power-h i s o w n, *Babel* (empty pride), and-*Arech* (slackness), and-*Achad* (selfish-ness), a n d-*Chaleneh* (all engrossing desire) in-the-earth of-*Shinhar* (civil revolution).

10. Et-telle-fut l'origine du règne-sien, *Babel* (la vanité), et-*Arech* (la mollesse), et-*Achad* (l'isolement, l'égoïsme), et-*Chaleneh* (l' ambition, l'envahissement), dans-la-terre de-*Shinhar* (la revolution civile.

11. From-that-earth, it-self, issued *Asshour* (right and lawful sway, source of happiness a n d grandeur) which-founded the selfsameness of-*Ninweh* (the growing strong, youth breeding out) and-w h a t-relates-to-p u b l i c-establishments at-home, a n d-what-relates-to-*Chalah* (the growing wise, old men ruling within).

11. H o r s-de-cette-terre elle-m ê m e, sortit-*Asshour* (le principe harmonique, le principe éclairé du gouvernement, l'ordre, le bonheur, résultant d e l'observation des lois), lequel-établit ce-qui-concerne-*Ninweh* (l'accroissement extérieur, l'éducation de-la jeunesse) et-ce-qui-concerne-les-institutions de-la-c i t é, et-ce-qui-concerne-*Chalah* (le perfectionement intérieur, le rassemblement des vieillards, le sénat).

---

lenists, he is startled at the depths into which the hierographic writer draws him, he will clearly feel why the Essenes, learned in these mysteries, have taken such pains to conceal them.

אתֿ־נִינֽוה, *the-selfsameness of Ninweh*…. Two contracted roots compose this word. The first, נוּן, presents in general the idea of extension, enlargement, propagation: נִין signifies properly *a son*. The second, נוֿה, designates an habitation, a colonization.

Moses who has skilfully profited by the name of *Babel*, taken in a bad sense, to make the principle of insubordination and of anarchy go forth, now avails himself of the name of *Ninweh*, to establish the principle of order and of legitimate government. It is thus, that in the course of this chapter, certain names of peoples and of cities, are

12. W'aeth-Ressen beîn Ninweh w-beîn Čhalah hiwa ha-Whir ha-ghedolah.

וְאֶת־רֶסֶן בֵּין נִינְוֵה וּבֵין כָּלַח הוּא הָעִיר הַגְּדֹלָה :

13. W - Mitzeraîm îalad æth-Loudîm wæth - Whonanîm w æth-Le-habîm w'æth-Naphethuhîm.

וּמִצְרַיִם יָלַד אֶת־לוּדִים וְאֶת־עֲנָמִים וְאֶת־לְהָבִים וְאֶת־נַפְתֻּחִים :

---

taken in the same spirit and used according to their hieroglyphic expressions.   In the primitive tongues, the rarity of words and the impossibility of drawing from neighbouring idioms, forced, as I have already stated, attaching to them a great number of significations.

וְאֶת־כלח, *and-what-relates-to-Chalah*....   The root כל which recalls all ideas of complement and integrity, expresses in the radical verb כּוּל, the action of seizing, of holding a thing together, of bringing it to perfection.   The root אז, which depicts a state of equilibrium and equality, being joined to it by contraction, forms with it the word כלח, which signifies literally, *an ancient, an old man*, that is to say, a man whom age and experience have led to perfection. Thence, by extension, the idea of a senate, of an assembly of old men, of a wise and conservative institution.

v. 12.   וְאֶת־רסן, *and-what-relates-to-Ressen*....   It is difficult to say whether the word רסן is the real name of a city as בבל and נינוה, or not; but, in any case, it cannot be denied that it may be used here in its grammatical acceptation, with admirable precision.

v. 13.   אֶת־לורים, *the-existence-of-the-Ludites*....   This root אוֹר indicating every emanation, which, governed by the sign of directive movement ל, forms the word לוֹד, in general, *an emanation, a propagation*: in particular, *an emanated individual, an infant*. Thence, the compound radical verb יְלוֹד, *to generate, to produce, to bring forth*, etc.

12. And-what-relates-to -
Ressen (the state's holding
reins) b e t w e e n - *Ninweh*
(youth breeding out), and-
C h a l a h (old men ruling
in) : and-it-was a-civil-safe-
guard most-great.

13. A n d-*M i t z e r a i m*
(overcoming power) begat
the-selfsameness of-the-*Lu-
dites* (pregnancies), a n d-
t h a t - o f-t h e-*Whonamites*
(material heaviness), and-
that-of-the-*Lehabites* (blaz-
ing exhalations), and-that-
of-t h e-*Naphethuhites* (hollowed caverns).

12. Et-c e-q u i-concerne-
Ressen (les r ê n e s du government) e n t r e - *Ninweh*
(l' accroissement extérieur,
la colonisation), et-*Chalah*
(le perfectionnement intérieur, le sénat) : et-elle-était
(cette institution centrale)
une-sauve-garde-civile très-
grande.

13. Et-*Mitzeraim* (l e s
forces subjuguantes) pro-
duisit l'existence d e s-*Lu-
déens* (les propagations), et-
celle-des-*Whonaméens* (l e s
appesantissements matér-
iels) et-celle-des-Lehabéens
(l e s exhalaisons enflam-
mées), et-celle-des-*Naphet-
huhéens* (les cavernosités).

ואת־ענמים, *and-that-of-the Whonamites....* This is the root עון
of which I have said enough, which is found generalized by the final
collective sign ם.

ואת־להבים, *and-that-of-the Lehabites....* The word להב comes
from the root הב or הוב which, designating in general, every kind
of uprising, is united to the sign of directive movement ל, to depict
the effect of flame.

ואת־נפתחים, *and-that-of-the-Naphethuhites....* The verb פתוח
which signifies *to crack, to split, to swell up,* etc., is used here in the
continued facultative, passive movement, plural.

v. 14. ואת־פתרסים, *and-that-of-the-Patherussites....* The root
רם, which contains all ideas of break, rupture, ruin, reduction into
impalpable parts, is presented in this instance, preceded by the root
פת which has been used in the preceding word.

ואת־כסלחים, *and-that-of-the-Chasseluthites....* The verb סלוח

14. W'æth-Phatherussîm
w'æth Chasseluhîm â s h e r
îatzâou mi-sham Phelishet-
hîm w'æth-Chaphethorîm.

וְאֶת־פַּתְרֻסִים וְאֶת־כַּסְלֻחִים
אֲשֶׁר יָצְאוּ מִשָּׁם פְּלִשְׁתִּים וְאֶת־
כַּפְתֹּרִים :

15. W-Chenahan î a l a d
æth-Tzîdon bechor-ô w'æth-
Heth.

וּכְנַעַן יָלַד אֶת־צִידֹן בְּכֹרוֹ
וְאֶת־חֵת :

16. W'æth - h a-Jeboussî
w'æth-ha-Æmorî w'æth - ha-
Ghirashî.

וְאֶת־הַיְבוּסִי וְאֶת־הָאֱמֹרִי וְאֶת־
הַגִּרְגָּשִׁי :

---

expresses the action of absolving sins.   It is used as finished facultative, plural, with the assimilative article כ.

פְלִשְׁתִּים, the-Phelishethites....   The verb פָלֹשׁ expresses the
action of dispersing, of throwing to the winds, and also of wandering.
It has the emphatic article ה changed to ת to form the plural facultative.

וְאֶת־כַפְתֹרִים, and-the-Chaphethorites....   The root תּוּר which
develops all ideas of tour, circuit, version, conversion, united to the
sign פ, forms the derivative verb פָתוּר, which signifies literally, to
turn one tongue into another, to translate, to make a version; and
figuratively, to change the life, to be converted, to pass from one
belief to another, etc.

v. 15. אֶת־צֹרְן, the-selfsameness-of-Tzidon....   One finds the
root of this word in צֹר, which contains the idea of that which
shows itself opposed, as adversary, enemy; that which uses perfidious,
insidious means to surprise, to deceive, to seduce, etc.   The analogous
word צִיר, develops every opposition which proceeds from force; as
צִיר , every opposition which comes from ruse.   The first depicts war,

14. And-that-of-the-*Pat-herussites* (b r o k e n out in crowds), and - that - of - the-*Chasseluthites* (t r i e d for atonement) : f r o m - which-issued-forth the-*Phelishethites* (s l i g h t e d), and-the-*Chaphethorites* (converts).

15. And-*Chanahan* (material existence) generated the-selfsameness o f-*Tzidon* (ensnaring foe) : first-born-his - o w n, and-that-of-*Heth* (dispirited amazement).

16. And-t h a t-of-the-*Je-bussites* (inward crushing), a n d-that-of-t h e - *Æmorites* (outward wringing), and-t h a t-o f - t h e *Girgashites* (chewing and chewing over and over).

14. Et-celle-d e s *Pathe-russéens* (les fractures in-finies), et-celle-des-Chasse-luthéens (les épreuves ex-piatoires) : de-qui sortirent de-la-même, l e s - *Phelishet-héens* (les égarés, les infi-dèles), e t-les-*Chaphethoré-ens* (les convertis, les fidè-les).

15. Et-*Chanahan* (l'exis-tence physique) produisit l' existence-de-*Tzidon* (l' insi-dieux adversaire) ; premier-né-sien, et-celle-de-*Heth* (l' abattement, la fatigue).

16. Et-celle-d e s-*Jebous-séens* (les refoulemens in-térieurs), et-celle-des-*Æmo-réens* (les exprimations ex-térieures), et-celle-des-*Gir-gashéens* (les remâchemens réitérés).

---

conquests, the glory of arms; the other, hunting, fishing, the gain and industry of commerce.

ואת־חת, *and-that-of-Heth....* This is the reaction of a use-less effort, it is elementary existence sharply driven back upon itself: such is the expression of the root חת.

v. 16. ואת־היבוסי, *and-that-of-theJebussites....* The com-pound radical verb יבוס, *to tread upon, to crush with the foot*, comes from the root בוס, which characterizes that sort of pressure by means of which one treads upon and crushes a thing to extract liquid and radical moisture.

ואת־האמרי, *and-that-of-the-Æmorites....* I have given the ety-mology of this verb אמור several times.

ואת־הגרגשי, *and-that-of-the-Girgashites....* The two distinct roots

17. W'æth-ha-H i w î w'
æth - ha - Harkî w'æth - ha -
Sçînî.

וְאֶת־הַחִוִּי וְאֶת־הָעַרְקִי וְאֶת־
הַסִּינִי :

18. W'æth-ha-Arwadî w'
æth - ha - Tzemarî w'æth-ha-
Hamathî: w'ahar na-phot-
zou mishephehôth ha - Çhe-
nahanî.

וְאֶת־הָאַרְוָדִי וְאֶת־הַצְּמָרִי וְאֶת־
הַחֲמָתִי וְאַחַר נָפֹצָה מִשְׁפְּחוֹת
הַכְּנַעֲנִי :

---

of which this word is composed, are גר, which designates all giratory movement executed upon itself, all chewing, all continued action;
and גש, which expresses the effect of things which are brought together, which touch, which contract; so that the meaning attached
to the word גרגש, appears to be a sort of chewing over and over,
of doing over again, of rumination, of continued contractile labour.

v. 17. ואת החוי, *and-that-of-the-Hiwites....*   The absolute verb
הוה , receiving the sign of potential manifestation in place of the
convertible sign, becomes the symbol of universal life היה: but if
the first character of this important word degenerates, and is changed
into that of elementary existence, it expresses in חיה only natural,
animal, bestial life: if it degenerated again still further, and if it
received the sign of material sense, it would finally become the symbol of absolute material life in עיה.   The word referred to in this
note is a plural facultative of the verb חיה, *to live.*

ואת־העֶרְקִי, *and-that-of-the Warkites....*   The word עֶרְקִי which
signifies literally, *the nerves*, expresses figuratively, the force and
energy which result therefrom.

ואת־הסיני, *and-that-of-the-Sinites....*   The root סן, which, in
a restricted sense is limited to characterizing the colour red, develops,
figuratively, every idea of hateful passion, animadversion, rage, com·
bat, etc.   It is well known what horror the Egyptians had for the
colour red.

v. 18. ואת־האֲרוָדִי, *and-that-of-the-Awardites....*   The com-

17. And that-of-t h e-*Hi-
wites* (animal lives), and-
that-of-the-*Wharkites* (brutish appetites), and - that -
of-the-*Sinites* (hateful and
bloody disposition).

18. And-that-of-t h e-*Ar-
wadites* (plundering de-
sire), and that-of-the-*Tzema-
rites* (hankering for power), and-that-of-the-*H a m -
athites* (most violent crav-
ing) : and-after-ward were-
scattered the-tribes of-the-
Chanahanites (material existing).

17. Et-celle-des-*Hiwéens*
(les vies animales), et-cel-
le-des-*Wharkéens* (les passions brutales), et-celle-des-
Sinéens (les passions hain-
euses).

18. Et-c e l l e-des-*Arwa-
déens* (les ardeurs du bu-
tin), et-c e l l e-des- *Tzema-
réens* (la soif du pouvoir)
et-c e l l e-d e s-*Hamathéens*
(les desirs insatiables) : et-
e n s u i t e furent-dispersées
les-tribus des-*Chenahanéens*
(les existences physiques).

pound ארור, comes from the two contracted roots אר-אור by the first,
אר, become ארה, is understood, an ardent desire to draw, to acquire,
to gather; by the second, אור, things in general, the riches which
one desires to possess.

ואת-הצמרי, *and-that-of-the-Tzemarites....*   The compound צמר
comes equally from the two contracted roots צם-מר : of which
the one, צם, designates literally *thirst;* and the other, מר, is well
known to us as containing all ideas of extension and of domination.

ואת-החמתי, *and-that-of-the-Hamathites....*   This is the root חם
taken in the sense of a covetous ardour, unceasingly excited,
whose expression is still increased by the addition of the emphatic
article ה changed to ת to form the plural.

v. 19. באכה, *by-dint-of....*   This is the root אך invested with
the emphatic article ה, and ruled by the mediative article ב.

גררה, *inward-wringing....*   The duplication of the character
ר , and the addition of the emphatic article in the root גר, increases
considerably its energy.   It is a sort of inward trituration ex-
ercised upon itself.

ער-עזה, *unto-stiffness....*   I have spoken of the root עו in v.
18, ch. II.

19.   Wa-îhî, gheboul ha-Chenahanî mi-Tzîdon b' âchah gherarah! had-hazah! h'âchah sedomah! wa-hamorah! w'âdmah! w'tzabîm had-lashah.

וַיְהִי גְּבוּל הַכְּנַעֲנִי מִצִּידֹן כֹּאֲכָה גְרָרָה עַד־עַזָּה כֹּאֲכָה סְדֹמָה וַעֲמֹרָה וְאַדְמָה וּצְבֹיִם עַד־לָשַׁע :

20.   Ælleh beneî-Ham l' mishephehoth-am li - lesho - noth-am b'âretz-oth-am b' gôîe-hem.

אֵלֶּה בְנֵי־חָם לְמִשְׁפְּחֹתָם לִלְשֹׁנֹתָם בְּאַרְצֹתָם בְּגוֹיֵהֶם :

21.   W-le-Shem îullad gam-houâ âbî chol-beneî-heber âhî Japheth ha-gadôl.

וּלְשֵׁם יֻלַּד נַּם־הוּא אֲבִי כָּל־בְּנֵי־עֵבֶר אֲחִי יֶפֶת הַגָּדוֹל :

סְרְמָה, *hidden-wiles*.... Two contracted roots compose the word here referred to. By the first, סוּר, is understood, a thing closed carefully, melted one in the other; thence, the French word *souder*: by the second, רוּם, a surd, silent thing; thence, *dumb*.

וְעֲמֹרָה, *and-overbearing*.... The verb אמֹר expresses the action of dominating with force, of oppressing. This is the verb אמֹר, *to declare his will, to manifest his power, to speak*, whose initial character א is changed into that of material sense עֲ.

וְאַרְמָה, *and-unmercifulness*.... It is necessary to guard against confusing this word with that which designates the homogeneous element: this one depends upon the root רוּם, of which I have spoken and which characterizes that which is mute, deaf, insensible as the tomb, inexorable, etc.

19. And-there-was t h e-utmost-bounds of-the-*Chena-hanites* (material existing) through-*Tzidon* (ensnaring f o e) by-dint-of i n w a r d-wringing unto-stiffness: by-dint-of hidden-wiles a n d-overbearing a n d - unmerci-fulness, a n d-w a r-waging, unto-the-swallowing-up (of riches).

19. Et-telle-f u t-l'exten-sion-t o t a l e des-*Chenahu-néens* (les existences physi-ques) par-le-m o y e n-de la-ruse, à-force-de contraction-intestine, j u s q u'à-l'affer-missement: à-f o r c e-de dé-tours-obscurs et-de-tyrannie et-d'insensibilité, et-de-guer-res, j u s q u ' à-l'engloutisse-ment (des richesses).

20. These-are the-issued-offspring-of-*Ham,* after-the-tribes-their-o w n, after-the-particular-speeches-of-them, in-the-lands-of-them; in-the-organic-bodies-their-own.

20. Tels-sont les-enfans de-*H a m,* selon-les-tribus-à-eux, selon-les-langues-à-eux, dans-les-terres-à-eux, dans-l e s-organisations-universel-les-à-eux.

21. A n d-through-*Shem,* d i d-it-become also, he-was t h e-father of-all-offspring-ultramundane, t h e-brother of-*Japheth,* the-great.

21. Et-envers-*Shem,* il-fut-engendré aussi, lui-qui-fut le-père-de-toutes-les-pro-ductions-ultra-terrestres, le-frère de-*Japheth,* le-grand.

וצבים, *and-war-waging....* The root צב is affected in general, by all ideas of rules given to a troop, an army, a multitude marching *en corps.*

ער-לשע, *unto-the-swallowing-up-of-riches....* The word referred to here is remarkable in its hieroglyphic form. Of the two roots from which it comes, the one לוע, designates properly *a yawn-ing jaw;* the other שוע, *cement,* that is to say, gold and silver con-sidered as *finance,* as political *cement* of states.

v. 20 and 21. All these terms have been explained.

v. 22. עילם, *Wheilan....* This is the word עולם of which I

22. Beneî Shem Wheî-
lam w'Asshour w'A r p h a-
cheshad w'Loud wa-Aram.

בְּנֵי שֵׁם עֵילָם וְאַשּׁוּר וְאַרְפַּכְשַׁד
וְלוּד וַאֲרָם :

23. W-beneî-Aram Houtz
w' Houl w-G h e t h e r wa-
Mash.

וּבְנֵי־אֲרָם עוּץ וְחוּל וְגֶתֶר וָמָשׁ :

---

have often spoken, in which the convertible sign is replaced by
that of potential manifestation and of eternity of time.

אַשּׁוּר, *Asshour*....   This word which is already found in v.
11. of this chapter, receives in this one a new force, by the influence of the generation of Shem to which Moses made him belong.   It comes from the root אוֹר, *light*, which being joined to the
sign of relative movement שׁ, forms the word שׁוּר, containing every
idea of luminous direction, of pure conduct, of order, of harmony,
of enlightened government; this word which takes again the sign of
stability and power א, forms the one of which we are speaking
אַשּׁוּר ; by which should be understood prosperity, welfare, glory,
blessing, and that which flows from immutable order and harmony.

וְאַרְף־כְּשַׁר, *and Arpha-cheshad*....   The two words that I separate here, are joined in the original; but this conjunction appears
to have been the consequence of a mistake of a copyist anterior to
Esdras.   The first word, אַרְף, comes from the root רף, which develops all ideas of mediative, remedial, restorative, curative cause.
United to the sign of stability and power א, it has formed that
name, famous in all the ancient mythologies, written Ὀρφεύς by the
Greeks, and by us, *Orpheus*.   The second word, כְּשַׁר, nearly as
famous, since it was the favourite epithet of the Chaldeans, is derived
from the root שׁר. applied to providential power, to productive nat-

22. The-issued-offspring of-*Shem* (that which is upright and bright) (were): *Wheilam* (everlasting time, eternity), and-*Asshur* (right and lawful sway, immutable o r d e r, holiness, felicity), and-*Arpha-cheshad* (restorer of providential n a t u r e), a n d-*Lud* (generative power), and-*A r a m* (universal elementizing).

23. A n d-the-issued-offspring of-*Aram* (universal elementizing) (w e r e) : *W h u t z* (substantiation), and-*Hul* (virtual striving), and-*Gether* (plenteous pressing), and-*M a s h* (harvest, reaped fruits).

22. Les-productions-émanées de-*Shem* (ce qui est élevé et brillant) (furent): *Wheilam* (la durée infinie, l'éternité), et - *Asshour* (le pouvoir légal, l'ordre immuable, l'harmonie, la béatitude) et-*Arpha-cheshad* (le principe médiateur d e l a nature providentielle), et-*Loud,* (la propagation), et-*Aram* (l'élémentisation universelle).

23. E t-l e s-productions-émanées d'*Aram* (l'élémentisation universelle) (furent) : *Whoutz* (la substantiation), et-*Houl* (le travail virtuel), et-*Gether* (la pression abondante), et-*M a s h* (la récolte d e s fruits, la moisson).

---

ure. Thence, the name, given to God Himself, שׁדי, *Providence.* In this instance this root שׁד, is inflected by the assimilative article כ.

ולוד, *and-Lud....* This word was explained in v. 13 of this chapter.

וארם, *and-Aram....* This is the elementary root אר of which I have frequently spoken, which is universalized by the final collective sign ם.

v. 23. עוץ *Whutz....* Here is the famous root עץ, *substance,* verbalized by the convertible sign ו.

וחול, *and-Houl....* It is useless to repeat all that I have said upon the subject of this root, whose purpose is to depict the effort of Nature in travail.

וגתר, *and-Gether....* This hieroglyphic word comes from two contracted roots: the first גת, designates literally *pressure;* the second, תר, the *abundance* which results.

24. W'A r p h a čheshad
ïalad æth- Shallah w-She-
lah ïalad æth-Heber.

וְאַרְפַּכְשַׁד יָלַד אֶת־שָׁלַח וְשֶׁלַח
יָלַד אֶת־עֵבֶר :

25. W-l' Heber ï u l l a d
sheneï banîm shem ha-æhad
Pheleg čhi b'ïamaï-ô niphe-
legah ha-âretz w-shem âhî-
ô Jaktan.

וּלְעֵבֶר יֻלַּד שְׁנֵי בָנִים שֵׁם הָאֶחָד
פֶּלֶג כִּי בְיָמָיו נִפְלְגָה הָאָרֶץ וְשֵׁם
אָחִיו יָקְטָן :

וּמַשׁ, *and-Mash*....   That is to say, the *harvest of fruits*,
necessary result of corporeity, of substantiation, of virtual effort, and
of the *abundance* brought about by pressure.

v. 24.   אֶת־שָׁלַח, *that-of-Shelah*....   That is to say, *the
luminous flash, the ray; inspiration, divine grace*: for this word,
chosen with great art by the hierographic writer, rests upon the two
contracted roots שׁל־לח, the first of which שׁל, is particularly assigned to the idea of a line drawn from one place to another, a stroke;
and the second לח, designates inherent power, vigour, projecting
force.
אֶת־עֵבֶר, *that-of-Wheber*....   The word עֵבֶר, whose literal acceptation is, that which passes further, which is beyond, receives
from the generation of Shem a figurative sense, relative to the
intellectual world, toward which the effort of this generation is
carried.

v. 25.   פֶּלֶג, *Pheleg*....   In v. 4. ch. VI. I have stated that the
root פַּל, developed invariably, the idea of a thing set apart,
distinguished, raised above the others.   This root, whose effort is
again increased by the addition of the root לג, applied to the
measure of extent, expresses here a moral distinction, a separation,
a classification among beings of a different nature.
Although I have avoided making observations upon this chapter,
wishing to leave to the sagacity of the reader the task of drawing
from the magnificent tableau which it presents, inductions and consequences, I cannot however refrain from remarking, as a thing

24. And-*Arpha - cheshad* (providential r e s t o r i n g cause) begot the-selfsameness of-*Shelah* (a c t u a l emission, e f f i c a c i o u s grace) : and-*Shelah* (divine, efficacious emission) begat that-of-*Wheber* (ultra-mundane).

24. E t - *Arpha - cheshad* (le principe médiateur providentiel) produisit-l'existence-d e-*Shelah* (l'émission active, la grâce divine, efficace) : et-*S h e l a h* (l'émission, la grâce divine) produisit celle-de-*Wheber* (c e qui est ultra-terrestre, audelà de ce monde).

25. And-toward-*Wheber* (ultra-mundane) was-it-begotten two-offspring: thename of-one was-*P h e l e g* (selection, separation), for by-the-days-his-own was-separated (divided in selected speeches) the-earth: a n d-the-name of-the-brother-his-own was-*J a k t a n* (lessening) (of evil).

25. Et-envers-*W h e b e r* (ce qui est ultra-terrestre) il-fut-engendré d e u x enfans: le-nom de-l'un-é t a i t *Pheleg* (l'élection, la-dialection), à-cause que-dans-les-jours-siens f u t-dialectisée (divisée en dialectes) le-terre: et-le-nom du-frère-sien fut-*Jaktan* (l'atténuation) (du mal).

---

which merits highest attention, that there exist in the three different generations set forth by Moses, three causes of division which are inherent in them, and which issue from three different principles. In the generation of *Japheth*, which symbolizes the extent, the cause of division is the generative principle; in that of *Ham*, which represents that which is curved and hot, this cause is thunder, for the purely physical part, and expiatory experiences, for the moral part; in that of *Shem*, finally, which is upright and bright, this cause is the providential mediative principle itself, which generating divine grace, produces that which is ultra-terrestrial and gives place to separation and to the attenuation of evil.

יקטן, *Jaktan....* The word קטן, which signifies that which is small, thin, slight, has received in this instance the initial adjunction י, which gives it a verbal force. It is, moreover, modified favourably by the influence of the generation of *Shem*.

26.   W'Jaktan îalad æth-
Almôdad w'æth-Shaleph w'
æth-Hatzar-maweth w'æth-
Jarah.

וַיִּקְטָן יָלַד אֶת־אַלְמוֹדָד וְאֶת־
שָׁלֶף וְאֶת־הֲצַרְמָוֶת וְאֶת־ יָרֵח ׃

27.   W'æth - Hadôram w'
æth-Aouzal w'æth-Dikelah.

וְאֶת־הֲדוֹרָם וְאֶת־אוּזָל וְאֶת־
דְּקְלָה ׃

28.   W'æth-Hobal w'æth-
Abi-mâel w'æth-Shebâ.

וְאֶת־עוֹבָל וְאֶת־אֲבִימָאֵל וְאֶת־
שְׁבָא ׃

---

v. 26. אֶת־אַלְמוֹדָד, *the-selfsameness-of-Almodad*....   One must
distinguish here two united words.   By the first, אל, should be understood a divine force; by the second, מוֹדָד, an action by means of
which every thing attains its measure and fills it.

וְאֶת שׁלֶף, *and-that-of-Shaleph*....   The word שׁלֶף recalls that
of שׁלח referred to in v. 24 of this chapter.   It is the reaction of
the action expressed by this one; so that in admitting that שׁלח
characterizes a virtual emission, as that of light or grace, for example, שׁלֶף will be its concomitant reflective emission: for the
root לף added to that of שׁל, *the luminous flash*, is applied to its
reflection or to its return unto itself.

וְאֶת־הֲצַר־מָוֶת, *and-that-of-Hotzar-moth*....   The two united words
which I separate here are worthy of remark.   The first הצר designates a scission operated upon a thing, and by means of which that
thing is found constituting several distinct parts.   It is composed
of the root רץ, applied to every idea of cutting, of division, of
scission, joined by contraction to the root צר, applied on the contrary,
to every idea of pressure, of compaction, of formation.   The second

26. And-*Jaktan* (lessening) begat the-selfsameness-of-*Almodad* (divine probatory mensuration) and-that-of-*Shaleph* (reflected emission) and-that-of-*H o t z a r-moth* (scission performed b y d e a t h); and-that-of-*Iarah* (brotherly sparkling show; the moon).

27. And-t h a t-of *Hadoram* (u n i v e r s a l brightness), and-that-of-*A w z a l* (godlike purified fire), and-t h a t-o f-*Dikelah* (ethereal sounding rarefaction).

28. And-that-o f-*Whobal* infinite orbicular diffusing), and-t h a t-of-*Abimael* (absolute fullness) and-that-of-*Sheba* (rest restoring).

26. Et-*Jaktan* (l'atténuation) produisit l'existence-d'*Almodad* (la mensuration probatoire e t divine), et-celle-de-*Shaleph* (l'émission réfléchie) et-c e l l e-de-*Hotzar-moth* (la scission opérée p a r la m o r t) et-celle-d'*Iarah* (la manifestation radieuse, fraternelle; la lune.)

27. E t-celle-d'*Hadoram* (la splendeur universelle), et-celle-d'*A u z a l* (l e f e u épuré et divin) et-celle-de-*Dikelah* (la raréfaction ethérée et sonore).

28. Et-c e l l e-de-*Whobal* (l'orbe infini), et-c e l l e-d' *Abimael* (le père de la plénitude), et-celle-de-*Sheba* (le retour au repos).

---

word מוּ‏ת is taken here, not only for *death*, but for its very cause, *mortality*.

וְאֶת־יָרַח, *and-that-of-Iarah*.... The word ירח signifies literally, *the moon*. It is composed, by contraction, of the two roots רא־אח, one of which characterizes visibility, and the other fraternity. These two roots, reduced to the syllable רח, receive the initial sign of potential manifestation י.

v. 27. וְאֶת־הֲדֹרָם, *and-that-of-Hadoram*.... The word הֲדֹר which signifies literally, *splendour, glory*, has received the sign ם which universalizes its meaning.

וְאֶת־אוּזָל, *and-that-of-Awzal*.... This is the root אשׁ applied to ether, fire, purified air, to which is united by contraction, the final אל. This word, taken as nominal verb, in אֹזִל, expresses the action of being carried rapidly from one place to another, to communicate sympathetically, in the same manner as an electric spark.

29.   W'æth-A ô p h i r w'   וְאֶת־אוֹפִר וְאֶת־חֲוִילָה וְאֶת־
æth-Hawilah w'æth-Jôbab:
ĉhol-ælleh beneî Jaktan.   יוֹבָב כָּל־אֵלֶּה בְּנֵי יָקְטָן :

וְאֶת־דִּקְלָה, *and-that-of-Dikelah*....   One finds in this word two
contracted roots, דק־קל: by the first, is understood a rarefaction pushed to extreme subtlety; by the second, a lightness raised to the simple
consistency of sound.   One feels clearly that there exist no words in
our modern tongues capable of expressing the ideas attached to
those of *Dikelah*, of *Awzal*, of *Hadoram*: for, whatever may be the
gases and the fluids which our physicists have discovered, they
have not yet attained to those known by the priests of Thebes.

v. 28. וְאֶת־עֹיבָל, *and-that-of-Whobal*....   The root עוּב, applied
to every elevation, to every orbicular depth, is united by contraction
to the root בל, which pushes the meaning to the limits of what is
possible.

וְאֶת־אֲבִימָאֵל, *and-that-of-Abimael*....   These terms have nothing difficult.

וְאֶת־שְׁבָא, *and-that-of-Sheba*....   This is the same word used by
Moses in v. 7. of this chapter: but the difference of the generation
places a great difference between the respective meaning which they
contain.   The repose produced by the igneous force would not be
the same as that emanated from the providential power.

v. 29.   וְאֶת־אוֹפִר, *and-that-of-Aophir*....   This is relative to
the aspect under which one has considered the word אוֹפִר, as some
have seen *gold*, and others, *ashes*: thus the hieroglyphic sense sometimes means noble and sometimes base.   To translate it exactly,
would require terms which we still lack.   This word formed with
deep skill, comes from the two contracted roots אוֹף־אר.   The first,
אוֹף, contains in itself the idea of a thing going to its end, attaining its goal; the second, אר, is well known to be the symbol
of the elementary principle.

וְאֶת־חֲוִילָה, *and-that-of-Hawilah*....   This word is presented in

29. A n d-that-of-*Aophir* (elementary fulfilled end), and-that-of-*Hawilah* (tried virtue) and-that-of *I o b a h* (shout, huzza!) a l l-those-were the-issued-offspring of *Jaktan* (manifested lessening) (of evil).

29. Et-celle-d'*Aophir* (la fin élémentaire), e t-celle-de-*Hawilah* (la vertu éprouvée), et-celle-de-*Jobab* (la jubilation, le cri d'allégresse!) tous-ceux-là-furent les-enfans de-*Jaktan* (l'atténuation) (du mal).

---

v. 7. of this chapter; but although it is always derived from the root חול or חיל, it has not, however, the same expression, on account of the generation of *Shem* which modifies it. Emerging from igneous force, it characterized energy; issued from providential power it is the emblem of virtue.

ואת־יובב, *and-that-of-Iobab*.... I do not wish to conceal from my readers that the word יובב, from which we make *jubilee* and *jubilation* after the Latin, was formed in the Egyptian tongue from an onomatopoetic root somewhat vulgar, and signified literally *to bark*. But, as the dog was, in the hieroglyphic style, the emblem of one of the most profound theurgic mysteries, his cry was, in that same style, the expression of the keenest and most exalted joy. In Hebrew as well as in Chaldaic, the word יבב, signifies an acclamation, a cry of cheerfulness, a general approbation. It is the same in the Syriac ܝܒܒ, and in the Ethiopic ፀቦ (*ibah*).

v. 30. ממשא, *from-harvest-spiritual-fruits*.... I have explained this word in v. 23, of this chapter.

ספרא, *of-spiritual-contriving*.... The vulgar meaning of this word is *book*. It is the name itself of the work of Moses, to which I have restored it. It is derived from the root סף, applied to every idea of addition, adjunction, accumulation, supplement, etc.

הר־הקדם, *to-the-height of-pristine-time*.... I have had occasion many times to speak of the word קדם, and particularly in v. 8, ch. II, where the same roots and the same words represented a great number of times, have always involved the same sense. The reader should also observe that in conformity with my promise, I have

30.   W a-î h î moshab'am   וַיְהִי מוֹשָׁבָם מִמֵּשָׁא בֹּאֲכָה
ma-meshâ b'âĉhah sepharah   סְפָרָה הַר הַקֶּדֶם :
har ha-kedem.

---

changed no character under pretext of reforming it.   My etymologies
are all supported by the same principles, are developed without effort, and succeed without contradiction. Therefore, as I have said,
my Grammar has proved my Translation; and my Translation, my
Grammar.   I arrive at the close of my labour with the innate
conviction of having satisfied my reader, if my reader, exempt from
prejudice, has put into his examination as much good faith as I have
put into my work.

v. 31 and 32.   All these terms are understood.   It is needless
for us to stop longer; but before passing on to the correct translation, I have still some observations to make, and I beg my readers
to give a moment's attention.

I have said in the Preliminary Discourse at the head of these
notes, that what I called THE COSMOGONY OF MOSES, was included in the first ten chapters of the *Berœshith*: considering these
ten chapters as a sort of sacred decade, wherein were developed,
following the signification of numbers, the birth of the Universe and
its principal vicissitudes.

I know very well that this *ancient custom of giving a certain
signification to numbers*, will not be in accordance with the taste of
the greater part of modern savants, who, accustomed only to hear
numbers spoken of under their purely mathematical relations, doubt
that one could without folly, attribute to them a meaning beyond
that which they express physically. These savants are quite excus-
able in scoffing at those who, without any real knowledge of antiquity have undertaken to speak a tongue of whose rudimentary
principles they are ignorant; I do not pretend to blame them.   On
the contrary, I find as they have, nothing more ridiculous than what
certain persons have written of numbers.   But let me make a
comparison.

Because there are bad musicians, must we eliminate music from
the *beaux arts?*   Because one can no longer penetrate the depths of
this art today, and because one is limited to the composition of
certain operas, and to the execution of certain symphonies, must one

30. And-such-was the-re-storing-place-of-them, from-harvest-spiritual-fruits, by-dint of-spiritual-contriving, to-the-h e i g h t of-pristine-time.

30. Et-tel-fut-le-lieu du-r e t o u r-à-eux, d e p u i s-la m o i s s o n-des-fruits-spirit-uels, à-force de-méditations-d'esprit, jusqu'au-s o m m e t de-l'antériorité des-temps.

---

charge Plato with falsehood for having said that music was the key to all knowledge? Is it necessary to believe that Buddha in India, Kong-tze in China and even the Scandinavian to whom has been given the name of Woden, consulted together at such distances, both of time and place, to say the same thing, if this thing had not had some foundation? Is it not more simple to think that we have lost certain underlying ideas concerning the manner of study-ing music; and that if we would, perhaps, consider this art from the standpoint that the Hindu sages, those of China, those of ancient Greece, and even the Druids, our ancestors, have considered it, we would find there the same moral resources and the same sublimities?

Plato who saw in music other things than the musicians of our day, saw also in *numbers*, a meaning that our algebraists no longer see. He had learned to see this meaning according to Pythagoras who had received it from the Egyptians. Now, the Egyptians were not alone agreed in giving to numbers *a mysterious signification*. It suffices to open certain ancient books to see that from the oriental limits of Asia to the occidental bournes of Europe, the same idea governed this subject. If I had not decided to omit citations in my notes, I could easily fill entire pages with them.

Therefore let us be reasonable. Can all antiquity be charged with folly? Can it be believed that Pythagoras was a man of weak mind, Plato foolish, Kong-tze ignorant? But if these men had just ideas, then there certainly did exist a *tongue of numbers*, since they never wearied speaking of it. Now what was this tongue? In what did it consist? It consisted in taking numbers in certain intellectual relations, in the same manner that one takes them today in their physical relations; so that, as an English geometrician can understand a problem of mathematics put down by a French

31.   Ælleh benei-S h e m
l'mishephehoth'am   li-lesho-
noth'am b'artzoth'am l'gôîe-
hem.

אֵלֶּה בְנֵי־שֵׁם לְמִשְׁפְּחֹתָם
לִלְשֹׁנֹתָם בְּאַרְצֹתָם לְגוֹיֵהֶם :

---

geometrician in algebraic characters and solve it without understanding the French tongue, so could a wise Chaldean grasp a mystery
of transcendental philosophy announced in hieroglyphic numbers by
an Egyptian without the least knowledge of his idiom: and as the
geometrician knows very well that the characters which he uses
have no power in themselves and that they are only the signs of
forces or physical quantities, the Chaldean sage knew also that the
numbers which served him were only *symbols* chosen to express the
forces of intellectual Nature.

The vulgar, it is true did not think the same; for the vulgar
is vulgar everywhere.   Not so very long ago there were some among
us who took the geometricians for sorcerers, and the astronomers
were menaced with burning.   ·The people of Memphis and Babylon,
as ignorant as those of Rome, did not separate the sign that they
saw, from the idea it was said to contain; for example, imagining
that the number *four*, which represented universal multiplicating
force, was that force itself.   Many men, usurping the title of sage
held to this thought: but it is an absurdity into which the true
sages never fell.   The symbol of the famous Tetrad was only
a simple *four* for Pythagoras when it was not attached to the idea
of the universal Motive Power; in the same manner as an *x* is only
an *x* for the algebraist who has not resolved to see the unknown
which he is seeking.

It is very important to know this.   In fact, it is because this
has not been known, that there has been so much irrational talk
for and against *numbers*. This tongue seems absolutely lost today
and I would have refrained from speaking of it, if Moses, whose
work I am translating had not used it in several places in his
Sepher.   Moreover, I have not pretended to reëstablish it; for that
enterprise would have demanded other labours.   I have only believed it useful to note the places where one cannot, without its
help, penetrate wholly the meaning of the hierographic writer.
These passages are those in which, under pretence of chronology

31. Those-are the-issued-offspring of-*S h e m*, after-the-tribes-of-t h e m, after-t h e-speeches-their-own, in-the-lands-of-t h e m, by-the-organic-bodies-their's.

31. Tels-sont-les-enfans-de *Shem*, selon-les-tribus-à-eux, selon-les-langues-à-eux, dans-les-terres-à-eux, d'a p-rès-les-organisations-univer-selles-à-eux.

---

he appears to fix the dates, or calculate the age of its cosmogonical personages. I heartily deplore the infinite pains that the savants, otherwise most estimable, have given themselves to excuse its frequent anachronisms, and to make the Hebrew text and the Samaritan, agree. They did not perceive that these were symbols which they submitted to their calculations; and that Moses, so rich and so grand in this way, could not have been so poor and petty. Indeed, a world whose creation did not go back six thousand years and which lasted only about 4200 years from its universal deluge, would be a world exceedingly modern in comparison with ours where the slightest ideas whether in history, or in physics, force us to go back to an incomparable antiquity.

Every time that one takes literally, the periods and the numbers of Moses, he is lost in an inextricable labyrinth. It will never be explained in a satisfactory manner why the Samaritan text which shortens the duration from the creation to the deluge by three cycles, lengthens on the contrary, that from the deluge to the call of Abraham, not only by the three suppressed cycles, but again by three more cycles; why the Hellenists having the two texts before them have followed neither, lengthening arbitrarily the duration from the creation to the deluge, by nearly eight cycles and that from the deluge to the call of Abraham by more than seven; which gives altogether a space of fifteen hundred years beyond the one fixed by the Hebrew text.

But these difficulties, insurmountable otherwise, disappear when one thinks that Esdras and the Hellenists had very strong reasons, the one, for being separated from the Samaritan text and the others, for altering this mysterious chronology. Esdras wishing, as we have already seen, to make the Hebraic Sepher forever distinguished from the Samaritan Sepher which he had anathematized, had no better means, without injuring the text, than that of changing

32, Ælleh mishephehôth beneî-Noah l'thô-ledoth'am b'gôie-hem w-me-ælleh nipredou ha-gôîm ba-âretz âhar ha-mabboul.

אֵלֶּה מִשְׁפְּחֹת בְּנֵי־נֹחַ לְתוֹלְדֹתָם בְּגוֹיֵהֶם וּמֵאֵלֶּה נִפְרְדוּ הַגּוֹיִם בָּאָרֶץ אַחַר הַמַּבּוּל :

---

the form of certain symbolic numbers which had no influence on the sacred doctrine; and the Hellenist Essenes, fleeing from every kind of profanation, could not better prove, that their intention had been not to unveil any of the Mosaic mysteries, than by changing completely those numbers, whose exact translation they could not give without exposing its meaning to the eyes of the profane: for not only the Chaldeans, but those of the Egyptians and the Greeks, initiated in the *science of numbers*, would have grasped the thought of Moses by the sole inspection of his chronology.

. An impartial reader who follows me attentively will easily understand, that in admitting with me the hierographic signification of the numbers alluded to in the Sepher, every difficulty relative to the pretended brevity of the duration of the world, as well as to the anachronisms, and differences, found between the two texts and the translation of the Hellenists, ceases; whereas, if one considers these numbers according to their arithmetical value, one of two things is necessary, either to regard Moses as an unlearned man, or to extinguish every historical and physical light which demonstrates the antiquity of the terrestrial globe.

Without explaining entirely the *symbolic signification of numbers*, because to do this it would be necessary to restore a science seemingly lost, a laborious and dangerous undertaking, I have said enough to put the reader on the path of discoveries. First I have given the interpretation of the Hebraic decade. This was all the more useful as I know that each chapter of the *Berœshith* bears the character of its number. Without this important consideration, and if I had not seen that the Cosmogony, properly so-called, was contained in a sort of hieroglyphic decade, I would not have translated this tenth chapter, which being only a sort of passing or link between two parts of the same whole, belongs still more to the

32. These-a r e the-tribes o f-t h e-i s s u e d-beings of-*Noah*, after-the-symbolical-progenies of-t h e m, in-the-organic-b o d i e s-their-own : a n d-through-t h o s e were-parted the-organic-natural-bodies, in-the-earth, after-the-great-swelling (of waters).

32. Telles-sont les-tribus des-êtres-émanés de-*N o a h ,* selon-l e s-charactéristiques-générations-à-eux, dans-les-organisations-constituantes-à-eux; et-par-ceux-là-même f u r e n t-diversifiées les-organisations-naturelles e n - la-terre, après-la-grande-intumescence (des eaux).

Geology which it begins, than to the Cosmogony which it finishes. I feel that this has need of an explanation.

The number *ten* has in particular in the tongue of numbers, that which is at once final and initial: that is to say, that it terminates the first decade and begins the second, containing thus two expressions and presenting itself at the same time as term and as principle. I beg the reader to examine the example of a thing somewhat difficult to understand otherwise.

First Decade	Second Decade	Third Decade

1.2.3.4.5.6.7.8.9.10.11.12.13.14.15.16.17.18.19.20.21.22.23.24.25.26.27.28. etc.

1. 2. 3. 4. 5. 6. 7. 8. 9.10.11.12.13.14.15.16.17.18.19. etc.

1. 2. 3. 4. 5. 6. 7. 8. 9.10. etc.

1. etc.

It can be seen in this example that the number 10 of the first decade, corresponds to number 1 of the second; so that if one follows the arithmetical progression, the numbers corresponding are found to be 10 and 1, 11 and 2, 12 and 3, etc. Always by adding the members of the complex numbers to form the simple number.

Now I must state for those of my readers who do not fear new and profound ideas, that the first ten chapters of the Beræshith do not correspond to the first decade such as is explained above, but to the second: so that they lead one to think that this book had a beginning composed of nine chapters, of which the first of the Beræshith formed the tenth. This beginning was consecrated to Theogony and was upon the essence of the Divinity. I have strong reasons for thinking that Moses, having received from the sanctuary of Thebes, these theogonic principles, and judging rightly that the Hebrews whom he had been called upon to lead, were in no condition to support them, he therefore suppressed them.   He limited himself to the Cosmogony and began his work in the manner that we have seen.

The first chapter, 10/1, was that of *Principiation*: there, all appears in power of being, in germ.

The second chapter, 11/2, was that of *Distinction*: the principle here passes from power into action.

The third, 12/3, was that of *Extraction*: a great opposition takes place.

The fourth, 13/4, was that of *Divisional Multiplication*: that is to say, of that sort of multiplication which takes place when a whole is divided into parts.

The fifth, 14/5, was that of *Facultative Comprehension*.

The sixth, 15/6, was that of *Proportional Measurement*.

The seventh, 16/7, was that of *Consummation*: the equilibrium is broken; a terrible catastrophe ensues; the Universe is renewed.

The eighth, 17/8, was that of *Accumulation*: the divided things returning to their common principles, becoming united.

The ninth, 18/9, was that of *Restoration Consolidated*: a new movement begins.

The tenth, 19/20, was that of *Aggregative and Formative Energy*: the natural forces unfold and act.

Cosmogony of Moses

Correct Translation

COSMOGONY OF MOSES

CHAPTER I.

Principiation.

1. Ælohim created in principle (the potential existence of) the Heavens and the Earth.

2. And the Earth was contingent potentiality in a potentiality of being: and Darkness (compressive and hardening force) was upon the Face of the Deep (infinite source of potential existence); and the Breath (Divine Spirit) of Ælohim, was pregnantly moving upon the face of the Waters (universal passivity).

3. And Ælohim said (declaring His Will) Light shall be: and Light was.

4. And Ælohim declared (did ken) this Luminous Essence good: and Ælohim made a division (caused a dividing motion to exist) between the Light and the Darkness.

5. And Ælohim called (declaring His Will) the Light, Day (luminous period, phenomenal manifestation), and the Darkness (sensible and material existence), Night (negative manifestation, nutation of things): then were evening and morning (west and east)—first day (first phenomenal manifestation).

6. And Ælohim said, An ethereal expanse shall be in the midst of the Waters (in the centre of universal passivity), and a rarefying force dividing the waters from the waters (division of their opposed energies).

7. And Ælohim made the ethereal expanse and divided the inferior faculties of the waters from their superior faculties: and it was so.

8. And Ælohim called (declaring His Will), the ethereal expanse, Heavens (exalted waters): then were evening and morning (west and east)—second day (second phenomenal manifestation).

9. And Ælohim said, The waters below the heavens shall be gathered unto one place, and Dryness shall appear: and it was so.

10. And Ælohim called the Dryness, Earth (terminating and final element), and the gathering place of the waters, he called Seas (aqueous immensity): and Ælohim saw that it was good.

11. And Ælohim said, The Earth shall bring forth shoots, —vegetating and germinating herb, with innate seed, a fruitful substance bearing fruit after its kind and having within itself its seminal power—on the Earth: and it was so.

12. And the Earth brought forth shoots, the vegetating and germinating herb, with innate seed after its kind, and a fruitful substance bearing fruit and having within itself its seminal power, after its kind: —and Ælohim saw that it was good.

13. Then were evening and morning (west and east) —third day (third phenomenal manifestation).

14. And Ælohim said, Centres of Light (luminaries) shall be in the ethereal expanse of the Heavens, to cause a movement of separation between the Day and the Night, and they shall be as signs to come, both for temporal divisions and for universal phenomenal manifestations, and for ontological mutation (of beings).

15. And they shall be as (sensible) Lights in the ethereal expanse of the Heavens to give (intelligible) Light upon the Earth: and it was so.

16. And Ælohim made (the potential existence of) that dyad of great luminous foci, the greater as symbolic

representation of the day (universal manifestation), and the smaller as symbolic representation of the night (negative manifestation) : and the stars (virtual forces of the universe).

17. And Ælohim placed them in the ethereal expanse of the Heavens to give (intelligible) Light upon the Earth.

18. And to act as symbolic types in the day and in the night, and to cause a movement of separation between the light and the darkness: and Ælohim saw that it was good.

19. Then were evening and morning (west and east) —fourth day (fourth phenomenal manifestation).

20. And Ælohim said, The Waters shall bring forth abundantly, vermiform and volatile principles with soul of life, moving upon the Earth and flying in the ethereal expanse of the Heavens.

21. And Ælohim created (the potential existence of) corporeal immensities, legions of marine monsters and (that of) all soul of life, animated with reptilian movement, whose principles the waters brought forth abundantly, after their kind, and (that of) every winged fowl after its kind: and Ælohim saw that it was good.

22. And Ælohim blessed them, saying, Be fruitful and multiply and fill the waters in the seas, and the birds shall multiply upon the earth.

23. Then were evening and morning (west and east) —fifth day (fifth phenomenal manifestation).

24. And Ælohim said, The Earth shall bring forth soul of life (animality) after its kind, quadruped and reptile and terrestrial animality after its kind: and it was so.

25. And Ælohim made (the potential existence of) terrestrial animality after its kind, and (that of) the quadruped after its kind, and all life trailing upon the ground after its kind: and Ælohim saw that it was good.

26. And Ælohim said, We will make Adam (univer-

sal man) in our reflected Shadow (image) after the laws of our assimilating action; and they (mankind) shall rule over the fish of the sea and over the birds of the air and over the quadruped and over all terrestrial animality and over all reptilian life moving upon the earth.

27. And Ælohim created (the potential existence of) Adam (universal man) in his reflected Shadow (image), in the shadow of Ælohim created He him: male and female (collective power, universal existence) created He them.

28. And Ælohim blessed them, and Ælohim said unto them: Be fruitful and multiply and replenish the earth and subdue it, and have dominion over the fish of the sea, and over the birds of the heavens and over every living thing that moveth upon the earth.

29. And Ælohim said, Behold, I have given you every herb germinating with innate seed, which is on the face of the whole Earth, and every vegetable substance bearing its own fruit and having in itself its seminal power: unto you it shall be for food.

20. And to all terrestrial animality, and to every bird of the heavens, and to every living reptilian thing that moveth upon the earth and having in itself the innate principle of the animated breath of life, every green herb shall be for food: and it was so.

31. And Ælohim saw (did ken) all that He had made (in potentiality), and behold it was very good. Then were evening and morning (west and east)—sixth day (sixth phenomenal manifestation).

————:-:————

CHAPTER II.

Distinction.

1. Thus were finished (in potentiality) the Heavens and the Earth and all the ruling law thereof (universal nature).

2. And Ælohim accomplished, in the seventh day (phenomenal manifestation), the sovereign work which He had made, and He returned to His Ineffable Self, in the seventh day (phenomenal manifestation), from all the sovereign work which He had made.

3. And Ælohim blessed the seventh day and sanctified (the symbolic existence of) it, because thereon He returned to His Ineffable Self from all the sovereign work, which Ælohim had created according to His efficient power.

4. Such is the sign (symbolic, hieroglyphic emblem) of the generations of the Heavens and of the Earth, when they were created, in the day (luminous manifestation) when YAHWEH Ælohim made (in principle) the Earth and the Heavens.

5. And the whole conception of Nature existed in the Earth before Nature was, and all its vegetative energy before it grew; for YAHWEH Ælohim had not caused it to rain upon the Earth, and Adam (universal man) did not then exist (in actual substance) to labour in the Adamic element.

6. But a virtual emanation went up from out the Earth and moistened the whole face of the Adamic element (homogeneous principle).

7. And YAHWEH Ælohim fashioned (the substance of) Adam (universal man) from (the sublimation of the most subtle parts of) the Adamic element, and breathed into his intelligence an exalted essence of lives, and Adam (universal man) became a similitude of the universal soul.

8. And YAHWEH Ælohim appointed an enclosure (organic circumference) in the sphere of temporal sensibility, (extracted) from the universal anteriority of time; and there He placed Adam whom He had fashioned (for eternity).

9. And YAHWEH Ælohim caused to grow from the Adamic element, every vegetative substance pleasing to the sight and good for food: and a substance of lives in the centre of the (organic) enclosure and its essential substance of the knowledge of good and evil.

10. And a river (luminous emanation) flowed from the sphere of temporal sensibility to water (vivify) the (organic) enclosure; and thence it divided and became (according to the quaternary power) four principles.

11. The name of the first (of those emanating principles) was Phishon (physical reality, apparent being); that which encompasseth the whole earth of Hawilah (virtual energy), natural source of gold (luminous reflection).

12. And the gold of this earth (emblem of luminous reflection of) good; there (the natural source of) Bedollah (mysterious separation) and the Stone Shoham (universal sublimation).

13. And the name of the second river (emanating principle) was Gihon (formative movement) : that which encompasseth the whole earth of Chush (igneous principle).

14. And the name of the third river (emanating principle) was Hiddekel (universal propagating fluid), that which goeth forth as (the vehicle of the principle

of) happiness (harmony) : and the fourth river (emanating principle) was Phrath (fecundating source).

15. And YAHWEH Ælohim took Adam (universal man) and placed him in the (organic) enclosure (of the sphere of temporal sensibility) to elaborate and guard it with care.

16. And YAHWEH Ælohim commanded Adam saying (declaring His Will), Of every vegetative substance of the (organic) enclosure thou mayest (freely) feed upon.

17. But of the physical substance of the knowledge of good and of evil, thou shalt not feed thereon: for in the day thou feedest thereon, becoming mutable, thou shalt die (pass into another state of being).

18. And YAHWEH Ælohim said, It is not good that Adam (universal man) should be alone (in his solitude) ; I will make him an auxiliary force (companion, counsel) emanated from himself, and formed in the reflection of his own light.

19. And YAHWEH Ælohim fashioned from the Adamic element all terrestrial animality of nature, and every bird of the heavens; and he brought them unto Adam (universal man) to see what name relative to himself Adam would call each species; and whatsoever name Adam assigned to each soul of life (relative to himself), that was its name (expression of its relation with the universal living soul).

20. And Adam assigned names to every quadruped, and to every bird of the heavens, and to all terrestrial animality of nature: but for Adam (universal man) was not found an auxiliary force (companion, counsel) as luminous reflection of himself.

21. And YAHWEH Ælohim caused a profound and sympathetic sleep to fall upon Adam (universal man) and he slept; and He broke from the unity, one of his involutions (exterior envelope, feminine principle) and shaped with form and corporeal beauty, its original inferiority (weakness).

22. And YAHWEH Ælohim restored this involution (exterior envelope) which He had broken from (the substance of) Adam, for (shaping the form of) Aïshah (volitive faculty, intellectual companion) and He brought her unto Adam.

23. And Adam said (declaring his thought), This is actually universal substance of my substance and corporeal form of my corporeal form: this one he called Aïshah (efficient volitive faculty, intellectual companion) for out of Aïsh (volitive principle, intellectual man) she had been taken in substance.

24. Therefore shall Aïsh (intellectual man) leave his father and his mother and shall cleave unto Aïshah (intellectual companion), and they shall be as one corporeal substance (one single being in one same form).

25. And they were both entirely uncovered (without corporeal veil to conceal their mental conceptions), Adam (universal man) and Aïshah (his volitive faculty) and they were not ashamed.

—————:-:—————

CHAPTER III.

Extraction.

1. Now Nahash (egoism, envy, covetousness, concupiscence) was an insidious passion (blind principle) in all elementary life which YAHWEH Ælohim had made: and it said (this passion Nahash) unto Aïshah (volitive faculty of Adam), Why, hath Ælohim declared, ye shall not feed upon all the substance of the organic enclosure?

2. And Aïshah (volitive faculty) said unto Nahash (covetous passion), Of the fruit growing substance of the organic enclosure, we may feed upon,

3. But of the fruit of the substance itself, which is in the centre of the organic enclosure, Ælohim hath said, Ye shall not feed upon it, ye shall not carry your desires (breathe out your soul) into it, lest ye cause your unavoidable dying.

4. And Nahash (insidious, covetous passion) said unto Aïshah: Not in dying shall ye cause your unavoidable death.

5. For Ælohim knoweth, that in the day ye shall feed thereon (on this substance), your eyes shall be opened (to the light) and ye shall be as Ælohim, conscious of good and evil.

6. And Aïshah (volitive faculty) saw that this substance (was) good for food and pleasant for the eyes, and that this substance was desirable to universalize the intelligence; and she took of the fruit thereof and did feed upon it and she gave also unto Aïsh (intellectual principle) united with her, and he did feed thereon.

7. And the eyes of them both were opened, and they knew that they were void of light (of virtue, sterile and unveiled in their dark principle) and they brought forth a shadowy covering, veil of sadness and mourning, and they made themselves pilgrims' cloaks.

8. And they heard the voice of YAHWEH Ælohim wafting itself to and fro in the organic enclosure like the spiritual breath of day, and Adam (universal man) hid himself and Aïshah (his volitive faculty), from the face of YAHWEH Ælohim, in the centre of the substance itself of the organic enclosure.

9. And YAHWEH Ælohim called unto Adam and said unto him, Where has thy will borne thee?

10. And he said, I heard Thy voice in the organic enclosure and I was afraid because I was void of light (unveiled in my dark principle) and I hid myself.

11. And He said, Who hath taught thee that thou wast void of light? If not (the use of) that substance whereof I commanded thee that thou shouldst not feed.

12. And Adam (universal man) said, Aïshah (volitive faculty) whom Thou gavest to be my companion, she gave me of that substance and I did feed upon it.

13. And YAHWEH Ælohim said unto Aïshah, Why hast thou done that? and Aïshah said, Nahash (insidious passion) caused my delusion and I fed upon it.

14. And YAHWEH Ælohim said unto Nahash, Because thou hast done this, cursed be thou, amongst all terrestrial animality, and amongst all elementary nature, according to thy tortuous inclination shalt thou act (grovellingly, basely), and upon elementary exhalations (corporeal illusions) shalt thou feed all the days of thy life.

15. And I will put antipathy (natural aversion) between thee and Aïshah (volitive faculty), and between

thy progeny and her progeny (productions of the volitive faculty); hers shall repress (centralize) the venomous principle (evil) in thee, and thine shall repress (centralize) the consequences of evil in her.

16. Unto Aïshah He said, I will multiply the number of thy physical hindrances (obstacles opposed to the execution of thy desires), and thy mental conceptions; and in sorrowful travail shalt thou bring forth thy productions: and unto Aïsh (intellectual principle) shall thy desire be and he shall rule in thee (act symbolically).

17. And unto Adam (universal man) He said, Because thou hast hearkened unto the voice of Aïshah (volitive faculty, intellectual companion), and hast fed upon the substance of which I commanded thee saying, Thou shalt not feed thereof; cursed be the Adamic element (homogeneous and like unto thee) because of thee: in painful travail shalt thou feed upon it all the days (phenomenal manifestations) of thy lives.

18. And harsh and rough (imperfect and disordered) productions shall germinate abundantly for thee; and thou shalt feed upon the bitter and withered fruits of elementary nature.

19. In continual mental agitation shalt thou feed upon it, until thy return (reintegration) unto the Adamic element (homogeneous and like unto thee); for out of the spiritual element wast thou taken and unto the spiritual element shalt thou be restored.

20. And Adam called the name of Aïshah (his volitive faculty), Hevah (elementary existence) because she was the mother of all (that constitutes) existence.

21. And YAHWEH Ælohim made for Adam and his intellectual companion, sheltering shapes (bodies) and enveloped them with care.

22. And YAHWEH Ælohim said, Behold Adam (universal man) is become like one of us, knowing good and evil; and now lest he put forth his hand and take

also of the Elementary Substance of lives, and feed thereon and live forever (immensity of time):

23. Therefore, YAHWEH Ælohim separated him from the organic sphere of temporal sensibility, to elaborate this Adamic element out of which he had been taken.

24. And He cast forth Adam (universal man) and from the universal anteriority of time, He caused to exist in the organic sphere of temporal sensibility, the Cherubim (collective being, like unto innumerable legions) and an incandescent flame of destruction whirling upon itself, to guard the way of the elementary substance of lives.

————:-:————

CHAPTER IV.

Divisional Multiplication.

1. And Adam (universal man) knew Hevah (elementary existence, his efficient volitive faculty); and she conceived and produced (the existence of) Kain (strong and mighty transformer, which seizes, centralizes and appropriates, and assimilates to itself); and she said, I have formed (by centralizing) an•intellectual being of the essence of YAHWEH.

2. And she added, bringing forth his brotherly self, (the existence of) Habel (gentle, pacific liberator, that which releases and extends, which evaporates and leaves the centre); and Habel was leader (director) of the elementary corporeal world, and Kain was servant of the Adamic element (homogeneal ground).

3. Now it was from the end of the seas (superficial phenomenal manifestations), that Kain caused to ascend of the productions of the Adamic element, an offering unto YAHWEH.

4. And Habel also caused (an offering) to ascend of the firstlings of his world and of their quintessence (most eminent virtues); and YAHWEH was saviour unto Habel and unto his offering.

5. But unto Kain and unto his offering He was not saviour; and Kain was very wroth and his face was downcast.

6. And YAHWEH said unto Kain, Why art thou wroth? and why is thy face downcast?

7. If thou doest well, shalt thou not bear the sign (of good in thee) and if thou doest not well, the sin lieth at the door (is upon thy countenance); and unto thee its desire, and thou, its symbolic representation.

8. And Kain declared his thought, unto Habel his brother; and they were existing together in productive Nature: and Kain (violent centralizer) rose up (was materialized) against Habel (gentle, pacific liberator) his brother, and slew him (conquered his forces).

9. And YAHWEH said unto Kain, Where is Habel, thy brother? and he said, I know not: am I my brother's keeper?

10. And he said, What hast thou done? the voice of the groaning generations of (future progenies which were to proceed from) thy brother riseth unto me from the Adamic element.

11. And now, cursed be thou, by the Adamic element whose mouth was opened by thine own hand, to receive the generations (future progenies) of thy brother.

12. When thou labourest in the Adamic element, it shall not yield its virtual force unto thee: staggering (agitated by a movement of uncertainty) and wandering (agitated by a movement of fear) thou shalt be upon the earth.

13. And Kain said unto YAHWEH, Great is my iniquity from that which I must endure (according to my purification).

14. Behold, Thou hast driven me out this day from the face of the Adamic element: and from Thy face must I hide myself and I shall be staggering (agitated by a movement of uncertainty) and wandering (agitated by a movement of fear) upon the earth: and it shall be that whosoever findeth me shall slay me.

15. And YAHWEH said unto him, Whosoever slayeth Kain (thinking to destroy him), sevenfold shall (instead) exalt him (increase his power sevenfold): and YAHWEH put a sign upon Kain, so that anyone finding him should not smite him.

16. And Kain withdrew from the face of YAHWEH and dwelt in the land of Nod (of banishment and exile, of troublous, agitated wandering) the temporal anteriority of elementary sensibility.

17. And Kain knew Aïsheth (his intellectual companion, his volitive faculty): and she conceived and brought forth (the existence of) Henoch (founder, central energy): then he builded a spherical enclosure (stronghold) and he called the name of this spherical enclosure after the name of his son Henoch.

18. And unto Henoch was born (the existence of) Whirad (excitative movement, interior passion, whirling motion): and Whirad produced Mehoujael (physical manifestation, objective reality): and Mehoujael produced Methoushael (abyss of death): and Methoushael produced Lamech (the knot which arrests dissolution, the pliant bond of things).

19. And Lamech took unto him two corporeal companions (physical faculties): the name of the first was Whadah (evidence, periodic return) and the name of the second was Tzillah (deep, dark, veiled).

20. And Whadah produced (the existence of) Jabal (aqueous principle, physical abundance, fertility): he who was the father (concentrating and appropriating force, the founder) of those who dwell in fixed and elevated abodes, and who recognize (the right of lawful) property.

21. And the name of his brother was Jubal (universal fluid, principle of sound, source of joy and moral prosperity): he who was the father (founder) of every luminous conception, and that which is worthy of loving admiration (arts and sciences).

22. And Tzillah also produced (the existence of) Thubal Kain (central diffusion, mercurial and mineral principle) who sharpened all (tools of) copper and iron (instructor of those who work in metals, excavate mines and forge iron): and the kindred of Thubal Kain was

Nawhomah (principle of aggregation, association of peoples).

23. And Lamech (the knot which arrests dissolution) said unto his corporeal companions (physical faculties) Whadah and Tzillah: Hearken unto my voice, ye companions of Lamech, listen unto my speech: for I have slain (destroyed) the intellectual individuality of me (that which is individualized by his volitive faculty) for my extension (free exercise of his forces), and the progeny (spirit of the race, particular lineage) for my formation (in the great family of peoples).

24. So sevenfold shall be exalted (the centralizing constitutive forces of) Kain (mighty transformer), and Lamech (flexible bond things), seventy and sevenfold (exalted).

25. And Adam (universal man) again knew his intellectual companion (efficient volitive faculty), and she produced a son, and called his name Sheth (basis, foundation of things): For thus, said she, hath Ælohim founded in me another seed (basis of another generation, emanated) from the mutation of Habel, whom Kain slew.

26. And unto Sheth likewise, was generated a son: and he called his name Ænosh (mutable being, corporeal man): then hope was caused (to support his sorrow), by calling upon (invocation of) the name of YAHWEH.

———:-:———

CHAPTER V.

Facultative Comprehension

1. This is the book of the (symbolical) generations of Adam (universal man) from the day when Ælohim created Adam; according to the assimilating action of Ælohim, made he his selfsameness (determined his potential existence).

2. Male and female (cause and means) created He them (collectively); and He blessed them and He called their (universal) name Adam, in the day when He created them (universally).

3. And Adam existed three tens and one hundred cycles (of temporal ontological mutation); and he produced according to his assimilating action, in his reflected shadow, an emanated being, and he called his name Sheth (basis and foundation of things).

4. And the days (luminous periods, phenomenal manifestations) of Adam, after he had brought forth (the existence of) Sheth, were eight hundred cycles (of ontological mutation): and he produced sons and daughters (many emanated beings).

5. And all the days (luminous periods) during which Adam (universal man) existed, were nine hundred cycles and three tens (of ontological mutation): and he passed away (returned to universal seity).

6. And Sheth (basis of things) existed five and one hundred cycles (of ontological mutation), and he produced Ænosh (mutable being, corporeal man).

7. And Sheth existed after he produced (the existence of) Ænosh, seven and eight hundred cycles (of on-

tological mutation), and he produced sons and daughters (many emanated beings).

8. And all the days (luminous periods) of Sheth were two and one ten and nine hundred cycles (of ontological mutation), and he passed away (returned to universal seity).

9. And Ænosh (mutable being, corporeal man) existed nine tens of cycles (of ontological mutation), and he produced Kainan (general usurpation).

10. And Ænosh existed after he produced (the existence of) Kainan, five and one ten and eight hundred cycles (of ontological mutation) and he produced sons and daughters (many emanated beings).

11. And all the days (luminous periods) of Ænosh were five and nine hundred cycles (of ontological mutation), and he passed away (returned to universal seity).

12. And Kainan existed seven tens of cycles (of ontological mutation), and he produced Mahollael (mighty exaltation, splendour).

13. And Kainan existed after he produced (the existence of) Mahollael, four tens and eight hundred cycles (of ontological mutation), and he produced sons and daughters (many emanated beings).

14. And all the days (luminous periods) of Kainan were ten and nine hundred cycles (of ontological mutation), and he passed away (returned to universal seity).

15. And Mahollael (mighty exaltation, splendour) existed five and six tens of cycles (of ontological mutation) and he produced Ired (steadfastness, perseverance, either upward or downward).

16. And Mahollael existed after he produced (the existence of) Ired, three tens and eight hundred cycles (of ontological mutation), and he produced sons and daughters (many emanated beings).

17. And all the days (luminous periods) of Mahollael were five and nine tens and eight hundred cycles

(of ontological mutation), and he passed away (returned to universal seity).

18. And Ired existed two and six tens, and one hundred cycles (of ontological mutation), and he produced Henoch (centralization, contrition).

19. And Ired existed after he produced (the existence of) Henoch, eight hundred cycles (of ontological mutation), and he produced sons and daughters (many emanated beings).

20. And all the days (luminous periods) of Ired were two and six tens and nine hundred cycles (of ontological mutation), and he passed away (returned to universal seity).

21. And Henoch existed five and six tens of cycles (of ontological mutation), and he produced Methoushaleh (abyss of death).

22. And Henoch followed in the steps of Ælohim, after he produced (the existence of) Methoushaleh, three hundred cycles (of ontological mutation), and he produced sons and daughters (many emanated beings).

23. And all the days (luminous periods) of Henoch were five and six tens and three hundred cycles (of ontological mutation).

24. And Henoch followed in the steps of Ælohim and (there was) naught of him (ceased to exist without ceasing to be); for Ælohim withdrew him unto Himself.

25. And Methoushaleh existed seven and eight tens and one hundred cycles (of ontological mutation), and he produced (the existence of) Lamech (the knot which arrests dissolution).

26. And Methoushaleh existed after he produced (the existence of) Lamech, two and eight tens and seven hundred cycles (of ontological mutation), and he produced sons and daughters (many emanated beings).

27. And all the days (luminous periods) of Methou-

shaleh were nine and six tens and nine hundred cycles
(of ontological mutation), and he passed away (returned
to universal seity).

28. And Lamech (pliant bond of things) existed
two and eight tens, and one hundred cycles (of ontological mutation), and he produced a son (emanated
being).

29. And he called his name Noah (repose of elementary Nature); saying, This shall rest us (our existence) and lighten our labour, and the physical obstacles of our hands, because of the Adamic element which
YAHWEH hath cursed.

30. And Lamech existed after he produced this son,
five and nine tens, and five hundred cycles (of ontological
mutation), and he produced sons and daughters (many
emanated beings).

31. And all the days (luminous periods) of Lamech
were seven and seven tens and seven hundred cycles (of
ontological mutation), and he passed away (returned
to universal seity).

32. And Noah (repose of elementary nature) was the
son of five hundred cycles (of ontological mutation):
and Noah produced (the existence of) Shem (that which
is lofty, bright) and (the existence of) Cham (that
which is curved, dark, hot) and (the existence of)
Japheth (that which is wide, extended).

CHAPTER VI.

Proportional Measurement

1. Now it was (it came to pass) because of the downfall of Adam (dissolution of universal man) by multiplying upon the face of the Adamic element, that daughters (sentient and corporeal forms) were abundantly produced unto them (the divisions of Adam).

2. And the sons (spiritual emanations) of Ælohim beheld the daughters (corporeal forms) of Adam that they were fair: and they took unto themselves of those physical faculties, whichsoever they desired most.

3. And YAHWEH said, My breath (vivifying spirit) shall no more be diffused (in bountiful profusion) upon Adam (universal man) during the immensity of time, because of his degeneration: inasmuch as he is corporeal, his days (luminous periods) shall be one hundred fold and two tens of cycles (of ontological mutation).

4. And the Nephilim (elect amongst men, noble illustrious ones) were upon the earth in those days: and also after that, sons (spiritual emanations) of Ælohim had come in unto (mingled with) daughters (corporeal faculties) of Adam (universal man) and they had produced through them those same Ghiborim (mighty men, those famous Hyperboreans) who were of old, corporeal men (heros) of renown.

5. And YAHWEH saw that the perversity of Adam (mankind) increased upon the earth and that every conception (intellectual production) of the thoughts of his heart diffused evil all that day (during that phenomenal manifestation, luminous period).

6. And YAHWEH renounced (withdrew His loving power from the existence of) Adam (mankind) on the earth, and He repressed Himself in His heart (evinced severity).

7. And YAHWEH said, I will efface (the existence of) Adam (mankind) which I have created, from the face of the Adamic element: from Adam (mankind) to the quadruped, the creeping kind and the bird of the heavens: for I renounce (the preserving care of) having made them.

8. But Noah (repose of nature) found grace in the eyes of YAHWEH.

9. These are the symbolic generations of Noah: of Noah, intellectual principle manifesting the justice of universal virtues in his generations (cyclic periods): Noah followed in the steps of Ælohim.

10. And Noah (repose of nature) produced three sons (triad of emanated beings): the existence of Shem (that which is lofty, brilliant), of Cham (that which is curved, dark, gloomy), and of Japheth (that which extends without limit).

11. And the earth was corrupt (debased, degraded) before the face of Ælohim: and the earth was filled with a violent degrading heat (dark and devouring).

12. And Ælohim looked upon the earth and behold it was corrupt, because every corporeal form had corrupted its own way (law) upon the earth.

13. And Ælohim said unto Noah (repose of nature), The end of every corporeal form draws near before my face: for the earth is filled with a violent degrading heat (dark and devouring) over the whole face of it: and behold, I leave the earth to its own destruction.

14. Make thee a Thebah (sheltering abode, enclosure, refuge) of preserving elementary substance: hollowed and roomed thou shalt make the Thebah: and thou shalt smear the interior and the exterior circumference with corporeal substance.

15. And thus shalt thou make it: three hundred fold of mother-measure the length of the Thebah (mysterious, sacred abode) : five tens of mother-measure the breadth of it and three tens of mother-measure the bulk (solidity) of it.

16. Gathering light, thou shalt make for the Thebah; and according to the mother-measure, the orbicular extent in its upper part: and the opening of the Thebah shalt thou place in its opposite part: the lower parts, thou shalt make twofold and threefold.

17. And I, behold I, do bring the great intumescence (of the waters) upon the earth, to destroy every corporeal form wherein is the breath of lives: from under the heavens, all that is upon the earth shall perish.

18. And I will establish My creative might with thee and thou shalt enter the Thebah, thou and thy sons (spiritual emanations) and thine intellectual companion (efficient volitive faculty) and the corporeal companions of thy sons (their natural faculties) with thee.

19. And of every living kind, of every corporeal form, two of every kind shalt thou bring into the Thebah (mysterious abode) to exist with thee: male and female shall they be.

20. Of fowl after its kind, of quadruped after its kind, of every creeping thing of the Adamic element after its kind, two of every species shall come unto thee to preserve existence there.

21. And thou shalt take unto thee of all food that is eaten: thou shalt gather it unto thee: and it shall be for food for thee and for them.

22. And Noah did all that Ælohim had commanded him: thus did he.

CHAPTER VII.

Consummation.

1. And YAHWEH said unto Noah, Come thou and all thine interior into the Thebah (sheltering abode) : for thee (thy selfsameness) have I seen righteous before My face in this generation (of perversity).

2. Of every pure quadruped kind, thou shalt take unto thee, seven-by-seven, the principle and the efficient volitive faculty: and of the impure quadruped kind, two-by-two, the principle and the efficient volitive faculty.

3. Of the fowl of the heavens also seven-by-seven, male and female, to preserve (the existence of) the seed upon the face of the whole earth.

4. For in this seventh day (luminous period, phenomenal manifestation), I will cause to rain (move the watery element) upon the earth, four tens of days (a great quaternion of light) and four tens of nights (great quaternion of darkness) : and I will efface all substantial, plastic nature that I have made, from the face of the Adamic element.

5. And Noah did all that Ælohim had commanded him.

6. And Noah was the son of six hundred cycles (of ontological mutation), when the great intumescence (of the waters) was upon the earth.

7. And Noah went, and his sons (emanated beings) and his intellectual companion (efficient volitive faculty) and the corporeal companions of his sons (their physical faculties) into the Thebah (mysterious abode) from the face (of the waters) of the great intumescence.

8. Of the pure quadruped kind and of the impure quadruped kind and of fowl and of every creeping thing animated with reptilian movement upon the Adamic element.

9. Two and two they came unto Noah (repose of nature) into the Thebah (sheltering abode), male and female, as Ælohim had commanded Noah.

10. And it was on the seventh of the days (luminous periods, phenomenal manifestations) that the waters of the great intumescence were upon the earth.

11. In the six hundredth ontological mutation of the lives of Noah, in the second neomenia, in the seventeenth day (luminous period) of that moon-renewal: in that same day were opened all the springs of the potential, universal deep, and the multiplying quaternions of the heavens were loosened.

12. And there was a falling of water (aqueous atmosphere) upon the earth unceasingly, four tens of days and four tens of nights (an entire quaternion of light and darkness).

13. Into the substantial principle of this day (seventh luminous period) went Noah (repose of elementary existence), and Shem (brilliant elevation), and Cham (dark inclination), and Japheth (extended space), sons (emanated productions) of Noah, and his intellectual companion (efficient volitive faculty), and the corporeal companions (physical faculties) of his sons with them, into the Thebah (place of refuge).

14. They, and all terrestrial animality after its kind, and every quadruped after its kind, and every creeping thing with reptilian motion after its kind, and every fowl after its kind: every thing that moves swiftly, everything that flies.

15. And they went unto Noah (repose of nature) into the Thebah (sheltering abode) two and two of every corporeal form having in itself the breath of lives.

16. And thus they went in, male and female of every corporeal form, as Ælohim had commanded: and YAHWEH finished and withdrew Himself.

17. And the great intumescence was four tens of days (luminous periods) upon the earth: and the waters increased greatly and they bore up the Thebah, which was lifted up above the earth.

18. And the waters prevailed and were greatly increased upon the earth: and the Thebah moved to and fro upon the face of the waters.

19. And the waters prevailed to their fullest extent upon the earth: and all the high mountains were covered, which are beneath the whole heavens.

20. Fifteen mother-measure above them did the waters prevail: and the mountains were wholly covered.

21. Thus perished (disappeared) every corporeal form moving upon the earth, of birds and of quadruped, of terrestrial animality and of every creeping thing moving with reptilian motion upon the earth and all Adam (mankind).

22. Everything having an emanated essence of the breath of lives (spiritual comprehension), perished in the exterminating intumescence.

23. And everything (plastic, substantial nature) was effaced from the face of the Adamic element: from Adam (mankind) to the quadruped, from the reptilian kind to the fowl of the heavens: and they were effaced from the earth: and there remained only Noah (repose of elementary nature), and that which was with him in the Thebah (holy retreat).

24. And the waters prevailed upon the earth five tens and one hundred days (luminous periods, phenomenal manifestations).

CHAPTER VIII.

Accumulation.

1. And Ælohim remembered (the existence of) Noah and (that of) all terrestrial animality and (that of) every quadruped with him in the Thebah (place of refuge) : and Ælohim caused a breath to pass over the earth, and the waters were checked.

2. And the springs of the deep (infinite source of potential existence) and the multiplying quaternion forces of the heavens were closed, and the falling of water (aqueous atmosphere) was exhausted from the heavens.

3. And the waters returned to their former state from off the earth by (the periodic movement of) flux and reflux: and the waters withdrew (shrank) at the end of five tens and one hundred days (luminous periods).

4. And the Thebah rested, in the seventh moon-renewal, on the seventeenth day (luminous period) of that moon-renewal, upon the heights of Ararat (first gleam of luminous effluence).

5. And the waters were agitated by (the periodic movement of) flux and reflux until the tenth moon-renewal: and in that tenth (month), on the first of the moon-renewal, the tops of the mountains (elementary firstlings, principles of nature's productions) became visible.

6. And it was at the end of four tens of days (the great quaternion), that Noah released the light of the Thebah, which he had made.

7. And he sent forth Ereb (western darkness) which

went to and fro (with periodic movement) until the drying up of the waters upon the earth.

8. And he sent forth Ionah (plastic force of nature, brooding dove) from him, to see if the waters were lightened from off the face of the Adamic element.

9. And Ionah found no place of rest to impart its generative force and it returned unto him into the Thebah, for the waters were still upon the face of the whole earth: and he put forth his hand (his power) and took it and brought it back unto him into the Thebah.

10. And he again waited a septenary of days (luminous periods) more, and again he sent forth Ionah from the Thebah.

11. And Ionah came back to him at the same time as Ereb (return of western darkness), and lo, an olive branch (a sublimation of igneous essence) was grasped in its mouth (its conceptive faculty): thus Noah knew that the waters were lightened upon the earth.

12. And he waited again a septenary of days (luminous periods) more, and he sent forth Ionah, and it (brooding dove, generative faculty) returned not again unto him.

13. And it was in the unity and six hundred cycles (of ontological mutation), in the very beginning, at the first of the moon-renewal, that the waters wasted away from upon the earth: and Noah elevated the shelter (vaulted superficies) of the Thebah and looked (considered) and behold they were wasted (the waters) away from upon the face of the Adamic element.

14. And in the second moon-renewal, in the seven and twentieth day of that moon-renewal the earth was dried.

15. And Ælohim spake unto Noah, saying,

16. Issue forth (produce thyself exteriorly) from the Thebah (sheltering place), thou and thine intellectual

companion (efficient volitive faculty), and thy sons (emanated productions) and the corporeal companions of thy sons (their physical faculties) with thee together.

17. All animal life that is with thee, of every corporeal form, of fowl and of quadruped and of every kind of reptile that creepeth upon the earth: let them produce (themselves exteriorly) with thee: and let them breed abundantly upon the earth and be fruitful and multiply upon the earth.

18. And Noah issued forth (was reproduced exteriorly) and his sons (emanated productions), and his intellectual companion (efficient volitive faculty) and his sons' companions (corporeal faculties) with him.

19. All terrestrial animality, all reptilian kind and every fowl: every thing creeping upon the earth after their kinds, issued forth (produced themselves exteriorly) from the Thebah.

20. And Noah raised up an altar (place of sacrifice) unto YAHWEH, and he took of every pure quadruped and of every pure fowl and raised a sublimation (caused an exhalation to rise) from the altar.

21. And YAHWEH breathed that fragrant breath of sweetness: and YAHWEH said within His heart, I will not again curse the Adamic element on account of Adam, because the heart of Adam (mankind) has conceived evil from his elementary impulses: I will not again smite all earth-born life (elementary existence) as I have done.

22. During all the days (luminous periods, phenomenal manifestations) of the earth, seed-time and harvest, cold and heat, summer and winter, and day and night shall not cease.

CHAPTER IX.

Restoration Consolidated.

1. And Ælohim blessed (the existence of) Noah and (that of) his sons (emanated productions), and He said unto them, Be fruitful and multiply and replenish the earth.

2. And the dazzling brightness of you and the awesome splendour of you shall be (impressed) upon all terrestrial animality and upon every bird of the heavens: upon all that receiveth original movement from the Adamic element, and upon every fish of the sea: into your hand (power) are they delivered.

3. Everything possessing in itself the principle of movement and of life, shall be food for you: even as the green herb have I given unto you all.

4. But the corporeal form which has in its soul, its similitude (blood assimilation, homogeneity) you shall not feed upon.

5. For your homogeneity (likeness of your soul), will I require (avenge) it: from the hand of every living being will I require it, and from the hand of Adam (mankind) and from the hand of Aïsh (intellectual man) his brother, will I require this Adamic soul (similitude).

6. Whoso sheddeth the blood (homogeneous, corporeal likeness) of Adam (mankind), through Adam shall his own blood be shed: because in the universal shadow (image) of Ælohim made He (the selfsameness of) Adam.

7. And you, universal existence, be ye fruitful and multiply; bring forth abundantly upon the earth and spread yourselves thereon.

8. And Ælohim spake unto Noah and unto his sons (his emanations) with him, saying,

9. And I, behold I will establish (in substance) My Creative Energy in you and in your generation after you:

10. And in every soul of life that is with you, of fowl, of quadruped and of all terrestrial animality with you: of all beings issued from the Thebah, (including) all terrestrial animality.

11. And I will establish (in substance) My Creative Energy in you: so that every corporeal form shall not be cut off any more by the great intumescence (of the waters): and neither shall there be any more a flood to destroy the earth.

12. And Ælohim said, This is the symbolic sign of the Creative Force (law) which I appoint between Me and you, and every soul of life that is with you, for perpetual ages (immensity of time).

13. My bow, I have set in the nebulous expanse: and it shall be for a symbol of the Creative Force (law) between Me and the earth.

14. And it shall come to pass, when I bring a cloud over the earth, that the bow shall be seen in the nebulous expanse.

15. And I will remember this Creative Law which is between Me and you and every soul of life in every corporeal form: and the great intumescence (of the waters) shall no more destroy every corporeal form.

16. And the bow shall be in the nebulous expanse, and I will look upon it, to remember the Creative Law (established) for the immensity of time, between Ælohim and every soul of life in every corporeal form that is upon the earth.

17. And Ælohim said unto Noah, This is the symbol of the Creative Force (law) which I have established (in substance) between Me and every corporeal form that is upon the earth.

18. Now, the sons (emanations) of Noah (repose of nature) issuing from the Thebah (sacred enclosure) were Shem (that which is elevated and shining), Cham (that which is dark, curved and hot), and Japheth (that which is extended and wide): and Cham was the father of Chanahan (material reality, physical existence).

19. These three were the sons (emanated beings) of Noah and of these was the whole earth overspread (shared, divided).

20. And Noah released (gave liberty to) Aïsh (intellectual volitive principle) of the Adamic element: and thus he cultivated that which is lofty (spiritual heights).

21. And being steeped with the spirit of his production, he intoxicated his thought (attained ecstasy) and (in his exaltation) he revealed himself in the centre (most secret place) of his tabernacle.

22. And Cham the father of Chanahan (physical, material existence), discovered the mysterious secrets of his father and he divulged them to his two brothers exteriorly (materialized them).

23. And Shem and Japheth took the left garment and raised it behind them, and went backward, and covered the secret mysteries of their father: and their faces (were turned) backward, so that the secret mysteries of their father they did not see.

24. And Noah awaked from his spiritual ecstasy and he knew what his youngest son (the least of his productions) had done unto him.

25. And he said, Cursed be Chanahan (physical, material existence): a servant of servants shall he be unto his brethren.

26. And he said, Blessed be YAHWEH Ælohim of Shem: and Chanahan shall be servant unto them (his people).

27. Ælohim shall give extension unto Japheth and he shall dwell in the tabernacles of Shem (brilliant elevation) : and Chanahan (physical, material existence), shall be a servant unto them.

28. And Noah existed after the great intumescence (of the waters), three hundred and five tens of cycles (of ontological mutation).

29. And all the days (luminous periods, phenomenal manifestations) of Noah (repose of nature) were nine hundred and five tens of cycles (of ontological mutation) : and he passed away (returned to universal seity).

———:-:———

CHAPTER X.

Aggregative and Formative Energy.

1. Now these (are) the symbolic generations of the sons (emanated productions) of Noah (repose of nature) : Shem, Cham and Japheth: and sons (emanated productions) were unto them after the great intumescence (of the waters).

2. And the sons (emanated productions) of Japheth (absolute extension) (were) : Gomer (elementary cumulation, aggregative force), and Magog (elasticity), and Madai (infinite commensurability and sufficiency), and Javan (generative ductility), and Thubal (diffusibility), and Meshech (perceptibility), and Thirass (modality, faculty of appearing under determined form).

3. And the sons (emanated productions) of Gomer (elementary cumulation) (were) : Ashechenaz (latent fire, caloric), and Riphath (rarity, centrifugal force), and Thogormah (density, universal corporization, centripetal force).

4. And the sons (emanated productions) of Javan (generative ductility) (were) : Ælishah (diluting and moulding energy), and Tharshish (intense, sympathetic principle), of Chittim (Chuthites, Scythians, the rejected, the barbarous) and of Dodanim (Dardanians, the elect, the civilized).

5. By these (faculties, or powers of repulsion and attraction) were differentiated the centres of will (interests, opinions and ideas of peoples), of social organizations in their lands: every principle (acting) after its own tongue, toward tribes in general, in their social organizations.

6. And the sons (emanated productions) of Cham (dark, hot inclination) (were): Chush (igneous force, combustion), and Mitzeraim (subjugating, victorious, oppressing power), and Phout (suffocating, asphyxiating energy), and Chanahan (physical and material existence).

7. And the sons (emanated productions) of Chush (igneous force, combustion) (were): Seba (radical moisture, principle of all natural productions), and Hawilah (natural energy, travail), and Sabethah (determining movement, cause), and Rahamah (thunder), and Sabethecha (determined movement, effect): and the sons (emanated productions) of Rahamah (thunder) (were): Sheba (reintegration of principles, electric repulsion), and Dedan (electric affinity).

8. And Chush (igneous force) produced Nimrod (principle of disordered will, of rebellion, anarchy, despotism): he who strove to be the dominator of the earth.

9. He who was a lordly adversary (proud opposer), before the face of YAHWEH: wherefore it is said: Even as Nimrod (principle of anarchical volition), lordly adversary before the face of YAHWEH.

10. And such was the beginning of his kingdom, Babel (vanity), and Arech (softness, dissolution), and Achad (selfishness), and Chalneh (ambition, all engrossing desire), in the land of Shinar (civil revolution).

11. Out of this land issued Ashour (principle of enlightened government, and the order and happiness resulting from the observation of laws), and founded Nineveh (exterior growth, colonization, education of youth), and the interior institutions of the city, and Chalah (perfecting of laws, assemblage of wise men, senate).

12. And Ressen (legislative power, reins of the government), between Nineveh (exterior growth, colonization) and Chalah (interior action of deliberation, senate): a very powerful civil safeguard.

13. And Mitzeraim (subjugating, victorious, oppressing power) produced (the existence of) Loudim (physical pregnancies), and (that of) Whonamim (material heaviness), and (that of) Lehabim (inflamed exhalations) and (that of) Naphethuhim (hollowed caverns).

14. And (that of) Phatherusim (infinite fragments), and (that of) Chaseluthim (expiatory trials, forgiveness of sins) from which issued forth Phelishethim (rejected, infidels) and Chaphethorim (converted, faithful).

15. And Chanahan (physical, material existence) produced (the existence of) Tzidon (insidious adversary, ruse) his first-born, and (that of) Heth (moral weakness, debasement).

16. And (that of) the Jebusite (inward crushing), and (that of) the Æmorite (outward wringing), and (that of) the Girgashite (continuous gyratory movement).

17. And (that of) the Chivite (bestial life), and (that of) the Wharikite (brutish passions), and (that of) the Sinite (hateful, bloody passions).

18. And (that of) the Arwadite (plundering desire), and (that of) the Tzemarite (thirst for power), and (that of) the Hamathite (insatiable desire) : and afterward the tribes of the Chanahanites (physical existences) were scattered.

19. And such was the general extent of the Chanahanites (physical existences) through Tzidon (insidious adversary, ruse) : by dint of intestine convulsion (they came) unto consolidation, by intrigues, and tyranny, and unmercifulness and wars (they came) unto swallowing up (of riches).

20. These are the sons (emanated productions) of Cham (that which is dark, curved, hot) after their tribes, after their tongues, in their lands (and) in their universal organizations.

21. And unto Shem (brilliant elevation) were sons (emanated productions) : he was the father of all ultra-

terrestrial productions, (and) the elder brother of Japheth (absolute extension).

22. The sons of Shem (upright and bright) (were): Heilam (infinite duration, eternity), and Ashur (lawful power, harmony and the happiness which results), and Arpha-cheshad (restoring principle of providential nature), and Lud (intellectual generation), and Aram (universal elementization).

23. And the sons of Aram (were): Hutz (substantiation), and Chul (virtual travail), and Gether (abundant pressing), and Mash (harvest of spiritual fruits).

24. And Arpha-cheshad (restoring principle of providential nature) produced Shelah (efficacious, divine grace), and Shelah produced Heber (that which is ultra-terrestrial, beyond this world).

25. And unto Heber were two sons: the name of the first was Pheleg (separation, classification), for in his days was the earth divided (classified): and his brother's name was Yaktan (attenuation of evil).

26. And Yaktan produced (the existence of) Almodad (divine, probatory mensuration), and (that of) Shaleph (reflected light), and (that of) Hotzarmoth (division caused by death), and (that of) Yarah (radiant, fraternal manifestation, the moon).

27. And (the existence of) Hadoram (universal splendour), and (that of) Auzal (purified, divine fire), and (that of) Dikelah (sonorous lightness, ethereal rarifaction).

28. And (the existence of) Hobal (infinite orbicular diffusion), and (that of) Abimael (father of absolute fullness), and (that of) Sheba (reintegration of principles, restitution of repose, redemption).

29. And (the existence of) Aophir (fulfillment of elementary principle), and (that of) Hawilah (proved virtue), and (that of) Yobab (celestial jubilation): all

these were the sons (emanated productions) of Yaktan (attenuation of evil).

30. And such was the place of their restoring (reintegration), from the harvest of spiritual fruits, by dint of spiritual travail (meditation), to the height (generative principle) of the anteriority of time.

31. These are the sons (emanated productions) of Shem (sublime, exalted), after their tribes, after their tongues, in their lands, after their universal organizations.

32. These are the tribes of the sons (emanated productions) of Noah (repose of elementary existence) after their symbolic generations, in their constitutional organizations: and of these were the natural organizations (general and particular) divided in the earth after the great intumescence (of the waters).

THE END

Made in the USA
Middletown, DE
23 April 2023

29339414R00210